An Introduction to Corpus Linguistics

Studies in language and linguistics

General editors: GEOFFREY LEECH, Lancaster University
and
JENNY THOMAS, University of Wales, Bangor

Already published:

AN INTRODUCTION TO CORPUS LINGUISTICS

GRAEME KENNEDY

 LONGMAN

London and New York

Addison Wesley Longman Limited
Edinburgh Gate
Harlow, Essex   CM20 2JE
England

and Associated Companies throughout the world

Published in the United States of America
by Addison Wesley Longman Inc., New York

First published 1998

ISBN 0 582 23154–X Paper
ISBN 0 582 23153–1 Cased

British Library Cataloguing-in-Publication Data

A catalogue record for this book is
available from the British Library

Library of Congress Cataloging-in-Publication Data

Kennedy, Graeme D.
      An introduction to corpus linguistics / Graeme Kennedy.
         p.   cm. — (Studies in language and linguistics)
      Includes bibliographical references (p.) and index.
      ISBN 0–582–23153–1. — ISBN 0–582–23154–X (pbk.)
      1. Computational linguistics—Methodology.   2. Discourse analysis—
Data processing.   3. English language—Data processing.   I. Title.
II. Series: Studies in language and linguistics (London, England)
P98.K44   1998
410'.285—dc21   97–39738
                                                                                      CIP

Set by 35 in 9/11 pt Palatino
Produced by Addison Wesley Longman Singapore (Pte) Ltd.,
Printed in Singapore

Contents

CONTENTS

CONTENTS

Author's acknowledgements

I owe a great deal to colleagues, students, friends and members of my family who have helped extend my involvement in corpus linguistics, and who, through their own research, comments and questions have encouraged, supported and enlightened me. The book owes a lot to Jane Dudley, Paul Nation and Robert Sigley, who each contributed in different ways.

Several graduate students who have worked with corpora during the last decade have also contributed to my own understanding of the nature, structure, acquisition and use of English. They include Morie Chan, Uthaivan Danvivath, Ann Devoy, Fang Xuelan, Susan Gardner, Mary Greenfield, He Anping, Alastair Ker, Jonathan Newton, Cucu Sutarsyah, Michelle Strand, Wang Sheng and Shunji Yamazaki.

I am grateful to the many authors who have given permission to reproduce data from their research. Every effort has been made to acknowledge data from published research wherever the source can be traced.

Corpus linguistics would not be the dynamic field of scholarship it has become without the work in corpus compilation and software design which many scholars have undertaken since the pioneering work of Randolph Quirk, Nelson Francis, Henry Kučera, Sidney Greenbaum, Geoffrey Leech and Jan Svartvik. Anyone working in the field of corpus linguistics today also owes a debt to a growing network of colleagues in many countries. In particular, I wish to acknowledge the work of Bengt Altenberg, who has supported many researchers with his bibliographical work; and also Stig Johansson and Knut Hofland, who, through ICAME and the Norwegian Computing Centre for the Humanities, have helped extend the availability of the major first-generation computer corpora on which corpus linguists have cut their teeth. I am especially grateful to Geoffrey Leech for his encouragement and painstaking editorial work, which did much to improve initial drafts of the book.

Publisher's acknowledgements

We are grateful to the following for permission to reproduce copyright material:

Association for Literary and Linguistic Computing for an extract from A Govindankutty, *ALLC Bulletin* (1973), 1, 3: 3; Guardian Syndication for the article ' "Doomsday rocks" rattle Nasa' by Simon Tisdall © *The Guardian Weekly* 19.4.92.

Brown University Library and the authors W. N. Francis and H. Kucera for 'Structure of the *Brown Corpus*' (our Table 2.2) from *Manual of Information to Accompany A Standard Corpus of Present-Day Edited American English, for Use with Digital Computers* 1964 (revised 1979); Inso Corporation and the authors W. N. Francis and H. Kucera for 'A lemmatized entry for *collect* and related words' (our Figure 3.3), 'Perfect and progressive verb forms in the *Brown Corpus*' (our Table 3.16), 'The tagset used for tagging the *Brown Corpus*' (our Figure 4.1) all from *Frequency Analysis of English Language: Lexicon and Grammar*' (1982); RELC (Regional Language Centre, Southeast Asian Ministers of Education Organization) for 'The 50 most frequent words used in an economics text compared with a corpus of the same size of general academic English (our Table 3.4) from Sutarsyah, Nation & Kennedy 'How useful is EAP vocabulary for ESP? – A Corpus-based Study' *RELC Journal 25, 2: 35–40,* 'Immediate right collocates of *at* occurring four or more times in the *LOB Corpus*, (our Table 3.27) from 'Collocations: Where grammar and vocabulary teaching meet' in Anivan, S. (ed.) *Language Teaching Methodology for the Nineties*. RELC Anthology Series No. 24, Regional Language Centre, 215–229, and 'Explicit devices marking causation in the *LOB Corpus*' (our Table 3.50) from Fang and Kennedy (1992: 68) in 'Expressing causation in written English' *RELC Journal 23, 1: 62–60*; Lund University Press and Bengt Altenberg for 'Relative proportions of major word classes in a sample (c. 50,000 words) from the *LLC*' (our Table 3.6) and 'Distribution of discourse items in a sample of 50,000 words from the *LLC*' (our Table 3.53) both from 'Spoken English and the Dictionary' (1990: 185, 183) also Lund University Press and Anna-Brita Stenstrom for 'Categories of discourse items in the *LLC*' (our Table 3.54) and 'Categories of discourse items in dialogue and monologue' (our Table 3.55) both from 'Lexical items peculiar to spoken discourse' – all four tables in *The London-Lund Corpus of Spoken English: Description and Research* (1990) edited by Jan Svartvik; *ICAME News* and Stig Johansson for 'Most distinctive nouns, verbs, adjectives and adverbs in two genres of the *LOB Corpus*' (our Table 3.8) from 'Word frequencies in different types of English texts' *ICAME News 5: 7–8* (1981); *ICAME News* and Eric Akkerman for 'Particles used with verbs in the *Brown Corpus*' (our Table 3.25) from 'Verb and particle combinations: Particle frequency ratings and idiomaticity' *ICAME News 8: 63* (1984); *ICAME News* for 'A fragment of a tagged version of the *LOB Corpus, horizontal format*' (our Figure 4.2); *ICAME Journal* and Kyto and Voutilainen for 'A sample of the output of the *ENGCG Parser*' (our Figure 4.15) from 'Applying the constraint grammar parser of English to the Helsinki Corpus' *ICAME Journal 19: 23–28* (1995); Rodopi and Henk Barkema for 'The occurrence of certain collocations in two corpora' (our Table 3.11) from 'Idiomaticity in English Nps' in Aarts, De Haan and Oostdijk (eds.) *English Language Corpora: Design, Analysis and Exploitation* (1993: 271); Rodopi and Karin Aijmer for 'Frequencies in spoken and written corpora of some individual hedges' (our Table 3.53) from 'Discourse variation and hedging' in Aarts and Meijs (eds.) *Corpus Linguistics II. New Studies in the Analysis and Exploitaton of Computer Corpora* (1986: 10); Rodopi and Geoffrey Sampson for 'A fragment of the *SUSANNE Corpus*' (our Figure 4.13) from 'A domesday book of English grammar' in Oostidjk and De Haan (eds.) *Corpus-based Research into Language: In Honour of Jan Aarts* (1994: 175); Rodopi and Nellche Oostdijk for 'Format of a parsed sentence using the Nijmegen approach to the automatic analysis of English' (our Figure 4.14) from *Corpus Linguistics and the Automatic Analysis of English* (1991: 162); Mouton de Gruyter for 'Most frequent verbs in Ota's Corpus, and their tense and aspect use' (our Table 3.13) and 'Use of modals in the *London-Lund* and *LOB* corpora' (our Table 3.20) both from Kennedy (1992) 'Preferred ways of putting things with implications for language teaching in Svartvik (ed.) *Directions in Corpus Linguistics*; Mouton de Gruyter and Bengt Altenberg for 'Amplifiers in recurrent combinations in the *LLC*' (our adapted Table 3.56) and 'Most frequent amplifier collocations in the *LLC*' (our Table 3.57) both from Altenberg (1991) 'Amplifier collocations in spoken English' in Johansson and Stenstrom (eds.) *English Computer Corpora*; Mouton de Gruyter and Matti Rissanen for 'Occurrence of periphrastic *do* in affirmative statements and of the progressive form in Early Modern English sub-periods in the *Helsinki Corpus* (excluding Bible transactions)' (our Table 3.62) from Rissanen (1992) 'The diachronic corpus as a window to the history of English' in

PUBLISHER'S ACKNOWLEDGEMENTS

Svartvik (ed.) *Directions in Corpus Linguistics*; Mouton de Gruyter for our Figures 4.9, 4.10 and 4.11 from Leech and Svartvik 'Running a grammar factory. The production of syntactically analyzed corpora or "treebanks" ' in Johansson and Stenstrom (eds.) *English Computer Corpora*; Oxford University Press for 'Relative frequencies of use of categories of quantification' (our Table 3.39) in 'Quantification and the use of English: A case study of one aspect of the learner's task' *Applied Linguistics Volume 8, No. 3*, also 'Frequencies of different types of postnominal modifiers in three registers (per 1,000 words)' (our Table 3.45) and 'Linguistic characterization of ten spoken and written resisters with respect to dimension 1 "Involved versus Informational Production", and dimension 5 "Non-Abstract versus Abstract Style" ' (our Figure 3.11) both from Biber, Conrad & Reppon 'Corpus-based approaches to issues in applied linguistics' *Applied Linguistics 51, 2: 173*, and 'Outline of major grammatical and discoursal units and structures which might be studied in a corpus' from 'The corpus as a research domain' in Greenbaum (ed.) (1996) *Comparing English Worldwide: The International Corpus of English*; Cambridge University Press and the author Douglas Biber for 'Features used in Biber's multi-feature, multi-dimensional analysis of variation' (our Figure 3.9) and 'Factorial structure of two text type dimensions' (our Figure 3.10) from *Variation Across Speech and Writing* (1988); Addison Wesley Longman for 'Some habitually spoken sequences in Australian and New Zealand English' (our Figure 3.4) from Pawley and Snyder chapter 'Two puzzles for linguistic theory: Native-like selection and native-like fluency' in Richards & Schmidt (eds.) *Language and Communication* (1983), and 'Semantic classes of apposition' (our Table 3.43) and 'Total number of appositions per genre' (our Table 3.44) from Meyer chapter 'A corpus-based study of apposition in English', also '*Must* in Australian, British and American English' (our Table 3.61) from Collins chapter 'The modals of obligation and necessity in Australian English', also 'Zero and *that* as object clause links in Late Middle English' (our Table 3.63) and 'Zero and *that* as object clause links in Early Modern English' (our Table 3.64) both from Rissanen chapter 'On the history of *that*/zero as object clause links in English', all five tables from Aijmer and Altenberg (1991) *English Corpus Linguistics: Studies in Honour of Jan Svartvik*; Blackwell Publishers and the Editorial Board of Studia Linguistica for 'Distribution of the fifteen most frequent causal links in *LLC* and *LOB*' (our Table 3.49) from Altenberg article 'Causal linking in Spoken and Written English' from *Studia Linguistica 38* (1984); Academic Press Inc. and G. Tottie for 'Distribution of negation types with *be, have* and lexical verbs' (our Table 3.51) from *Negation in English Speech and Writing* (1991).

CHAPTER ONE

Introduction

In the language sciences a corpus is a body of written text or transcribed speech which can serve as a basis for linguistic analysis and description. Over the last three decades the compilation and analysis of corpora stored in computerized databases has led to a new scholarly enterprise known as corpus linguistics. The purpose of this book is to introduce the various activities which come within the scope of corpus linguistics, and to set current work within its historical context. It brings together some of the findings of corpus-based studies of English, the language which has so far received the most attention from corpus linguists, and shows how quantitative analysis can contribute to linguistic description. It is hoped that, by concentrating in particular on some of the results of corpus analysis, the book will whet the appetites of the growing body of teachers and students with access to corpora to discover more for themselves about how languages work in all their variety. The book is intended primarily for those who are already familiar with general linguistic concepts but who want to know more of what can be done with a corpus and why corpus linguistics may be relevant in research on language. Corpus linguistics is not an end in itself but is one source of evidence for improving descriptions of the structure and use of languages, and for various applications, including the processing of natural language by machine and understanding how to learn or teach a language.

The main focus of this book is on four major areas of activity in corpus linguistics:

- corpus design and development (Chapter 2)
- corpus-based descriptions of aspects of English structure and use (Chapter 3)
- the particular techniques and tools used in corpus analysis (Chapter 4)
- applications of corpus-based linguistic description (Chapter 5)

Readers may choose to work through the book in the above order or to begin with the sections dealing with corpus-based descriptions of English

(Chapter 3) in order first to become more familiar with some of the results of corpus analysis. In focusing on the contribution of corpus linguistics to the description of English and on some of the central issues and problems which are being addressed within corpus linguistics, the book also attempts to bring together disparate work which is often hard to get hold of. However, such is the speed of development and change in corpus linguistics at the present time that anyone writing about it must be conscious that it would be easy to produce a Ptolemaic picture of the field – with the world distorted and with Terra Australis Incognita, the Great Southern Continent, both misconceived and misplaced. Work relevant for corpus linguistics is being done in many fields, including computer science and artificial intelligence, as well as in various branches of descriptive and applied linguistics. It would not be surprising if some of the scholars contributing to corpus linguistics from these and other perspectives found that their work is inadequately represented here. However, they can be assured that such neglect is not intended.

Because corpus linguistics is a field where activity is increasing very rapidly and where there is as yet no magisterial perspective, even the very notion of what constitutes a valid corpus can still be controversial. It also needs to be understood at the outset that not every use of computers with bodies of text is part of corpus linguistics. For example, the aim of Project Gutenberg to distribute 10,000 texts to 100 million computer users by the year 2001 is not in itself part of corpus linguistics although texts included in this ambitious project may conceivably provide textual data for corpus analysis. Similarly, contemporary reviews of computing in the humanities show the enormous extent of corpus-based work in literary studies. While some of the methodology used in literary studies resembles some of the activity being undertaken in corpus linguistics, research on authorial attribution or thematic structure, for example, does not come within the scope of this book. Nor does the book attempt to cover systematically the wide range of corpus-based work being undertaken in computational linguistics in such areas of natural language processing as speech recognition and machine translation.

Although there have been spectacular advances in the development and use of electronic corpora, the essential nature of text-based linguistic studies has not necessarily changed as much as is sometimes suggested. In this book, reference is made to corpus studies which were undertaken manually before computers were available. Corpus linguistics did not begin with the development of computers but there is no doubt that computers have given corpus linguistics a huge boost by reducing much of the drudgery of text-based linguistic description and vastly increasing the size of the databases used for analysis. It should be made clear, however, that corpus linguistics is not a mindless process of automatic language description. Linguists use corpora to answer questions and solve problems. Some of the most revealing insights on language and language use have come from a blend of manual and computer analysis. It is now possible for researchers with access to a personal computer and off-the-shelf software to do linguistic analysis using a corpus, and to discover facts about a language which have never been noticed or written about previously. The most important skill is not to be able to program a computer or even to manipulate available software (which, in any case, is increasingly user-friendly). Rather, it is to be able to ask insightful questions which address real issues and problems in theoretical, descriptive and applied language studies. Many of the key problems and challenges in corpus linguistics are associated with the following questions:

- How can we best exploit the opportunities which arise from having texts stored in machine-retrievable form?
- What linguistic theories will best help structure corpus-based research?
- What linguistic phenomena should we look for?
- What applications can make use of the insights and improved descriptions of languages which come out of this research?

In answering these and other questions corpus linguistics has potential to provide solutions and new directions to some of the major issues and problems in the study of human communication.

1.1 Corpora

The definition of a corpus as a collection of texts in an electronic database can beg many questions for there are many different kinds of corpora. Some dictionary definitions suggest that corpora necessarily consist of structured collections of text specifically compiled for linguistic analysis, that they are large or that they attempt to be representative of a language as a whole. This is not necessarily so. Not all corpora which can be used for linguistic research were originally compiled for that purpose. Historically it is not even the case that corpora are necessarily stored electronically so that they can be machine-readable, although this is nowadays the norm. As discussed in Section 2.2, electronic corpora can consist of whole texts or collections of whole texts. They can consist of continuous text samples taken from whole texts; they can even be made up of collections of citations. At one extreme an electronic dictionary may serve as a kind of corpus for certain types of linguistic research while at the other extreme a huge unstructured archive of texts may be used for similar purposes by corpus linguists.

Corpora have been compiled for many different purposes, which in turn influence the design, size and nature of the individual corpus. Some current corpora intended for linguistic research have been designed for general descriptive purposes – that is, they have been designed so that they can be examined or trawled to answer questions at various linguistic levels on the prosody, lexis, grammar, discourse patterns or pragmatics of the language. Other corpora have been designed for specialized purposes such as discovering which words and word meanings should be included in a learners' dictionary; which words or meanings are most frequently used by workers in the oil industry or economics; or what differences there are between uses of a language in different geographical, social, historical or work-related contexts.

A distinction is sometimes made between a corpus and a text archive or text database. Whereas a corpus designed for linguistic analysis is normally a systematic, planned and structured compilation of text, an archive is a text repository, often huge and opportunistically collected, and normally not structured. It is generally the case, as Leech (1991: 11) suggested, that 'the difference between an archive and a corpus must be that the latter is designed or required for a particular "representative" function'. It is nevertheless not always easy to see unequivocally what a corpus is representing, in terms of language variety.

Databases which are made up not of samples, but which constitute an entire population of data, may consist of a single book (e.g. George Eliot's *Middlemarch*) or of a number of works. These corpora may be the work of a single author (e.g. the complete works of Jane Austen) or of several authors (e.g. medieval lyrics), or all the editions of a particular newspaper in a given year. Some projects have assembled all the known available texts in a particular genre or from a particular historical period. Some of these databases or text archives described in Section 2.4 are very large indeed, and although they have rarely yet been used as corpora for linguistic research, there is no reason why they should not be in the future. In many respects it is thus the use to which the body of textual material is put, rather than its design features, which define what a corpus is.

A corpus constitutes an empirical basis not only for identifying the elements and structural patterns which make up the systems we use in a language, but also for mapping out our use of these systems. A corpus can be analysed and compared with other corpora or parts of corpora to study variation. Most importantly, it can be analysed distributionally to show how often particular phonological, lexical, grammatical, discoursal or pragmatic features occur, and also where they occur.

In the early 1980s it was possible to list on a few fingers the main electronic corpora which a small band of devotees had put together over the previous two decades for linguistic research. These corpora were available to researchers on a non-profit basis, and were initially available for processing only on mainframe computers. The development of more powerful microcomputers from the mid-1970s and the advent of CD-ROM in the 1980s made corpus-based research more accessible to a much wider range of participants.

By the 1990s there were many corpus-making projects in various parts of the world. Lancashire (1991) shows the huge range of corpora, archives and other electronic databases available or being compiled for a wide variety of purposes. Some of the largest corpus projects have been undertaken for commercial purposes, by dictionary publishers. Other projects in corpus compilation or analysis are on a smaller scale, and do not necessarily become well known. Undertaken as part of graduate theses or undergraduate projects, they enabled students to gain original insights into the structure and use of language.

1.2 The role of computers in corpus linguistics

The analysis of huge bodies of text 'by hand' can be prone to error and is not always exhaustive or easily replicable. Although manual analysis has made an important contribution over the centuries, especially in lexicography, it was the availability of digital computers from the middle of the 20th century which brought about a radical change in text-based scholarship. Rather than initiating corpus research, developments in information technology changed the way we work with corpora. Instead of using index cards and dictionary 'slips', lexicographers and grammarians could use computers to store huge amounts of text and retrieve particular words, phrases or whole chunks of text in context, quickly and exhaustively, on their screens. Furthermore the linguistic items could be sorted in many different ways, for example, taking account of the items they collocate with and their typical grammatical behaviour.

Corpus linguistics is thus now inextricably linked to the computer, which has introduced incredible speed, total accountability, accurate replicability, statistical reliability and the ability to handle huge amounts of data. With modern software, computer-based corpora are easily accessible, greatly reducing the drudgery and sheer bureaucracy of dealing with the increasingly large amounts of data used for compiling dictionaries and other information sources. In addition to greatly increased reliability in such basic tasks as searching, counting and sorting linguistic items, computers can show accurately the probability of occurrence of linguistic items in text. They have thus facilitated the development of mathematical bases for automatic natural language processing, and brought to linguistic studies a high degree of accuracy of measurement which is important in all science. Computers have permitted linguists to work with a large variety of texts and thus to seek generalizations about language and language use which can go beyond particular texts or the intuitions of particular linguists. The quantification of language use through corpus-based studies has led to scientifically interesting generalizations and has helped renew or strengthen links between linguistic description and various applications. Machine translation, text-to-speech synthesis, content analysis and language teaching have been among the beneficiaries.

AN INTRODUCTION TO CORPUS LINGUISTICS

Some idea of the changes which the computer has made possible in text studies can be gauged from a report in an early issue of the *ALLC Bulletin*, the forerunner of the journal *Literary and Linguistic Computing*. A brief report by Govindankutty (1973) on the coming of the computer to Dravidian linguistics captures the moment of transition between manual and electronic databases. The text he was working with of 300,000 words is small by today's standards, but what took the researcher and his long-suffering colleagues nearly six years of data management and analysis could, 20 years later, be carried out in minutes.

> It took nearly six years' hard labour and the co-operation of colleagues and students to complete the Index of Kamparāmāyaṇam, the longest middle Tamil text, in the Kerala University under the supervision of Professor V. I. Subramoniam. The text consists of nearly 12,500 stanzas and each stanza has four lines; each line has an average of six words. All the words and some of the suffixes were listed on small cards by the late Mr. T. Velaven who is the architect of this voluminous index. Later, the cards were sorted into alphabetical order and each item was again arranged according to the ascending order of the stanza and line. Finally, each entry was checked with the text and the meaning and grammatical category were noted. The completed index consists of about 3,500 typed pages (28 × 20 cm).
>
> While indexing, some suffixes such as case were listed separately. This posed some problems when I started to work on the grammar of the language of the text. When it was necessary to find out after what kind of words and after which phonemes and morphemes the alternants of a suffix occur, it became necessary again to go through all the entries. Though I have tried to work out the frequency of all the suffixes, for want of time it was not completely possible. However, the frequency study helped to unearth different strata in the linguistic excavation and indirectly emphasized that it is a *sine qua non*, at least, for such a descriptive and historical study.
>
> Though it took a lot of time, energy and patience, the birth of an index brought with it an unknown optimism in the grammatical description. After completing the index and the grammatical study of Kamparāmāyaṇam, three months ago I started indexing Rāmacaritam, an early Malayalam text, using small cards. This project is being carried out in the Leiden University with the guidance of Professor F. B. J. Kuiper. While I was half my way through the indexing, Dr. B. J. Hoff of the Linguistics Department informed me of the work done in the Institute for Dutch Lexicology with the help of a computer. When I discussed the problems with Dr. F. de Tollenaere, who is the head of this institute, he outlined with great enthusiasm how a computer can be utilized for this purpose. Immediately, I started transcribing the text and now it is being punched on paper tape, using an ARBA paper tape punch at the Institute. This paper tape punch, having an extra shift, has twice the eighty-eight standard possibilities, which results in one hundred and seventy-six different punching codes, which for the computer has the value of one hundred and seventy-six characters. Moreover, a coding system makes it possible to have up to two hundred and seven possibilities, which are also available at the output stage, as the Institute has at its disposal a print train with two hundred and seven symbols.

To a present-day corpus linguist, even the laborious data entry by punched paper seems quaintly archaic, and Govindankutty's task could now be undertaken on a personal computer accessed directly through a keyboard.

Until the mid-1980s corpus linguistics typically involved mainframe computing and was largely associated with universities having access to large machines. In the 1970s, with shared access to a standard mainframe, it could take an hour or more to make a concordance consisting of all the instances of a word such as *when* in a one-million-word corpus. By the late 1980s, the time taken to run such a program had been reduced to minutes. In the 1990s, the same job can be done just as quickly on the faster personal computers running at 60 or more megahertz. Hard disk drives of 500 megabytes or more on personal computers and input from a CD-ROM are now common, thus facilitating storage and rapid analysis.

In the early 1980s a captive computer scientist or friendly computer programmer was almost indispensable to assist many aspiring corpus linguists to cope with inevitable technical problems associated with data management and the programming skills necessary for corpus analysis. By the 1990s, improvements in personal computers of the kind already mentioned, and the availability of commercial software packages designed for corpus analysis, have meant that most corpus linguists can now concentrate not on how to program and use a computer but on problems and issues in linguistics which can be addressed through a corpus.

1.3 The scope of corpus linguistics

Corpus linguistics is based on bodies of text as the domain of study and as the source of evidence for linguistic description and argumentation. It has also come to embody methodologies for linguistic description in which quantification of the distribution of linguistic items is part of the research activity. As Leech (1992: 107) has noted, the focus of study is on performance rather than competence, and on observation of language in use leading to theory rather than vice versa.

It would be misleading, however, to suggest that corpus linguistics is a theory of language in competition with other theories of language such as transformational grammar, or even more that it is a new or separate branch of linguistics. Linguists have always needed sources of evidence for theories about the nature, elements, structure and functions of language, and as a basis for stating what is possible in a language. At various times, such evidence has come from intuition or introspection, from experimentation or elicitation, and from descriptions based on observations of occurrence in spoken or written texts. In the case of corpus-based research, the evidence is derived directly from texts. In this sense corpus linguistics differs from approaches to language which depend on introspection for evidence. In his celebrated work, *Coral Gardens and their Magic*, Malinowski (1935: 9) wrote about the paradigm shift which he considered was necessary in the linguistics of the day.

> The neglect of the obvious has often been fatal to the development of scientific thought. The false conception of language as a means of transfusing ideas from the head of the speaker to that of the listener has, in my opinion largely vitiated the philological approach to language. The view set forth here is not merely academic: it compels us, as we shall see, to correlate other activities, to interpret the meaning – text; and this means a new departure in the handling of linguistic evidence. It will also force us to define meaning in terms of experience and situation.

Linguists may not see the necessity for such a sea change today. However, it is the case that corpus linguists often have different concerns from many other linguists. Corpus linguists are concerned typically not only with what words, structures or uses are possible in a language but also with what is probable – what is likely to occur in language use. The use of a corpus as a source of evidence however is not necessarily incompatible with any linguistic theory, and progress in the language sciences as a whole is likely to benefit from a judicious use of evidence from various sources: texts, introspection, elicitation or other types of experimentation as appropriate. Any scientific enterprise must be empirical in the sense that it has to be supported or falsified on evidence and, in the final analysis, statements made about language have to stand up to the evidence of language use. The evidence can be based on the introspective judgment of speakers of the language or on a corpus of text. The difference lies in the richness of the evidence and the confidence we can have in the generalizability of that evidence, in its validity and reliability. The boundaries, therefore, between corpus-based description and argumentation and other approaches to language description are not rigid, and linguists of varied theoretical persuasions now use corpora for evidence which is complementary to evidence obtained from other sources.

Corpus linguistics, like all linguistics, is concerned primarily with the description and explanation of the nature, structure and use of language and languages and with particular matters such as language acquisition, variation and change. Corpus linguistics has nevertheless developed something of a life of its own within linguistics, with a tendency sometimes to focus on lexis and lexical grammar rather than pure syntax. This is partly a result of using methodologies such as concordancing where the contextual evidence available in a single line of wide-carriage computer printout of 130 characters is sometimes too limited for the analysis of syntax or discourse.

Work in corpus linguistics is currently associated with several quite different activities. Scholars working in the field tend to be identified with one or more of them. The first group of researchers consists of corpus makers or compilers. These scholars are concerned with the design and compilation of corpora, the collection of texts and their preparation and storage for later analysis.

A second group of researchers has been concerned with developing tools for the analysis of corpora. Important contributions to software development especially for the syntactic analysis of corpora have been associated particularly but not exclusively with researchers in computational linguistics. These researchers have been concerned with the use of corpora to develop, among other things, algorithms for natural language processing and the modelling of linguistic theories.

A third group of researchers consists of descriptive linguists whose main concern has been to make use of computerized corpora to describe reliably the lexicon and grammar of languages, both of the linguistic systems we use and our likely use of those systems. It is the probabilistic aspect of corpus-based descriptive linguistic studies which especially distinguishes them from conventional descriptive fieldwork in linguistics or lexicography. That is, corpus-based descriptive linguistics is concerned not only with what is said or written, where, when and by whom, but how often particular forms are used. The measurement of the distribution of words and grammar has encouraged new ways of studying the linguistic basis of variation in text types, language change and regional and other varieties of language. The corpus provides contexts for the study of meaning in use and, by making available techniques for extracting linguistic information from texts on a scale previously undreamed of, it facilitates linguistic investigations where empiricism is text based.

A fourth area of activity, which has been among the most innovative outcomes of the corpus revolution, has been the exploitation of corpus-based linguistic description for use in a variety of applications such as language learning and teaching, and natural language processing by machine, including speech recognition and translation.

At the present time in corpus linguistics, some researchers tend to focus on issues in corpus design, others on methods for text analysis and processing, and still others, probably the majority, on corpus-based linguistic description and the application of such descriptions. These various concerns are discussed in Chapters 2–5 of this book.

Although the scope of corpus linguistics may be defined in terms of what people do with corpora, it would be a mistake to assume that corpus linguistics is simply a faster way of describing how a language works, or is about the nature of linguistic evidence. Analysis of a corpus by means of standard corpus linguistic research software can and frequently does reveal facts about a language which we might never previously have thought of seeking. Altenberg's (1991a) study of amplifier collocations in English, for example, raised questions about semantic

9

classes of maximizers and boosters such as *perfectly* or *awfully* which probably would not have been asked without the evidence of a corpus. He found for example that frequent maximizers such as *quite* tend to collocate with non-scalar words (*quite obviously*) while *absolutely* has a greater tendency than other maximisers to collocate with negatives (*absolutely not*). The major shift in methodology associated with corpus linguistics comes not from theory but rather from what the use of corpora makes possible.

As we have seen, corpus linguistics goes beyond the use of corpora as a source of evidence in linguistic description. It also revives and carries on a concern of some linguists with the statistical distribution of linguistic items in the context of use. From the 1920s there was, especially in the United States and the United Kingdom, a tradition of word counting in texts in order to discover the most frequent, and arguably therefore the most pedagogically useful, words and grammatical structures for language teaching purposes. The work of Thorndike and West described in Section 3.1.1 was particularly notable in this regard.

From the 1930s, Prague School linguists undertook quantitative studies (mainly of Czech, English and Russian) of the frequency of certain grammatical processes, the relative frequencies of different parts of speech, the location and distribution of information in the sentence, and the statistical distribution of syllable types and structures. Some of this work was directed towards comparative stylistic analysis (e.g. Krámský, 1972) and some towards quantitative comparisons of varieties of English (e.g. Dušková, 1977). Such Prague School quantitative studies, which were carried out manually, differ from modern computer corpus-based studies particularly in the size of the corpora and in their representativeness. Dušková, for example, studied 10,000 finite verb forms from 10 plays to draw conclusions about the functions and use of the preterite and the perfect in British and American English, but it is not clear why these 10 plays were chosen as representative of contemporary English. Nevertheless, the Prague School focus on quantitative studies was commendable at a time when orthodox linguistics eschewed them. Other quantitative studies were directed towards discovering the 'statistical laws' of text.

The work of the American philologist George Zipf, from the 1930s, was concerned with such quantitative analyses as the relation between the frequency of words in text and text length, the frequency of words and their antiquity, and the relation between the rank order of an item in a word frequency list and the number of occurrences or tokens of that item in a text. Zipf (1949) sets out his famous 'law' which held that the relationship between the frequency of use of a word in a text and the rank order of that word in a frequency list is a constant (f.r=c).

As noted above, the earliest computerized corpora compiled for linguistic research from the 1960s required the use of mainframe computers, and researchers frequently had to design their own software for analysis.

Initial interest was often in lexis, including word counts, but it was quickly apparent that a computer corpus facilitated the study of permissible or likely word sequences or collocations (are we more likely to write *different from*, *different to* or *different than*?) and grammatical and stylistic characteristics of particular authors and genres. There was a particular interest in what characterized 'scientific style', 'newspaper style' and 'literary or imaginative style'.

With a corpus stored in a computer, it is easy to find, sort and count items, either as a basis for linguistic description or for addressing language-related issues and problems. It is not surprising, therefore, that a wide range of research activities have come to be within the scope of corpus linguistics. Analyses can contribute to the making of dictionaries, word lists, descriptive grammars, diachronic and synchronic comparative studies of speech varieties, and to stylistic, pedagogical and other applications. With appropriate software it is easy to study the distribution of phonemes, letters, punctuation, inflectional and derivational morphemes, words (as variously defined), collocations, instances of particular word classes, syntactic patterns, or discourse structures. Recent work at Birmingham University described by Renouf (1993) shows how new words and new uses can be identified in corpora at the time these words enter journalistic use.

The scope and current concerns of a field of scholarship can sometimes be seen or defined through the topics which make up conference programmes and the content of specialist journals. In the 1990s the topics which appear on conference programmes and in journals which cover corpus linguistics include improved ways of annotating corpora, the tagging of parts of speech and the senses of polysemous word forms, improved automatic parsing, identification of collocations, phraseological units and discourse structure, text categorization, research methodology in the face of more and bigger corpora, and the application of this work in lexicography, syntactic description, translation, speech and handwriting recognition, and language teaching. Educational applications are increasingly on the agenda. At Lancaster University in 1994 and 1996 the pedagogical significance of electronic corpora was the subject of conferences on the teaching of linguistics and the teaching of languages.

In March 1993, a Georgetown University Round Table meeting in Washington, DC, on corpus-based linguistics identified the following topics as those in particular need of investigation and dissemination at a time when linguistics was returning to more text-based approaches to language:

- the design and development of text-speech corpora
- tools for searching and processing on-line corpora
- critical assessments of on-line corpora and corpus-processing tools
- methodological issues in corpus-based analysis

- applications and results in linguistics and related disciplines, including language teaching, computational linguistics, historical linguistics, discourse analysis and stylistic analysis

The scope of computer corpus-based scholarship can also be measured by some of its achievements. In lexicography the revision of the *Oxford English Dictionary*, its publication in electronic form on CD-ROM and the publication of new learners' dictionaries of English by other major publishers were all based on corpora. The completion of the 100-million-word *British National Corpus* in 1994 set a new standard in corpus design and compilation. Another important international standard set in corpus preparation and formatting has been in the gradual adoption of the Standard Generalized Markup Language (SGML) through the Text Encoding Initiative (TEI) (see Section 2.6.5). In the analysis of corpora there have been improvements in the accuracy of the automatic grammatical tagging and parsing of texts. There has also been a substantial and rapidly growing amount of descriptive detail on the elements and structure of languages (particularly English) arising from corpus-based research. These achievements will be considered in more detail in Chapter 3.

CHAPTER TWO

The design and development of corpora

Major corpora of English, their structure, organization and intended functions are described in this chapter. In the late 1990s no overview can be exhaustive. There are probably several hundred corpus compilation projects under way internationally for various languages. Some have been compiled by individual researchers, have been designed to serve particular purposes, are finite in size and have as few as 50,000 words. Others which have been compiled for research with commercial outcomes consist of hundreds of millions of words and continue to grow. Many of the corpora described are available for researchers for the cost of the tape or CD-ROM. Others are accessible only at particular sites, while a few are available for research on-line through the Internet on a fee-for-service basis.

2.1 Pre-electronic corpora

Corpus-based research is often assumed to have begun in the early 1960s with the availability of electronic, machine-readable corpora. However, before then there was a considerable tradition of corpus-based linguistic analysis of various kinds occurring in five main fields of scholarship:

1 biblical and literary studies
2 lexicography
3 dialect studies
4 language education studies
5 grammatical studies

2.1.1 Biblical and literary

One of the first significant pieces of corpus-based research with linguistic associations involved using the Bible as a corpus on which to base commentaries or criticism. From the 18th century, lists and concordances of words used in the Bible were made in an attempt to show that the various parts of the Bible were factually consistent with each other. Alexander Cruden, a London bookseller, proofreader, morals campaigner and prison reformer, born in Aberdeen in 1701, produced the most famous of these for the Authorized (King James) Version of the Bible. First published in 1736, Cruden's Concordance was a monumental piece of laborious scholarship which went through 42 editions even before 1879. It included concordances not only for what the author considered to be the major content words in the Bible but also some function words such as *how, you, he, once, between* (but not *on, she* or *with*) and certain collocations such as *how long, how many, how much, how much less, how much more, how often, all the nations*. Figure 2.1, reproduced from the 1769 3rd edition, illustrates a typical entry from Cruden. It records all places where *dry* and *ground* co-occur in the Bible, and not only as immediately adjacent pairs. After Cruden's work was first published, the works of established authors such as Shakespeare were similarly concordanced and indexed for various scholarly purposes.

dry *ground*	
behold the face of the *ground* was *d.*	*Gen* 8:13
Israel shall go on *d. ground* in the sea.	*Ex* 14:16, 22
stood firm on *d. ground* in Jordan. Israel passed on *d. ground.*	*Josh* 3:17
Elijah and Elisha went over on *d. ground.*	*2 Ki* 2:8
he turneth water-springs into *d. ground.*	*Ps* 107:33
he turneth *d. ground* into water-springs.	35
I will pour floods upon the *d. ground.*	*Isa* 44:3
He shall grow as a root out of a *d. ground.*	53:2
She is planted in a *d.* and thirsty *ground.*	*Ezek* 19:13

Figure 2.1 Concordance for *dry ground* from Cruden (1769)

2.1.2 Lexicographical

In a discussion of studies based on pre-electronic corpora, Francis (1992) reminds us that the use of corpora for lexicography goes back at least to the early 17th century. Samuel Johnson built on the work of his predecessors over the previous 150 years and recorded on slips of paper a large corpus of sentences from 'writers of the first reputation' to illustrate meanings and uses of English words. Johnson worked with some six assistants to assemble over 150,000 illustrative citations for the approximately 40,000 headword entries in his *Dictionary of the English Language*. It is likely that the corpus formed from these sample citations came to well over one million words.

As noted earlier, the *Oxford English Dictionary* (*OED*) was similarly corpus-based. When the twelfth and final volume of the *OED* was published in 1928, it was the culmination of 71 years of sustained work on a corpus of the canon of mainly literary written English from about

AD 1000. Working manually with text is hugely time-consuming and labour intensive as the first editor of the *OED*, James Murray, discovered. Murray, his successor Henry Bradley, and two editors involved in earlier preparation had all died before the work was completed. Some 2,000 volunteer readers collected about five million citations totalling perhaps 50 million words to illustrate the meanings and uses of the 414,825 entries which appeared in the dictionary. The sheer scope of the task of managing this vast amount of information without a computer and the effect on Murray's family can be gauged from the commentary on the project written by his granddaughter (Murray, 1977). Over 350 volumes of early manuscripts from *Beowulf* to the 17th century were edited and published for the first time by the Early English Text Society beginning in 1864, initially to make accessible part of the corpus from which the citations for the dictionary were to be extracted.

Subsequent supplements to the *Oxford English Dictionary* were able to make use of several million more citation slips which had been compiled since the first volume was published in 1884. This huge corpus for lexicographical research, and its analysis and description, is one of the greatest pieces of linguistic scholarship in English or any language, and it was done without the contribution of speed, accuracy and exhaustiveness which the computer can bring to the task.

Editorial work for a second edition of the *Oxford English Dictionary* began in 1984 and, when published in 1989, the text included the original edition and the supplements published in 1928 and 1972–86 as well as new material. The second edition contains over 447,000 word forms defined and illustrated in some 2.4 million quotations, and is available both in electronic form and as hard copy.

Parallel to the work on the *OED* in the latter part of the 19th century, another great corpus of citations was being assembled to inform and illustrate later editions and incarnations of Noah Webster's *An American Dictionary of the English Language*, which had been published in 1828. According to Francis (1992: 22) the third edition of Webster's *New International Dictionary* published in 1961 had available a corpus of over 10 million citation slips to validate and illustrate the meanings and uses of the almost half a million headword entries which it contained. *Webster's Third* was probably the last major English dictionary to be completed without an electronic database.

2.1.3 Dialect

Alongside the lexicographical work on the *OED* and *Webster's*, an interest in linguistic variation in regional dialects also led some 19th-century linguists to assemble and interpret corpora of various kinds. Most of the work was on lexical variation in the choice of words for particular concepts, and possible variant forms of particular words, both in spelling and pronunciation. The *English Dialect Dictionary* (Wright, 1898–1905) and *The Existing Phonology of English Dialects* (Ellis, 1889) were two monumental results of specialized corpus-based studies of lexical variation in dialects of the United Kingdom.

2.1.4 Language education

Some of the most influential corpus-based research in the first half of the 20th century had a pedagogical purpose. Thorndike (1921) compiled a corpus of 4.5 million words from 41 different sources to make a word frequency list which was initially intended to lead to better curricula materials for teaching literacy to native speakers of English in the United States. Three-quarters of the corpus came from the Bible and classic works of English fiction published in the 19th century, including some of the novels of Charles Dickens, with the remainder of the corpus coming from letters, newspapers and school readers. During the 1930s, Thorndike's corpus was updated in collaboration with Lorge (Thorndike & Lorge, 1944). Their corpus was increased to 18 million words from a wider range of textual sources, although there was still a heavy representation of classics, including volumes of Gibbon's *Decline and Fall of the Roman Empire*. The lexical analysis of this corpus and the published works which derived from the research of Thorndike and Lorge were enormously influential for the teaching of English in many parts of the world over the next 30 years, and are discussed further in Section 3.1.1.

Whereas Thorndike's corpus work had been undertaken with learners of English in United States schools in mind, an earlier corpus was produced in Germany to gather statistical information on the use of words and letters of the German language in order to improve the training of stenographers, who, of course, in an age before dictaphones, tape recorders and photocopiers, had a vital role recording the daily discussions and decisions made in government and business. According to Bongers (1947), the German researcher, J. W. Kaeding needed the help of over five thousand assistants over a period of years to process the corpus of over 11 million words he used in the 1890s to undertake his analysis. Following Thorndike's pioneering work, other pre-electronic corpora were assembled for teaching purposes in several countries for languages including Dutch, French, German, Italian, Latin, Russian and Spanish.

Other corpora were compiled in the 1950s and 1960s to study aspects of the lexico-grammar of English with pedagogical purposes in mind. Notable among these was a corpus of about half a million words of written British English assembled in India by H. V. George and his colleagues in Hyderabad from novels, plays and non-fiction sources including newspapers. Some of the analyses carried out on this corpus and other smaller ones compiled for pedagogical purposes in Japan, North America and in Europe are described in Chapter 3.

2.1.5 *Grammatical*

Corpora have long been one of the sources for the compilation of descriptive grammars. The major descriptive grammars of English of the first half of the 20th century often used newspapers and novels as a source of examples to illustrate grammatical features or constructions. The work of Jespersen (1909–49) is probably the best known, but Kruisinga (1931–32) and Poutsma (1926–29) are among those who produced grammars based on somewhat informal corpora of various sizes rather than on introspection.

More structured and systematic corpora for grammatical studies were subsequently assembled by Fries in the United States. This work was a precursor of later work in descriptive linguistics and sociolinguistics but has often not received the recognition it deserves. Fries used a corpus of letters written to the US government by persons of different educational and social backgrounds as a basis for describing social class differences in usage in his *American English Grammar* (1940). He recorded, for example, the incidence of the past participle *done* used as a preterite among less well-educated correspondents, and noted that *they sung* or *it sunk* were commonly used in standard educated American English of the time. He noted that the subjunctive had virtually disappeared among all groups, while the passive occurred six times as often in the letters written by well-educated writers as compared with the less well-educated. In a later study for *The Structure of English* (1952), Fries used a 250,000-word corpus of recorded telephone conversations. In both these works Fries had to rely on the manual analysis of non-computerized corpora.

The most important pre-electronic corpus assembled particularly for grammatical description was the *Survey of English Usage (SEU) Corpus* (Quirk, 1968). In a sense, the *SEU Corpus*, while initially pre-electronic and not able to be analysed by computer, marked the transition between earlier non-computerized corpus-based description and the development of modern corpus linguistics. When Randolph Quirk founded the Survey in 1959, the aim was to collect 200 samples, each of about 5,000 words, representative of spoken and written British English, to form a corpus of one million words which could be used as a basis for describing the grammar and usage of educated adult native speakers of British English. The corpus samples of spoken English were taken from a wide range of genres which reflected different degrees of formality and intimacy, monologue, dialogue, different topics in different contexts including conversations, interviews, lectures, seminars, committee meetings and telephone discussions. The corpus was distinctive because half of the texts had their origin in speech and half in writing, as Table 2.1 shows. In spite of its range, the corpus had a notably academic and formal public flavour, even in some of the face-to-face conversations, a feature which has had to be taken into account in the construction of

Table 2.1 Structure of the *SEU Corpus*

I	**Texts of written origin (100)**		

    A Printed (46)
    Informative (28)

press	(8)
academic (arts and science)	(13)
administrative	(4)
legal	(3)

    Instructional (6)
    Persuasive (5)
    Imaginative (7)

    B Non-printed (36)
    Correspondence (21)

social	(13)
non-social	(8)

    Personal diaries (4)
    Continuous writing (11)

imaginative	(5)
informative	(6)

    C Scripted to be spoken (18)
    Talks (6)
    Plays (4)
    News (3)
    Scripted oration (3)
    Stories (2)

II Texts of spoken origin (100)

    A Monologue (24)
    Spontaneous (18)

oration	(10)
commentary	(8)
sport	(4)
non-sport	(4)

    Prepared but unscripted oration (6)

    B Dialogue (76)
    Face-to-face conversation (60)

surreptitiously recorded	(34)
non-surreptitiously recorded	(26)

    Telephone conversation (16)

later corpora. Nevertheless, the structure of the written half of the *SEU Corpus* was, as we shall see, a precursor of the structure of the first major electronic corpora.

The *SEU Corpus* contains texts produced between 1953 and 1987 and was originally available to be consulted on 6" × 4" paper slips filed at University College London. There is a slip for each word token in the corpus. Each slip includes 17 lines of text, with overlap of text between adjacent slips. Each slip is marked as being an example of one of 65 grammatical features and some 400 function words or phrases. The spoken English texts are also marked for prosodic features. The grammatical features identified provided the basis for later 'tagsets' used in the automatic tagging and parsing of corpora from the 1980s. It would be hard to exaggerate the importance of the *SEU Corpus*. Not only did it have to break new ground in establishing a principled basis for corpus design, but also it initiated and made possible a large number of studies of corpus-based English grammar by many scholars, including the most complete description of contemporary English grammar, *A Comprehensive Grammar of the English Language* (Quirk et al., 1985).

For many reasons, the collection, transcription and processing of the *SEU Corpus* took over 25 years and was not completed until 1989. Technology overtook it, however, and the spoken section was able to be published separately in electronic form from 1980 as the *London–Lund Corpus*, which is discussed in Section 2.3.1.4.

The hard copy of the original one-million-word *SEU Corpus* was also subsequently converted to an electronic database. For copyright reasons, the half of the corpus derived from written sources is not able to be consulted outside the Survey premises at University College in London, but it continues to be a valuable point of reference. The Survey premises have for over three decades been one of the leading centres in the world for corpus-based research, and innumerable scholars from many countries have found it to be a hospitable and stimulating environment for investigating the grammar of English.

2.2 Types of electronic corpora

As we have seen in Section 1.1, bodies of text of various kinds available in machine-readable form can be used as corpora for linguistic analysis. These corpora can differ in a number of ways according to the purpose for which they were compiled, their representativeness, organization and format. In the corpus linguistics literature, several different types of electronic corpora are sometimes distinguished.

Some corpora have been assembled simply to make available a text base for unspecified linguistic research. Such corpora, which may be called **general corpora**, consist of a body of texts which linguists analyse to seek

AN INTRODUCTION TO CORPUS LINGUISTICS

answers to particular questions about the vocabulary, grammar or discourse structure of the language. Are speakers or writers of American English, for example, more likely to say or write *in certain circumstances* rather than *under certain circumstances*? Is British usage the same? What prosodic, lexical or syntactic devices are used most frequently to initiate turn-bidding interruptions in discourse? The *SEU Corpus* was an early example of a general-purpose corpus which has been used especially for research on grammar (see Section 2.1.5). A general corpus is typically designed to be **balanced**, by containing texts from different genres and domains of use including spoken and written, private and public. Attempts may be made to include texts according to their perceived or possible typicality or influence in a language. Thus a greater proportion of samples from wide-circulation newspapers or best-selling novels might be included than from some other sources. General or balanced corpora are sometimes referred to as **core corpora**, which can be used as a basis for comparative studies.

Corpora which are designed with particular research projects in mind are sometimes called **specialized corpora**. Corpora assembled by major commercial publishers as sources of word frequency data and citations for the compilation of modern dictionaries are of this kind. Specialized corpora have also been assembled to study topics as varied as child language development (Carterette & Jones, 1974) or the English used in petroleum geology exploration, drilling and refining (Zhu, 1989). Corpora may be even more specialized and consist of examples of people disagreeing with each other in radio interviews, or of teachers' directives in high-school classrooms. Leech (1992: 112) has described the development of **training corpora** and **test corpora** as specialized corpora to facilitate the building of models of language and of language processing. Major types of specialized corpora include those compiled for studies of regional or sociolinguistic variation. **Dialect corpora, regional corpora, non-standard corpora** and **learners' corpora** come into this category.

Spoken language is by far the commonest mode or use of language, yet most corpus-based grammatical and lexical studies of English have so far been based on the analysis of **written corpora**. It is much slower and more difficult to make **spoken corpora** because transcription, ideally involving complex phonetic and prosodic features, is much more time-consuming and expensive to undertake. Nevertheless, specialized corpora of spoken language have been available for several years and new spoken language corpora currently being compiled will almost certainly reveal quite new insights into the essential nature of language and language use.

Corpora may also be broadly characterized according to the way they represent a language. On the one hand, a corpus can consist of a total statistical population. For example, a corpus consisting of the complete works of Charles Dickens or of all the editions of the *New York Times* between 1940 and 1990 represents a total population of text. The corpus is not representative of an entity. It is that entity. On the other hand, a one-million- (or 100-million-) word linguistic corpus which seeks to be representative of a language or language variety in a particular year (e.g. written or spoken New Zealand English in 1986) should ideally be sampled systematically from all the spoken and written English produced in that country in that year so that it represents the language as fairly as possible. Such a **sample-text corpus** is designed to be a representative sample of the total population of discourse. That population is not necessarily 'the language as a whole'. Texts can be sampled from sub-populations, according to regions, genres, or groups of users (e.g. school-children, women, journalists or immigrants). The individual speakers or writers who are included in such corpora may be anonymous, as is sometimes the case in journalistic writing or radio broadcasts. The extent to which a corpus can ever be considered to represent a language in general is currently a matter of some contention. In practice, whether a finite sample of a language could ever 'represent' the vast amount of a language produced in even a single day is always likely to be, in the final analysis, an act of faith.

A sample text corpus may consist of complete texts sampled from a population of complete texts (sometimes called a **full-text corpus**) or it may consist of samples of a specified size taken from complete texts. Particular corpora tend to be suitable for particular types of analysis and some corpora are simply not suitable for certain types of research. For stylistic or discourse studies, for example, a corpus which consists of 2,000-word samples extracted from many texts may not be able to capture reliably the internal structural characteristics of full texts where introductory and concluding sections may be expected to have different linguistic features. Such studies may require the use of full text corpora.

Corpora can consist of the 'raw' orthographic text of transcribed speech or of writing and contain a minimum of annotations which identify such divisions as paragraphs and line numbers. The original 'raw' text can also be annotated or pre-processed linguistically to show the word class of each word in the text by means of a grammatical **tag** or label which is attached to each word. Corpora can also be **parsed** to show the sentence structure and the function in the sentences of the different word classes. The **tagging** and **parsing** of corpora can now be undertaken automatically with increasingly high levels of reliability (see Section 4.1). Some corpora, such as the *Brown*, *LOB* and *London–Lund* corpora are also available in **concordanced** versions where all occurrences of any word are listed together in context (see Section 4.2.2).

A somewhat special case of pre-processed text being used for research occurs where the corpus is not itself a collection of texts, but is a collection of citations or a listing produced by previous corpus analysis. Some dictionaries, word lists and psycholinguistic databases which were originally based on corpus analysis have themselves become available in electronic form and are used in various fields of linguistic research. Researchers including Janssen (1990) and Vossen (1991) have used such corpora for phonological and semantic description. The electronic versions of the *Oxford English Dictionary* (*OED*) or the *Longman Dictionary of Contemporary English* (*LDOCE*) contain huge numbers of brief citations or sentences to illustrate meanings and uses and are rich storehouses of potential information on the English language. It is possible to examine such corpora to find answers to questions both trivial and consequential. In the case of the *OED* it is not difficult to find out what proportion of the headwords are of, say, Arabic origin, and to list these according to the year in which they were first noted being used in English. From the *LDOCE* it is possible to list all words with the same suffix (e.g. *-y*) or all headwords which are hyphenated (e.g. *number-crunching*) or all words or uses of words which have been noted as taboo, slang or derogatory.

The corpora types described above are typically finite in size and, indeed, for electronic corpora one million running words became a kind of unofficial standard size from 1964 until the early 1990s. More recently, however, some corpora have been compiled containing vast amounts of text which are added to, often opportunistically, and which are not necessarily balanced and structured, so that text does not systematically and proportionately come from particular genres or registers. New texts, from daily newspapers and other sources, may actually replace material which was in the corpus earlier. These **dynamic corpora**, sometimes also referred to as **monitor corpora**, are open-ended language 'banks' which are limited only by the financial resources and technology needed to maintain them. Sinclair (1992) conceived of them as huge, changing bodies of language of no finite size, flowing across a set of filters which extract linguistic evidence. Svartvik (1992) has noted that, instead of attempting to represent languages in finite collections of text, corpora compiled in the future are likely to become much more diverse to serve a range of purposes.

The types of corpora mentioned so far in this section have been **synchronic corpora**. A synchronic corpus is an attempt to represent a language or a text type at a particular time. The *Brown Corpus*, for example, contains written texts of American English published in 1961 (see Section 2.3.1.1). A **diachronic corpus**, on the other hand, represents a language over a period of time. The diachronic part of the *Helsinki Corpus of English Texts* (see Section 2.3.2.4), for example, contains English texts covering the period from about AD 700 to AD 1700 and can be used, among other things, for studying language change.

Such has been the growth in corpus-building activity since the mid-1980s, made possible by various technological advances in the capture, storage and processing of text, that scholars in many language-related fields now have a wide range of choices for selecting appropriate corpora to seek answers to particular research questions about the nature, structure and use of languages. Some of the results of corpus-based research on English are described in Chapter 3.

2.3 Major electronic corpora for linguistic research

2.3.1 First generation corpora

2.3.1.1 THE BROWN CORPUS

The *SEU Corpus*, begun in 1959, was the last major pre-electronic corpus (see Section 2.1.5). Only two years later, in 1961, on the other side of the Atlantic, planning began for the compilation of the first machine-readable corpus for linguistic research. Any account of corpus-based linguistic analysis must take as a reference point the pioneering *Brown University Standard Corpus of Present-Day American English*, commonly known as the *Brown Corpus* (Francis & Kučera, 1964). The *Brown Corpus* was significant not only because it was the first computer corpus compiled for linguistic research, but also because it was compiled in the face of massive indifference if not outright hostility from those who espoused the conventional wisdom of the new and increasingly dominant paradigm in US linguistics led by Noam Chomsky. Following the publication of Chomsky's own stimulating but controversial ideas in *Syntactic Structures* (1957), transformational generative grammarians increasingly took the position that the aims of linguistic theory should not be to record linguistic behaviour but rather to describe and account for what users of a language know. This movement carried all before it for a period and changed the direction of most linguistic research away from descriptive studies of performance to the modelling of competence. Chomsky, among others, argued against the use of corpora and statistically based, probabilistic models of competence derived from linguistic performance. In 1958, for example, Chomsky is reported to have argued that corpora were inadequate as a basis for describing grammatical rules on the grounds that 'Some sentences won't occur because they are obvious, others because they are false, still others because they are impolite' (Leech, 1991: 8). Five years later Chomsky is reported to have trivialized the relevance of statistical analyses of frequency of occurrence of linguistic items, when he spoke to a Linguistic Society of America Summer Institute audience by suggesting that although *I live in New York* is more frequent than *I live in Dayton, Ohio*, this did not have relevance for linguistic theory or description (see Halliday, 1991: 42; Biber & Finegan, 1991: 204).

It was in such an unsupportive environment that Nelson Francis and Henry Kučera began what must have seemed a huge and somewhat daunting task to compile a synchronic corpus of approximately one million words representative of the written English printed in the United States in the year 1961. Given the enormity of the task, and the available technology, this pioneering work was completed with remarkable speed, in that the corpus was available on computer tape with an accompanying manual by 1964.

The structure of the *Brown Corpus* consists of 500 samples each of about 2,000 words of continuous written English. The resulting corpus contains approximately 1,014,300 words. As Table 2.2 shows, the samples in the *Brown Corpus* were taken from a large number of text categories, from both informative and imaginative prose but excluding verse and drama.

Table 2.2 Structure of the *Brown Corpus* from Francis and Kučera (1964)

Text type		Daily	Weekly	Sub-category total	Category total	Proportion of the corpus (%)
I	**Informative prose (374 samples)**					75.0
A	**Press: reportage**					
	political	10	4	14		
	sports	5	2	7		
	society	3	0	3		
	spot news	7	2	9		
	financial	3	1	4		
	cultural	5	2	7		
	Total				44	8.8
B	**Press: editorial**					
	institutional	7	3	10		
	personal	7	3	10		
	Letters to the Editor	5	2	7		
	Total				27	5.4
C	**Press: reviews (theatre, books, music, dance)**	14	3		17	3.4
D	**Religion**					
	books			7		
	periodicals			6		
	tracts			4		
	Total				17	3.4

Table 2.2 continued

Text type		Daily	Weekly	Sub-category total	Category total	Proportion of the corpus (%)
E	**Skills and hobbies**					
	books			2		
	periodicals			34		
	Total				36	7.2
F	**Popular lore**					
	books			23		
	periodicals			25		
	Total				48	9.6
G	**Belles lettres, biography, memoirs etc.**					
	books			38		
	periodicals			37		
	Total				75	15.0
H	**Miscellaneous**					
	government documents			24		
	foundation reports			2		
	industry reports			2		
	college catalogue			1		
	industry house organ			1		
	Total				30	6.0
J	**Learned**					
	natural sciences			12		
	medicine			5		
	mathematics			4		
	social and behavioural sciences			14		
	political science, law, education			15		
	humanities			18		
	technology and engineering			12		
	Total				80	16.0

continued overleaf

Table 2.2 continued

Text type		Daily	Weekly	Sub-category total	Category total	Proportion of the corpus (%)
II	Imaginative prose (126 samples)					25.0
K	General fiction					
	novels			20		
	short stories			9		
	Total				29	5.8
L	Mystery and detective fiction					
	novels			20		
	short stories			4		
	Total				24	4.8
M	Science fiction					
	novels			3		
	short stories			3		
	Total				6	1.2
N	Adventure and western fiction					
	novels			15		
	short stories			14		
	Total				29	5.8
P	Romance and love story					
	novels			14		
	short stories			15		
	Total				29	5.8
R	Humour					
	novels			3		
	essays etc.			6		
	Total				9	1.8
GRAND TOTAL					500	100.0

The samples were 'selected by a method that makes it reasonably representative of current printed American English' (Kučera & Francis, 1967: xvii). The corpus was not intended to be representative of any assumed model of stylistic quality, but rather to serve as a standard of comparison for 'studies and analyses of present-day English'.

In establishing the categories and their subdivisions, there was an important link with the *Survey of English Usage Corpus*, which had been started shortly before in London. The categories for the *Brown Corpus* and the number of samples in each category were largely established at a conference at Brown University in February 1963 (Francis & Kučera, 1982: 5) in which Francis and Kučera were joined by Randolph Quirk, the director of the *SEU Corpus* project, as well as by prominent US scholars including Philip B. Gove, editor of *Webster's Third International Dictionary*, Patricia O'Connor and John B. Carroll. Francis and Kučera (1964) describe in detail the methods of random sampling used, as well as bibliographic details of the texts, copyright permission, and the coding conventions used for dealing with such things as abbreviations, formulas, foreign languages, quotations and punctuation. Many of the texts were sampled from local libraries. Table 2.2 shows the actual number of samples in each category of the corpus.

The texts in the *Brown Corpus* were originally card-punched with 70 characters per line plus locational information identifying the texts and line numbers. The corpus on 100,000 cards was then transferred to magnetic computer tape and became available for mainframe computers as well as more recently for microcomputers by means of diskette or CD-ROM. It is available in a number of versions or formats including one in which most punctuation has been removed. There is also a grammatically tagged version with each word assigned one of over 80 tags to specify its word class. Details about the availability of different versions of the *Brown Corpus* and several other corpora are available from the International Computer Archive of Modern and Medieval English (ICAME) at the Norwegian Computing Centre for the Humanities, Bergen (see Section 2.7).

The careful planning of the structure of the *Brown Corpus*, with the selection of text categories to represent a broad range of stylistic aspects of written American English, set a standard for corpus-based research. Another important standard set early for corpus research was the principle of free access. For over thirty years the *Brown Corpus* has been made available at cost for scholarly research all over the world without payment of copyright fees or any attempt to recover the costs involved in compiling the corpus in the first place. For both compiling the corpus and making it available so freely, Francis and Kučera are owed an enormous debt of gratitude by researchers on the English language, and particularly by the corpus linguists who have followed in their footsteps.

2.3.1.2 THE *LANCASTER–OSLO/BERGEN (LOB) CORPUS*

In 1964, when the *Brown Corpus* became available, the compilers expressed the hope that 'the Corpus may further prove to be standard in setting the pattern for the preparation and presentation of further bodies of data in English or in other languages' (Francis & Kučera, 1964: 2). Between 1970 and 1978 a corpus of written British English was compiled at the University of Lancaster and the University of Oslo in collaboration with the Norwegian Computing Centre for the Humanities at Bergen. The *Lancaster–Oslo/Bergen (LOB) Corpus* (Johansson et al., 1978) was intended to be a British English counterpart to the *Brown Corpus*. Like the American corpus, the *LOB Corpus* contains 500 texts of about 2,000 words each, all published in 1961, to give about one million words of running text in total. The categories in the two corpora are the same and the stratified random sampling principles used are also identical, although the sampling was of course based on different bibliographic sources and there are different weightings in the selection of news-papers. There were also small differences in the number of texts in some categories, and the *LOB Corpus* samples are more consistently grouped into subject categories than those in the *Brown Corpus*. These and other differences are described in detail in Johansson et al. (1978: 10–40). There were, for example, not surprisingly, in Category N (adventure and west-ern fiction) fewer westerns and more general adventure stories in *LOB* than in its American counterpart. However, the differences do not signi-ficantly alter the comparability of the two corpora.

It was recognized by the compilers that a one-million-word corpus is too small to represent adequately the incidence of particular low fre-quency items which may not be present at all, or are likely to occur in distorted proportions according to the choice of topics contained in the texts. As Johansson (1980: 26) noted, however,

> The true 'representativeness' of the *LOB Corpus* arises from the deliberate attempt to include relevant categories and subcategories of texts rather than from blind statistical choice. Random sampling simply ensured that, within the stated guidelines, the selection of individual texts was free of the conscious or unconscious influence of personal taste or preference.

Although the *LOB Corpus* contained texts produced in 1961, the same year as those included in the *Brown Corpus*, because *LOB* was compiled more than a decade after *Brown*, the compilers were able to take advant-age of developments in computer technology, and in the method used for coding items such as sentence-initial markers and abbreviations. The *LOB Corpus* became available on magnetic tape for mainframe com-puters, and subsequently on cartridge, diskette, microfiche and CD-Rom with versions for MS-DOS, Macintosh and Unix platforms. As well as the original text version of the *LOB Corpus*, partly analysed versions are available with the addition of grammatical tags to each word and in *Key Word in Context (KWIC)* concordances. The full range of versions of the *LOB Corpus*, including the computer requirements for each, is available from ICAME at the Norwegian Computing Centre for the Humanities, Bergen (see Section 2.7).

When the *LOB Corpus* became available as a matching corpus to the *Brown Corpus*, designed to facilitate comparative studies of written American and British English, it was soon apparent that reliable comparative studies of high frequency lexical items and grammar would be possible. Johansson (1980) suggested that it could be argued that the corpora were similarly constructed in that their frequency of use of high frequency grammatical words was similar, thus validating the categorization and sampling techniques employed. The results of some comparative studies of the *Brown* and *LOB* corpora are described in Chapter 3.

2.3.1.3 OTHER FIRST-GENERATION CORPORA MODELLED ON THE *BROWN CORPUS*

Three corpora modelled on the structure and size of the *Brown Corpus* have been produced for written varieties of Indian, New Zealand and Australian English. Because they have a similar structure to the *Brown* and *LOB* corpora they inevitably invite comparison with the earlier corpora. The *Kolhapur Corpus of Indian English* (Shastri, 1988) drew its samples from written material published in India in 1978. While the samples came from the same 15 genres as were used for *Brown* and *LOB*, the *Kolhapur Corpus* had slightly different weightings among the various categories of imaginative prose and between full-length novels and short stories, thus reflecting different cultural emphases. Essentially, there were only about half as many samples from the science fiction, adventure, western fiction, romance and love story categories as in the *Brown* or *LOB* corpora. The general fiction category was enlarged to make up the total of 500 samples.

Both the *Wellington Corpus of Written New Zealand English* and the *Australian Corpus of English* (*ACE*), also known as the *Macquarie Corpus of Written Australian English*, take 1986 as the baseline year for the selection of samples for published material, 25 years after 1961, the year from which the texts for the *Brown* and *LOB* corpora were selected. Bauer (1993a, b) describes difficulties in matching the six *Brown/LOB* categories of imaginative writing (K–R) in published New Zealand fiction, with the resulting decision to put all the fiction together in a single category. The comparatively small amount of publishing in New Zealand when compared with the output in the UK and USA also meant that for some text categories, *Wellington Corpus* samples had to include material published over a four-year period (1986 to 1990). Although the *Wellington Corpus* was designed to be able to be compared with *Brown* and *LOB* rather than being representative of written New Zealand English as such, Bauer (1993a: 2) notes that as a consequence one major type of fiction published in New Zealand, namely fiction written for children of various ages, was not included. Nevertheless, comparative studies of the New Zealand and Australian corpora with the other similarly structured corpora have revealed that they can be used as a basis for studying certain lexical and syntactic tendencies of the different varieties of English, as Collins (1991a, b) and Bauer (1993b) have shown.

Other corpus compilation projects related to the first-generation corpora include the *Corpus of English-Canadian Writing* project at Queens University in Kingston, Ontario, and containing the same written genre categories as the *Brown* and *LOB* corpora (with the addition of categories for feminism and computing) but intended to be three times as big. Thirty years after the texts in the *Brown* and *LOB* corpora were produced, a project at the University of Freiburg was established to compile parallel corpora of written American and British English texts produced in 1991. These later corpora modelled on *Brown* and *LOB* should enable researchers to document ongoing grammatical change in written English over the three decades (Sand & Siemund, 1992).

The first-generation corpora modelled on the *Brown Corpus* were important achievements which launched a large variety of studies, but they suffered from certain drawbacks. First, the size of the corpora at approximately one million words is obviously somewhat arbitrary and limiting (although this does not necessarily lead to unreliable research, as Biber (1993a, b) has suggested). One million words of running text was very large by most criteria in the early 1960s. However, it became clear that, for reliable information on lexical use, much larger corpora are needed especially for less frequent words. A corpus must be big enough to provide a substantial number of instances of a particular linguistic feature from a number of different texts in order to give us a reliable picture of how that feature is used.

In considerable numbers of studies of English grammar using the first-generation corpora, it has been difficult to find substantial or interesting differences between the regional varieties. Leitner (1991) has questioned whether using common genre categories for the selection of texts in corpora representing different regional varieties of English can make for valid comparative studies, since cultural norms may not be adequately reflected. He argued that it should not be assumed that Indian English is used with the same socio-political or technological presuppositions, or in the same categories, as American or British English. If we use corpora to make contrastive lexico-syntactic studies of different varieties of English it is likely that we will find that the main differences are not in the structures used but rather in the frequency with which these structural features are used in the different varieties. That is, rather than the presence or absence of items or structures in the different varieties, we are likely to find quantitative differences in their relative frequency of use.

One problem in undertaking comparative studies with the *Brown* and *LOB* corpora arises from statistical skewing derived from differences in sample size. In *Brown*, it was claimed that each '2,000-word sample' ends at the first sentence ending after 2,000 words. The average length of sample is actually 2,028.6 words, giving a total size for the 'one-million'-word corpus of 1,014,312 words. Sections A–J of the corpus (informative prose), which has 75% of the samples, actually has 83% of the additional 14,312 words over the one-million-word notional size. Section H, which notionally makes up 6% of the corpus, has about 18% of the additional material. In making comparisons between genres, this additional material could conceivably distort the quantitative analysis, although it is unlikely to affect the results when the corpus as a whole is being analysed.

In making comparisons between corpora, the overall length of each corpus can be significant. As we have seen, the *Brown Corpus* has 1,014,312 words of text. Even though the *LOB* compilers followed strictly the pre-scribed procedure used in *Brown* to make each sample, the *LOB Corpus* has 1,006,825 words according to the manual (Johansson et al., 1978). Seven-and-a-half thousand words difference in a corpus of more than one million words may be trivial, but it could make detailed comparisons less accurate than they should be. It is not a shortcoming of the corpora, but the software used in corpus analysis can also give quite widely diver-gent measures of the number of words in a corpus. Although the *LOB Corpus* 'officially' has 1,006,825 words, a mainframe computer reading the tape or a PC reading a CD-ROM for a concordance program can indicate that as many as 1,123,380 'words' were counted, if the software included aspects of the markup or computer coding as text. Word counts can also vary depending on whether numbers are counted or how hy-phens are treated.

However, in spite of such problems, considering the vast number of changes in the storage capacity, methods of text capture, and software which have occurred since 1961, it is really quite astonishing that the first-generation corpora have stood up so well to the needs of researchers on the English language. The ICAME bibliography (Altenberg, 1991b) records many hundreds of studies based on the *Brown* and *LOB* corpora in particular and they continue to be important sources for analysis, description and comparative purposes.

2.3.1.4 THE *LONDON–LUND CORPUS* (LLC)

The *Survey of English Usage* (*SEU*) *Corpus* compiled at University College London from 1959 was, as we have seen, part of the first generation of modern corpora but it was never intended to be computerized. The orthographically transcribed spoken half and the written half were both filed and analysed on paper in some 100 filing cabinet drawers at Uni-versity College.

In 1975, however, the *Survey of Spoken English* (*SSE*) was set up at Lund University in Sweden by Jan Svartvik initially to make available in electronic, machine-readable form the spoken part of the *SEU Corpus*.

The original 87 texts of transcribed speech totalling some 435,000 words were supplemented by 13 more texts to produce the complete *London–Lund Corpus* (*LLC*) of one hundred 5,000-word texts. The total of about half a million words made up by far the biggest and most widely used electronic corpus of spoken English available until the mid-1990s. The *LLC* adopted a less detailed prosodic analysis than had been used in the original corpus transcription, but it was still very rich, including as it does the following features:

> tone units (including the subdivision where necessary into subordinate tone units), onsets (the first prominent syllable in a tone unit), location of nuclei, direction of nuclear tones (falls, rises, levels, fall-rises etc.), boosters (i.e. relative pitch levels), two degrees of pause (brief and unit pauses alone or in combination) and two degrees of stress (normal and heavy). Also indicated are speaker identity, simultaneous talk, contextual comment ('laughs', 'coughs', 'telephone rings' etc.) and incomprehensible words (i.e. where it is uncertain what is said in the recording).
> (Greenbaum & Svartvik, 1990: 15)

The accurate orthographic transcription, prosodic notation and data entry of a spoken corpus of this size was a monumental effort and the *LLC* is not only important in its own right for the study of spoken British English but it is also a very important baseline record of data collected over a 25-year period from 1959 by which other corpora of spoken English can be evaluated.

The 87 spoken texts in the original version or the 100 texts in the full version have been used by researchers in many countries for studies which go well beyond the study of phonology. The detailed annotation has also facilitated numerous studies of lexis, grammar and especially discourse structure and function. The *LLC* presents some problems, however, for researchers. The texts recorded were of speakers who were predominantly highly educated adults. Many were academics or persons working in an academic environment (see Greenbaum & Svartvik, 1990: 20–45). The range of genre categories is narrow in comparison with the categories represented in, say, the more recent *International Corpus of English* (see Section 2.3.3.4) or in the informal use of English in daily social life. The prosodic notation shown in Figure 2.2 can make the corpus awkward to work with for some grammatical or collocational studies, and some researchers have found it helpful to strip the notation out of the corpus and deal with 'raw' orthographically transcribed text when studying certain lexico-syntactic or discourse features.

Thirty-four 'conversation' texts from the 100 texts in the *LLC* have been printed in hard copy as a book (Svartvik & Quirk, 1980), and the complete version of the *LLC* is now available on computer tape as well as on CD-ROM. These can be obtained through ICAME (see Section 2.7).

```
1  1  1   10  1  1  B  11   ((of ^Spanish)) . graph\ology#                    /
1  1  1   20  1  1  A  11   ^w=ell# .                                         /
1  1  1   30  1  1  A  11   ((if)) did ^y/ou _set _that# -                    /
1  1  1   40  1  1  B  11   ^well !J\oe and _l#                               /
1  1  1   50  1  1  B  11   ^set it betw\een _us#                             /
1  1  1   60  1  1  B  11   ^actually !Joe 'set the :p\aper#                  /
1  1  1   70  1  1  B  20   and *((3 to 4 sylls))*                            /
1  1  1   80  1  1  A  11   *^w=ell# .                                        /
1  1  1   90  1  1  A  11   "^m/\ay* I _ask#                                  /
1  1  1  100  1  1  A  11   ^what goes !\into that paper n/ow#                /
1  1  1  110  1  1  A  11   be^cause I !have to adv=ise# .                    /
1  1  1  120  1  1  A  21   ((a)) ^couple of people who are !d\oing [dhi: @]  /
1  1  1  130  1  1  B  11   well ^what you :d\/o#                             /
1  1  1  140  1  2  B  12   ^is to - - ^this is sort of be:tween the :tw\/o of /
1  1  1  140  1  1  B  12   _us#                                              /
1  1  1  150  1  1  B  11   ^what *you* :d\/o#                                /
1  1  1  160  2  1  B  23   is to ^make sure that your 'own . !c\andidate     /
1  1  1  170  1  1  A  11   *^[\m]#*                                          /
1  1  1  160  1  2  B  13   is . *.* ^that your . there's ^something that your /
1  1  1  160  1  1  B  13   :own candidate can :h\/andle# - -                 /
```

Figure 2.2   A fragment of the *LLC*

Some of the results of descriptions of English which have been based on the *LLC* are discussed in Chapter 3.

2.3.2   *Corpora of English compiled for specialized purposes*

2.3.2.1   CORPORA FOR LEXICOGRAPHY

Beginning in the late 1960s a number of electronic corpora were compiled for specialized purposes, especially, but not exclusively, for lexicographical projects of various kinds. Algeo (1988) reported the compilation of a corpus of about five million words drawn from the 18th century to the present which had been compiled for studying characteristic Briticisms in the English language. The corpus was initially on 110,000 slips but in its computerized form promises to be not only the basis for a dictionary of Briticisms but a source for the diachronic study of British English and a reference source for comparative linguistic and cultural studies especially between British and American English. The potential value of the corpus can be seen in the light it can throw on such phenomena as the possible source of the discourse item *you know*. Algeo (1988: 56) notes that:

> it has been widely assumed, on both sides of the Atlantic, that *you know* is an Americanism that has recently begun corrupting the purity of the tongue. However, a hundred and fifty years ago, Americans bemoaned it as a Briticism.

Algeo cites an 1835 issue of the *New Yorker* which contains the following:

> *you know* is a phrase that an Englishman throws in at the turn of every sentence, when he is hunting for a new idea or the words to fill the coming one – just as he has three adjectives for all the purposes of conversation, *clever,* . . . *nice* . . . and *nasty* . . . and with whomsoever you talk, of any education, man or woman, you will have them all before ten minutes are over

Another early electronic corpus compiled in the United States but for a very different lexicographic purpose was the *American Heritage Intermediate (AHI) Corpus*. This large commercial corpus of 5.09 million words of text was based on a 1969 survey of US schools and consists of 10,043 samples, each 500 words long, from publications which were widely read among American schoolchildren aged 7 to 15 years. This corpus has been described as the culture talking to its children (although it was in fact the **written** input to which children of the time were exposed at school). The original purpose of the corpus was to produce a citation base for the *American Heritage School Dictionary*. The word frequency lists published from the corpus have been the most comprehensive available for that genre. The *AHI Corpus* covered various school subject fields including reading, English and grammar, composition, literature, mathematics, social studies, spelling, science, music, art, religion, home economics, library fiction, non-fiction, reference and magazines.

The careful rationale for the sampling is described in Carroll et al. (1971). At the time it was compiled, the corpus had to be entered on punched cards, and it was not lemmatized (i.e. *sleep, Sleep, slept, sleeps, sleepy, sleeping,* etc. would all be counted as separate word forms or types), thus making it necessary to interpret carefully the word frequency tables which were produced from the corpus. Although the 1,000 most frequent types accounted for 74% of all the words in the corpus (and 5,000 types accounted for 89.4%), the frequency information for the remaining words was less reliable. The compilers of the corpus estimated that a corpus of up to 500 million words would be necessary to provide valid relative frequencies of the rarer words in the *AHI Corpus* and there is no reason to doubt that this would hold for other general corpora. The occurrence of hapax legomena (types which appear only once in a corpus) is a matter of chance in a particular corpus, arising from the particular topics represented in the sampling. Thus, whether or not the word *surcingle* appears in a corpus (and how many times it occurs) depends on whether horse riding or wearers of cassocks are mentioned in part of the discourse sampled. For this reason it is easy to overestimate the probability of occurrence of the low frequency words of a language which happen to occur in a particular corpus.

The *AHI Corpus* was one of the first computer-based databases for lexicographical purposes and the resulting dictionary a forerunner of a number of innovative, commercial, corpus-based dictionary projects which were published from the 1980s, including the *Longman Dictionary of Contemporary English* and the *Collins Cobuild English Language Dictionary*. These are discussed further in Section 2.3.3.

2.3.2.2 DICTIONARIES AS CORPORA

While electronic corpora have been used to make dictionaries, the other side of the coin is that some dictionaries have themselves been used as rather specialized kinds of corpora. For example, the development of systems for the automatic processing of natural languages for purposes such as translation requires detailed information about the possible meanings of individual words. At present, published dictionaries are the best practical source of information on the various senses of words. For this reason, machine-readable versions of dictionaries on computer tape or CD-ROM have been used for research on automatic sense disambiguation, among other things. Probably the best-known electronic dictionary used as a corpus in the 1980s was the *Longman Dictionary of Contemporary English* (*LDOCE*), which was available on tape for a number of research teams.

In the 1990s the publication of major standard dictionaries in electronic form has opened the way for a wide variety of research activities analysing the lexicon of particular languages and has facilitated the development of a probabilistic dimension in lexicography through associated word frequency studies. The most significant event was the publication of the *Oxford English Dictionary* (second edition) in electronic form. The *OED2* has over half a million entries, 2.4 million illustrative quotations and occupies some 572 megabytes of disk space. On CD-ROM, with the superb accompanying search-and-retrieval software developed specially for the dictionary, the headwords and citations in the *OED2* constitute a specialized corpus which can be used for an unprecedented variety of research activities. The late Anthony Burgess, in his *Observer* review of the electronic version of the *OED*, described this work as one of the major technological achievements of the century. The electronic version of the *OED* is marked up so that the retrieval software can readily locate every item in a particular category. For example, words can be located not only for definitions but also so that files can be made of words with particular morphological characteristics, words belonging to particular word classes, variant forms, words which had their first recorded use in the same year, words borrowed into English from particular languages (e.g. all words of Russian origin in English), all quotations in the dictionary from particular writers, and so on.

Although it is neither a dictionary nor a corpus of texts, the *Oxford Psycholinguistic Database* similarly provides a specialized lexical database useful for corpus linguistics research by bringing together a rather heterogeneous collection of information on some 99,000 English words likely to be of use in psycholinguistic research. Some 27 properties are provided for each word, including the number of letters, phonemes and syllables; information on word class; whether the word is dialectal, concrete or 'imageable'; and frequency data from several corpus studies based on the *Brown* and *London–Lund* corpora among others. The information in the database is categorized so that the user can retrieve individual parameters (e.g. all adverbs) or combinations (e.g. all adverbs beginning with the letter *a* and ending in *-ly*) or all words normally acquired by children before the age of six and with a specified frequency in one or more of the corpus word counts. The easy-to-use software is designed to run on Macintosh systems. Improvements in the design and content of the *Oxford Psycholinguistic Database*, as with any corpus or database, are still possible. One issue is the extent to which the word frequency data on American usage taken from the Thorndike–Lorge count made in the 1930s or the *Brown Corpus* of written American English from the year 1961 is reliable for psycholinguistic research in the UK or elsewhere in the 1990s or beyond. This issue applies more widely, of course, to the use of any corpus. For example, it is still an open question how well many of the texts which make up the *London–Lund Corpus*, which was compiled in the 1960s, accurately reflect contemporary spoken British English in the 1990s. Comparative studies of the stability of varieties of a language and of the nature and direction of language change are among the most needed areas of corpus-based research and can be expected to attract even more interest among scholars as new corpora become available for analysis.

Edwards (1993: 296) has described the characteristics of some of the other lexical databases which may be useful for corpus linguists, including the *MRC Psycholinguistic Database* and both the *CELEX Relational Database*, which contains lexical data on the vocabulary of Dutch, English and German, and the *Acquilex Project*, which also contains lexical data from a number of languages.

2.3.2.3 CORPORA FOR STUDYING SPOKEN ENGLISH

Whereas the *London–Lund Corpus* of spoken English has been used for lexical, grammatical and discourse analysis as well as for prosodic studies, the *Lancaster/IBM Spoken English Corpus* (*SEC*) (Knowles et al., 1992) has been designed and used most particularly for detailed prosodic research. The corpus consists of about 52,600 words of the spoken standard British English (RP) of adults sampled between 1984 and 1987 from 11 categories including radio news broadcasts, university lectures, religious broadcasts, broadcast fiction, poetry, dialogue and propaganda. One particular advantage of this corpus is that it is available in several versions including in orthographic transcription, with or without punctuation, grammatically tagged with the CLAWS tagset (see Section 4.1.2), parsed, and prosodically transcribed, showing features of stress, intonation and pauses.

A phonetic transcription and a digitized sound version now available on CD-ROM greatly enhance the usefulness of this valuable corpus for many kinds of phonological analysis, although because the corpus does not contain information on the social or educational background of its speakers there are certain limitations on its use for sociolinguistic analyses. For anyone considering the compilation of such a corpus, Knowles (1993) gives a telling description of the huge amount of detailed and painstaking work necessary in preparing even small amounts of text for analysis.

Another potentially important corpus under construction in the 1990s is the *Corpus of Spoken American English* (*CSAE*) (Chafe et al., 1991), designed to provide the first large computerized corpus of spoken American English as used by adults, and one of the few large spoken corpora compiled since the *London–Lund Corpus* of British English. Originally intended to be of about 200,000 words but more recently described as having up to one million words, *CSAE* will be made up of at least 80 hours of the transcribed naturally occurring speech of some 900 speakers, including dialogue and monologue, spontaneous and planned, face-to-face and telephone conversations, arguments, service encounters, sales pitches, workplace talk, business and political meetings, counselling, lectures, sermons, prayers, talk shows, radio phone-ins, broadcast news and sports commentaries. Although the *CSAE* is not designed specifically for dialect research, there is a range of speakers of different ages from different regional, ethnic, gender, religious and social groups. When completed, the transcribed corpus will also be linked to the original sound recordings of speech. This linking of visual and auditory versions on CD-ROM should facilitate a whole variety of research studies in addition to the obvious comparisons with written varieties and with other spoken varieties of English.

The Human Communication Research Centre (HCRC) at the Universities of Edinburgh and Glasgow has produced the *Map Task Corpus* (Anderson et al., 1991). It is available on eight CD-ROMs from the HCRC with transcribed speech linked to audio. In 16 hours of unscripted speech, a 147,000-word corpus was collected from 128 two-person conversations between 64 young adult Scottish students at the University of Glasgow. Unlike most spoken language corpora, the speech was collected in an experimental setting, with the interlocutors being engaged in a task in which one member of each pair had to draw a route on a schematic map on the basis of the discussion. There was systematic control of such factors as gender, friendship patterns and whether or not the interlocutors had eye contact. It will be of considerable interest to find out whether such a carefully designed task-based way of eliciting spoken language results in a corpus which is linguistically similar to spoken texts collected as people go about their ordinary lives. One of the strengths of the HCRC corpus is that it should make available a more fine-grained and controlled source of data for the study of variability in speech than is often possible from the topics and interactions which occur in the randomly selected texts which are normally part of corpora of spoken language.

One of the largest corpora of a particular variety of spoken English is the *Wellington Corpus of Spoken New Zealand English* (Holmes, 1995). This one-million-word corpus, which complements the *Wellington Corpus of Written New Zealand English* (Bauer, 1993a), was designed to reflect as much as possible casual conversation in informal contexts collected between 1988 and 1993. The composition of the corpus is formal monologue 12%, semi-formal speech including elicited monologue 13%, and informal dialogue 75%. The completed corpus of 500 samples each of about 2,000 words has been orthographically transcribed with minimal prosodic markup of features such as pause length. It will be particularly useful for studying lexical, grammatical and discoursal characteristics of New Zealand spoken English and for comparative studies of age and gender differences across these linguistic levels.

2.3.2.4 DIACHRONIC CORPORA

The study of language change is most naturally corpus based. It is scarcely surprising therefore that in the mid-1990s some of the most vigorous activity in corpus-based research has been in diachronic studies of English. With the earliest periods of a language it is possible for corpora to be more or less exhaustive collections of all known written records of the language. For example, the *Complete Corpus of Old English* prepared at the University of Toronto consists of 3,022 texts, the entire population of surviving Old English texts. Available now in electronic form, this corpus was published in 1981 as the basis for a definitive *Dictionary of Old English*. As we have seen in Section 2.3.2.2, the citations in the *Oxford English Dictionary* constitute a corpus made for lexicographical purposes. This corpus consists of quotations from mainly literary works – covering over eight centuries. The first specialized electronic diachronic corpus of English however is the *Helsinki Corpus of English Texts: Diachronic Part*. Compiled at the University of Helsinki between 1984 and 1991 (Kytö, 1991; Kytö & Rissanen, 1992), the corpus consists of some 400 samples of continuous text, with a total of 1.5 million words covering the period from Old English to Early Modern English (*c.* 750 to *c.* 1700). The genres include letters, sermons, diaries, legal and official documents and plays. The corpus is available from ICAME untagged for both mainframe computers and for personal computers on diskette or CD-ROM (see Section 2.7). The texts in the *Helsinki Corpus* are coded according to some 25 parameters including not only the author's age and gender but also the date of the manuscript, whether it is dialect, whether the text was intended to be private (e.g. a letter) and whether the writer and addressee had equal social standing. Because of the coding, computer searches can thus be directed at predefined parameters. Rissanen (1992: 187) has pointed out that although in theory it is possible to focus only on texts fulfilling particular parameters, e.g.

private letters written by middle-aged wives to their husbands between 1500 and 1640, or religious treatises written in the E. Midland dialect between 1250 and 1420

it was not always possible to code all the parameters with accuracy.

Compiling a corpus means an endless series of compromises. Just as a corpus will never reliably reflect all the language in all its varieties and modes of existence, so, too, parameter coding can never hope to give a complete and valid description of the samples.
(1992: 188)

Rissanen has described the difficulties involved in the compilation of a diachronic corpus to ensure adequate chronological, regional, socio-linguistic and generic coverage. Careful construction of the corpus is necessary if reliable comparative data is to be obtained. For example, study of the use of *hope* (noun and verb) in Early Modern English may show tentatively that women writers in Early Modern English used the word *hope* in private letters 60% more often than men writers. However, such a finding can only be of interest if the sampling is representative and the parameters are reliably encoded. The diachronic study of pronoun usage in various genres is another example where reliable text-type classification is crucial.

Two corpora of regional varieties of Early Modern English complement the *Helsinki Corpus*. These are corpora of early American English and older Scots English. Both were also compiled in Helsinki (Kytö, 1993). The *Corpus of Early American English* is intended to represent the period from the very earliest foundations of the first overseas variety of English from the beginning of the 17th century.

A further section of the *Helsinki Corpus* covers samples of British regional rural dialects collected in the 1970s. Preliminary analysis by Ihalainen (1991a) indicates that the use of electronic corpora will make possible the production of a new generation of more detailed and accurate grammars of English dialects including perhaps the redrawing of some dialect boundaries for phenomena such as the use of *done* as a past tense for *do* (*I went out and done a bit of gardening*).

The various sections of the *Helsinki Corpus* have offered easy access to machine-readable text for diachronic studies. Other diachronic corpus projects in the early 1990s also hold great potential for research. For example, a rich general-purpose diachronic corpus for a particular period has been provided in the *Century of Prose Corpus* (Milić, 1990). It has approximately half a million words of literary and non-literary English sampled from 120 authors published between 1680 and 1780. The 10 text categories range from biography, history and fiction to letters, essays and polemics, and they sample works ranging from major writers such as Boswell, Burke, Gibbon and Swift to the less well known. Compilers of diachronic corpora have numerous special problems to overcome. They have to achieve integrity of texts in their corpora through selecting appropriate scholarly editions; they have to transcribe manuscripts, and, where optical scanning fails, they have to ensure accurate keyboarding as a means of text input. The *Century of Prose Corpus* is not coded for as many parameters as the *Helsinki Corpus*, but nevertheless provides a valuable resource for research on the linguistic characteristics of writers and genres of the period, for descriptive and comparative purposes.

In the early 1990s there was a rapid increase in the number of English diachronic corpus projects. This is evident in reports by Kytö et al. (1994) and Kytö and Rissanen (1996) which describe such projects dealing mostly with more than one genre. Some of these corpora have been designed and annotated to accommodate research questions which were not possible in earlier corpora, including the way in which a three-way relationship involving variation across time, genre and idiolect may provide the context for language change (Wright, 1993). These new corpus projects will make possible computerized analysis of texts spanning over 12 centuries of English from the earliest extant Old English documents up to the present in several regional varieties. For example, the *Archer Corpus* project (Biber & Finegan, 1995) begins where the *Helsinki Corpus* left off by providing a 1.7-million-word collection of spoken and written texts from the mid 17th century to the present.

2.3.2.5 CORPORA FOR RESEARCH ON LANGUAGE ACQUISITION

The study of language acquisition and development is crucially dependent on transcriptions of interaction between and among children and caregivers in natural situations. Over the last three decades many rich and important bodies of language acquisition data have been recorded and transcribed for particular purposes. The *Child Language Data Exchange System* (*CHILDES*) has since the mid-1980s brought together bodies of mainly child language acquisition data from over 500 children to form a very large database, most of which has been reformatted according to a common set of transcription conventions. In addition, a set of over 20 software programs for analysing the texts has been developed and is available on a non-profit basis with the corpus on the same CD-ROM. Full details on the content, structure, transcription and coding systems as well as the software for analysis for the *CHILDES Database* are available in MacWhinney and Snow (1990) and in MacWhinney (1991). The *CHILDES Database* and the accompanying corpus analysis software have already influenced the way in which research is carried out on language acquisition. In particular, they hold promise for improving our understanding of the factors which control the process of acquisition through the ability to describe patterning of a probabilistic nature in large amounts of data.

The *CHILDES Database* is large and consists of some 20 million words. The majority of the transcripts are of the acquisition of English but the corpus as it grows is potentially a major source of data for comparative studies as well. This means not only comparing different languages, but also acquisition of first and second languages, or acquisition of normal and impaired language. For example, researchers may wish to compare how linguistic means for marking comparisons of quantity are made. Instead of being dependent on a possibly unrepresentative diary study of a single child, the database makes it possible to retrieve all instances of comparison from different studies of different children in different contexts and to provide descriptions of the relative frequency of the devices used. Using the *CHILDES Database*, many hypotheses can be tested which were simply beyond the scope of the data gathered and transcribed in individual diary studies. Another advantage of the *CHILDES Database* is that it contains the corpora used in some of the classic and most influential studies of child language acquisition, including the large longitudinal studies of Adam, Eve and Sarah undertaken by Brown and his students at Harvard in the 1960s and beyond, as well as data collected for well-known studies by Bloom, Clark, Fawcett, Fletcher, Berko-Gleason, Snow, Wells, Slobin and Weir. The corpus compiled by Carterette and Jones (1974) of conversations among American interlocutors from children beginning elementary school to adults is also included in the *CHILDES Database* in both orthographic and phonemic notation. The *Child Language Analysis* (CLAN) software can be used for a large variety of analyses of texts including finding the mean length of utterance, the frequency of particular words or phrases, particular collocations, or the extent to which adult and child interlocutors repeat or expand upon ('imitate') each other's speech. Admittedly, much of the hypothesis testing and theory building associated with language acquisition research requires experimental designs involving comprehension of input rather than observational studies of speech production based on a corpus. The *CHILDES Database* has nevertheless opened up possibilities for the study of language development which could only be dreamed of before the era of electronic corpora.

While the *CHILDES Database* is a repository of many different kinds of language acquisition data, the *Polytechnic of Wales (POW) Corpus* is a purpose-built electronic corpus for investigating the acquisition and development of syntactico-semantic structures by children. The *POW Corpus* consists of approximately 65,000 words of the informal spoken language of 120 children aged from 6 to 12 years in South Wales. The electronic version is not marked up with prosodic information. However, the corpus has been grammatically parsed manually in terms of a version of systemic functional grammar (Halliday, 1985). The data was controlled for the gender, age and socio-economic status of the children and includes adult–child interviews and spontaneous speech among child peers.

The grammatical model used means that the phrase markers for the *POW Corpus* can be very large and complex whether being represented in linear form or in a hierarchical tree diagram (Souter, 1993). The *POW Corpus* nevertheless provides a detailed and sophisticated grammatical analysis of language acquisition data and is available for scholarly research through ICAME (see Section 2.7).

Corpora have also been assembled for research on second or foreign language acquisition. These include the *European Science Foundation Second Language Databank* (*ESFSLDB*) of transcribed speech collected for the longitudinal study of the learning of Dutch, English, French, German or Swedish by adult immigrants from different language backgrounds including Punjabi, Spanish, Turkish, Finnish, Italian and Moroccan Arabic (Perdue, 1993).

Study of the characteristics of English as a foreign language will be facilitated by several important corpora. An *International Corpus of Learners' English* (*ICLE*) is being developed at the Catholic University of Louvain in Belgium (Granger, 1993). The corpus is compiled from written texts produced by advanced learners of English from a number of countries including Belgium, China, France, Germany, the Netherlands and Sweden. The texts come from 500-word student essays. Each learner variety has a minimum of 400 essays, thus making up national subcorpora of approximately 200,000 words each. Study of the general characteristics of interlanguage, the transitional forms used by learners of a second language, should also benefit from this corpus.

Whereas the *ICLE* is designed primarily for academic research, a large corpus of learners' English has been developed for academic research, lexicography and for the preparation of commercial language teaching materials (Warren, 1992). The *Longman Corpus of Learners' English* (*LCLE*) totals approximately 10 million words and is made up of samples of written English from sources including examination answers, letters, reports, diaries and student essays from learners of English of over eight different levels of proficiency from over 160 different language backgrounds.

Interlanguage studies of the written English of mainly Cantonese learners of English will be facilitated by the completion of the five-million-word *Hong Kong University of Science and Technology* (*HKUST*) *Corpus* (Milton & Tong, 1991). The corpus will be probably the largest machine-readable corpus yet produced of the written English of Chinese learners and also one of the largest corpora of any single group of learners. It is intended that it will be available with grammatical and discourse feature tags.

The use of this corpus to describe the rule base of the written English of learners of Chinese background is intended to inform the development of English teaching materials.

2.3.2.6 OTHER CORPORA FOR SPECIAL PURPOSES

As Greenbaum (1992: 171) noted in paraphrasing Ecclesiastes, 'Of making many corpora there is no end'. In addition to the established general or comparative corpora mentioned earlier in this section, there are, as we have seen, increasing numbers of corpora being compiled for special purposes. Some of them will doubtless be used for other comparative purposes. Although the word 'corpus' is sometimes used to label a machine-readable version of even a single book or quite small collections of texts, the majority of these corpus projects for specialized purposes have settled on a corpus size of between about 100,000 and two million words of running text in length.

In 1985 it was probably a reasonable expectation to be able to list all the electronic corpora compiled for linguistic research for all languages. It is however no longer possible to be sure that any list of available corpora, even for English, is fully comprehensive or up to date. Among the specialized corpora of English texts compiled since the 1970s which can be relevant for linguistic research, however, there are a few which can give some idea of the scope of specialized corpus compilation.

Since the early 1970s a group led by Jan Aarts at the University of Nijmegen has been associated with a number of important corpus-building and corpus-analysis projects which have as one of their major goals the grammatical description of English. The *Nijmegen Corpus* consists of about 132,000 words of British English from 1962 to 1968. Six 20,000-word extracts of written, mainly literary, English from six authors and 12,000 words of transcribed sports commentary make up the corpus. The *Nijmegen Corpus* is analysed in terms of a very large set of labelled trees or phrase markers, and is intended to be used with the *Linguistic Data Base* (*LDB*) also developed at Nijmegen (see Section 4.1.4).

As Oostdijk (1991: 14) has pointed out, experience with the *Nijmegen Corpus* highlighted various shortcomings in the way in which linguistic knowledge could be formalized for the analysis of texts. In a sense, work on the 1.5-million-word *Tools for Syntactic Corpus Analysis* (*TOSCA*) *Corpus* project at Nijmegen grew out of earlier developmental work on the smaller *Nijmegen Corpus*. The *TOSCA Corpus* is linguistically analysed and consists of 75 samples each of 20,000 words from various fiction and non-fiction genres in written British English. The samples are larger than in most corpora of this size, in accordance with the compilers' views on the need for samples of a certain minimum size as a foundation for quantitative studies. The texts which make up the *TOSCA Corpus* are intended to be representative of written-to-be-read, published, educated contemporary British English prose produced between 1976 and 1986 (see Oostdijk, 1988a, 1991; van Halteren & Oostdijk, 1993). Forty-five samples come from 21 non-fiction genres including, for example, (auto)biography, history, literary criticism, politics, women's studies, chemistry, economics, physics. There are 30 samples from 9 fiction genres, including, for example, horror, humour, love and romance, and general fiction.

At the Hong Kong University of Science and Technology a one-million-word corpus of the English of computer science has been developed, intended to assist the teaching of English for computer science students in Hong Kong (Fang, 1993; James, 1996). The corpus consists of three 2,000-word samples from each of some 166 English language textbooks used in computer science courses in the early 1990s.

Other specialized corpora with a similar applied linguistic purpose include the *Jiao Tong University Corpus for English in Science and Technology* (*JDEST*) and the *Guangzhou Petroleum English Corpus* (*GPEC*) produced in China. Both are designed to facilitate lexical analysis of particular registers, including counts of high frequency words. The *JDEST Corpus* was compiled in the 1980s and consists of about one million words from written English texts in mainly the physical sciences, engineering and technology. The *GPEC* consists of about 411,000 words comprising 700 texts from the petroleum industry from written American and British English sources of the mid-1980s.

In 1993, Stenström and Breivik announced the development of a corpus of London teenager language (*COLT*), being a half-million-word corpus of the English of 13–17 year-olds. After its completion in 1994, *COLT* was incorporated into the *British National Corpus*.

The commercial publication of corpora such as those described by Murison-Bowie (1993), each of one million words of running text produced from newspapers or from academic writing in many genres, with analytical software for use on microcomputers, now means that individual researchers, language teachers or scholars working independently who have contributed so much to language studies in earlier generations can undertake original investigations outside academic institutions.

Corpora of languages other than English are also increasingly numerous. For example, the European Corpus Initiative (see Section 2.7) has produced a 93-million-word corpus which includes texts from most of the major European languages and some others including Chinese, Malay and Japanese. A large corpus of 27 million words of text from Dutch newspapers has been made available for research through the Institute for Dutch Lexicography at Leiden University. A corpus of 28 million sentences of written Japanese and a much smaller corpus of transcribed spoken Japanese are reported to have been produced for the Japanese Electronic Dictionary Research Institute. Bilingual corpora have also been compiled containing parallel texts from pairs of languages such as English, Finnish, French, German, Greek, Norwegian, Spanish, Swedish and Welsh.

With continuing improvements in text capture and storage, the design of new software for analysis, and the further development of methodological paradigms for computer corpus research, corpus compilation projects and research based on these corpora can be expected to develop vigorously in the comparatively near future.

While most of the corpora discussed so far were compiled as text bases for various kinds of linguistic investigation, much of the grammatical analysis of these corpora was what might be called lexical grammar, focusing on the behaviour of particular words in context. It was not long however before groups of researchers, especially those with an interest in computational linguistics and applications of natural language processing, saw the need for improving on unanalysed raw corpora by having a grammatical label or 'tag' attached to each word in the corpus. It is possible to carry out grammatical tagging by hand. Thus, in the sentence *Liz returned to her job*, tags can be attached to each word to show that *Liz* is a proper noun, *returned* is a finite past tense verb, *to* is a preposition, *her* is a possessive pronoun, and *job* is a singular countable noun. The tagged sentence might look like this –

Liz_NP returned_VB to _PE her_PP job_NN

Manual tagging of all the words in a large corpus is slow work, however, and therefore attempts were made to develop automatic grammatical tagging systems. Working initially with the *Brown Corpus* in the 1960s, researchers have developed increasingly sophisticated automatic word-class annotation systems and have also made some progress in developing automatic parsers which map out the structure and functions of sentence constituents. Grammatically annotated and analysed corpora are described further in Section 4.1.

2.3.3   Second generation mega-corpora

As we have seen, most of the first-generation publicly available machine-readable corpora were modelled on the *SEU* and *Brown* corpora in size or in the way they set out to represent a particular variety of a language. Until the 1980s, one million words, the size of the *SEU* and the *Brown* corpora, was what Leech (1991: 22) called the 'going rate'. Although in the 1960s and 70s, corpora of one million words (or even less) had been a lot of text to capture, store, manage and analyse, it became obvious that they were too small for most kinds of lexical and semantic analysis (see Section 2.5.3). Fortunately, developments in technology for text capture and storage came at the right time and made bigger corpora possible, so that by the 1990s corpora of 100 million words or more became available.

2.3.3.1 THE *COBUILD* PROJECT

The first major machine-readable corpus-based lexicographical project since the *American Heritage* project of the 1970s was also the first major mega-corpus project. The *Cobuild* project, which made use of the *Birmingham Collection of English Text*, was a joint venture between a major commercial publisher, Collins, and a research team based in the English Department of the University of Birmingham, hence *Cobuild* (*Collins Birmingham University International Language Database*). From a commercial perspective, the corpus has usually been referred to as the *Cobuild Corpus*, but it is also widely known as the *Birmingham Corpus*, and both terms are used in the present text. The task of compiling the corpus, which was to be the basis initially for the production of a new English dictionary, began in 1980. A full account of this innovative dictionary-making project is contained in Sinclair (1987).

According to Renouf (1987: 3), the so-called *'Main' Cobuild Corpus* was designed initially to represent the English language as it was 'relevant to the needs of learners, teachers and other users, while also being of value to researchers in contemporary English language'. To this end, the structure and content of the corpus were designed according to certain principles. These included: 25% of the corpus should be from spoken texts; the corpus should reflect broadly general rather than technical language; the corpus should reflect current usage from 1960 and after, and preferably very recent 'naturally occurring' text, rather than scripted drama. Prose, including fiction, was included, but not poetry. The texts were selected from speech and writing produced by adults aged 16 or over and were of 'standard', not regional, dialects, predominantly British English (70%), with some American (20%) and other regional varieties.

The written texts were not selected randomly but were chosen using criteria such as that they should be from the more popular, established and widely read works. Authorship was 75% male and 25% female. Spoken texts came from a variety of transcripts including radio broadcasting and university archives of oral interviews and lectures. With the addition of further newspaper and journalistic texts, the *Main Corpus* consisted of approximately 7.3 million words by August 1982. Some idea of the scope of the *Cobuild Corpus* can be seen in the Introduction to the *Collins Cobuild English Language Dictionary*, which lists the sources used.

By the time the *Cobuild Dictionary* was published in 1987, the *Main Corpus* had been supplemented by a continually growing 13-million-word *'Reserve' Corpus* of fiction and non-fiction, selected not according to a preconceived framework giving a balance of genres, but especially according to variety of topic.

The published description and analysis of the combined *Main* and *Reserve Cobuild Corpus* in Renouf (1987) was detailed as to the categorization of texts into primary discourse functions (e.g. survey, procedure, argument, narrative, historical fiction, letter, face-to-face informal conversation) and also as to topic, date of publication, author's gender and author's regional variety of English. In the first instance, however, the *Cobuild Corpus*, like most others, has tended to be used as a whole rather than being cited in published genre studies. There was also a smaller subcorpus containing about one million words representative of the English used in texts and course books for learners of English (the *TEFL Corpus*). This was compiled as part of the *Cobuild* project to be a point of reference for future developments in curriculum design for teaching English as a foreign language.

The *Cobuild* project broke new ground, not only because of the size of the computer corpus but because it associated corpus making with a particular commercial research and development project to produce corpus-based dictionaries, grammars and language teaching courses. Inevitably the size of the corpus as well as commercial and copyright considerations have meant that access to the corpus has not been as easy as for the first generation of computer corpora. Nevertheless, during the 1980s researchers from various parts of the world were welcomed to Birmingham to work with some of the contents of what was at that time the largest and most modern corpus available.

Late in 1990, John Sinclair, the director of the *Cobuild* project, announced that the corpus database was being expanded into a huge corpus-building initiative called *The Bank of English*, a corpus of potentially hundreds of millions of words. By 1997 the size of this monitor corpus was reported to be over 300 million words and growing. A dynamic element was thus introduced to the corpus by which new text was continually added to the database for analysis by sophisticated software to detect new words and uses of words. Early research results from this corpus are described in Renouf (1993). Blackwell (1993) has described some of the problems associated with working with such vast amounts of data, including, for example, about 2.5 million words per month of new text coming from one single newspaper. Typographical errors, unwanted electronic 'control' instructions from computer files, incompatibility of hardware and software and markup of text all help to make the compilation of such a dynamic, ever-changing monitor corpus something of a challenge. Because the content of a monitor corpus changes, the ideal of accountability through the reproducibility of results has to be considered in a new light. While the future is unclear on the eventual scope and use of *The Bank of English* corpus, its *Cobuild* precursors set new standards in the management and use of mega-corpora, and the dictionaries based on it have been well received and widely used.

2.3.3.2 THE *LONGMAN CORPUS NETWORK*

The *Longman Corpus Network* is a commercial database consisting of three major corpora, the *Longman/Lancaster English Language Corpus* (LLELC), the *Longman Spoken Corpus* (LSC), and the *Longman Corpus of Learners' English* (LCLE) already described in Section 2.3.2.6. Each of these has different design features and purposes but together they were compiled as a basis from which reliable descriptions of English could be made, especially for the compilation of dictionaries for non-native speakers of English (Summers, 1991). As well as having an independent existence within the *Longman Corpus Network*, the *LSC* has since become a major part of the Longman contribution to the much larger *British National Corpus* project (see Section 2.3.3.3).

In the late 1980s, in collaboration with Geoffrey Leech, who had directed the compilation of the *LOB Corpus* at Lancaster University between 1970 and 1976, Della Summers and her team began compiling the *Longman/Lancaster English Language Corpus*. It was intended to be a 'well-balanced' corpus of 20th-century English, covering British, American and other major varieties of native-speaker English in both spoken and written varieties, and to eventually contain up to 50 million words. Like the *Cobuild Corpus*, the new corpus was designed to overcome the limitations for lexicography of the 'standard' one-million-word corpora and to be

> representative of the standard language in a very general sense, not restricted to a regional variety (e.g. British English or a local dialect) or a narrow range of text types (e.g. scientific texts, newspaper writing, language of a particular social class).
> (Summers, 1991: 4)

The principle of representativeness was intended to be achieved by selecting texts in two ways. Half the corpus (the 'Microcosmic' half), consisting only of books, was compiled by random selection procedures using Whitaker's *Books in Print* as the source of titles. Only books for adults written after 1900 were included. The other half of the corpus was selected through a mixture of pragmatic measures, such as influentialness and popularity, to gather a broad range of objectively defined text types according to predetermined ratios. The corpus was weighted by having approximately 58% informative and 42% imaginative texts which were sampled in chunks of up to 40,000 words from over 2,000 books, periodicals and even unpublished sources. In including such a high proportion of imaginative writing, it was argued that fiction is a more influential genre than non-fiction and has a higher readership based on library-lending statistics and best-seller lists. However, it might also have been argued that newspaper English has an even more massive and diverse readership, such that journalistic genres have become the most widely read and influential of all written genres of the late 20th century.

The *LLELC* can be made available from the publisher at cost and under licence as a non-analysed or untagged corpus for academic research. Its overall structure and its various constituent genre subject fields are outlined in Figure 2.3. Rather than being organized according to general genre categories such as 'academic' or 'press', as was the case in several of the first-generation corpora, the *LLELC* has a topical basis according to general subject fields, it being argued by Summers (1991: 7)

1 NATURAL AND PURE SCIENCE (6%) Maths Physics Chemistry Biology Astronomy	6 ARTS (7.9%) Visual arts Architecture Performing Media Literary Design
2 APPLIED SCIENCE (4.3%) Engineering Communications Technology Computing Energy Transport	7 BELIEF AND THOUGHT (4.7%) Religion Philosophy Occult Mythology Folklore
3 SOCIAL SCIENCE (14.2%) Sociology Geography Anthropology Medicine Psychiatry Psychology Law Education Linguistics	8 LEISURE (5.7%) Food Travel Fashion Sport Household Antiques Hobbies Gardening
4 WORLD AFFAIRS (10.4%) History Government Politics Military Archaeology Economics Development	9 FICTION (40%) General fiction Historical fiction Science fiction Romantic fiction Mystery Adventure
5 COMMERCE AND FINANCE (4.4%) Business Finance Industry Employment Occupations	10 POETRY, DRAMA, HUMOUR (2.3%)

Figure 2.3 Subject fields included in the *LLELC*

that the approach was more appropriate for lexical research. Within these 10 'superfields', individual subjects can be separately identified. Thus the vocabulary used in relation to tennis can be studied within sport as part of Superfield 8.

2.3.3.3 THE BRITISH NATIONAL CORPUS (BNC)

Whereas in the 1960s the systematic compilation of one-million-word corpora was a huge task, by the 1980s, as we have seen, improved technology and a better appreciation of the shortcomings of one-million-word corpora for some purposes encouraged more ambitious enterprises. Between 1991 and 1995 the *British National Corpus* was undoubtedly the most ambitious corpus compilation project yet attempted. Begun as a collaboration between major academic, commercial publishing and publicly funded institutions, with the British government paying half of the cost, the project was established to produce a corpus of about 100 million words of contemporary spoken and written British English. The corpus was designed to be representative of British English as a whole and not just one particular genre, subject field or register. Oxford University Press, Longman Group (UK) Ltd, W. & R. Chambers, the British Library and the Universities of Oxford and Lancaster brought together their respective strengths and experience in electronic text management and publication, lexicography and corpus analysis, to design, develop and annotate this corpus. Because the *BNC* has a principled structure for the collection of spoken and written text and is finite in size, it is likely to be a major point of reference for British English, just as the *SEU*, *Brown* and *LOB* corpora were for first-generation corpus research. The *BNC* was designed to be well balanced, with a wide range of genres from written and spoken English, and to be widely accessible for educational, academic and commercial purposes.

The 4,124 texts in the *BNC* come from 90% written and 10% spoken sources. Even though the 10-million-word spoken section was at the time the largest collection of spoken English ever assembled, Leech (1993b) has noted that the *BNC* still does not redress the severe imbalance between spoken and written data which has been characteristic of most corpora. The texts in the *BNC* from written sources consist of about 75% 'informative' prose, all post-1975, and about 25% 'imaginative' (literary works), all post-1960. The proportion of imaginative text samples is possibly higher than the proportion of fiction among published output during the sampling period, but imaginative text was considered to warrant 25% in light of what was judged to be the continuing influential cultural role of literature and creative writing. The informative prose section of the *BNC* consists of texts from the categories shown in Table 2.3, with the proportion of texts in each category being based loosely on the

Table 2.3 Structure of the informative prose section of the *BNC*

	% of informative prose section	% of total written section
Natural and pure science	6.8	5
Applied science	13.3	10
Social and community	13.3	10
World affairs	20.0	15
Commerce and finance	13.3	10
Arts (rock & pop, dance, theatre, etc.)	13.3	10
Belief and thought (religion, philosophy, etc.)	6.7	5
Leisure (sports, gardening, etc.)	13.3	10
Total	100.0	75

pattern of book publishing in the UK during the last twenty years or so, as shown by the *British National Bibliography* and other published sources.

For the written section of the corpus, about 60% is taken from books, about 25% from periodicals, about 5% from published brochures and other ephemera, about 5% from unpublished letters, essays, minutes, etc., and the remainder from such sources as plays or speeches which have been 'written-to-be-spoken'. The written corpus is also planned to represent different so-called 'levels' of British English, with about 30% coming from more literary or technical 'high' style, about 45% being 'middle' and about 25% a more informal or 'low' style.

For the 10-million-word spoken part of the *BNC*, there are two major sources of text (Crowdy, 1993). To get coverage of text types, context-governed material was collected consisting of recordings of the following: educational and informative events in lectures, tutorials and classrooms; news reports; business events such as demonstrations, consultations and interviews; official and public events such as sermons, political speeches, public meetings and parliamentary debate; leisure events such as sports commentaries, club meetings, broadcast phone-ins and chat shows. These texts were collected systematically in 12 regional sampling areas throughout the United Kingdom.

The second type of spoken text consists of up to 2,000 hours of transcribed recordings made by 124 volunteers (and their interlocutors) from all walks of life, recruited systematically from 38 different parts of the UK from four different socio-economic groupings and with balanced coverage of male and female speakers of a wide range of ages between 15 and 60+. Each volunteer recorded, as unobtrusively as possible on a small portable recorder, all their conversations over a two-day period.

All participants were told they had been recorded and given the chance to have the tape erased. Details were also systematically kept of various details of the situation of discourse and the interlocutors. These include the setting, activity at the time of recording, location, time, date, audience, degree of spontaneity, topic, gender of participants, age, race, occupation, education, social group, relationship between interlocutors, dialect, etc. All the spoken text is transcribed orthographically with pauses (vocalized and non-vocalized), hesitations, false starts, overlapping speech and repetitions indicated, and some paralinguistic features such as 'shouting or whispering'. There is little prosodic information and no phonetic features are marked (Crowdy, 1994). The *BNC* will therefore not be used for research requiring fine-grained phonetic analysis, although original recordings may eventually be available.

The *BNC* was from the beginning envisaged not as a passive database for casual research. With the very considerable cost of such a corpus compilation project, and the involvement of commercial publishers interested in producing better lexicographical and grammatical reference books, the project was envisaged as contributing to information technology in the 1990s and beyond through the development of more sophisticated processing of natural language by computers. It was also envisaged as providing a pattern for similar national corpus developments for other countries and other languages.

Sampling is always a major issue in corpus design and the *BNC* has set new standards in the way it has been designed to be representative. For a corpus to be 'representative' there must be a clearly analysed and defined population to take the sample from. But because we cannot be confident we know all the possible text types nor their proportions of use in the population, a 'representative' sample is at best a rough approximation to representativeness, given the vast universe of discourse. The *BNC* consists of text samples which are each generally no longer than 40,000 words. The method of sampling from the universe of spoken and written English available was a principled one involving text both as a produced phenomenon (as sampled from national bibliographies) and as a received phenomenon (as sampled from best-seller lists, library loan figures, and circulation figures). This illustrates the importance of some element of subjective judgment in designing a corpus. For example, the fact that a book is published is, of course, no guarantee that it is widely read (or read at all). On the other hand, quite ephemeral writing such as junk mail may be read by large numbers of people. Thus book best-seller lists, library-lending statistics and periodical circulation figures can only partially reflect receptive use and influence. Since reception measures of popularity, or production measures of representativeness, in themselves tell only part of the story, the *BNC* compilers employed layered sampling involving four selection features: domain, time, medium (books, periodicals, leaflets, unpublished, etc.) and level. Layered sampling was intended to act as a control on the collection of texts so as to ensure that the corpus was representative of a broad range of styles of English. Thus sampling was based not only on the production and on the reception of the text, but on the nature of the text itself as representing a certain kind of language. This approach to sampling was undertaken in the expectation that linguistic analyses of the corpus could be used both to describe 'modern British English' as a whole and for comparative studies between different parts of the corpus.

As a kind of control to monitor the intuitive categories of sampling, about half the texts in the published books and periodicals category were randomly selected from catalogues (such as *Books in Print*) without regard for the target proportions of the 'domain', 'time' or 'level' features of selection. Once randomly picked, these texts were then classified according to the selection feature categories.

In addition to the four selection features with specified target proportions for selecting texts, the *BNC* has a second set of 'classificatory features' for which no target proportions are set, but which make possible comparative studies. These 'classificatory features' include text composition (single authorship or multiple authorship of a collection of smaller texts), subject field, gender, age and ethnic group of author, and target age group of the text.

The texts in the *BNC* have been annotated and entered into the corpus using an encoding system which makes use of the Standard Generalized Markup Language (SGML) and conforms to the TEI (Text Encoding Initiative) (see Section 2.6.5). Automatic word-class tagging was carried out using advanced versions of the CLAWS tagging system developed at Lancaster University (see Section 4.1.2).

The sheer size of the *BNC* posed challenges for text capture, tagging, storage and processing capacity. The 100 million words make up over 6.25 million sentences. Errors are inevitable in transcription (e.g. *there/ their*), and spelling errors in the original written texts, or from optical scanning (*clear* read as *dear*) cannot all be corrected in a corpus of that size. Similarly, grammatical tagging cannot be expected to be exhaustively checked and corrected for such a huge corpus within the time and budget available. To proof-read thoroughly the text of a 100-million-word corpus, allowing 45 minutes for 1,000 words, would take approximately 75,000 hours, or the work of 40 people for about a year. To thoroughly check the accuracy of tagging in the same way could be expected to take much longer, even with machine assistance.

It is always hard to predict the use to which a corpus will be put and the discoveries about a language which will be revealed by research on that corpus. Although until 1996 its use was restricted to researchers from within the European Community, it seems certain that the *BNC* will become an international benchmark for corpus linguistics, an indispensable basis for the description of British English, and for research

AN INTRODUCTION TO CORPUS LINGUISTICS

on theories of language, sociolinguistic variation and applied linguistic studies. In addition, studies in these traditional areas may be complemented by research on the nature and process of corpus compilation and the nature and extent of well-formedness in text. Further information about the *BNC* and a smaller 'sampler' version can be obtained at the following e-mail address: natcorp@oucs.ox.ac.uk, or on the World Wide Web at http://info.ox.ac.uk/bnc/.

2.3.3.4   THE *INTERNATIONAL CORPUS OF ENGLISH* (ICE)

The most ambitious corpus project for the comparative study of English worldwide is the *International Corpus of English* (*ICE*) (Greenbaum, 1996b). As a whole, *ICE* will be a mega-corpus, but its component parts are more modest in size. In 1988, the late Sidney Greenbaum, Director of the Survey of English Usage at University College London, proposed the development of a large corpus for the comparative study of both spoken and written forms of regional varieties of English throughout the world. The *ICE* project envisages the compilation of up to 20 parallel subcorpora, each consisting of one million words of the English used by adults over the age of 18 who have received formal education through the medium of English to at least the completion of secondary school, in countries such as the UK, USA, Canada, Australia and New Zealand where English is the dominant or major first language, as well as in countries such as India, Nigeria, Singapore or regions such as the Caribbean where English may be an additional official language or a second language of a significant part of the population. The spoken and written texts are selected from the period 1990–93. Some national corpus compilation teams may supplement their one-million-word core corpus with additional categories and texts or add a larger monitor corpus, or even in some cases compile additional parallel corpora to take account of regional or sociolinguistic variation within a country (Greenbaum, 1991). The *ICE* project will enable researchers to use each regional corpus independently for descriptive research and also to undertake comparative studies. For example, researchers will be able to find out which varieties of English are most likely to say or write *different from* rather than *different to*, which varieties use *see a movie, see a film, go to the pictures, go to the movies* or *go to the cinema*, and who says *they will side* someone rather than *side with* them. It will, of course, also be possible to see what proportion of uses of a phenomenon such as the splitting of infinitives and the doubling of negatives is normal in different varieties. The *ICE* project promises to make available for systematic investigation for the first time corpora from many regional varieties of English, and to make possible very detailed grammatical comparisons of different regional varieties of English worldwide. It has been suggested that one consequence of the *ICE* project may be to help standardize some of the newer institutionalized national varieties of English and show which aspects of English – particularly morphological and syntactic – show the greatest diversity. The *ICE* subcorpora are, however, likely to be too small for much specialized lexical analysis beyond words of relatively high frequency of occurrence.

The first section of *ICE* to be completed for analysis was the British subcorpus (*ICE-GB*). The structure of *ICE-GB* is shown in Figure 2.4. The other (regional) subcorpora will have approximately identical structures. Like the *Brown* and *LOB* corpora, each subcorpus of *ICE* is made up of 500 text samples each of about 2,000 words. Whereas all of the *Brown* and *LOB* corpora and 50% of the *SEU Corpus* were from written sources, only 40% of *ICE* comes from written sources. The 300 texts of spoken origin in *ICE* include a larger amount of public dialogue than did *SEU*,

---

Spoken (300)

DIALOGUE (180)

Private (100)
   direct conversations (90)
   distanced conversations (10)
Public (80)
   class lessons (20)
   broadcast discussions (20)
   broadcast interviews (10)
   parliamentary debates (10)
   legal cross-examination (10)
   business transactions (10)

MONOLOGUE (120)

Unscripted (70)
   spontaneous commentaries (20)
   unscripted speeches (30)
   demonstrations (10)
   legal presentations (10)
Scripted (50)
   broadcast news (20)
   broadcast talks (20)
   speeches (not broadcast) (10)

Written (200)

NON-PRINTED (50)

Non-professional writing (20)
   student untimed essays (10)
   student examination essays (10)
Correspondence (30)
   social letters (15)
   business letters (15)

PRINTED (150)

Informational (learned) (40)
   humanities (10)
   social sciences (10)
   natural sciences (10)
   technology (10)
Informational (popular) (40)
   humanities (10)
   social sciences (10)
   natural sciences (10)
   technology (10)
Informational (reportage) (20)
   press news reports (20)
Instructional (20)
   administrative/regulatory (10)
   skills/hobbies (10)
Persuasive (10)
   press editorials (10)
Creative (20)
   novels/stories (20)

Total 500 samples, each of 2,000 words

Figure 2.4 Structure of the *ICE*

---

which was collected 30 years earlier, perhaps reflecting a more pervasive presence of broadcasting. There is also no longer a category of surreptitiously recorded texts, reflecting changes in the accepted ethics of research methodology. *ICE* has more varied categories of monologue than the oration and commentary subcategories which made up most of the monologue texts in the *SEU Corpus*. The spoken texts are transcribed orthographically (with pause marking) and not prosodically, in order to ensure greater speed and consistency in transcription. It is intended that recordings of the spoken texts will be available for any researcher wishing to study their prosodic characteristics.

In the sections of *ICE* of written origin, there are traces of the structure of earlier corpora, but the judgment of the international advisory board for *ICE*, consisting of 16 distinguished corpus linguists drawn from many countries, as to how to represent the language, has led to different emphases. For example, in the *Brown* and *LOB* corpora, 25% of the corpus was of imaginative written prose. In the *SEU Corpus*, 7% of the written texts (or 3.5% of the whole corpus) was of imaginative writing. In *ICE*, similarly, only 10% of the written texts (or 4% of the whole corpus) is rated as 'creative' writing. In the sources of text of journalistic origin, the proportions were 17.6% of *Brown* and *LOB*, 8% of the written part of *SEU* (4% of the whole corpus) and 15% of the written parts of *ICE* or 6% of the whole corpus.

Parallel to the compilation of the subcorpora which will eventually make up the whole corpus, the *ICE* project has included the development of a sophisticated grammatically focused software package for corpus analysis. Custom-built utility programs are available for searching for words, parts of words, tags, tag combinations, concordancing, frequency analysis, and for displaying markup or stripping it entirely or selectively with user-friendly Windows interfaces. Other corpora, including the original *SEU Corpus* of the 1960s, can of course be analysed with the same software, thus making possible a range of comparative synchronic and diachronic studies.

The new generation of mega-corpora is likely to dominate work in corpus linguistics for a considerable period. However, while definitive lexical descriptions and large commercial projects will be crucially dependent on them, such mega-corpora may not be appropriate or easily accessible for individual academic researchers interested in outcomes such as making a list of the 500 most frequent words used in economics. Small corpora which can be stored and analysed on a personal computer can reveal reliable information about the linguistic behaviour of very high frequency function words such as prepositions, and high frequency grammatical features such as relativization. The most frequent content words in specific registers and discourse processes such as turn-taking can also be effectively studied in small corpora. It is important therefore not to overlook the value of working with small corpora of one million words or less in the period ahead – especially until software for accessing and analysing mega-corpora becomes easily available, both for researchers who are not engaged in large projects, and for teachers interested in exploiting corpora in the classroom.

2.4 Electronic text databases

In general, corpus linguists have worked with corpora which have been specifically designed for linguistic research. These corpora have usually been planned to be representative of a range of categories of text, and structured especially so that generalizations can be made about a language or languages. They have often been grammatically tagged or parsed to facilitate linguistic research. As Lancashire and McCarty (1988) and Lancashire (1991) make clear, however, the compilation of huge computerized text databases has been proceeding apace for many ancient and modern languages not only for linguistic analysis and lexicography, but also in fields such as legal, historical and literary studies.

In a general sense, databases are collections of information which are designed to facilitate data entry and retrieval. Linguistic corpora, at one extreme, are a subset of databases which have been designed and structured specifically to be used for linguistic description and analysis. Archives, at the other extreme, are usually unstructured repositories of texts. Apart from the forty or so corpora available in the early 1990s designed specifically for linguistic studies, it would be difficult to exaggerate the sheer quantity of human language which is now stored in electronic form and which is potentially available for linguistic analyses of various kinds, including studies of the lexicon, grammar and discoursal characteristics of varieties of a language in particular contexts of use. It is no longer possible to reliably estimate how much data is stored in this way, but the volume may be guessed at when we consider that most of the world's major newspapers, for example, are now composed at computer keyboards and typeset from computer tape. A single daily edition of a major British daily may typically contain up to 150,000 words of text, stored as over 800 k of data. The digitized text can be sent by telephone line or satellite link to printing sites and eventually to archives. In some cases the electronic newspaper enters a database with dozens of other daily papers from around the world for access via the Internet through libraries and personal computers. There is nothing in principle which prevents corpus-based linguistics being carried out on archives, text bases, or individual digitized texts which have been compiled for other purposes. As we have seen, the electronic *OED*, for example, can be used for synchronic or diachronic lexical studies, and Lancashire (1991: 154) summarizes some of the major points of entry to this huge lexical database.

One of the earliest modern computerized text databases was the monumental piece of work organized by Roberto Busa to produce the *Index Thomisticus*. The card punching of this 10.6-million-word database took from 1962 to 1966. Publication began in 1973 of almost forty volumes of all the works of Thomas Aquinas, including indexes, concordances, word frequency tables and other analyses. The result was a reference work for students of scholastic philosophy and also a database for the linguistic analysis of medieval Latin.

Since the 1970s one of the most remarkable and valuable repositories of machine-readable texts has been the *Oxford Text Archive (OTA)* (Burnard, 1988). Based at Oxford University Computing Services, *OTA* contained by the early 1990s over 2,000 texts or collections of texts from some forty languages including Arabic, Armenian, Coptic, Danish, Dutch, English, Finnish, French, Fufulde, Gaelic, German, Greek, Hebrew, Icelandic, Italian, Kurdish, Latin, Latvian, Malayan, Mayan, Pali, Portuguese, Russian, Sanskrit, Serbo-Croatian, Spanish, Swedish, Turkish and Welsh.

Many of the texts in the *OTA* have been converted to a markup which is compatible with the SGML-based Text Encoding Initiative (TEI) standard (see Section 2.6.5). The texts are stored as plain ASCII character files and are compatible with standard software text analysis programs such as the *Oxford Concordance Program (OCP)* (see Section 4.3.1). Many of the texts are freely available without copyright restriction and there is licensed access via the Internet. The catalogue can be accessed through ota@ox.ac.uk. Texts are also available from *OTA* for academic use on tape, diskette or cassette. In addition to its own huge holdings of text, *OTA* also maintains lists of machine-readable texts available at other major centres including Cambridge, Louvain, Pisa, Philadelphia and Provo.

There are many other large databases or archives providing a choice of texts which can be used for linguistic analysis. A few major ones are mentioned here to give an idea of the variety and extent of what is available. Further information on these and other databases is reported in Edwards (1993).

The *Bell Communications Research Corpus* (also known as the *Bellcore Corpus*) is a very large archive of modern English collected in the USA. It includes about 200 million words of newspaper wire service text, about 50 million words of other journalistic writing, and sundry other bodies of text including the *Brown Corpus* and some English dictionaries. The Association for Computational Linguistics Data Collection Initiative (ACL DCI) (Church & Liberman, 1991) makes available in TEI-conformant SGML markup a large number of texts of mainly American English, including, for example, selections from the *Wall Street Journal*, the report of the Challenger Shuttle Inquiry, scientific abstracts, classic US novels, as well as transcripts of a vast amount of Canadian parliamentary proceedings (*Hansard*) in bilingual French/English aligned format. The European Corpus Initiative (ECI) was established in 1992 and the multilingual texts in its database form a kind of corpus archive. The first ECI multi-lingual corpus contains about 100 million words in 27 mainly European languages. The texts range from 34 million words from a German newspaper, the *Frankfurter Rundschau*, 4 million words from the French newspaper *Le Monde*, 2.5 million words of mainly technical writing and light fiction in Modern Greek, as well as text from 45 other corpora. Another vast resource, particularly for historical and lexicographical studies of the French language, is the *Trésor de la Langue Française* project, a joint French–US project notable for its systematicity. Developed at Nancy and the University of Chicago, this text base of over 170 million words of written French from the 17th century to the present comes from over 2,600 separate texts, including literary, historical, philosophical and scientific works.

The *Masterpiece Library* contains a varied selection of 1,338 mainly literary texts from the public domain as well as a version of the Bible, the Koran, the complete works of Shakespeare and US government documents such as the Constitution, all indexed for rapid retrieval and analysis. Other text bases of specifically literary texts, assembled as repositories of examples of the canon of a particular period or genre, have also become available. The *Century of Prose Corpus* and the *Augustan Prose Sample* are examples of such selections. But it is the vast comprehensive databases of all the known literary works of a period or genre in a language which provide hitherto unattainable opportunities not only for literary and stylistic studies but also for lexical and particularly diachronic linguistic studies. Not surprisingly perhaps, these commercially produced text databases are not cheap, costing initially up to £9,000 per CD-ROM. They have already proved to be valuable research text bases in many universities throughout the world. Most of the canon of English poetry from the Anglo-Saxon period to 1900 is available in the *Chadwyck-Healey English Poetry Full-Text Database*. Over 4,500 volumes of poetry from 1,350 major and minor poets have been brought together in a single machine-readable database with sophisticated search and retrieval software to aid literary scholarship. The *Chadwyck-Healey English Verse Drama Full-Text Database* extends the *English Poetry Full-Text Database* by including more than 1,500 verse dramas by some 430 named authors and 230 anonymous works covering the late 13th century to the end of the 19th century.

Huge comprehensive bodies of Classical Greek and Latin literature have also become available in machine-readable form. The *Thesaurus Linguae Graecae* contains about 8,000 works by approximately 3,000 authors covering 14 centuries from Homer in the 8th century BC to the 6th century AD. The *Patrologia Latina* of all the known writings of over 1,000 Late Ancient and Early Medieval Latin writers in theology, philosophy, history and literature was published by Migne in the 19th century in 221 volumes. Published in machine-readable form by Chadwyck-Healey as

The *Patrologia Latina Database*, it promises to enrich studies in all disciplines concerned with a thousand-year period of European history. It is impossible to foresee the applications in thematic, stylistic, lexicographical, historical and other linguistics studies which may be made of these huge databases.

The problem for corpus-based linguistic studies will be a shortage not of text data but of suitable software and methods to answer significant research questions: questions which will stimulate research on these vast text bases and throw light on the nature, function and use of natural languages.

2.5   Issues in corpus design and compilation

Linguistic corpora are intended to be the basis for the analysis and description of the structure and use of languages and for various applications. However, Johansson (1994: 13) may very well have been correct in the mid-1990s to have noted that 'the verb most frequently collocating with *corpus* is probably *compile*'. From the 1960s to the 1990s, the compilation, structure and size of corpora have been the subject of continuing attention among corpus linguists.

Issues in corpus design and compilation are fundamentally concerned with the validity and reliability of research based on a particular corpus, including whether that corpus can serve the purposes for which it was intended. Issues have included whether a corpus should be a static or dynamic sample of a language, how best it can be representative of a language or a genre, how big a corpus should be to be representative or to serve particular purposes, and how big the text samples should be.

2.5.1   Static or dynamic

The issue referred to in Section 2.2 of whether a corpus should present a static or dynamic picture of a language is an important one. A corpus can be a static collection of texts selected in some principled way, intended to be typical of the whole language or an aspect of the language at a particular time. The first-generation one-million-word corpora were like this. The *SEU Corpus*, for example, attempted to select text samples from different domains of use of spoken and written British English in such a way that the corpus could be taken as synchronically representative of English. A great deal of care is typically taken in designing the structure of such a corpus, with deliberate inclusion of particular genres, of a particular sample size. The great grammars of English such as Quirk et al. (1985), which were based on the *SEU Corpus*, took for granted that the corpus was a kind of snapshot of British English. Such a corpus, like a photograph of a scene, aims to capture the main features of the landscape. However, even if the design is exemplary, obviously not all local varieties can be included in such a static corpus and only certain major genres get to be included. Such corpora are a series of static snatches of the language – small samples even from within texts rather than whole works by authors. The nature of a sample corpus is such that it freezes the language at a point in time but, because of its careful structuring with fixed numbers of texts and text types, it can be used for comparative purposes with similarly structured corpora. Small or large corpora can be static. Even the very large *British National Corpus* of 100 million words is of this type.

An alternative view of corpus design is that of the dynamic or monitor corpus (Sinclair, 1991). A monitor corpus, more analogous to a moving picture than a snapshot, is so-called because it provides the means to monitor changing patterns of usage over time. Potentially vast amounts of text are collected over a period of time and passed through software which filters out relevant information for the descriptive purpose in hand, summarizing aspects of the language, and noting new structures or word forms or changing uses or collocations of older word forms. Such a dynamic collection of texts is constantly growing and changing with the addition of new text samples. Sinclair (1991: 25) describes the notion of the monitor corpus as holding the state of the language at any one time. The hundreds of millions of words, however, would gradually 'get too large for any practicable handling and will be effectively discarded'. The composition and size of the monitor corpus is thus constantly changing and this may therefore make it unsuitable for comparative studies of, say, relative frequency of items in different varieties of the language. The monitor corpus is an entirely different enterprise, therefore, from the static sample corpus. The data collection for a monitor corpus is often opportunistic and necessarily not 'balanced'. Quantity of text replaces planning of sampling as the main compilation criterion. Because of the expensive resources needed in computer hardware for capture, storage and processing of text, and the sophisticated software and technical expertise needed for analysis, work with monitor corpora may be less accessible to individual researchers and many academic institutions, and seems likely to be undertaken mainly by consortia of large commercial and governmental agencies or specialist research centres. Individual researchers may have to pay for access to such monitor corpora on a fee-for-service basis. Yet, corpus-based research, like most linguistic research, is often solitary and non-corporate and involves an interaction between text and the linguist's mind assisted by the computer. Therefore it would be a pity if work with monitor corpora were effectively restricted to only a small number of researchers. Questions of access notwithstanding, mega-corpora of the monitor type do promise to provide rich insights (especially for lexicographers and diachronic linguists) into the processes of language change and the use of low frequency words. The place of static sample corpora nevertheless seems to be assured for research on high to medium frequency vocabulary, and for phonological, morphological, syntactic and much discourse-focused research.

2.5.2 *Representativeness and balance*

Linked to the issue of whether a corpus should be static or dynamic is the issue of how to achieve valid and reliable grounds for selecting what texts go into a corpus. Questions associated with 'representativeness' and 'balance' are complex and often intractable. Leech (1991) has suggested that a corpus is 'representative' in the sense that findings based on an analysis of it can be generalized to the language as a whole or a specified part of it. The structure of the early sample corpora such as *Brown* or *LOB* was carefully designed so that they could be considered to be representative of written American and British English respectively. The notions of representativeness and balance are, of course, in the final analysis, matters of judgment and can only be approximate.

However, the issue is really 'representative of what?' In light of the perspectives on variation offered by several decades of research in discourse analysis and sociolinguistics, it is not easy to be confident that a sample of texts can be thoroughly representative of all possible genres or even of a particular genre or subject field or topic. And yet it remains a legitimate goal for the compilation of a corpus to be representative of a language. After all, generalizations are an essential part of science and we have no difficulty accepting generalizations about the human body in the diagrams in an anatomy text even when we know that every person's body is different from those diagrams. In phonology, we have little difficulty accepting generalizations about the sound systems of a language even when every speaker of the language sounds different. The great dictionaries and grammars of English are all generalizations about the language in this sense.

Another issue in corpus design is the balance or weighting between the different sections in a general corpus. Most of the early corpora were heavily weighted in favour of written texts or were made up entirely of written texts. With current technology written text is much easier to collect into a corpus, and even in the largest of the structured second-generation sample corpora, the *British National Corpus*, only 10% of the 100 million words is from spoken sources. The balance between spoken and written texts in the smaller *ICE* is 60% spoken texts and 40% written texts, so this is one of the few corpora with the balance weighted in favour of spoken texts. Even within a written corpus the question of what genres to include is not straightforward. There is, for example, no comprehensive taxonomy of genres from which to select.

The issue of balance arises also in corpora that are designed to represent not the language as a whole but one specific domain, genre, topic or subject field, and can be totally avoided only by corpora consisting of everything published in an historical period, the complete works of an author, or any other total population of text (see Section 2.2). Balance in a corpus is not addressed by having equal amounts of text from different sources, say, spoken or written English. No one knows what proportion of the words produced in a language on any given day are spoken or written. Individually, speech makes up a greater proportion than does writing of the language most of us receive or produce on a typical day. However, a written text (say, in a newspaper article) may be read by 10 million people, whereas a spoken dialogue involving the purchase of a pair of shoes may never be heard by any person other than the two original interlocutors. Similarly, a broadcast conversation on radio or television will reach many more ears than a commercial encounter involving just a customer and a salesperson.

Within a written corpus, balance is equally intractable. Sinclair (1991: 20) suggested that for a general written corpus the minimal criteria for the selection of texts might include the distinction between fiction and non-fiction; book, journal or newspaper; formal or informal; with control of age, gender and origin of the authors. How to get a balance between the few writers and speakers who are prestigious and the great majority of text producers and speakers who have no special claims to fame is not simple, and corpus compilers have devised increasingly sophisticated ways of attempting to achieve representativeness and balance, as evidenced by the sampling methods devised for the *British National Corpus* described in Section 2.3.3.3.

Many of the most important issues in achieving representativeness in a large corpus have been discussed by Summers (1991), who noted that even a written corpus of 30 million words is small when compared with the population of written text from which it is sampled. Experience in corpus compilation convinced her that such was the difference in the content and language of journalistic texts when compared with imaginative and academic texts or ephemera that for lexical studies in particular the original purpose or topic of a text heavily influenced the reliability of the lexical analysis. On the basis of this experience, Summers argued in favour of an initial sampling approach 'using the notion of a broad range of objectively defined document or text types as its main organizing principle' (1991: 5). This balance of text types can then be modified or fine-tuned on the basis of internal analysis of the corpus. Summers outlines a number of possible approaches to the selection of written texts, including: an 'elitist' approach based on literary or academic merit or 'influentialness'; random selection; 'currency', or the extent to which text is read, thus favouring journalistic texts and current best-sellers; subjective judgment of 'typicalness'; availability of text in archives; demographic sampling of reading habits; empirical adjustment of text selection to meet linguistic specifications. A pragmatic approach is of course to use a combination of these approaches and to select from a broad range of sources and text types, taking account of currency and influentialness.

The particular year or years from which texts are selected is significant too. Classic texts from earlier periods may or may not continue to be widely read or have influence. On the other hand, religious works such as the King James version of the Bible translated several hundred years ago may continue to have contemporary influence.

One particular issue is faced by compilers of representative regional corpora which are designed to be used for comparative purposes: What are the criteria for inclusion? We live in an age of the international movement of peoples as immigrants or travellers, and of the globalization of print and broadcast media. Many countries, particularly since the 1940s, have seen considerable changes in the composition of their populations. Even where corpus compilers decide that the speech and writing of immigrants from other English-speaking countries should not be included in a particular subcorpus, this has not been unproblematical. In the case of Australia, for example, census figures in the 1980s showed that as many as one out of every three Australians was born outside that country. Many had immigrated from the United Kingdom or New Zealand, bringing and often retaining their characteristic prosodic, lexical and grammatical usage. If there were any significant differences between Australian and British or New Zealand English, these could be diluted by the influence of immigrants, and yet it is this influence or mix which is part of the use of English in Australia. To further confound the picture, popular culture, especially television, is pervasively international. British and Australian soap operas appear on each other's screens.

Similar issues arise from the influence of immigrants who are native speakers of languages other than English. The *ICE* project illustrates some of the difficulty involved in deciding whose language gets to be included in a corpus. It has been estimated that in 1980 as many as 25% of the Australian population were not native speakers of English (Kaplan, 1980). In many cases English continues not to be their most frequently used language at home. In planning a corpus sample, those responsible for compiling the various subcorpora of *ICE* have had to decide whether texts from native speakers of a language other than English or of another regional variety of English can be included, and if so, how long a period of residence should be required.

Bauer (1991) and Holmes (1996) described some of the problems in deciding who could be described as a New Zealander or, rather, a speaker of New Zealand English and, in doing so, illustrate well this aspect of the problem of selecting text. Potential subjects for inclusion in a corpus on grounds of residency, citizenship or even being born in the new country all create problems for the corpus compiler. If being born in the country is the criterion, then it may also be necessary to exclude people who have spent substantial periods overseas. On the other hand, even if a child's parents were immigrants, maybe receiving schooling in the new country would be enough to be counted as a local. Yet, a child born in New Zealand could be taught at school by one or more teachers who were themselves immigrants from Glasgow, Sydney, Toronto or Bangkok and not native speakers of the local variety of English. Residency or citizenship as criteria permit the inclusion of persons who may rarely speak English at all and then only in a strongly accented way. In order to avoid these problems and other subjective factors, including prejudging who 'sounds like' a speaker of a local variety and thus prejudging what the corpus is intended to reveal – namely what constitutes New Zealand English – Holmes (1996) reported that for the purposes of the *ICE* project a speaker of New Zealand English was someone who had lived in New Zealand since before the age of 10, had not returned from an overseas trip within the last year, and who had not spent more than 10 years or over half his or her lifetime overseas. People of any first language background were eligible for inclusion so long as these criteria were fulfilled and 12% of the total number of participants were Maori, the same proportion as in the total population.

Although it could be argued that the age of 5 (the beginning of elementary schooling) could be more appropriate than 10 as the criterion for inclusion, it is also worth remembering that people who speak a nonnative variety of English are not necessarily unrepresentative of users of English in a country. During his term as US Secretary of State in the 1970s, Henry Kissinger, for example, was as much a representative of the US government and American English as the Presidents he served, and yet his English accent was probably not typical of the majority of his fellow citizens.

Criteria such as those mentioned above constitute a best effort to reconcile competing factors in the criteria for inclusion in a particular corpus. They represent a pragmatic solution since there is no objectively valid criterion to use to define 'speaker of a language'. The effects of age, age of beginning learning a language, experience of travel, education, occupation and ethnicity are among the factors which need to be considered when selecting spoken or written text for inclusion in a corpus.

Very careful planning is necessary for designing a structured corpus such as *ICE* to ensure systematic representation (rather than random sampling) of text varieties, yet certain comparisons between the subcorpora are likely to prove difficult or unreliable. For example, in selecting texts for each subcorpus, sociolinguistic variation is 'kept in mind' but is not necessarily systematic in the selection of texts. Gender, age, socioeconomic or ethnic background and other sociolinguistic comparisons may not therefore be reliable. Not all countries, especially where English is a second language, find it easy to get examples of all text categories. Just as it was not easy to find westerns in societies outside the USA for compilers making corpora modelled on the *Brown Corpus*, so also for the *ICE* project classroom lessons could not be classed as dialogues in some countries where they are rather closer to monologue. Similarly, in the *ICE* project, class lessons could be from secondary or tertiary level as long as the participants were 18 years of age or older. The style of discourse might be quite different depending on the level, the subject and the country concerned. The level of education normally affects the speech of both long-term residents and newly arrived immigrants and what is standard and non-standard is not easy to define. In Caribbean English, creole is sometimes interspersed with English in various contexts and domains of use. In the end, some differences between ideolects may be easier to detect than those between some regional varieties.

In societies where the education of girls is less extensive than for boys, it may not be meaningful to compare linguistic characteristics of male and female participants. Difficulties in making comparisons may arise equally from written or spoken texts. Comparisons made between newspapers or other journalistic texts in two or more corpora are also not necessarily straightforward because it is not always easy to find the source of articles and to be sure they represent local use. Reports and articles may be taken initially from overseas wire services before being edited to conform to local space and stylistic conventions.

2.5.3 Size

Issues associated with how to make a corpus representative or balanced or able to be used for comparative purposes are essentially issues concerning the quality of a corpus. There are also related issues associated with the quantity of text. These issues are concerned not only with the total number of words (tokens) and different words (types) in a corpus, but with how many categories the corpus should contain, how many samples the corpus should contain in each category, and how many words there should be in each sample. Although questions of size and representativeness affect the validity and reliability of the corpus, it has to be stressed again that any corpus, however big, can never be more than a minuscule sample of all the speech or writing produced or received by all of the users of a major language on even a single day.

Until the late 1970s the first-generation corpora of one million words seemed vast. On mainframe computers it could take hours to run concordance searches. By the mid-1980s, using software which pre-indexed a corpus, it took seconds to run a concordance search of a one-million-word corpus on a personal computer. The new generation of corpora such as the *Cobuild* and *Longman/Lancaster* corpora were able to be much bigger, partly because the technology, including optical scanning, used for 'capturing' text made their compilation much easier. Sinclair (1991: 20) was able to suggest that 10–20 million words might constitute 'a useful small general corpus' but 'will not be adequate for a reliable description of the language as a whole'. It was argued that corpora of finite size were inherently deficient because any corpus is such a tiny sample of a language in use that there can be little finality in the statistics. Sinclair (1991: 9) pointed out that even projected billion-word corpora will show remarkably sparse information about most of a very large word list.

The issue is how many tokens of a linguistic item are necessary for descriptive adequacy. In a typical text (or a corpus of one million words), 40 to 50% of the word types occur only once. In the case of polysemous words, at least half of the attested meanings of words occur only once. Rundell and Stock (1992) in their overview of corpus-based lexicography note that *break* occurs 8,267 times in the *Longman/Lancaster Corpus*, but that the uses of *break* as in *news breaking* and *breaking someone's serve* in tennis are not frequent enough to provide the kind of evidence needed by lexicographers on which to base a fully adequate dictionary entry. More than one instance of use of an item is needed as a basis for description. But if once is too little, how many tokens are enough to discover the patterns of collocation, of polysemy, of morphological characteristics and of the likelihood of occurrence of a given form or meaning? For example (on the evidence of the *LOB* and *Brown* corpora), the word *circumstance* occurs about 90% of the time in written American and British English in its plural form (*circumstances*). This information is available from two corpora totalling two million words which produced 210 tokens of *circumstance(s)*. On the other hand, a high frequency word such as *at* in English typically has about 5,500 tokens in a one-million-word corpus. This is more than enough for most descriptive purposes, including providing a picture of the distribution of the major meanings of this preposition. It is hard to cope with the manual analysis necessary for lexicography or lexical grammar if there is too much data. About 1,000 tokens of a word in concordance format is normally the maximum which analysts such as lexicographers can get their minds around. When there are too many tokens of an item in a corpus, it is possible to make a convenient subset, for example, by sampling every nth token. Linguists and lexicographers then require support on how best to sample from a statistical perspective, and often sophisticated technical advice on how to carry it out. There is currently a need for more sophisticated, publicly available software to assist linguists to sample and work with the large amounts of data which are produced when analysing high frequency items in the large corpora.

Some idea of the scope of the problem of having potentially too much evidence resulting from the size of large corpora can be seen from initial analyses of the *Bank of English* and *BNC* data. In the one-million-word *LOB* or *Wellington* corpora, about 100 word types occur more than 1,000 times. In a 100-million-word corpus, about 8,000 word types can be expected to occur more than 1,000 times. These 8,000 types account for about 95% of the tokens in the corpus. The remaining 5% of the tokens (about five million words) may consist of half a million or more different word-types. Thus, although it is the case that for the descriptive adequacy of low frequency phenomena such as collocations very large corpora are necessary, there is no point in having bigger and bigger corpora if you cannot work with the output. A vast collection of texts is not necessarily a corpus from which generalizations can be made. A huge corpus does not necessarily 'represent' a language or a variety of a language any better than a smaller corpus. At this stage we simply do not know how big a corpus needs to be for general or particular purposes. Rather than focusing so strongly on the quantity of data in a corpus, compilers and analysts need also to bear in mind that the quality of the data they work with is at least as important.

For the study of prosody, a corpus of 100,000 words will usually be big enough to make generalizations for most descriptive purposes, so long as we can be sure that speech is spontaneous. A robustly reliable analysis of the use of verb-form morphology can be undertaken on a corpus of half a million words. Studies of many syntactic processes and high frequency vocabulary generally require corpora of between half a million and one million words. The availability of the new 100-million-word structured corpora such as the *BNC* will enable some of the issues associated with size and representativeness to be settled empirically by making possible comparisons with analyses carried out on smaller, differently structured corpora such as *Brown, LOB* or *ICE*. It will then be possible to see the extent to which size, text categories, or overall structure affect the use of particular linguistic items or levels. Overall corpus size needs to be set against diversity of sources to help achieve representativeness. Within any text category, it is generally the case that the greater the number of individual samples, the greater the reliability of the analysis of the linguistic variables. In the final analysis, of course, a corpus is more or less adequate according to the extent to which the corpus matches the purposes to which it is put.

Related to the general issue of overall corpus size is the issue of the size of the individual samples drawn from texts which make up the corpus. In the first-generation electronic corpora such as *Brown* and *LOB*, 2,000-word randomly selected samples were used. Some of these texts were whole documents, but most were only parts of documents. However, because texts have different discourse characteristics in introductory and concluding sections, for example, it is possible that the use of parts of documents could distort the overall picture of the language represented in the corpora. On the other hand, the use of whole documents in a structured corpus may cause an equally distorted picture because it results in fewer texts (often of disproportionate size) and thus the range of authors is reduced.

Further, the *Brown Corpus* and the corpora modelled on it were compiled with texts representing various recognized 'folk' varieties of language use. Not surprisingly, some researchers were concerned over whether such general corpora with 15 such varieties of use adequately represented the vast range of varieties which potentially could be included, and, further, whether the number of samples of a particular variety and the size of each sample were adequate for comparative purposes. Oostdijk (1988b) suggested that the text samples in the standard corpora might be too small and that samples of up to 20,000 words might be necessary.

Biber (1990) studied the distribution of 10 linguistic features across 55 'pairs' of samples from LOB and LLC texts. Each of the two samples in each pair consisted of 1,000 running words taken from the same text. The texts came from a wide range of spoken and written genres. He compared the internal variation between the two texts in each pair and concluded that text samples of 2,000–5,000 words are big enough to represent their text categories. Further, he argued that the typical number of samples within each genre (20–80 texts) in a corpus such as *LOB* is adequate for the kinds of studies of variation typically undertaken, namely correlation-based analyses.

Biber (1993b) has further argued that quantity of data alone cannot solve issues in corpus design involving the kinds and number of texts to be included, the selection of samples from particular texts and the size of each sample. These matters must also be based on theory. Equally necessary is a thorough definition of the target population of text types which are to be represented in the corpus. However, a theoretical foundation based on well-attested sampling methods such as those developed in the social sciences is not enough. Biber argued that pilot studies were needed to fine-tune the structure of a corpus to make it more representative. Empirical research on the pilot corpus should thus be used to confirm or modify the various design parameters. In this sense, corpus design can be iteratively upgraded. Biber's own work has made use of the multivariate techniques of factor analysis and cluster analysis for the study of linguistic variation in corpora (see Section 3.5). By using linguistically defined rather than situationally defined or a priori folk categories for establishing text types, Biber has broken new ground. Such analysis, he suggests, can be used in corpus design to confirm the range and types of variation in a corpus and within registers, and the extent to which types or items are represented. Biber's work has thus argued for a qualitative as well as a quantitative basis for corpus design, and it should encourage continuing use of corpora of the order of one million words for grammatical studies.

Biber's innovative typological approach to text types which are identified by factor analysis of the grouping of linguistic items in texts nevertheless assumes the validity of the traditional linguistic variables (e.g.
passive voice) as pictured in standard descriptive grammars. However,
one of the promises of corpus-based analysis is that it will identify
new variables, new patterns of word relationships and possibly new
grammatical features. Sinclair (1989) has illustrated this well in a corpus-
based account of the preposition *of*, where he demonstrates that this
most frequent of English prepositions fails to exhibit some of the defining characteristics of the word class which have been described in earlier
grammars.

2.6 Compiling a corpus

There are, as we have seen, many linguistic corpora available but these
will not always suit the purposes of every potential user wishing to
do corpus-based research. Sometimes a particular subsection of a larger
corpus can be downloaded on to a PC for analysis for the study of,
say, sports commentaries or the language of courtrooms. Research on a
particular writer or genre, however, may require texts which are not yet
part of a corpus to be available in machine-readable form for analysis.
In which case, linguists may need to compile their own corpus. This
section outlines the main steps in compiling a corpus, including the
various matters which have to be considered, decisions which have to
be made, and tasks which have to be undertaken in the compilation process. There are three main stages in corpus compilation: corpus design,
text collection or capture, and text encoding or markup.

2.6.1 Corpus design

General issues associated with corpus type, size and composition have
been considered in Section 2.5. When compiling a new corpus, even if
it is small, it is sensible for compilers to assume that it may eventually
be used for comparative purposes. Careful planning and principled ways
of selecting texts for a corpus are therefore highly desirable to ensure
comparability and compatibility of corpora and their ability to be used
or referred to by other researchers. The optimal design of a corpus is
highly dependent on the purpose for which it is intended to be used.
The compiler of a corpus should, if possible, have a clear idea of what
kinds of analyses are likely to be undertaken and whether they justify
the large amount of effort involved in making the corpus. Essentially if
the aim is to undertake linguistic or sociolinguistic analysis to uncover
systems or the use of those systems, then careful thought needs to be
given to the type, content, structure and size of the corpus.

In Section 2.2 the various types of corpora were described. In the following discussion it is assumed that in normal circumstances a purpose-built corpus for particular research is likely to be on a relatively small, finite scale and will be a synchronic or diachronic corpus of spoken and/or written texts. The corpus may consist either of a total population of texts (e.g. all the works of a particular author) or of a sample of texts from a given population. A number of matters need to be kept in mind in deciding on the appropriate type of corpus. If the corpus is to be a synchronic corpus, the year or years in which the texts were produced or published must be decided on. If the corpus is to be a diachronic one, then the period to be covered is obviously relevant – there must be systematic chronological coverage of the period or of the end points of the period to ensure that there is adequate data on which to base studies of language change. Rissanen (1992: 189) has reminded compilers of diachronic corpora of the desirability of adequate coverage of genre, geographical region, gender, age, sociolinguistic background and level of education of the persons who originally spoke or wrote the texts. It is, however, often difficult to achieve such coverage.

Just as the research aims of the corpus compilers must determine the type of corpus, so early decisions need to be made on the content. Perhaps the most fundamental decision concerns whether spoken or written texts (or both) should be included, and if both then the proportion of each. If spoken language texts are to be part of the corpus, careful thought needs to be given to which genres should be included. The categories included in recent corpora such as the *ICE* or the *BNC* are the result of careful planning decisions and can be a guide to other corpus compilers. The categories shown in Figure 2.5 are among those which have been included in previous corpora and which might be considered for inclusion in a corpus of spoken texts.

There may, of course, be good grounds for including only one category of use in a corpus of spoken texts (e.g. committee meetings), but whatever the decision on content, for a structured corpus, the decision should be a principled one by which text types are deliberately included or excluded.

A list of examples of text categories could similarly be drawn up when considering the structure and content of a corpus of texts from written sources, as outlined in Figures 2.3–2.4 and Table 2.3.

One thing that corpus compilers quickly discover is that texts do not always fit easily into a priori categories. A compiler of a corpus of written Samoan would discover, for example, that Samoan newspapers often contain more than 'news'. A substantial amount of imaginative prose fiction, including short stories, as well as religious and cultural content, is frequently also part of a newspaper. A corpus sampled from Samoan newspapers thus has to take account of wider categories than spot news reports and editorial content.

- **Monologue**
  - formal
    - written to be read aloud
    - prepared but unscripted public speech
  - less formal
    - academic lectures
    - commentaries on public occasions
    - sports commentaries
    - demonstrations
- **Dialogue**
  - face-to-face dialogue
  - public discussion (e.g. on radio)
  - business or professional transactions, e.g.
    - client and professional
    - workplace interaction between colleagues
    - commercial (sales) transaction
  - informal
    - within family
    - between friends
  - telephone dialogue
    - between interlocutors known to each other
    - between interlocutors unknown to each other
  - structured interaction
    - interview
      - formal, e.g. arts programme
      - less formal, e.g. with survivors and witnesses to events such as accidents
    - debate
    - committee meeting

Figure 2.5 Categories of spoken texts

Linked to the content of the corpus is the question of structure. If both spoken and written texts are to be included, a decision is needed on the relative proportions of each. Any proportion chosen is likely to be quite arbitrary or, at best, a matter of informed judgment. As already mentioned, even for an individual, no one knows for sure what proportion of the language we produce or are exposed to is through speech or writing respectively. Taken over a whole community, it is simply impossible to get a balance which represents actual use of the language. This question of balance is, of course, not a problem if the corpus consists of a total population (e.g. all editions of a newspaper in a given year).

In structuring the proportions of texts from different text categories in a corpus, it is sometimes useful to do a pilot survey of a domain in advance to find out the proportions of different text types occurring naturally in language use. For example, in designing a corpus of spoken Maori used in radio and television broadcasts, Boyce (1996) undertook a preliminary analysis of the amount of broadcast time spent on TV and radio stations each week in different activities. On one radio station the proportions shown in Table 2.4 occurred.

Table 2.4 Analysis of broadcast activities on a Maori radio station

Activity	%
News	15
Documentary	5
Sports and cultural events commentary	4
Panui or public notices (e.g. deaths, weather, advertisements)	3
Continuity announcing	17
Music	56
Total	100

Since the purpose of the corpus was to study the high frequency lexical items of modern spoken Maori, it was decided to collect texts in the proportions shown in Table 2.5.

Table 2.5 Structure of a corpus of broadcast Maori

Activity	%
News (monologue and interviews)	30
Documentary	25
Sports and cultural events commentary	20
Panui	10
Continuity announcing	5
Other (including talkback)	10
Total	100

Thus, in the proportions collected, there was a heavy reduction in the amount of continuity announcing with its repetitive, formulaic announcement of the time or of particular musical items. Similarly, even though music included traditional songs, these were not sampled as providing examples of modern spoken Maori. The surveying of domains of use in this way can only be a rough guide for designing the structure of a corpus. It has, of course, to be matched against the purpose of the corpus.

In deciding on the size of a corpus, the practical problems associated with handling large amounts of text should never be underestimated. Although one million words is seen as being small for many purposes, compiling a one-million-word corpus is a very big undertaking if it involves any spoken text. There is nothing magic about one million words and no advantage in compiling a corpus of that size if a corpus of 200,000 words will do the job intended. As noted in Section 2.5.3, on the evidence of Biber's research, sample sizes of 2,000–5,000 words of text will be reliable for many linguistic studies, excluding perhaps some studies of discourse, where larger samples involving cohesion or the characteristics of introductory, developmental and concluding sections of texts may be needed.

A systematic description of extralinguistic variables to be taken account of in designing the content and structure of a corpus has been provided by Atkins et al. (1992: 7–9). Some of the major ones include text origin, participants, medium (spoken or written) genre, style, setting, factuality, topic, date of publication or speech event, authorship (including gender, age, nationality), age and size of intended audience or readership. For some of these variables it is nevertheless sometimes difficult or impossible to achieve balance. In collecting texts of conversations, the relationship between the interlocutors may have a marked effect on the kind of data collected for some variables. For example, texts which record workplace interactions can be more or less formal depending on whether the encounter is between equals in such matters as gender, age, status or knowledge of the topic. If an encounter is between interlocutors who are not comparable in one or more of such variables it can affect patterns of interruption, turn-taking and feedback.

If the corpus is to be a sample of text from a given population and we have decided on the type, content, structure and size of our corpus, the next step is to select the actual texts which will make up the corpus. Of course, as has already been noted, if the corpus consists of a total population of texts, sampling is not necessary. However, even when the corpus is to consist of the complete works of a particular author, decisions may still have to be made as to which edition of a work is to be included.

The purpose of sampling adequately is so that, on the basis of the sample, generalizations can be made reliably and validly about a population as a whole. But as we have seen, a linguistic population is normally so large (in terms of the number of speech acts produced) and so indefinable (in terms of the possible range of text types) that a random sample, stratified according to text types, is probably not feasible. Published written texts can be sampled on the basis of bibliographic resources such as *Books in Print*. Spoken texts are harder to sample. However, we can attempt to avoid excessive bias in the selection of spoken texts included in a corpus by taking some practical measures. If it is necessary to sample a large community, two particular sources of advice may be relevant. Although public opinion pollsters sometimes have a bad record in forecasting election results, they have in many cases a good deal of experience and understanding of the structure of large populations and methods of stratified random sampling which can be relevant for a corpus compiler. Several decades of research in sociolinguistics has also provided informed understanding of linguistically relevant domains of use, genres and population groups.

Two particular situations which sometimes create problems in sampling are when texts are smaller than the sample size decided on and when the sampling period could introduce unwanted bias into a corpus. If a sample size of 2,000 words is decided on, this will represent about 11–13 minutes of speech at the normal speech rate of 150–175 words per minute. However, many speech events such as commercial encounters or telephone conversations are much shorter than this. As the compilers of the *SEU Corpus* found in the 1960s, in such cases it may be necessary to combine several speech events to form a text of the size decided on for the corpus. Junk mail or brief newspaper articles may similarly have to be assembled into composite corpus texts of the appropriate sample size.

Newspapers frequently contain many quite brief articles of only a few hundred words on community events, editorial opinion, letters, short stories, reports of sports events and public announcements. If sample sizes of 2,000 words have been decided on, and the sampling procedure indicates that the first item on a particular page of a particular edition of a newspaper should be included, it is frequently the case that the item to be sampled may be much less than 2,000 words in length. Therefore a systematic procedure is needed by which the sample is compiled by adding further text from the next item or items of the same text category in that edition.

Ultimately, when including texts from journalistic sources, the corpus compiler has to keep an eye on diversity of topics and issues. Certain days of the week or times of the year often tend to have items on particular topics and so can bias the content of the corpus. There is likely to be much more mention of snow or Christmas in December in the United Kingdom than in May. Bell (1991: 23) overcame this problem by means of a 'constructed week' by which newspapers are randomly selected from over several weeks or months so that a 'composite' week of seven days is compiled. Thus, events associated with particular national festivals or holidays, an aircraft hijacking over several days, or a parliamentary election campaign which might dominate the content of a newspaper or broadcast news over any one week are not permitted to bias the sampling excessively.

For journalistic texts there can be further problems in sourcing the texts. A newspaper article may have been edited by several persons and may even have originated overseas in the case of international wire service items. In broadcast news, a bulletin read by a 30-year-old female news-reader might have been written by a 60-year-old male, or vice versa.

2.6.2 *Planning a storage system and keeping records*

A corpus of one million words typically requires 8–10 megabytes of disk space. If it is grammatically tagged, then a further 3–5 megabytes will normally be needed. A parsed version could require another 30 megabytes. The hardware to store computer corpora is no longer a problem, and technology is developing very rapidly. A single DAT tape can provide the necessary back-up for a one-million-word corpus many times over and a single CD-ROM can hold hundreds of megabytes of data. However, texts in a corpus are of limited value unless they can be accessed easily, together with 'header' information on the source of the text linked with the computer file. Before data is collected, therefore, the compiler should plan a systematic method of referencing, to link the electronic texts in the computer file back to the original audio or video tape which recorded the broadcast interview or conversation, or to the actual book, edition, page number and paragraph where sampling is to begin and end. This is considered further in Section 2.6.5.

A catalogue of files should be kept and, of course, all material should be backed up and stored securely and separately from the working copies of texts and the working electronic files. In addition to the storage and cataloguing of texts and their electronic version on computer, it is normally essential to plan to collect and catalogue as much information as possible about the authorship or source of texts. In the case of spoken or written texts, it is important to note when and where the text was recorded or collected. In the case of spoken text, the corpus compiler should note who was present, any relevant relationships among participants, the topic, whether the discourse was planned or impromptu, and the degree of formality. In the case of broadcast material, however, it is often very hard to get information on the participants, and yet this can be crucial for much corpus-based research. Experience suggests that it is essential to attempt to collect such information as soon as possible after a broadcast. Here good working relationships with the broadcasters can be enormously facilitative. Holmes (1996: 180) provides an example of a questionnaire for use in the collection of background information on participants contributing spoken texts to a corpus. It is useful to collect information on where people grew up as well as their place of birth, and on where they have lived as well as how long they have lived in one or more places.

Figure 2.6 summarizes the major context features which it was considered desirable to collect for each spoken language text in the *British National Corpus* (BNC), to be displayed in the markup for each text.

2.6.3   Getting permission

Corpus compilers, like other users of texts, must follow the same rules and legal requirements as other members of the community. Before texts are copied into a corpus database, compilers must seek and gain the permission of the authors and publishers who hold copyright for a work, or the informed consent of individuals whose rights to privacy must be

---

Setting (e.g. car, office, train)
Activity (e.g. watching TV)
Location (town or district where discourse occurred)
Time
Date
Audience (number of participants and number of people within earshot)
Spontaneity (a range from scripted to unscripted)
Topic
Gender
Age
Race
First language or language variety of other participants
Occupation
Education
Social group
Relationship to person recording (e.g. family, stranger)
Dialect of person recording

Figure 2.6 Context features of spoken texts recorded for the *BNC* (Crowdy, 1993: 264)

---

recognized. If the use of the corpus is likely to have commercial value, it is of course likely that copyright holders will require fees for the incorporation of their texts in the corpus. Some corpora, including *Brown* and *LOB*, are available without copyright restriction for non-commercial research purposes (see Section 2.7). Some corpora are simply not publicly available.

However, while corpus compilers must observe copyright law and the rights of individuals to confidentiality under privacy legislation, it is often the experience of many corpus linguists that if permission is sought, copyright holders make reasonable efforts to facilitate genuine research. The process is sometimes slow and tedious. It is not always clear who holds copyright; publishers are sometimes taken over by other companies; authors of articles sometimes prove difficult to trace; some works which are no longer subject to copyright in a particular edition are not free to be published in another. It is fairly safe to assume that separate permission will have to be sought for every text incorporated into a corpus. Sometimes, if all texts in the corpus have a single publisher, blanket permission can be obtained for research purposes. Similarly, the publisher of a single text may give permission for an electronic version to be made of a text for the purposes of linguistic analysis, on condition that the electronic version is destroyed when the analyses have been undertaken. For example, the writer of a thesis on the use of the passive voice or on vocabulary in medical text might receive one-off permission of this kind.

For the collection of spoken text, the key issue is that there be no invasion of personal privacy, particularly as enshrined in local legislation on individual rights. Unauthorized bugging with concealed microphones or cameras, as was sometimes done before the 1970s, is now generally considered to be unethical and unacceptable unless there is informed

consent from participants, including guarantees that there will be no possibility of their being identified. However, as some compilers of spoken
corpora for research purposes have found, many participants are willing
to give permission in advance for surreptitious recordings to be made
at an unspecified time in the future so long as they have the right to
listen to data collected and to have erased any parts of a recording with
which they feel embarrassed or uncomfortable. In some confidential contexts such as business transactions or professional consultations, it may
simply not be possible either to get permission or to collect naturalistic
speech unaffected by the recording situation.

Where spoken texts are collected from the public domain, permission
must normally be sought from the appropriate authority such as the
owner of the broadcasting station or TV network, and sometimes these
authorities have been known to exact heavy fees even when the station
or network is publicly owned. In general, the more public the domain,
the easier it is to get permission to incorporate a text in a corpus, but
what is considered public may vary from community to community.
Among New Zealand Maori, the marae is a public forum within and
between tribal groups where strict rules of protocol are observed in discussion and debate. What is said within the marae is, however, private
to that context and the right to record debate cannot be taken for granted.
Debate in a national parliament, on the other hand, normally does not
involve limitations on recording, and indeed, it may be broadcast, which
can make it easier for the corpus compiler.

Overall, whenever texts are collected from whatever source it is important that good records are kept about the texts, including where and
when they were collected and as much as possible about the source, both
to facilitate subsequent research and so that in the event of permission
being sought to incorporate the texts in a corpus as little time and expense
as possible has to be spent obtaining that permission. Corpus compilers
should collect a few more texts than are actually required within each category of a proposed corpus to allow for the need to fill gaps where permission subsequently cannot be obtained to incorporate particular texts.

2.6.4 *Text capture*

Once the design, content and structure of a corpus have been determined, the individual texts in the predetermined categories have to be
collected or captured.

2.6.4.1 WRITTEN TEXTS

There are three ways of entering written texts into a computer file. At
some stage in its life, any text which goes beyond a handwritten form
has to be typed either on to a page or, most commonly nowadays, dir-

ectly into a computer file. For texts which already exist in a typewritten form but are not in a word processor, rekeyboarding may be the most economical way of entering data if the corpus is to be small, but it can be a slow and expensive way of capturing text, nevertheless. An experienced touch typist who can type 60–80 words per minute can be expected to achieve about 10,000 words in an eight-hour day, allowing for interruptions and rest times. Keyboarding into a computer file is, of course, faster than the card-punching methods which had to be used to enter data into the *Brown Corpus* in the early 1960s.

Texts which are not yet available in a typed form, including spoken texts, have to be keyboarded at some stage, whereas sometimes other texts which are to be part of a corpus already exist in a machine-readable form. Nowadays, books, major newspapers and magazines and even many small community papers are typically typeset from computerized files. Publishers are sometimes willing to allow corpus compilers to access these computer tapes so that particular texts can be directly incorporated into a corpus. Some major newspapers such as the *Guardian* or the *Independent* in the United Kingdom are available on CD-ROM and permission (subject to payment of a fee in some cases) may be sought to transfer partial files to a corpus being compiled for particular purposes. Newspaper publishers' tapes sometimes require a lot of editing ('cleaning') to ensure that advertising, printer controls and other markup features are not incorporated into the corpus when they are not wanted.

If a corpus is being compiled to facilitate a study of, say, an aspect of student writing, it is sometimes possible, with informed consent of course, to get student essays which have been typed on a word processor submitted on a disk to enable the work to be directly transferred to the corpus database.

The third main way of capturing written text is through scanning, which has revolutionized the capture of text. Although the original Kurzweil Data Entry Machine (KDEM) from the 1970s was potentially able to convert printed text into computerized form at least twice as fast as a typist could keyboard the text, the machine was expensive and had difficulty with some varieties of fonts, bolding or italics, and poor quality print. With good copy, it could read 250–300 words per minute. Nowadays, a scanner and the requisite optical character recognition (OCR) software can be purchased for US$500 or less. Although these scanners, which operate rather like photocopiers, work better than ever, character recognition systems are still not error-proof. Renouf (1987) has described some of the problems which were encountered in scanning texts in the early 1980s into the *Cobuild Corpus*. Subsequent checking and editing of files which have been keyboarded or scanned can be time-consuming and costly if done to a high standard.

Over a decade later, many of these problems continue to confront the corpus compiler who uses scanning to capture texts. Changes in font size, the colour and quality of the paper used, the occurrence of tables, abbreviations, footnotes, running heads and variations in page layout can all interfere with straightforward scanning and make necessary a great deal of manual editing. Words broken across lines, for example *occur-red, attain-ment, assem-bled* may be digitized as separate words. Abbreviated forms such as *I've, don't, she's* can be misscanned and have a consequent effect on word counts. Typical misreadings of letters are 'o' for *a* ('cor', 'overage', 'hove' for *car, average, have*) 'd' for *cl* ('dear', 'dean' for *clear, clean*), 'm' for *in, ni* or *ir* ('mnate', 'ml', 'am' for *innate, nil, air*), 'j' for *u* ('jnit' for *unit*), 'c' for *e* ('casy' for *easy*), 'l' for *1*; 'ij' for *y*. Some of these misreadings will not be detected by a spelling checker and so careful manual checking of each screenful of text may be required if high levels of accuracy are called for. Technical developments in scanning and OCR software which allow the user to 'train' the machine to work with an entirely new non-Latinate alphabet are already available and their costs are likely to fall.

2.6.4.2 SPOKEN TEXTS

Spoken language is all around us and yet it is harder and more expensive to compile a corpus of spoken text than it is of written text because of the additional steps necessary to get the electronically recorded spoken text into a written or transcribed form ready for capture.

Monologue or dialogue can be collected directly from participants on audio or video tape. Alteratively, some genres can be collected with permission either as publicly broadcast or in a prerecorded form ready for broadcast on radio or television. Sometimes suitable texts for a corpus are available as high quality recordings in the archives of radio or television stations.

When the compiler needs to record speech, the desired quality of recording can be an important consideration. If delicate transcription is required, with a great deal of prosodic detail, then high quality recordings or source tapes are necessary. Digital recordings generally provide better quality for narrow or delicate transcription, but this has to be balanced against cost, convenience of use, obtrusiveness of recording and so on. The miniaturization of equipment has resulted in the use of unobtrusive Walkman-sized audio recorders with lapel microphones which can provide satisfactory quality recording for many purposes. Such equipment was used for compiling the *British National Corpus*. Equipment for recording telephone conversations is cheap and readily available, but quality recordings and permission to record or keep a recording may not be so readily obtained.

Sometimes if a large chunk of speech is recorded, the sample for the corpus can be collected from within the larger chunk. This can be useful when collecting spoken text from children, who may take some time to accept the presence of the tape recorder as natural. Where there are large groups of people in, say, meetings or tutorial groups, it may be hard to pick up what was said and also who said what. Not all tape recording is thus subsequently able to be transcribed and used.

As Edwards (1992: 129) has noted, 'The transcript is central to corpus linguistic approaches to spoken discourse.' However, as is known by anyone who has had to transcribe substantial amounts of text, transcription can be time-consuming, expensive and fraught with difficulties. Tape-recorded monologue or dialogue typically contains 7,000–9,000 words per hour. In corpus compilation, it is of course hard to get an accurate word count of spoken text until after the tape has been transcribed. It may take about 10 hours to transcribe orthographically one hour of recording with a minimum of prosodic information marked up. It can take up to 25 hours to transcribe a single hour of recorded monologue with minimal prosodic detail and full TEI conformant markup, and considerably longer if there is dialogue. And yet, unless there is sufficiently detailed transcription, much important research is simply impossible to undertake. Word and sentence stress and intonation can have a substantial effect on meaning. Length of pauses and hesitations, correct alignment of simultaneous speech, and feedback devices are minimal prerequisites for most discourse studies. The excellence of the transcription of the LLC is one of the reasons it has proved to be such a rich and enduring basis for research on prosody and discourse, even though the original recordings are not generally available.

It is very important to have clear conventions for transcribing prosodic phenomena and we should not underestimate the need for systematic training and regular interaction among transcribers so that there is consistency of practice. The conventions developed for the ICE project (Greenbaum, 1996b) and the specifications described by Crowdy (1994) for the British National Corpus project provide good examples of broad orthographic transcription systems which are well attuned to the kinds of use likely to be made of contemporary corpora. Knowles (1993) has described some of the problems associated with more detailed prosodic transcriptions of spoken texts in a machine-readable corpus, and some possible solutions.

For research on discourse and grammar, and for many applications in such fields as language teaching, less delicate transcription will normally be adequate for most purposes. In transcription of dialogue it is not always easy to decide when one unit of conversation begins and another ends. The boundaries are often fuzzy and conversations lose their way, are interrupted by other events, or simply peter out. Crowdy (1994) describes some practical steps which were taken in transcribing the texts in the BNC into conversational units. The minimal features noted in the transcription included speaker turns, overlapping speech, the punctuation of 'sentence-like' units, pauses, certain paralinguistic features such as whispering or laughing, non-verbal sounds, and contextual comments such as 'eating biscuits'. See Leech et al. 1995.

A transcription is an imperfect written approximation of a speech event which exists initially as a dance of air molecules. The level of delicacy or amount of detail in a transcription is, as noted earlier, related to the use to which the transcription will be put. But many corpus compilers do not always know what use will be made of their labours. For this reason, Edwards (1992) and others have sought to develop standards or principles for corpus transcription which are clear and easy to use, expandable and able to be used in different computer systems.

Once a spoken text is transcribed and typed on a word processor it is already in an electronic form and further keyboarding or scanning is not normally necessary. Whether spoken or written texts are being compiled into a corpus, it is important before data accession to check that the text selected is usable. Thus after transcription and data entry it is essential to check that captured text is of high quality and as free as possible of error. Spelling checkers do not find errors such as the transcription of 'there' for *their* or the scanning of *clear* as 'dear'. Proof-reading, revision and editing are important to ensure the integrity of the texts in the corpus. The need for systematic backing up of data and secure storage off site cannot be overemphasized. The cost in time, money and convenience if data is lost is too dreadful for most compilers to contemplate.

2.6.5 *Markup*

Anyone compiling a corpus which consists of electronic versions of texts taken from many different sources soon learns that inconsistent methods of encoding the text and signposting the different parts of the text can cause confusion. The conventions for indicating such text features as line breaks, line numbers, word breaks and boundaries, hesitations, chapters, sections, paragraphs, headings, or printer controls, can vary considerably, with the consequence that software may not always be able to distinguish between the real text and the codes which have been used to markup the text structure, format and other visible or audible features of text. If software is being used to count the number of words in a text, for example, such confusion can have obviously undesirable outcomes.

In the 1980s, an international standard for the electronic encoding of text was developed from within the publishing industry in order to facilitate the portability of electronic manuscripts, enabling them to be re-used in different contexts on different equipment, thus saving the cost of repeated typesetting. Because of its power, flexibility and independence of particular software systems, the Standard Generalized Markup Language (SGML) has become increasingly accepted outside the publishing industry as the standard way of encoding electronic texts, for use by parliamentarians, builders of expert systems, governmental bodies and corporations, as well as by linguists, and other scholars. Bryan (1988) provides an introduction to how to use SGML and Goldfarb (1990) is the standard comprehensive reference work.

SGML (ISO 8879: 1986) enables electronic texts originally keyboarded on different word processors to be edited, searched, analysed or typeset consistently. The SGML tags define the typeface, page layout and so on in a way that has been variously described as a kind of style manual or syntax for the descriptive markup of electronic texts. In addition to various more informal outlines on SGML available as freeware, there is at least one commercially available tagger (Light, 1994) which adds SGML markup to electronic texts either when they are being keyboarded or when they already exist, and operates in conjunction with a normal word processor.

One of the most powerful advantages of SGML as a markup system is that the features which have been marked up can be displayed in different ways. For example, speaker turn-taking can be displayed in time order, with a speaker listed on the line below the previous speaker, or alternatively each speaker can be given a column adjacent to the other speaker, with utterances and responses arranged on the same line.

In addition to the standardized system for encoding features of texts which SGML provides, there is also a need for agreement on what features about a text should be encoded. The *Text Encoding Initiative* (Sperberg-McQueen & Burnard, 1994) is a complex application of SGML sponsored by three of the major professional associations which work with computer texts: the Association for Computers and the Humanities (ACH), the Association for Literary and Linguistic Computing (ALLC) and the Association for Computational Linguistics (ACL) (see Section 2.7). This pioneering international project involving six years' work by many scholars was set up to attempt to establish guidelines for encoding machine-readable text, including what should be encoded, and how this should be done so that texts could be exchanged independently of the hardware or software in use.

The *TEI Guidelines* were designed to apply to any texts regardless of the language, the date of production or the genre. As a framework, the document type definition (DTD) is modular and extensible to cater for features which researchers might wish to encode beyond the minimal core, including, for example, hypertext, figures and tables, and text types in a corpus. Ide and Véronis (1995) have edited a volume on the significance and design features of the Text Encoding Initiative and on issues and problems in the encoding of specific text types, including poetry and prose, spoken texts and large corpora.

Although approaches to markup are still being developed, anyone compiling a corpus could do worse than become familiar with the experience of the compilers of the *British National Corpus* in developing and applying markup which conformed to the Text Encoding Initiative proposals. Burnard (1992a) describes the set of features which were tagged in the first instance to give full bibliographic information about a spoken or written text, and these are discussed by Burnage and Dunlop (1993). A very complex set of tags marks the internal organization of each text, including, for example, paragraphs <P>, quotations <QUOTE>, titles <CAPTION>, to more specific features of the text such as underlining. With increased detail in tagging or parsing comes a seemingly exponential increase in the complexity of the representations. Figure 2.7 contains a fragment of a text from the *BNC* showing part-of-speech tags < > preceding each word and SGML markup.

CB8 2667 172 32 <s n=2667> <w AJ0>Blue <w NN1>cheese <w NN2>lovers <w VM0>will <w VVI>welcome <w AT0>a <w AJ0>new <w AJ0-NN1>French <w AJ0>blue <w NN1>cheese <w PRP>from <w AT0>the <w NN2>Pays <w UNC>de <w NN1-NP0>Bresse <w PRP>in <w AJ0>eastern <w NP0>France<c PUN>.

Figure 2.7 A fragment from the *BNC* showing SGML markup

The cost and manual effort of marking up a corpus can be very great indeed, as Atkins et al. (1992) have noted. The level of detail of markup has to be related to the potential use of the corpus. If, for example, the focus is on the corpus as a whole rather than on separate genres or text types, then complex markup is probably not justifiable. However, as noted earlier, the problem is that it is sometimes difficult to be sure in advance what use will be made of a corpus and the extent to which it will need to be transferable to other contexts in the future. Atkins et al. have provided a minimal list of features of written and spoken texts which it may be useful to encode in a TEI-conformant way. These include, in the case of written texts, quotations, lists, headings, abbreviations, initials and acronyms, front and back matter of books (prefaces, appendices, etc.), chapters, sections and proper names. Spoken texts may encode, for example, speaker turn-taking, interruptions, overlapping speech, dialectal forms, orthographically normalized conventions of sentence structure, pauses (including pause length) and inaudible speech.

The *TEI Guidelines* are an intricately detailed account of the possible information structure of many text types and may eventually serve other purposes than text encoding. However, the corpus compiler has flexibility as to how much detail is marked-up for any particular corpus. In initial stages, corpus compilers can conveniently use simplified variants of markup, which involve rather little change to the text as captured.

It is to be hoped that the Text Encoding Initiative will help establish norms for those compiling electronic corpora for a wide variety of research purposes as to the levels of markup and the features which should be marked. When we move beyond the representation of formal organizational features of text, however, to the tagging of word classes, there are few signs yet that there can be compatibility of tagsets between different corpus projects (see Section 4.1.2).

2.7 Organizations and professional associations concerned with corpus design, development and research

As noted earlier, work with corpora has developed in association with three main disciplinary fields: descriptive linguistics, computational linguistics and literary studies. For many corpus linguists, their work is essentially doing descriptive linguistics using corpora as the source of evidence, and encompassing lexicographical, phonological, grammatical and discourse studies including studies of variation. Work with corpora is often cross-disciplinary, however, and is undertaken for other purposes than linguistic description. Computational linguistics involving work on machine translation, or the automatic analysis of speech or writing, is now a very large field, overlapping and interacting with more narrowly focused corpus-based linguistic descriptions. In fact, for some researchers, corpus linguistics is seen as being a sub-branch of computational linguistics (see Section 5.2). Humanities research in language and literature has also involved corpus compilation and the corpus-based analysis of the structure, style, content and authorship of mainly literary texts. The professional associations, centres and bibliographic resources in each of these three main fields are highly developed and have fostered research as well as keeping researchers in touch with progress in corpus-based studies.

For corpus linguists with an interest in the description of English, the International Computer Archive of Modern English (ICAME) has been the major resource. (ICAME, The Norwegian Computing Centre for the Humanities (NCCH), Harald Hårfagresgt. 31, N-5007 Bergen, Norway. E-mail: icame@hd.uib.no. The World Wide Web site is: http://www.hd.uib.no). Established in 1977 by linguists and information scientists working with machine-readable texts, and renamed the International Computer Archive of Modern and Medieval English in 1996, ICAME aims to collect and distribute information about machine-readable corpora, to publish research on corpora, to build up an archive of corpora and to distribute these to researchers. An annual conference has been held since 1979, and the *ICAME Journal* (originally *ICAME News*) has appeared once a year since 1976, reporting on the ICAME conferences as well as publishing research and reviews. The *ICAME Bibliography* (Altenberg, 1991b) is the most exhaustive, specialized source of information in English on published studies based on computer corpora. Many of the major first-generation corpora are available at cost from ICAME in various forms including CD-ROM. The ICAME CD-ROM contains the *Brown, LOB, Kolhapur, London–Lund* and *Helsinki* corpora in various versions and formats, along with *WordCruncher, TACT* and *Free Text Browser* software for corpus analysis. This ICAME collection is one of the most valuable sources of text for corpus-based linguistic analysis, not only because it provides a convenient way of studying some of the classic one-million-word corpora but also because of the accompanying software for corpus analysis. ICAME also provides access to information on corpora and corpus-based research through various directories available by file transfer protocol from the NCCH file servers.

It would be hard to exaggerate the part played by ICAME through the Norwegian Computing Centre for the Humanities in the development of corpus linguistics. It has provided for corpus linguists a low-cost service of very high quality, without which the rapid development of the field from the 1980s would not have been possible. As a further indication of the growth of corpus linguistics, a major new journal, *The International Journal of Corpus Linguistics*, was launched in 1996.

The major bibliographic overview in all corpus-using fields is the *Humanities Computing Yearbook* (Lancashire & McCarty, 1988; Lancashire, 1991). This indispensable resource provides a comprehensive survey of computing activities in the main disciplinary fields, including individual languages, and includes published research as well as sources of corpora and software, centres for archives and research, and professional associations. Published research has been brought together on an annual basis since 1991 in *Research in Humanities Computing* (Hockey & Ide, 1991). Surveys of available corpora by Taylor et al. (1991), Leech and Fligelstone (1992), and Edwards (1993) are valuable overviews from which to begin to explore the world of corpus linguistics.

The major professional association in computational linguistics is the Association for Computational Linguistics (ACL). Based in North America but international in its scope, ACL also has a European chapter. Annual conferences are sponsored and a quarterly journal, *Computational Linguistics* (formerly *The American Journal of Computational Linguistics*), has been published since the 1970s. ACL publishes research on natural language processing by computer.

There are two major professional associations in corpus-related language and literature studies. The Association for Computers and the Humanities (ACH) has since the 1960s been concerned not only with the development and analysis of text databases for literature and language studies but also with other computing-related work in historical, anthropological and other humanities and social science research. ACH has published a journal, *Computers in the Humanities*, since the 1960s.

From the late 1960s to 1980 the Association for Literary and Linguistic Computing (ALLC), initially associated with the Literary and Linguistic Computing Centre at Cambridge, kept scholars in touch through the publication of a bulletin which reported activity mainly in Western Europe on projects to make databases of texts with indexes and concordances. The databases were mainly of literary texts. The bulletin also reported on conferences on the use of computers in literary and linguistic research. In 1980 the *ALLC Journal* was launched and this was merged with the *ALLC Bulletin* in 1986 to produce *Literary and Linguistic Computing,* a journal which has become indispensable in the field. The Association for Literary and Linguistic Computing is concerned with all aspects of computing applied to literary texts, including research on language and language use. ALLC and ACH hold joint annual conferences, alternating between North America and Europe, and have, together with ACL, jointly sponsored the Text Encoding Initiative to establish standards for encoding text in computer databases (see Section 2.6.5).

A more recent body set up in 1989 to encourage computing in literary, linguistic and other humanities fields in the United Kingdom is the Computers in Teaching Initiative Centre for Textual Studies (CTI Centre) based at Oxford University. The overview of resources published in Davis et al. (1992) includes up-to-date information on text sources and tools for text analysis. The Centre's first director, Susan Hockey, has taken many important initiatives in computer corpus work, and has more recently taken over the direction of the Centre for Electronic Texts in the Humanities (CETH) established by Princeton and Rutgers Universities in the United States in 1991 to be a North American focus for the acquisition and dissemination of electronic text files in the humanities.

More and more academic and commercial bodies have compiled and published linguistic databases of various kinds for various purposes since the late 1980s. Two organizations have been particularly active. The Linguistic Data Consortium (LDC), based at the University of Pennsylvania, has published a large number of corpora, mostly on CD-ROM at a reasonable price. In 1994 alone, 15 new corpora were published by LDC. Information about the LDC and the corpora it distributes can be accessed on the World Wide Web: http://www.ldc.upenn.edu . The more recently established European Corpus Initiative (ECI) has also distributed corpora on CD-ROM and can likewise be accessed on the World Wide Web: http://www.cogsci.ed.ac.uk/elsnet/eci.html.

CHAPTER THREE

Corpus-based descriptions of English

A major reason for compiling linguistic corpora is to provide the basis for more accurate and reliable descriptions of how languages are structured and used. This chapter reports the results of some of the corpus-based research on English, and illustrates some of the ways in which the use of corpora can contribute to linguistic description.

Corpus-based studies have approached the description of English from many perspectives. In addition to major lexicographical projects, there have been many corpus-based articles, theses and books published on a wide variety of topics over the last three decades, particularly on aspects of English lexis, morphology, syntax and discourse. This research literature is listed in Altenberg (1991b) and is broadly classified in Figure 3.1. Most of these descriptive studies include quantitative information on the distribution of linguistic features in particular genres or for different functions in speech or writing. Taken as a whole, they nevertheless present a rather unsystematic coverage of aspects of English. For example, in the studies of verb forms shown in Figure 3.1, there are no studies listed of the most frequent of all English verb forms (apart from the operators *is*, *have* and *do*) – namely the finite stem(+s) used for the simple present tense, nor are there studies of the non-finite present and past participles, which happen to be very frequent in English. In the noun phrase studies, *a, the, some, any* and a few quantifiers have been the subject of corpus-based analyses but there are many determiners which have not been studied. Only a few of the hundred or so prepositions of English and a small collection of adverbials have featured. One of the more systematically explored phenomena has been discourse particles, which is somewhat ironical perhaps when spoken corpora have been in such short supply. Studies of syntactic processes have covered a number of the major processes in English but often only within one genre or variety of the language.

There has nevertheless accumulated over the last 70 years, assisted since the 1960s by computerized corpora and computer software for analysis, enough corpus-based information on the English language to

Figure 3.1 A classification of corpus-based research on English (1960–93) (from Kennedy, 1996b)

I   Word-class and lexically focused studies

1 Verb forms

  • transitive verbs
  • infinitives
  • distribution and use of modals *shall, should, will, would, can, could, may, might, need*
  • *going to, will, is, isn't, is not, have, get, do*
  • progressive, preterite, perfect, subjunctive, passive voice
  • verb+particle combinations, prepositional verbs, verbs ending in *-alise*

2 Noun phrases

  • NP types
  • articles, quantifiers, *some, any*
  • *man, one, your, who, whom, what, whose, of which*
  • *both ... and, neither ... nor, all but, nothing, no, not*
  • classifying adjectives
  • referential pronouns, reciprocal pronouns, pronominal chains
  • noun phrases with *of*
  • *'s* genitive

3 Prepositions

  • *around, to, between, through, of*

4 Adverbials

  • *only, really, literally, directly, closely, increasingly, also, too, -ly* adverbs
  • adverbial stance types

5 Miscellaneous

  • *if not, even if, even though, but,* existential *there*
  • high frequency vocabulary, lexical density, cohesive devices, adjective–noun collocations

II   Syntactic processes

1 NP complexity

2 Premodification

3 Postmodification (including relativization)

4 Subordination

  • conditional clauses
  • nominal clauses
  • causal linking and ordering strategies
  • temporal *as* clauses

5 Complementation

  • infinitival complement clauses
  • *for/to* infinitive clauses
  • *to*+infinitive and *of*+infinitive

6 Topicalization

  • *tough*-movement
  • extraposed gerundial subject clauses
  • cleft and pseudo-cleft constructions

continued overleaf

Figure 3.1 continued

   7 Ellipsis

- conjunction-headed abbreviated clauses
- gapping

   8 Co-ordination

- contrastive linking

   9 Adverbial usage

- adverbial fronting
- sequences of spatial and temporal adverbials

  10 Miscellaneous

- comparatives
- apposition
- *do* support
- negation
- *by* agents
- tag questions

III Miscellaneous topics in spoken English

- impromptu speech, carry-on signals in conversation, speech rate, turn-taking, slips of the tongue, pauses, segmentation, phraseology, contractions, tone units, intonation, prosodic units, tone contrasts, discourse tags, lexical items peculiar to spoken discourse, questions and responses in conversation
- discourse particles and hedging devices
- *sort of, kind of, you know, actually, in fact, anyway, now, just, oh, ah, you see, I mean, to begin with, for example, yes, no, well*

IV Variation

- historical drift in genres
- word frequencies in US and UK English
- linguistic characteristics of different genres
- gender-related differences in spoken English
- differences in speech and writing
- comparison of UK and US written English

---

demonstrate the strengths of this approach to linguistic description. Because the grammatical tagging and parsing of corpora with high levels of accuracy continues to be time-consuming and difficult work, there has been a strong tendency for corpus-based studies to focus on unanalysed corpora, and particularly on individual words or morphemes. Thus lexically based grammar has thrived within corpus linguistics more than it has in non-corpus-based approaches to language description.

Descriptive language studies at the level of the word and above can be categorized according to the levels of lexis, morphology, syntax, discourse and pragmatics. Semantic studies and comparative studies of variation are undertaken both within and across these levels. In the following sections, examples of corpus-based descriptions of English will be given at the various levels. These studies have varied enormously in size and representativeness, but most of them have included statistics on use as well as descriptions of systemic possibility, thus distinguishing them from linguistic descriptions which lack a distributional focus. In some cases, the research described in this section has been selected not just for its intrinsic descriptive significance but because there are pedagogical applications which go beyond descriptive adequacy, and which can have an impact on English language curriculum design and teaching practices.

3.1 Lexical description

The most obvious use of corpora for lexical description is in lexicography. As already noted in Section 2.1.2, the *Oxford English Dictionary* was originally the culmination of the painstaking manual analysis of a corpus representing a thousand years of linguistic history, including the canon of English literature. There are now very few large contemporary dictionaries of English which do not make the claim that they are computer corpus based. Dynamic monitor corpora can be used not only to identify the set of different words or 'types' in a language, and to show when new types enter the language, but corpora can be used to identify the various senses or uses of particular types and their relative frequencies. This capacity to study the use of word forms and collocations in context by means of concordancing software was most notably exploited first in the *Cobuild* project (Sinclair, 1987), where the comparatively large size of the corpus at the time made it possible to find enough examples of the occurrence of less frequent types to have some confidence in the validity and reliability of the descriptive lexical entries.

It is now almost inconceivable that worthwhile and comprehensive lexical descriptions can be undertaken without a corpus. In the *London–Lund Corpus* of spoken English, for example, the polysemous word *good* occurs over 800 times and as an adjective has over 20 senses including agreeable (*good mood*), suitable (*a good fit*), large (*a good crowd*), enjoyable (*a good film*), high quality (*a good car*), skilful (*a good cook*), tasty (*a good meal*), fine (*good weather*), virtuous (*be good, good behaviour*), valid (*the licence is good*), desirable (*a good report*), valuable (*good value*).

Good also occurs as a discourse particle in other contexts as part of exclamations (*Good heavens!*), greetings (*Good afternoon*), to change topics or end conversation (*Good, let's leave it at that*), and in various backchannel functions to show a listener's understanding and to support an interlocutor. The relative frequencies in the *LLC* of the major uses of *good* are shown in Table 3.1.

The *London–Lund Corpus* is, of course, a small corpus of spoken British English mainly from the 1960s. Other corpora which are more representative of other varieties of English and which are large enough to

Table 3.1 Uses of *good* in the *LLC*

Use	%	%
Discourse particle		32.4
Greetings	7.2	
I understand	1.0	
To end conversation	2.1	
To express satisfaction	6.4	
Exclamation	6.0	
To change topic	2.7	
Others	7.0	
skilful or *competent*		14.3
suitable		7.4
enjoyable		7.0
desirable		7.0
high quality		5.2
helpful or *agreeable*		3.7
large		3.7
valid		3.2
virtuous		3.0
Miscellaneous		13.1
Total		100.0

provide a more reliable basis for lexicography may give quite different pictures of the use of *good*. Whereas about a third of the uses of *good* in the *LLC* are as discourse particles, greetings or exclamations for example, none of these uses appears in the genre of written academic English (section J) in the *LOB Corpus*.

The value of a corpus for identifying neologisms has been illustrated by Renouf (1993). In approximately 2.5 million words of text, published in editions of the London *Times* newspaper during March 1991, researchers found 5,374 new word types which had not yet appeared in dictionaries (e.g. *poserphone, wetware, empurple, indifferentness, kissergram, extracurricularly, televangelism, euroconvertible, de-yuppify, vatable, size-ist, Lebanonisation, bureaucratitis, dogs dinnerish, retro-twang*). Some 337 of the new types occurred more than once (e.g. *videograb, microflat, self-quotation*). Many neologisms, of course, have a short shelf life, but computer software which can filter out from vast amounts of text the new word forms (and the new contexts in which familiar words occur) will make the lexicographer's job both more interesting and more challenging in that criteria need to be developed to determine whether and when a new form should be legitimized in a dictionary. More recently Renouf made available to teachers of English a list of words in context, selected from 11,699 neologisms which had been identified from a corpus made up of issues of the *Independent* newspaper from January to March 1994. The list includes such choice neologisms as: *complainy, dial-a-video, bespokesman, cleavage-wielding, event-driven, fruitcakeland, infotainers, over-housed, unbusy, anarchitecture, bimboisation, bonkable, crashworthiness.*

As dictionaries become increasingly based on huge computer corpora which are continuously kept up to date, we may expect more specialized dictionaries routinely to include statistical information on the occurrence of types in different genres, and words which commonly collocate with them. Corpus-based dictionaries used for teaching and learning languages are already beginning to use colour codes or symbols to indicate whether types or meanings of types typically belong to particular frequency levels in the language. In this way, teachers and learners should ideally be able to identify readily the most frequent 500, 1,000, 2,000, 3,000 and 5,000 types or meanings in a language or important genre. Such information is important for curriculum design and for giving teachers and learners part of the basis of information to help decide where pedagogical focus might be directed most profitably.

3.1.1 Pre-electronic lexical description for pedagogical purposes

Whereas lexicographical studies have, until recently, typically described the lexicon without statistics, for much of the 20th century there has been a tradition of corpus-based lexical studies with statistical information for pedagogical purposes. Even before the development and use of computers for linguistic analysis since the 1960s, there were several large and impressive lexico-statistical studies designed to provide a scientific basis for language teaching and especially for the teaching of English to both native speakers and speakers of other languages. From the early 1920s, partly in response to the waves of immigration to North America, and also because of the demand for English language teaching in British colonies, particularly in Asia and Africa, there were several major projects designed to discover the most frequently used words in English. This work was reviewed by Fries and Traver (1940) and by Bongers (1947). Thorndike (1921) established the relative frequency of each of the words in his 4.5-million-word corpus which included classical literary works and books read by younger children (see Section 2.1.4). The Thorndike word count, which of course had to be done manually, subsequently formed the basis for major change in first and second language teaching initially in the United States and subsequently wherever English was learned or used. The principle of 'vocabulary control' in the design and editing of reading materials for both first and second language learners of English owes much to Thorndike's pioneering work, and the so-called 'reading movement' (Coleman, 1929) became the conventional wisdom in the United States and elsewhere for about 25 years from the early 1930s.

Essentially, it was argued that learners of a language should be exposed first to reading the most frequently occurring words in the language. Although there were often bitter debates between advocates of vocabulary control in language education and the proponents of Basic English during the 1930s, the two movements had something in common in that they each sought to establish a core vocabulary which, in the case of Basic English, could be used to express all concepts or, in the case of the 'reading movement', should form the basis for learning to read.

Vocabulary research was undertaken with major support from the Carnegie Corporation in the 1930s. Conferences in the USA and the UK brought together leading linguists and English language teaching specialists including West from India, Palmer from Japan, Sapir and Thorndike from the USA and Faucett from China. The report based on the *Carnegie* project (Faucett et al., 1936) articulated the principle that high frequency of occurrence as determined by the analysis of texts should be a major determinant of the lexical content of language instruction. Significantly for subsequent research, the project gave support to lexico-statistical analysis of the distribution of word meanings and not only of word forms. Until that time, forms such as *bow, bright, too, date* were simply counted as single types even though they are polysemous and in some cases belong to more than one word class.

Thorndike's earlier work was revised as *The Teacher's Wordbook of 30,000 Words* (Thorndike & Lorge, 1944). The revision was based on a larger corpus of about 18 million words. The textual sources were selected from school textbooks, children's classic stories such as *Little Women* and *Black Beauty*, English poetry, the US Constitution, the Bible, writers such as Jane Austen, Thackeray, Dryden, Defoe, Gibbon, Emerson and Thoreau, the *Encyclopaedia Britannica*, the *Ladies' Home Journal* and the *Saturday Evening Post*. Lorge's analysis of the vocabulary of magazines ensured that literary classics were complemented by more contemporary reading matter.

Because the corpus-based Thorndike–Lorge wordlist indicated the number of occurrences of each word per million words, and listed separately those words which occurred at least 50 times or 100 times per million words, the work was an easily accessible reference to guide teachers in selecting vocabulary for teaching and for rewriting reading material for learners within a high frequency vocabulary. The agenda of the authors went beyond this, however, in suggesting that 'graduation from senior high school may be made conditional upon knowledge of at least 15,000 words'. They added that

> much could be said about the use of the list by lawyers (especially in examining witnesses), preachers, lecturers, writers of textbooks, writers of propaganda and advertisements, and others. But to all such the list may be left to speak for itself.
> (Thorndike & Lorge, 1944: xii)

segmentCORPUS-BASED DESCRIPTIONS OF ENGLISH

Lorge (1949) later published a revision of earlier work he had undertaken with Thorndike describing the frequency of use of the different
meanings of the 500 or so commonest words of English as they occurred
in about 4.5 million words of text. This work in turn influenced probably the most well-known and persistent corpus-based description of
the English lexicon for pedagogical purposes, Michael West's *General
Service List of English Words* (1953), which updated the *Carnegie* project
of 1936 and built on the work which Thorndike began 30 years before.
West's book presents a description, based on Thorndike's research, of
the most frequent 2,000 words in the written English of the time, supplemented by information on the frequency of the meanings or uses of
these words, based on the work of Lorge. Figure 3.2 contains the entry
in the *General Service List* for *mind*. Users of the book today may wonder if it is credible for *mind* to be listed as a noun for 89% of its uses
and only 10% as a verb. They may also wonder how representative was
the corpus which found *insect* among the 2,000 most frequent words but
not *spider*, or *wine* but not *beer*. Similarly, *right* is listed as a noun as
in *human rights* for almost 50% of its uses, whereas the use of *right* to

MIND	1458e			
mind, n.		(1a)	*(seat of emotion)*	
			His mind was filled with sad thoughts	
		(1b)	*(seat of reason)*	
			A cultivated mind	54%
		(2)	*(Phrases concerned with the memory)*	
			Call to mind	
			Bear in mind	12%
		(3)	*(Phrases concerned with decision)*	
			An open mind	
			Speak one's mind	
			Know one's mind	
			Change one's mind	
			?[Have a good mind to]	9%
		(4)	*(Phrases concerned with temperament)*	
			In a good (bad) state of mind	
			Peace of mind	12%
		(5)	*(Phrases concerned with sanity)*	
			In his right mind	
			Out of his mind	2%
mind, v.		(1a)	*(consider; be careful of)*	
			Don't mind me!	
			Mind what I say	
			Mind you do!	
			Mind the step!	2%
		(1b)	*(attend to)*	
			Mind the baby	1%
		(2)	*(object to, care about)*	
			Do you (would you) mind if I smoke?	
			I do not mind (what you do)	
			Never mind!	7%
/-minded			Absent-minded *etc.*	1%

Figure 3.2 The entry for *mind* in West's *General Service List of English Words*

95

mean the opposite of *left* is only 8% and *right* as an adjective meaning correct (*you're right*) is only 9% of uses. This may have been because the Thorndike–Lorge corpus was biased towards more literary and formal styles of writing, and did not include speech at all. Nevertheless, partly for want of anything better, West became an indispensable source of reference in applied linguistics to check unbridled intuitions about language use, and for the design of curricula and teaching materials.

From the late 1930s, descriptions of the lexicons of other European languages were published. Shortly after the *General Service List of English Words* appeared, for example, Gougenheim et al. (1956) published a description of the use of high frequency vocabulary and grammatical structures from a corpus-based analysis of spoken French.

At about the same time as studies of the lexicon for pedagogical purposes were proceeding, there was also research on statistical regularities in such matters as the frequency of use of different phonemes, syllable structures, letters of the alphabet, word lengths and the proportions of nouns in the most frequent 1,000 types. This research was undertaken by Zipf, Dewey and others and reviewed by Miller (1951).

Perhaps the most important outcome of the early corpus studies was the recognition that, in whatever textual source, a small number of different word types make up most of the actual word occurrences or tokens. In general terms in large corpora this research may be summarized as in Table 3.2, although there can be some variation in the proportion of a text which is made up of the most frequent 2,000–5,000 words. In samples of spoken English, for example, 50 function words and discourse particles can sometimes account for up to 50% of the total tokens.

Table 3.2 Approximate proportions of different word types at different frequency levels in texts

% of total word tokens in a text	No. of different word types
95	3,000–15,000
90	2,000–3,000
80	1,000–1,500
70	600–800
50	50–100
25	10–15

There was thus a strong pedagogical motivation behind some of the most notable corpus-based studies of the lexicon from the 1920s to the end of the 1950s, when interest in this kind of research waned temporarily. Availability of computerized corpora and changes in the conventional wisdom about the role of form-focused language teaching led again to renewed attention to lexical description especially from the 1980s (see Section 5.3).

3.1.2 Computer corpus-based studies of the lexicon

The availability of computerized corpora from the mid-1960s made possible a new generation of statistically based descriptions of the lexicon, and in fact changed the nature of lexical studies by making possible rapid and comprehensive analysis of huge amounts of data with complete accountability. With a computerized corpus and appropriate software, both significant and more trivial but nevertheless interesting facts about the lexicon of a language can be uncovered.

As shown in Table 3.2, between 50 and 100 English words typically account for half of the total word tokens in any text. A comparison of the rank ordering of the 50 most frequent words in various corpora shows both remarkable consistency and systematic differences. Table 3.3 lists the 50 most frequent word forms in the 20-million-word *Birmingham Corpus* (Sinclair & Renouf, 1988), which includes about 1.5 million words of spoken English, compared with the rank ordering of these 50 words in five other much smaller corpora. The various corpora differ not only in size. There is geographical diversity (UK, USA, New Zealand), diversity in the period of text production (1961 in the case of *Brown* and *LOB*, the 1980s in the case of the *Birmingham* and *Wellington* corpora), variation across written as well as spoken texts (e.g. *LOB* is written whereas *LLC* is spoken), and writing both for children (*American Heritage Corpus*) and mainly for adults (e.g. *Brown*).

Although there are some striking differences in the rank ordering of the 50 most frequent words, reflecting the nature of the different corpora (e.g. the high frequency of *I* and the relatively lower rank of *had* and *were* in the spoken corpus, and major disparities in the relative frequencies of gender-specific pronouns), there is also, however, a striking consistency in the content of the lists. All of the words except *said* are function words. Even in the 100 most frequent words in the *Birmingham Corpus* there are only about a dozen content words.

One of the problems in counting word types based on graphic word forms, as in Table 3.3, is that such lists can be misleading. A word type such as *have* can be a full verb or an auxiliary, just as *like* can be a verb, adjective, noun, preposition or conjunction with quite different senses. On the other hand, different forms of the same word (e.g. *been* and *being*) will routinely be counted by machine as different types unless further processing is undertaken.

Thus rather than counting *book, books* or *am, is, are, was, were* as separate types, it has become quite normal in corpus studies to list under the same headword or lemma the inflectional variants (see Section 4.1.1). Francis and Kučera (1982: 1) defined a lemma as 'a set of lexical forms

Table 3.3 Rank order of the 50 most frequent word types in the *Birmingham Corpus* compared with other corpora

	Birmingham Corpus	Brown Corpus	LOB Corpus	Wellington Corpus	American Heritage Corpus	London–Lund Corpus
the	1	1	1	1	1	1
of	2	2	2	2	2	5
and	3	3	3	3	3	3
to	4	4	4	4	5	4
a	5	5	5	5	4	6
in	6	6	6	6	6	9
that	7	7	7	10	9	8
I	8	20	17	12	24	2
it	9	12	10	9	10	10
was	10	9	9	8	13	13
is	11	8	8	7	7	11
he	12	10	12	16	11	18
for	13	11	11	11	12	20
you	14	33	32	31	8	7
on	15	16	16	13	14	16
with	16	13	14	14	17	32
as	17	14	13	15	16	29
be	18	17	15	17	21	21
had	19	22	21	23	29	55
but	20	25	24	26	31	15
they	21	30	33	27	19	24
at	22	18	19	18	20	26
his	23	15	18	24	18	85
have	24	28	26	29	25	19
not	25	23	23	25	30	35
this	26	21	22	22	22	14
are	27	24	27	20	15	42
or	28	27	31	32	26	44
by	29	19	20	19	27	65
we	30	41	40	36	36	23
she	31	37	30	28	54	72
from	32	26	25	21	23	53
one	33	32	38	40	28	36
all	34	36	39	41	33	33
there	35	38	36	35	37	38
her	36	35	29	33	64	96
were	37	34	35	30	34	64
which	38	31	28	39	41	43
an	39	29	34	34	39	81
so	40	52	46	48	57	30

Table 3.3 continued

	Birmingham Corpus	Brown Corpus	LOB Corpus	Wellington Corpus	American Heritage Corpus	London–Lund Corpus
what	41	54	58	58	32	34
their	42	40	41	38	42	112
if	43	50	45	56	44	48
would	44	39	43	44	59	51
about	45	57	54	54	48	37
no	46	49	47	51	71	25
said	47	53	48	49	43	76
up	48	55	52	46	50	61
when	49	45	44	45	35	67
been	50	43	37	43	75	68

having the same stem and belonging to the same major word class, differing only in inflection and/or spelling'. Figure 3.3 is an example of a lemmatized entry for the various forms, variants and derivatives of the word *collect* in the *Brown Corpus*. Each type also has a grammatical tag selected from a set of 87 tags to indicate word classes, and these are

collect	verb	78-15-060
collect	VB	16-11-016
collects	VBZ	5-04-005
collected	VBD	7-04-007
collected	VBN	36-09-029
Collected	VBN-TL	1-01-001
collecting	VBG	13-08-011
collectible	**JJ**	**1-01-001**
collection	**noun**	**92-14-046**
collection	NN	82-14-042
collection	NN-HL	1-01-001
Collection	NN-TL	1-01-001
collections	NNS	8-05-008
collective	**adjective**	**31-08-019**
collective	JJ	30-08-018
collective	JJ-HL	1-01-001
collective	**NN**	**1-01-001**
collective-bargaining	**NN**	**1-01-001**
collectively	**RB**	**4-03-004**
collector	**noun**	**16-08-010**
collector	NN	7-03-003
Collector	NN-TL	1-01-001
collector's	NN$	0-00-000
Collector's	NN$-TL	1-01-001
collectors	NNS	7-04-006

Figure 3.3   A lemmatized entry for *collect* and related words
(from Francis and Kučera, 1982: 91)

shown in the middle column (e.g. VBZ means the -s form of the verb). The numbers on the right of each entry show the number of tokens of that type in the *Brown Corpus*, the number of genres (out of a possible 15) in which the word form occurs, and the number of samples (out of a possible 500) in which it occurs.

Other lemmatizing schemes can be less restrictive and include as part of the same lemma all the inflected forms of *collect, collectible, collection, collective, collective-bargaining, collectively* and *collector*. Francis and Kučera (1982) also include a rank list of lemmas in the *Brown Corpus*. Such a list can thus be expected to show many fewer types in a corpus than an unlemmatized list. The lemma *go*, for example, represents 13 separate types with a total of 1,848 tokens in the *Brown Corpus*, namely *go, Go, g'ahn, goes, went, gone, gonne, Gone, going, goin, goin', Going, gonna*. Some of these, of course, are rare, non-standard spellings.

In most corpora, many of the words which occur do so only once. These words are known as 'hapax legomena' (from Greek = 'something said only once'). In a short newspaper item of about 200 words, as many as 150 words may be hapax legomena. In large representative corpora, the proportion of hapaxes is normally much smaller. For example, in the *American Heritage Intermediate Corpus* (Carroll, Davies & Richman, 1971), which is an unlemmatized corpus of 5,088,721 words, 35,079 of the 88,741 different types are hapaxes (39.5%).

Nevertheless, the fact that almost 40% of the words in a corpus of over five million words occur only once shows that a corpus of even that size is not a sound basis for lexicographical studies of low frequency words. There are simply not enough instances of many words in such a corpus to form a clear picture of their linguistic ecology – their range of senses, the company they keep, the grammatical structures they occur in, and so on.

In research on the relationship between the size of a corpus and the number of different word types found in it, Sharman (1989) studied a one-million-word corpus of written American English broadly representative of journalistic texts. We might expect that, although the number of different words would increase as a corpus increases in size, there would come a point when no new words would appear. It is clear however, that this point is not likely to occur in a corpus of one million words, nor perhaps in any general corpus, however large. Sharman found that there was an almost linear relationship between vocabulary size and corpus size. A new word appeared in the text approximately every 30 words on average. While it is true that some of the 'new' words discovered as the word count proceeds through the corpus are proper nouns, this does not account for the observed relationship. It is not yet clear how big a corpus must be for the curve to level off. Sharman's study also confirmed the statistical regularities in language proposed by Zipf (1949) and others forty years earlier.

In specialist corpora within a single genre or subject field, or in small corpora, the list of the most frequent 50 or so words which make up about 50% of all the tokens in English texts can be substantially different from those shown in Table 3.3. This can be illustrated in Table 3.4 –

Table 3.4 The 50 most frequent words used in an economics text compared with a corpus of the same size of general academic English (from Sutarsyah, Nation & Kennedy, 1994: 41)

Rank	Economics text		General academic texts	
1	the	22,905	the	23,890
2	of	12,710	of	14,591
3	be	10,686	be	14,021
4	a	9,952	and	8,455
5	and	8,323	in	8,077
6	in	7,010	to	7,867
7	to	6,502	a	7,857
8	that	4,392	that	3,400
9	*price	3,080	have	3,217
10	for	2,912	this	3,143
11	it	2,674	it	3,071
12	we	2,534	for	3,060
13	have	2,514	as	2,574
14	*cost	2,251	by	2,351
15	by	2,034	with	2,110
16	this	2,003	they	2,056
17	*demand	1,944	on	1,956
18	on	1,882	which	1,631
19	as	1,831	he	1,590
20	they	1,820	not	1,544
21	*curve	1,804	or	1,542
22	at	1,797	at	1,535
23	*firm	1,743	from	1,518
24	*supply	1,590	can	1,242
25	*quantity	1,467	we	1,205
26	can	1,442	but	1,103
27	*margin	1,427	*use	974
28	will	1,378	one	922
29	*economy	1,353	some	894
30	from	1,337	there	894
31	*produce	1,237	do	793
32	if	1,202	more	744
33	*income	1,183	other	704

continued overleaf

Table 3.4 continued

Rank	Economics text		General academic texts	
34	do	1,165	all	694
35	with	1,135	than	666
36	*market	1,101	if	662
37	but	1,090	*make	656
38	or	1,058	may	636
39	each	1,038	I	615
40	*labour	1,004	only	608
41	*increase	1,002	no	595
42	*consume	995	when	581
43	than	977	*year	577
44	not	974	so	571
45	more	963	such	558
46	other	957	would	556
47	*total	946	who	550
48	*change	927	two	546
49	*rate	915	also	529
50	when	910	any	528

a list of the most frequent 50 types (lemmatized) in a single economics text of about 320,000 words, compared with the most frequent 50 types in a similarly sized corpus consisting of 160 two-thousand-word samples from the combined general academic sections (Section J) of the *LOB Corpus* and the *Wellington Corpus*. The more narrowly focused the corpus (academic English compared with 'general' English, or the English of economics compared with general academic English), the more content words find their way into the higher frequency levels. Thus, for example, in the economics text 18 of the 50 most frequent words are content words (marked with an asterisk *); in the academic English corpus only 3 of the most frequent 50 types are content words; in the *Birmingham Corpus* only one word in the most frequent 50 word types, namely *said*, is unequivocally not a member of a closed class of function words. In 'general corpora' beyond about the most frequent 150 words, content words begin to predominate. For corpus-based studies of function words, a diverse corpus from a wide range of texts and genres is needed. For the description of content words, a more homogeneous (special purposes) corpus may be more valuable.

As shown earlier in Figure 3.3, some corpora are available with grammatical tags assigned to each word token in the texts. One of the advantages of tagged corpora, which are discussed in more detail in Section 4.1, is that they can provide information not only on whether an individual form occurs more often, say, as a noun or a verb, but tagging can also show the frequency and distribution of word classes in a corpus. Table 3.5, for example, shows the word-class rank order in the one-million-word *Brown* and *LOB* corpora, and also their frequencies in the two major subdivisions of each corpus, informative and imaginative prose. It can be seen that nouns are more frequent in the genres which make up the informative prose sections of each corpus and the complexity of the noun phrase also accounts for the higher proportion of adjectives, determiners and prepositions in informative prose.

Table 3.5 Relative proportions of major word classes in the *Brown* and *LOB* corpora
(based on data from Francis & Kučera, 1982: 547; Johansson & Hofland, 1989: 15)

Word class	% of total corpus (1,000,000 words in each)		% of informative prose (A–J)		% of imaginative prose (fiction) (K–R)	
	Brown	LOB	*Brown*	LOB	*Brown*	LOB
Nouns	26.80	25.2	28.50	26.9	21.77	20.0
Verbs	18.20	17.8	17.02	16.4	21.69	21.9
Determiners and quantifiers	14.16	14.2	14.84	15.2	12.11	11.4
Prepositions	12.04	12.2	12.77	13.1	9.87	9.6
Adjectives	7.07	7.3	7.65	7.8	5.35	5.7
Pronouns	6.56	7.1	4.75	5.0	11.94	13.1
Conjunctions	5.92	5.5	5.94	5.5	5.86	5.4
Adverbs	5.23	5.5	4.73	5.0	6.72	7.2
Others*	4.02	5.2	3.80	5.2	8.49	5.8
Total	100.00	100.0	100.00	100.0	100.00	100.0

* Includes *wh-* words, *not*, *there*, foreign words and interjections. Numerals are included as quantifiers.

The relative proportions of the word classes in these two corpora of written American and British English may be compared with Altenberg's (1990) analysis of the relative proportions of the word classes in a 50,000-word sample from the *London–Lund Corpus* (*LLC*) of spoken British English. As shown in Table 3.6, fewer nouns and a considerable proportion of discourse items characteristic of spoken English are noteworthy. In

Table 3.6 Relative proportions of major word classes in a sample (c. 50,000 words) from the *LLC* (Altenberg, 1990: 185)

Word class	%
Verbs	20.1
Pronouns	17.3
Nouns	14.3
Discourse items	9.4
Prepositions	9.2
Adverbs	9.0
Determiners	7.9
Conjunctions	6.3
Adjectives	6.0
Predeterminers	0.3
Miscellaneous	0.2

particular, the discourse items are more frequent than some content-word categories. It should be noted, however, that the guidelines used in tagging the three corpora differed on matters of detail, so that these figures should not be interpreted as reflecting precise differences between the language of the three corpora.

Johansson and Hofland (1989) have shown the frequency of occurrence in the *LOB Corpus* of certain tag combinations involving nouns (NN), verbs (VB), adjectives (JJ) and adverbs (RB). Table 3.7 shows that some sequences such as adjective+noun or noun+noun are very frequent indeed, whereas certain other combinations occur much less frequently.

Johansson and Hofland (1989) have also analysed the occurrence of the 40 most frequent sequences of word-class tags at the beginnings and ends of sentences. Among the 40 most frequent combinations of two-, three-, four- or five-tag sequences, all 40 of the final sequences end in a noun. The three most frequent sequences are adjective+noun (4,312), definite article+noun (3,233), preposition+noun (2,552). Their analysis suggests that the ends of sentences may be more predictable grammatically than the beginnings, in that the 40 most frequent combinations whether two, three, four or five tags in length cover more of the sentences in the corpus than do the 40 most frequent initial combinations.

Lexical studies of corpora can also contribute to register studies. In a study based on the *Brown Corpus*, Johansson (1978) compared the lexicon of Section J (learned and scientific writing) with the corpus as a whole, and calculated whether a word is proportionately more or less frequent in the learned and scientific English than in the whole corpus. He noted

Table 3.7 Frequency per million words of certain tag combinations in informative prose and imaginative prose in the *LOB Corpus* (based on Johansson & Hofland, 1989, Vol. 2: 3)

	Relative frequency per million words	
Tag combination	Informative prose	Imaginative prose
NN NN		
(e.g. *child care*)	11,507	5,427
NN JJ		
(e.g. in *the enquiry proper*)	932	743
JJ NN		
(e.g. *good care*)	30,854	21,928
JJ VB		
(e.g. in *when will the enquiry proper start*)	20	24
JJ JJ		
(e.g. in *good medical care*)	2,991	2,238
JJ RB		
(e.g. in *that's difficult too*)	231	318
RB JJ		
(e.g. *extremely low*)	3,631	3,268
RB RB		
(e.g. in *work extremely hard*)	1,175	1,220

certain characteristics of the vocabulary of scientific English, including a disproportionate use of words such as *discussion, argument, result, conclusion, analysis, experiment, measurement, sample, probability, distribution, class, group, type, species, items, characteristics, typical*. Certain relational words are disproportionately more frequent in scientific English, including *same, similar, different, distinct, equivalent, equal, average, normal, relative, difference, increase, change*. Comparative adjectives and adverbs are similarly disproportionately frequent, whereas locative adverbs of space or time are disproportionately less frequent in scientific texts than in general written American English.

In a later study of the lexical characteristics of different registers, Johansson (1981) compared Section J (academic texts) with Sections K–R (imaginative prose fiction) in the *LOB Corpus*, and identified by means of a 'distinctiveness coefficient' the nouns, verbs, adjectives and adverbs which were most particularly associated with the two varieties. Johansson's ranking of the most 'distinctive' words included those shown in Table 3.8.

Table 3.8 Most distinctive nouns, verbs, adjectives and adverbs in two genres of the *LOB Corpus* (from Johansson, 1981: 7–8)

Nouns		Verbs		Adjectives		Adverbs	
Academic texts	Fiction	Academic texts	Fiction	Academic texts	Fiction	Academic texts	Fiction
constants	mister	measured	kissed	thermal	damned	theoretically	impatiently
axis	sofa	assuming	heaved	linear	asleep	significantly	softly
equations	wallet	calculated	leaned	radioactive	sorry	approximately	hastily
oxides	cheek	occurs	glanced	structural	gay	hence	nervously
equation	living-room	assigned	smiled	finite	miserable	relatively	upstairs
theorem	cafe	emphasized	hesitated	transient	dear	respectively	faintly
coefficient	wrist	obtained	exclaimed	physiological	silly	commonly	quietly
ions	darling	executed	murmured	numerical	empty	separately	abruptly
correlation	sigh	tested	gasped	magnetic	stiff	consequently	eagerly
electrons	gun	corresponding	hurried	conceptual	dreadful	similarly	upright
impurities	gaze	vary	flushed	residual	afraid	rapidly	tomorrow
oxidation	clip	bending	cried	differential	deadly	thus	downstairs
parameters	fist	varying	eyed	stationary	sweet	furthermore	gently
nickel	trail	loading	staring	statistical	ashamed	sufficiently	anyway
electron	lounge	measuring	paused	negative	lovely	therefore	maybe
impurity	cheeks	determine	whispered	relative	faint	secondly	swiftly
diagram	lips	isolated	waved	experimental	calm	ultimately	presently
ion	cigarette	dissolved	nodded	theoretical	silent	readily	suddenly
parameter	stairs	resulting	frowned	integral	nice	effectively	somewhere
coefficients	footsteps	defined	shivered	mechanical	funny	generally	back
oxygen	dad	occur	muttered	chemical	worried	widely	slowly
sodium	lawn	stressed	shared	internal	tired	strictly	desperately
equilibrium	receiver	illustrates	flung	initial	stupid	mainly	sharply

For each word class, what the lists show is those items which occur in one variety but are highly unlikely to occur in the other. The lists also demonstrate that the life of the mind is richly diverse in its cognitive and social dimensions.

Lexical studies which use dictionaries as a rather special kind of corpus have also flourished with the development of machine-readable versions of dictionaries, usually derived initially from the computer tapes used in typesetting. In fact, some studies could only have been undertaken with such machine-readable databases. The 1978 first edition of the *Longman Dictionary of Contemporary English* (*LDOCE*) and the 1974 edition of the *Oxford Advanced Learner's Dictionary* (*OALD*) were made available by their publishers in machine-readable form for research purposes, and a number of interesting studies resulted which threw light on the nature of the lexicon. Several of the early studies on the *LDOCE* are reported in Boguraev and Briscoe (1989). The various authors indicated how much remained to be done to capture adequately the richness of senses of words within the confines of dictionary entries, and to overcome some of the major problems of using dictionary entries for establishing the senses of lexical items in natural language processing systems.

Vossen (1991) also reports a study of the semantic information in the *LDOCE* entries which illustrates the potential descriptive information made available. The dictionary contains 23,800 entries which are labelled as 'nouns'. Of these, 67% are listed as having one sense, 20% have two senses, 6.5% have three senses, and 2.5% have four senses. The remaining 600 or so nouns have between 5 and 27 senses listed, with an average of about 7. Thus, for a relatively small number of nouns such as *line, point, head, place, time, service, thing, body*, polysemy is a major characteristic. Although this study suggests that two-thirds of nouns are not polysemous, it is the high frequency nouns such as those above which are polysemous. There is apparently a strong correlation between frequency of use and degree of polysemy, just as there is between word length and morphological regularity. Monosyllables are often able to occur as different parts of speech without affixation. Polysyllables are more likely to undergo derivation by affixation, thus producing distinctive forms for each word class.

An interesting, very similar relationship appears to occur with the verbs and adjectives listed in the *LDOCE*. For the 7,921 entries listed as verbs, 55% have one sense, 23.8% have two, 10% have three and 4.4% have four senses. The remaining 469 verbs each have between 5 and 43 senses listed, with an average of about 6 senses each. For the 6,922 listed adjectives, 63.4% have a single sense, 24.2% have two senses, 7% have three and 2.6% have four senses. The remaining 184 have between 5 and 21 listed senses, with an average of about 6.

3.1.3 Collocation

It is over 250 years since Cruden identified the repeated co-occurrence of certain words in the Bible, and this observation was illustrated in Section 2.1.1 with the words *dry* and *ground* from his celebrated *Concordance*. In the 1930s, the British linguist H. E. Palmer, working as an English language teaching specialist in Japan, undertook corpus-based research on recurrent combinations of English words, which resulted in a description of over 6,000 such collocations. This research led Palmer (1933: 7) to conclude that collocations 'exceed by far the popular estimate of the number of simple words contained in our everyday vocabulary', thus calling for a reconsideration of the nature of vocabulary.

Since the late 1960s, computer-assisted analysis of corpora has made it possible to carry forward the early work of Palmer and others, and to reveal previously unrecognized patterns of word use in everyday language which do not fit easily into either of the traditional categories of lexis or grammar. Rather, they seem to straddle lexis and grammar and at times suggest the necessity for some redefinition of the notion of a word.

Firth (1957: 14) referred to a collocation as 'actual words in habitual company' but it is possible to define 'habitual company' in a number of ways so as to give the notion of collocation more or less restricted senses. We have already considered the use of software to show the frequency with which various tag combinations occur in a corpus. However, the identification and counting of collocations depends on how collocation is defined. A number of scholars have explored the phenomenon and have considered the significance for linguistic theory of the fact that some words can have a tendency to occur in the company of other words in certain contexts, e.g. *pouring rain, statistically significant, intrinsic value, strong tendency*. Even before the work of Palmer and Firth, the study of words in combination was popular in certain prescriptive educational contexts. Second or foreign language learners have often made efforts to learn the 'idiomatic' use of a language, or to learn set phrases appropriate for different contexts. Thus, teachers have encouraged their students to learn *pull my leg* (rather than *pull my legs*), *call it a day* or *step on the gas* (rather than **name it a day* or **walk on the gas*). On the other hand, teachers of native speakers of English have often discouraged them from any tendency to use set phrases, on the ground that clichés should be avoided. For imaginative writing, originality has usually been highly prized, and many schoolchildren have been encouraged to avoid word sequences which offend the sensitivities and sensibilities of particular teachers. In some English-speaking contexts, certain word sequences are sometimes quite unfairly picked on as clichés, Americanisms, Briticisms, Australianisms or whatever. However, although it may be true that particular word sequences are sometimes overused, it is not a moral issue or grounds for chauvinism. Examples of word sequences which have been criticized as clichés in the last decade or so in New Zealand newspapers include:

a good time was had by all
at this point in time
in times of rapid social change
as part of our strategic plan
we have hopefully not heard the last of . . .
the flavour of the month/decade

Since the late 1950s the most influential forces in linguistic theory have also supported the notion that language use is most naturally innovative. Within transformational-generative theory, for example, the position taken by Chomsky (1959: 57) was largely unchallenged.

> We constantly read and hear new sequences of words, recognize them as sentences and understand them. It is easy to show that the new events that we accept and understand as sentences are not related to those with which we are familiar by any simple notion of formal (or semantic or statistical) similarity or identity of grammatical frame.

In characterizing language as innovative, Chomsky was here referring specifically to the sequencing of words in sentences and was arguing against the Skinnerian conceptualization of the sentence simply as a left-to-right finite state Markov process or verbal chain in which the probability of a word's occurrence was determined by the occurrence of the words preceding it. The generative approach to language tends to downplay the use of prefabricated, ready-made sequences of words, although there is no reason why many sentences cannot be treated as partially lexicalized rather than purely syntactically generated. Thus, in the sentence *I haven't time at the moment*, the phrase *at the moment* can be treated as a prepositional phrase or, alternatively, as a lexicalized unit equivalent to one of the uses of *now*. Historically, lexical units such as *breakfast* have syntactically analysable origins.

The extent to which users of a language have free choice in the use of words in rule-governed or grammatical sequences or whether we tend to choose prefabricated sequences has been characterized by Sinclair (1991: 109) in terms of two complementary 'principles', namely 'the open-choice principle' and 'the idiom principle'. In fact actual language use is rarely a choice between such polar opposites but is on a cline between these extremes.

The open-choice principle involves the potential to generate unique sentences based on grammatical rules and individual lexical items, and could be seen as 'an analytical process which goes on in principle all the time, but whose results are only intermittently called for' (1991: 114). The idiom principle on the other hand recognizes that, just as there are tendencies for physical, cognitive or social phenomena to be associated, so this will be reflected in language. Thus the possible tendency of these words to co-occur – *ice* and *cold*, *cry* and *tears*, *noise* and *loud/soft* – could merely reflect nature. Whatever the reason, the idiom principle is manifested in the use of 'a large number of semi-preconstructed phrases that constitute single choices, even though they might appear to be analysable into segments' (Sinclair, 1991: 110). It is argued that some combinations are so tightly bound or lexicalized that they form units which behave as if they were single items, e.g. *at least* or *of course*, while others are less strongly lexicalized.

An interest in recurring word combinations has also come from a number of other sources within linguistics. In addition to lexicographical research resulting in dictionaries of collocations (e.g. Benson et al., 1986), some research on language acquisition has focused on the phenomenon of collocation. Wong-Fillmore (1976: 614) concluded that 'The strategy of acquiring formulaic speech is central to the learning of language'. Peters (1980) similarly suggested that unanalysed sequences of words had a significant role among the units of language acquisition and proposed ways for identifying such unanalysed sequences. Nattinger and De Carrico (1992) have extended the observation by suggesting that since first language learners can be seen to use unvarying, apparently unanalysed, prefabricated chunks of speech (e.g. *what's that*, *give me*), then second language teaching might similarly be concentrated around the establishment of what they call 'lexical phrases'.

One of the most influential cases for taking recurring word combinations seriously within linguistic theory was made by Pawley and Syder (1983). Although their evidence was not based on corpus analysis, they argued that there were numerous examples of recurring word combinations at the phrase, clause and multi-clause level in Australian and New Zealand English, and of course other varieties. The examples of what they called 'habitually-spoken sequences' in Figure 3.4 are without doubt only a tiny sample of word sequences which recur in English.

Work in corpus linguistics has demonstrated the extent to which particular sequences of words recur in English. Nowhere has this been more strikingly illustrated than in a study by Altenberg (1991a) which showed that about 70% of the words of running text in the half-million-word *London–Lund Corpus* are part of recurrent word combinations. Most of the combinations are two to three words in length, but some have more than five words. Altenberg focuses on amplifier collocations and shows that a few are used a great deal, but even those with only two tokens in the corpus are often strikingly familiar. Some of the common collocations in the *LLC* include *very much*, *so many*, *quite clear*, *perfectly willing*, *dead against*, *completely different*, *deeply divided*, *incredibly young*.

It is, however, one thing to use a corpus to discover recurring word sequences. It is quite another matter to decide the status of these recurring

Did you have a good trip?	How are you going to do that?
How is everyone at home?	Once you've done that the rest is easy.
How long are you staying?	I see what you mean.
He's not in. Would you like	It's as easy as falling off a log.
to leave a message?	I'll believe it when I see it.
Can I take a message?	You don't want to believe everything you hear.
He's busy right now.	I knew you wouldn't believe me.
Would you like to wait?	You can't believe a word he says.
I can't wait any longer.	If you believe that you'll believe anything.
Would you like some more?	It just goes to show, you can't be too careful.
Have some more.	There's nothing you can do about it now.
I enjoyed that.	That's easier said than done.
I don't regret a single moment.	You're not allowed to do that.
Have you heard the news?	

Figure 3.4   Some habitually spoken sequences in Australian and New Zealand English
(from Pawley & Syder, 1983: 206–207)

sequences. The patterning of speech or writing based on recurring sequences of words can be characterized in many ways. Some sequences allow for no alteration (*it's as easy as falling off a log*). Others allow certain changes (*at the moment / at certain moments*, etc.), and others are relatively free within a framework (*too . . . to, an . . . of*). Some researchers, such as Benson et al. (1986), have even viewed collocations as a set of grammatical frames (e.g. noun+noun; SVO to O; noun+*that*-clause).

For a systematic, exhaustive description of recurring word sequences in a corpus, clear criteria are needed. A dictionary definition of collocation, such as that of the *LDOCE* – 'a habitual combination of words which sounds natural' – seems intuitively right but empirically problematical. How often does a combination have to recur to be 'habitual', and who decides what 'sounds natural'? Does a combination have to be 'well-formed' or canonical to be a collocation (e.g. *Wannanother one?*)? Do collocations have to be syntactic or are they primarily semantic? Do collocations have to consist of adjacent words or can they be discontinuous (e.g. <u>the distinction between</u> . . . , <u>the distinction</u> we frequently draw <u>between</u> . . .)? Can a sequence which occurs only once in a particular corpus but which is intuitively recognized by native speakers as a sequence they have heard before be listed as a collocation nevertheless? How big does a corpus have to be in order to establish that a collocation does exist? Are there degrees of collocationality based on the flexibility of the bonding between words (e.g. whether substitution of an inflection or a word is possible – e.g. *the tip of the iceberg, the tip of the problem*). Can we lemmatize collocations so that similar or inflectionally related sequences are counted as a single collocational type (e.g. tense changes *Do you need a hand?*, *Did you need a hand?*)? Are degrees of collocationality able to be established on the basis of the number of tokens of a type in a particular corpus? For example, in the *LOB Corpus*, we find the following:

(a)	at London Airport	8 tokens
(b)	between friends	4 tokens
(c)	between you and me	0 tokens

Native speakers of English can rate these phrases in terms of 'natural-ness' of collocation, with (a) being typically judged to be the least natural and (c) the most natural. It is also an open question whether a syntactic framework can be a collocation, enabling *at London Airport* and *at LA International Airport* to be considered as a single type.

Different researchers have answered these and other questions differently and the positions they have taken affect our conclusions about the pervasiveness of collocations, with consequences for the description of the lexicon and for linguistic theory.

The leading researcher on collocations in the *Brown Corpus*, Kjellmer (1982: 25), noted that a characteristic of collocations was that they were combinations which co-occur 'more often than the frequencies in the corpus of the constituents of the combination would lead us to expect'. This criterion would select not only combinations such as *another one* or *last week* but also non-grammatical combinations such as *although he* or *and the*. Kjellmer (1987: 133) proposed that in a one-million-word corpus such as *Brown*, a particular sequence of words must occur more than once in identical form and be grammatical if it is to be accepted as a collocation. The obvious problem with this criterion is that in such a small corpus some sequences which occur only once (and therefore do not count as collocations) are nevertheless immediately recognizable as recurring in the language. An example noted by Kjellmer is *yesterday evening*. On the other hand, the non-*ad hoc*, principled approach allows sequences such as *a night* or *of the night* to fit the criterion for collocation status and yet they might be considered to be so predictable as to be uninteresting. In the *LOB Corpus*, one of the most frequent words recurring alongside *without* is *and*: *and without*. On the other hand, *do without, without question, without comment* or *without reference* seem intuitively to have a greater claim to be considered as collocations.

Formal similarity as a criterion for collocational status can also confound different syntactic structures or processes, as in the following pairs of examples.

(a) I had no use for it *at all*.
(b) We were aware of his influence *at all* times.
(c) I'm *used to* her sarcastic remarks.
(d) He *used to* live next door.

Insisting on exact formal identicalness of sequences in order for them to be classed as collocations also misses certain regularities in language use. In the *LOB Corpus*, the words in Figure 3.5 occur once each with *among*, and yet because these individual sequences do not recur they

chief among	among friends
first	his very friendly acquaintances
foremost	our friends and acquaintances
peerless	our acquaintances
principal	his intimates
unique	his kindred
unparalleled	consanguineal kin

Figure 3.5   Some items which occur once with *among* in the *LOB Corpus*

might be denied collocational status on formal grounds. From a semantic point of view, however, the words in each group preceding or following *among* have much in common.

Figure 3.6 contains the contexts in which each of the 12 tokens of the word-type *silk* occur in the *Brown Corpus*. What is immediately apparent is that the word *silk* in this corpus is usually found in the environment of a colour. Eight of the 12 tokens explicitly name the colour of the silk. The last example merely mentions that it was 'a shade which matched her hair, skin, housepaint, and cats'. We can only speculate as to why colour rather than texture or weight are features considered worthy of

---

Mrs Thomas Jordan selected a black taffeta frock made with a skirt of fringed tiers and worn with *crimson silk* slippers.

Mrs Eustis Reily's *olive-green* street length *silk* taffeta dress was embroidered on the bodice with gold threads and golden sequins and beads.

Her favorite cocktail dress is a Norell, a *black* and *white* organdy and *silk* jersey.

a new Turkish Empire embracing 'the union of all Turks throughout Central Asia from Adrianople to the Chinese oases on the *Silk* Trade Route'.

It was amazing how they had herded together for protection: an enormous matriarch in a quilted *silk* wrapper, rising from the breakfast table; a gross boy in his teens, shuffling in from the kitchen with a sandwich in his hands;

Here he sketched, sitting in their flowing gowns of linen and *silk*, young girls not yet twenty, some about to be married, some married a year or two.

Martha Schuyler, old, slow, careful of foot, came down the great staircase, dressed in her best lace-drawn *black silk*, her jeweled shoe buckles held forward.

Finally she had come down; Winston had heard her shaking out the skirt of her new *pink silk* hostess gown.

Dark *gray* sports jacket, lighter *gray* slacks, *pink* flannel shirt, *black silk* necktie.

He was a man in his late forties, with *graying* hair, of medium height; he looked dapper in a lightweight summer suit, *brown silk* tie and *green-tinted* soft collar.

Suddenly a treble auto horn tootley-toot-tootled, and, thumbing hopefully, I saw emergent in windshield flash: *red* lips, streaming *silk* of *blonde* hair and – ah, trembling confusion of hope, apprehension, despair – the leering face of old Herry.

Her uniform was of rich, raw *silk*, in a *shade* which matched her hair, skin, housepaint, and cats.

Figure 3.6   *Silk* in the *Brown Corpus*

---

mention. There seems little doubt that such semantic collocations are quite pervasive in English.

Words which frequently occur in each other's company are not necessarily contiguous. We have already seen that *silk* and colour words in the *LOB Corpus* have a tendency to occur in the same sentence. There are also discontinuous collocations which are more syntagmatic. In the *LOB Corpus, at* occurs frequently with *time* or *moment*, as Table 3.9 shows.

It might be argued that *at* and *time* and *at* and *moment* can be separated by up to four words in the corpus and still in a very real sense be considered to form a collocation. Sinclair (1991: 117) suggested that a span of up to four words each side of a word is the environment in which collocation is most likely to occur although, of course, computer software makes it possible to explore much larger spans, including the size of a whole text. In such a case, however, to say that two or more words can both occur in a whole text may not be saying anything very significant.

It is clear that if we insist that collocations must be immediately adjacent, then significant patterning can be lost. This is illustrated also in a comparison of the words which collocate with the word *circumstances* in the *Brown* and *LOB* corpora. Table 3.10 shows that, in these corpora of written English, *circumstances* tends to be preceded by *in* in British English and by *under* in American English. In each case, however, the collocation is typically discontinuous and insistence on adjacency would mask the patterning.

Another issue in corpus-based collocational research is the extent to which sequences of words which occur only once in a corpus but which are subjectively recognizable as being idiomatic should be listed. In the *LOB Corpus*, for example, the following sequences occur once only, and yet a number of them at least are easily recognized by native speakers of English as familiar or recurrent. By Kjellmer's criterion, none would be listed as collocations because they occurred only once in the corpus.

at a bad time	not at all common
at a certain point	not at all convinced
at a certain time	not at all surprised
at a glance	(peace) at any cost
at a loose end	at dusk
at a rough guess	at frequent intervals
at a stretch	at his mercy
at a standstill	at the very best
(didn't do) at all badly	at first glance
(she couldn't think) at all clearly	at one extreme

The size of a corpus obviously affects the chances of a particular sequence of words recurring. Kjellmer (1991: 115) suggested that one-million-word corpora are 'large enough to contain a considerable part of the English

Table 3.9 Two discontinuous collocations with *at* in the *LOB Corpus*

at + ___ + time(s)	No. of tokens	*at* + ___ + moment(s)	No. of tokens
at the same time	92	at the moment	34
at the time	77	at that moment	11
at times	30	at this moment	8
at this time	28	at any moment	6
at a time	26	at the very moment	3
at that time	24	at the same moment	2
at any time	21	at the last moment	2
at the present time	20	at one moment	2
at one time	17	at every moment	2
at all times	8	at a moment when	2
at no time	3	at the right moment	1
at such times	3	at the present moment	1
at certain times	3	at the next moment	1
at time A	3	at another moment	1
at other times	3	at that same moment	1
at some time	2	at that strange moment	1
at some time or other	2	at any given moment	1
at most times	2	at a crucial moment	1
at one and the same time	2	at a particular moment	1
at a bad time	1	at certain moments	1
at a good time	1	at necessary moments	1
at a certain time	1	at unguarded moments	1
at any given time	1	at that self same moment	1
at any other time	1	Total	85
at just the right time	1		
at much the same time	1		
at some earlier time	1		
at some future time	1		
at the right time	1		
at the wrong time	1		
at the appointed time	1		
at various times	1		
at varying times	1		
at feast times	1		
at question time	1		
at feeding time	1		
at exactly the appropriate time	1		
at just about the time	1		
at half time	1		
Total	386		

Table 3.10 Collocations with *circumstances* in the *Brown* and *LOB* corpora

	Brown (US)	LOB (UK)		Brown (US)	LOB (UK)
in the circumstances	0	6	under the circumstances	7	1
in no circumstances	0	1	under no circumstances	5	1
in these circumstances	2	6	under these circumstances	2	3
in such circumstances	1	4	under such circumstances	0	0
in certain circumstances	0	3	under certain circumstances	2	2
in some circumstances	0	3	under some circumstances	0	0
in different circumstances	0	1	under different circumstances	2	0
in similar circumstances	1	1	under similar circumstances	2	0
in any circumstances	1	1	under any circumstances	0	0
in normal circumstances	1	0	under normal circumstances	1	0
Total	6	26		21	7

phrases in current use'. However, the question of how much constitutes a 'considerable part' is not resolved. Barkema (1993) took a random set of 'received expressions' and compared their frequencies in the *Birmingham Corpus* when it contained 20 million words and in the one-million-word *Brown Corpus*. He showed that a corpus of even 20 million words is not big enough to provide sufficient examples for research on the use of some collocations, and a one-million-word corpus is too small to catch some collocations at all. While it could be argued that it is not the size of the *Brown Corpus* that makes the difference but rather its earlier date and the fact that it is a corpus of written American English only, the information which Barkema has provided in Table 3.11 suggests that corpus size may indeed be crucial. Even in the *Birmingham Corpus*, the following collocations commonly listed in dictionaries are among those which did not occur: *baker's dozen, black frost, blue gum, breach of promise, compassionate leave, complementary colours, false pride, fortified wine.*

Table 3.11 The occurrence of certain collocations in two corpora (from Barkema, 1993: 271)

	Birmingham Corpus (20 million words)	*Brown Corpus* (1 million words)
compare notes	11	1
dead centre	4	4
black and blue	15	0
catch someone red-handed	3	0
read between the lines	9	1
the happy few	5	0
the last straw	2	0
the man in the moon	1	2
a different kettle of fish	4	0
the man in the street	7	1
broken home	8	1
you name it	3	1
better late than never	1	1
what a shame	3	1
not to put too fine a point on it	1	0

The occurrence of collocations, like the occurrence of hapax legomena, is, however, also influenced by topic diversity in a corpus and not by size alone. *Breach of promise* and *fortified wine* both occur in the one-million-word *Wellington Corpus*.

The view that collocations are 'fixed and often fossilized building blocks' (Kjellmer, 1987: 135) not only allows no place for discontinuous collocations but also would seem to minimize the possibility of lemmatization. In Table 3.10 above we have examples of collocations with *circumstances* in the *Brown* and *LOB* corpora, which could in a sense be viewed as variants or allomorphs of a single collocation – *under/in . . . circumstances*.

One of the most inclusive approaches taken by corpus linguists to the notion of collocation is that of Renouf and Sinclair (1991), who have suggested that collocational patterning can be usefully described in terms of 'frameworks' consisting of two designated function words with an intervening lexical word. They used a one-million-word corpus of spoken British English and a 10-million-word corpus of written British English from the *Birmingham Corpus* to show how central to English are 'frameworks' such as those shown in Table 3.12.

Table 3.12 Some English 'frameworks'

Framework	Examples
a + ___ + of	a lot of; a pair of
be + ___ + to	be able to; be allowed to
too + ___ + to	too late to; too much to
for + ___ + of	for most of; for fear of
had + ___ + of	had enough of; had heard of
many + ___ + of	many thousands of; many kinds of

They show that over 50% of the occurrences in the written corpus of the words *couple, series, pair* and *lot* are in the framework *a + ___ + of*, and that a surprisingly high proportion of the occurrences of words such as *piece, quarter, variety, member, number, kind, sort, matter* and *result* also occur in that framework. Such patterning appears to be quite widespread in English. For example, Figure 3.7 shows the 88 occurrences in the *LOB Corpus* of the frame *from* (NP) *to* (identical NP).

Renouf (1992: 308) used an 18-million-word written corpus and a 1.3-million-word spoken corpus from the *Birmingham Corpus* to explore the recurrence of longer strings consisting of words from the most frequent 150 in each corpus. She found that collocational sequences such as the following, which contain six words in each case, tended to recur, in some cases many times:

in such a way as to
at the same time as the
all you have to do is
what do you think of the

Such strings do not always fit comfortably into traditional grammatical analyses but could be greatly expanded in number if high frequency words from, say, the top 500 or 1,000 words had been included in the study.

travel from airport to airport
transference from blood vessel to blood vessel
moved from boardroom to boardroom
jumping from boulder to boulder
it varied from child to child
caressed his mouth from corner to corner
read the volume from cover to cover
changes in demand and supply from country to country
is almost constant from day to day (4)
vary a great deal from factory to factory
on the basis of trial and error from farm to farm
follow up the building work from floor to floor
making a detour from gate to gate (2)
are likely to vary from group to group (2)
changes vary from head to head
travel . . . from hotel to hotel
travel . . . from Harry's bar to Harry's bar
the most patient showing from hour to hour
they vary from individual to individual
it varies from industry to industry
may vary from language to language (2)
he moved . . . from lodging house to lodging house
varies from place to place
his fingers moved from pocket to pocket
tramping from point to point
up and down, from pole to pole
small changes from quarter to quarter
she moved from regatta to regatta
as one moves on from room to room
vary greatly from school to school
extending from shoulder to shoulder
shook his head from side to side
bearing tidings from sheikdom to sheikdom
by jumping from site to site
vary very little from society to society (2)
going from strength to strength
from time to time (34)
from transom to transom
travel from village to village
we egged her on from week to week
washing lines from window to window
vary from workshop to workshop
with some variation from year to year (6)

Figure 3.7   From (NP) *to* (identical NP) in the *LOB Corpus*

Very frequently recurring sequences such as *at the same time as the . . . ,
had it not been for . . . , this is not to say that . . . , if you see what I mean* simply
confirm that sequences of words which have been lexicalized to varying
degrees are basic, pervasive units in the language. Pawley and Syder
(1983) and Nattinger and De Carrico (1992) have noted that not only
do these units serve efficiently as prefabricated units to assist psycholinguistic processing, but they also serve as macro-organizers in discourse
to show relationships (e.g. *this ties in with . . .*), to shift topics (e.g. *so now
let's turn to . . .*), and to highlight important points (e.g. *now, I'd like to
give you . . .*). They have suggested that the normal use of a language

involves the selection of such 'prefabricated' groups of words and the stringing of these groups together. From this point of view we might consider the following sentence to consist of a series of overlapping frameworks which flow into each other with the last element of one frame forming the beginning of the next: *The pathologist gave an outline of a series of things which the patient could have died of.*

The pathologist gave
an outline of
  of a series of
    of things which
      which the patient could have died of.

It might be thought when considering the large number of tokens of a collocation such as *at (the) moment* (see Table 3.9) that there is a special or even unique semantic relationship between a word such as *moment* and the preposition *at*. Regrettably perhaps for collocational theory this does not seem to be the case. The word *moment* occurs 316 times in the *LOB Corpus*. On 197 of these occurrences (62%) it follows a preposition.

at (the) moment	85
for (a) moment	81
in (a) moment	9
from (that) moment	8
after (a) moment	8
of (the) moment	6
Total	197

While *at* is, by a narrow margin, the most frequent preposition before *moment*, it is only 43% of the prepositional antecedents. A similar picture emerges with the prepositional antecedents of the word *time*, where *at, by, for, from* and *in* all figure prominently.

Formally identical collocations can indeed be strikingly different semantically, as noted in Kennedy (1990: 226). In the *LOB Corpus at the turn of* occurs five times as follows:

1   at the turn of a knob
2   at the turn of the stairs
3   at the turn of the path
4   at the turn of the century
5   at the turn of Leo's key

Semantically each token has little in common with the others. In context, the first is an adverbial of manner, the next two are locative and the last two are temporal. In the same corpus, *at once* occurs 98 times. In 89 of the tokens, *at once* means 'immediately' (*I replied at once*). In the remaining 9 tokens, *at once* means 'simultaneously' (*I can't be everywhere at once*).

While there seems little doubt that collocations may be considered to include a range of types of differing degrees of fossilization and flexibility, it seems to be similarly the case that some collocations are more recognizably lexicalized than others, although this is no simple matter of frequency. For example, *no hope* and *pretty good* may be less frequent than *the three*, but the last is unlikely to be recognized as lexicalized. *The White House* is clearly lexicalized, however, as is *on foot* and not **on feet*. Kjellmer (1984: 164) raised this issue as one of 'collocational distinctiveness' and suggested that the degree of lexicalization of a collocation depends on one or more of the following:

(a)   absolute frequency of occurrence
(b)   relative frequency of occurrence
(c)   length of sequence (*a glass of water* could be considered to be more distinctive than *a glass*)
(d)   distribution of sequence over texts
(e)   distribution of sequence over text categories
(f)   structure of sequence

Thus the fact that *consist of* is absolutely more frequent than *consist in* in the *Brown Corpus* makes *consist of* more distinctive under (a). For (b) the relative frequency of occurrence takes account of the actual as against the expected frequency of co-occurrence of the two or more items in a sequence.

Ways of assessing distinctiveness can now be based on empirical rather than intuitive means. Software developed for the *British National Corpus* enables researchers to calculate the statistical significance of the difference between the actual co-occurrence of words in the corpus as against the expected co-occurrence based on the frequency of the individual words. Thus, for example, the most distinctive collocates of *Christmas* include *day, eve, tree, cards* and *present* whereas *greetings, holiday, mail* and *service* have lower distinctiveness.

The development of software which can identify recurrent patterning at the level of the structural framework and of individual collocations, especially those which may be lemmatized or discontinuous, should open up important new territory for research in descriptive linguistics. Indeed, corpus linguistics may make one of its most significant contributions to linguistic description by helping redefine the boundary between lexis and grammar, thus enriching our understanding of linguistic structure and psycholinguistic processes.

3.2   Grammatical studies centred on morphemes or words

The analysis of the range of topics in English corpus linguistics published over the last three decades and summarized in Figure 3.1 shows that various aspects of the distribution and use of verb-form morphology, prepositions, conjunctions and adverbials have been among the most prominent items studied. Although the published research on corpora is not yet systematically comprehensive, the following sections illustrate some of the kinds of information which corpus-based descriptive studies of morphology can make available.

3.2.1 Verb-form use for tense and aspect

Analysis of the *Brown* and *LOB* corpora shows that verbs make up almost 20% of the words in the corpora (see Table 3.5). Joos (1964: 74) identified some 224 grammatically possible finite verb forms or combinations of forms in English. It is therefore perhaps not surprising that F. R. Palmer (1965: 1) suggested that 'learning a language is to a very large degree learning how to operate the verbal forms of that language'.

Even before the age of the computer, corpus-based studies made significant contributions to our understanding of the use of the English verb-form system. Many of these studies were motivated by pedagogical concerns because the high frequency of verbs overall and their difficulty for learners of English as a second or foreign language meant that teachers needed an indication of which were the most frequently and widely used forms.

Ota (1963) studied verb-form use in American English. He worked with a corpus of about 150,000 words, consisting of over 10 hours of unrehearsed radio conversations and interviews, transcribed as about 300 pages of text, 10 TV drama scripts, and about 30,000 words of written academic English. Ota's corpus included 17,166 finite verb forms of which 977 were part of passive-voice constructions. His detailed study of 'the probable and improbable rather than the possible and impossible' (1963: 14) was an early example of corpus research which broke new ground even though the work needs replication with larger corpora and over a wider variety of genres. Ota described the relative frequency of use of the most commonly used verbs and the tenses and adverbials most commonly used with each of those verbs. He found, for example, that the adverbials *today* and *this year* are more likely to be linked to past tense verb forms than to simple present (e.g. *What did you do today? I bought a car earlier this year*).

Table 3.13 shows that 7 verbs *be, think, have, know, say, want, go* made up 50% of the finite verb tokens in Ota's corpus and together with the remaining 9 verbs listed accounted for over 61% of the finite verb tokens in the corpus. For language teachers, the fact that finite forms of the verb *be* made up nearly a third of all finite verbs in the corpus was a valuable indicator of where pedagogical time might profitably be invested. Table 3.13 also shows that these frequent verbs tend to be associated with particular verb-form uses. Because Ota's corpus was made

Table 3.13 Most frequent verbs in Ota's corpus, and their tense and aspect use (from Kennedy, 1992: 347)

Most frequent verbs	% of the 17,166 finite verbs in Ota's corpus	Verb-form use (%)				
		Simple present	Present progressive	Simple past	Past progressive	All other verb-form uses
be	30.7	79.0	0.05	17.0	0	3.9
think	5.0	87.8	1.3	9.7	0.3	1.0
have	4.0	66.0	1.3	23.7	0.1	8.9
know	3.6	88.7	0	8.2	0	3.1
say	2.6	37.4	2.5	50.0	0.7	9.4
want	2.4	81.1	0	17.7	0.2	1.0
go	1.7	32.1	27.5	26.5	2.4	11.5
get	1.5	47.7	9.2	36.6	1.1	5.4
do	1.5	29.3	22.4	23.6	1.9	22.8
come	1.4	33.6	11.2	39.0	3.3	12.9
have to	1.3	74.8	0.4	24.3	0	0.5
see	1.3	65.0	0.9	23.0	0	11.1
make	1.3	36.6	8.8	29.2	0.9	24.5
mean	1.2	82.6	0	15.4	0	2.0
feel	0.9	68.7	3.3	22.7	0.7	4.6
take	0.9	27.5	9.4	38.9	2.0	22.2
	61.3					

up largely of spoken English, his finding that for most of the verbs the present tense is more frequent than the past, was consistent with other studies. The overwhelming predominance of use of the simple present over the present progressive is also revealed even for most of the dynamic verbs. Ota also noted that stative verbs in his corpus were not only rarely found with a progressive verb form but were also up to ten times more likely to be found with first-person subjects (or a second-person subject in the case of questions) than with any other subjects, *I/we want* or *know,* or *do you want* or *know* being much more frequent than *he/she wants* or *knows.*

The summary in Table 3.13 of the main verb-form uses of the 16 most frequent verbs in Ota's corpus opens up the question of verb-form use in general. Other major studies based on pre-electronic corpora showed that, although there may be 224 grammatically possible finite verb forms or combinations of forms in English, they have vastly different probabilities of being used in speech and writing. Whereas Ota's study was of American English, Joos (1964) and George (1963a) undertook pioneering studies of British English. Joos studied over 9,100 finite and non-finite verb forms in a single book, an account of a courtroom trial (Sybil Bedford's *The Trial of Dr Adams*). Table 3.14 shows the rank order of the 23 most frequent finite verb-form types found among the 8,038 finite verb-form tokens in Joos's corpus. These 23 forms cover 95% of all the finite verb tokens. Another 56 forms in the corpus accounted for the remaining 5% of the tokens. One hundred and forty-five of the 224 possible forms Joos identified did not occur at all in the book he analysed. It is likely that Joos's text, reflecting the legal domain of the courtroom, has a higher proportion of complex verb forms, including those containing modals used for hypothesizing in cross-examination, than would be the case in many other genres. However, the overall picture is nevertheless similar to Ota's and shows the dominance of the simple present and the simple past. A similar finding came from a study undertaken by George (1963a) at the Central Institute of English in Hyderabad, India. George analysed 108,783 successive finite and non-finite verb forms in a mainly written corpus of about 500,000 words with a heavy emphasis on expository writing from British newspapers, non-fiction, and reference books, as well as some texts selected from novels and plays.

Table 3.15 summarizes the findings of Ota, George and Joos on the uses of the finite verb forms associated with the eight most frequent tense and aspect uses of the English verb. In spite of the great differences between the three corpora in size, structure and composition, a clear picture emerges. Spoken English, whether spontaneous or scripted, is dominated by the simple present (particularly the verb *be*). Written English, especially in narrative texts, tends to have frequent use of the simple past. However, as Francis and Kučera (1982: 545) have noted, analysis of the *Brown Corpus* shows that, in written American English at

Table 3.14 Rank order of the most frequent simple and complex finite verb forms (adapted from Joos, 1964: 77–79)

Rank	Verb forms	Examples	No. of tokens	% of finite forms
1	Simple present	no good *comes* of these cases	2,853	35.5
2	Simple past	the doctor *went* away	2,143	26.7
3	Present perfect	they *have decided* not to call the doctor	319	4.0
4	Past passive	Morphia and heroin *were* commonly *used*	292	3.6
5	Present passive	both morphia and heroin *are administered*	249	3.1
6	*would* + infinitive	If there were, I *would take* them	219	2.7
7	*can* + infinitive	as colourless as one *can make* them	208	2.6
8	Past progressive	when he *was prescribing* for her	177	2.2
9	Present progressive	*are* you *standing* there . . . as a trained nurse	175	2.2
10	Past perfect	*had* you *made* any inquiries	164	2.0
11	*will* + infinitive	I *will* certainly *help* you	115	1.4
12	*may* + infinitive	asks if he *may put* a further question	90	1.1
13	*do*	And you still *say* so? I *do*	83	1.0
14	*did*	*did* the doctor *ask* for anything? – He *did*	80	1.0
15	*would have* + p.p.	*would* you *have expected* the doses	77	1.0
16	*must* + infinitive	you *must believe* me	65	0.8
17	*might* + infinitive	whether he *might say*	65	0.8
18	Present perfect passive	cases where this amount *has been given*	63	0.8
19	*should* + infinitive	he told me I *should prepare* a codicil	59	0.7
20	*could* + infinitive	I did not think you *could prove* murder	56	0.7
21	*might have* + p.p.	He *might have given* hyoscine	34	0.4
22	*can be* + p.p.	justice *can be done*	32	0.4
23	*could have* + p.p.	you *could have asked* this question	27	0.3
				95.0

Table 3.15 Relative frequencies of use of finite verb forms

Verb forms	Ota (1963)		George (1963a)		Joos (1964)
	Spoken US English (%)	Written US English (%)	UK English plays (scripted speech) (%)	Written UK English (%)	Written UK English (%)
Simple present	64.4	26.4	67.6	38.4	39.6
Simple past	18.3	58.5	14.4	48.2	31.3
Present perfect	4.8	2.7	5.3	3.1	4.0
Past perfect	0.4	3.4	0.9	4.1	2.0
Present progressive	5.4	0.9	4.4	1.4	2.2
Past progressive	0.9	1.1	0.4	1.4	2.2
Present perfect progressive	0.5	0.1	0.6	0.1	0.2
Past perfect progressive	0.01	0.2	–	0.1	0.1
All other verb forms	5.3	6.6	6.4	3.2	18.4

Note: George's and Joos's data combined active and passive voice. Ota's data included active voice only.

least, the past tense does not dominate in informative written language. Joos's study is of written text which attempts to record the spoken language of the courtroom and includes a more even balance between simple present and simple past.

In all three studies, perfect and progressive aspects are relatively infrequent, with the present perfect and the present progressive being more frequent than the past perfect and past progressive in spoken English, and the reverse being the case for written English. Studies by Dušková and Urbanová (1967) and Krámský (1969) based on small corpora have been discussed in Kennedy (1992: 347) and show similar distributions of verb-form use. It is worth remembering that the very high frequency of the simple present and simple past in all these studies is in part a reflection of the very high frequency of use of the verb *be*, which is rarely used with perfect or progressive aspect.

The robustness of these findings based on the manual analysis of relatively small corpora received support from computerized analysis of the *Brown Corpus*. Francis and Kučera (1982: 555) report the use of all perfect and progressive forms in that one-million-word corpus, as shown in Table 3.16.

Table 3.16 Perfect and progressive verb forms in the *Brown Corpus* (from Francis & Kučera, 1982: 555)

Genre	Perfect forms Number	%	Progressive forms Number	%
A. Press: reportage	469	5.94	297	3.76
B. Press: editorial	367	6.99	231	4.40
C. Press: reviews	188	5.96	88	2.79
D. Religion	210	6.16	73	2.14
E. Skills and hobbies	326	4.92	142	2.14
F. Popular lore	588	6.32	251	2.70
G. Belles lettres	1,075	7.15	362	2.41
H. Miscellaneous	233	5.45	90	2.10
J. Learned	739	5.54	210	1.57
K. General fiction	563	7.45	320	4.24
L. Mystery and detective	511	7.52	268	3.94
M. Science fiction	109	6.78	52	3.24
N. Adventure and western	518	6.40	328	4.06
P. Romance and love story	601	7.30	348	4.23
R. Humour	148	6.82	83	3.82
Whole corpus	6,645	6.47	3,143	3.06

There are slightly more uses of the perfect in imaginative genres (K–R) than in the informative genres (A–J). The genre differences are more substantial in the use of the progressive, with the proportion of progressive in the general fiction section being almost three times as great as the proportion in the learned section, and the proportion in Sections A–J being much lower overall than in Sections K–R.

Whereas Ota (1963) had quantified the tendency of particular verbs to be associated with particular verb-form endings, Kjellmer (1992) has shown from the *Brown Corpus* that it is possible to find common semantic elements in verbs which have a tendency to be used in the present tense or the past tense. The verbs in the corpus which are most 'present-tense prone' are 'verbs of organization or abstract relations' (1992: 331), including *amount, illustrate, derive, define, distinguish, promote, conform, exceed, strengthen, influence, affect, reinforce* and *utilize*. Verbs such as these typically occur with abstract subjects in expository or discursive types of text in the *Brown Corpus*. Verbs which are 'past-tense prone' include *exclaim, pause, peer, mutter, smile, lean, laugh, toss, climb, roar, swing, stumble, flee, whisper, stare, yell, nod, sigh* and *grin*. These are 'verbs of physical action or expression'. They almost always have human subjects, and are found especially in narrative genres.

George (1963b: 35) suggested that in their lack of statistical data contemporary descriptions of English were like geographical descriptions of the world's countries which neglected to mention their sizes. One of the innovations in his study was that he counted tokens of some 168 categories of form and function among the finite and non-finite verb forms in his half-million-word corpus. In addition to the important analysis of tense and aspect use summarized in Table 3.15, George noted the overall distribution of finite and non-finite uses of verb forms. Table 3.17 shows that over 50% of the verbs in his corpus of written British English were non-finite.

Table 3.17 Distribution of English finite and non-finite verb forms (adapted from George, 1963a)

Verb-form type	%
finite stem form (including 3rd person singular)	20
non-finite stem form (infinitive)	22
(finite) past tense form	27
(non-finite) past participle	20
(non-finite) present participle	11
	100

The comprehensive description of verb-form use in the *Brown Corpus* (Francis & Kučera, 1982: 545) uses a different taxonomy for its analysis of written American English, providing separate analyses for operators and modals, and separate counts for the informative and imaginative genres. Since finite and non-finite uses of the base forms are not separately described, the analysis is not easily comparable with George's study. For each of the verb-form types listed in Table 3.17, George's analysis provides a distributional account of the various syntactic and semantic or functional roles of that type. By way of illustration, Table 3.18 shows how the non-finite *-ed* form or so-called past participle is used in George's Hyderabad corpus. Furthermore, in this corpus over a third of the non-finite *-ing* forms do not function as verbs. In fact the most frequent use of the stem+*ing* form is as an adjective in a noun phrase. Analysis of a corpus of spoken English may, of course, give a somewhat different picture. However, until such new analyses become available based on more representative corpora, the results of the studies by Ota, Joos, George, and Francis and Kučera continue to provide distributional analyses of verb-form use which are rich in detail and which can provide food for thought for anyone interested in the use of English and in language pedagogy. A few forms and functions are used a great deal, and the rest are rarely used in most contexts. A besetting problem in language pedagogy has often been that whereas frequent uses are sometimes neglected altogether, rare and idiosyncratic uses receive much

Table 3.18 Uses of the past participle
(adapted from George, 1963a)

Use	% of past participle use	% of all verb forms
As a participle of occurrence The letter was *opened* No fault was *found* with the work	41.6	8.3
As a participle of state I was *delighted* to hear it We found our friends *excited* about it	16.7	3.3
Used in perfect aspect She had *heard* the news	27.0	5.5
As an adjective the yellow *varnished* walls a *determined* person	11.7	2.3
Miscellaneous Her bag *clutched* under her arm	3.0	0.6
	100.0	20.0

greater attention in descriptions of English and get disproportionate attention from teachers and learners. A case in point has been that syllabuses have tended to give priority to the present progressive over the simple present. With modern machine-readable corpora it will now be possible to undertake comprehensive analyses of verb-form use in different genres and varieties of the language.

3.2.2 Modals

Francis and Kučera (1982) noted that 7.6% of the verb forms in the *Brown Corpus* are modals. A study by Coates (1983) of how modals are used in samples of the *London–Lund* and *LOB* corpora is an influential example of corpus-based analysis which skilfully brings together a consideration of form and function in English modals. Coates made use of representative samples of about 200 tokens from each of the modals in each of the two corpora. The total number of tokens of each modal in the corpora is shown in Table 3.19.

Table 3.19 Frequency of nine modals in the *London–Lund* and *LOB* corpora
(adapted from Coates, 1983: 23)

LLC (spoken British English)		LOB (written British English)	
will	4,286	would	3,002
can	3,528	will	2,804
would	3,521	can	2,141
could	2,000	could	1,744
must	1,158	may	1,323
should	1,123	should	1,285
may	879	must	1,131
might	723	might	775
shall	495	shall	352
Total	17,713	Total	14,557

Note: In the *LLC* the actual frequencies in the corpus have been adjusted to be equivalent to the one million running words of the *LOB Corpus*.

There are differences between the spoken and written use of modals, thus making overall generalizations difficult. While *would* is the most frequent modal in written British English, it is relatively less important than *will* in spoken English. Kennedy (1992: 351) has summarized the major functions of the auxiliaries in Coates's analysis (see Table 3.20). Coates has shown that there are some notable differences between the

Table 3.20 Use of modals in the *London–Lund* and *LOB* corpora (from Kennedy, 1992: 351)

Modal	Root use (%)							Epistemic use (%)	Hypothetical use (%)	Other (%)
	Obligation-necessity									
must	53 (65)							46 (31)		1 (4)
need	87							13		
should	42 (51)							18 (12)	21 (9)	19 (28)
ought	84 (84)							9 (13)		7 (3)
		Possibility	**Ability**	**Permission**						
can		65 (64)	21 (25)	5 (3)						9 (8)
could		25 (30)	12 (29)	2 (2)				4 (7)	56 (32)	
may		4 (22)		16 (6)				74 (61)		6 (11)
might		1		1				54	44	
					Obligation	**Willingness**	**Intention**			
will						13 (8)	23 (14)	58 (71)		6 (7)
shall					2 (34)	19 (9)	18 (19)	61 (35)		1 (3)
would						4 (6)			11 (5)	1 (3)
should							1 (3)	83 (83)	21 (9)	1 (3)

Note: Percentages from the *LOB Corpus* (written English) are in parentheses.

two corpora in the semantic functions of some of the modals. *Shall*, for example, is used to express obligation much more in written than spoken texts.

For some of the modals the root meaning is the most frequently used, but for others the major function is epistemic, to express degrees of certainty (e.g. *You must be absolutely exhausted*) or hypothetical (*If I could be there, I'd tell her what I thought*). The epistemic use of *must, should, may* and *shall* is relatively more frequent than the root use in spoken rather than written English. There appear to be significant differences between genres in the relative frequency of the root and epistemic uses of some of the modals. For example, the epistemic use of *must* is proportionately about twice as frequent in Section J (academic texts) as in the *LOB Corpus* as a whole.

Corpus-based research can also show that there are substantial differences between the modals in the kinds of complex verb-phrase structures in which they occur. Table 3.21 lists the major verb structures and the extent to which the modals in Section J of the *LOB Corpus* are used in those structures.

Will, would, might and *shall* all have over 60% of their tokens in the modal+infinitive structure (*will go, might happen*, etc.). *Can*, on the other hand, has a majority of its tokens in the modal+*be*+past participle structure (*can be done*). Rather tellingly, from a pedagogical viewpoint, seven of the nine possible structures have few or no tokens at all in Section J of the *LOB Corpus*.

A more comprehensive corpus-based study of English modal verbs by Mindt (1995) provides detailed analyses of the verb-phrase structures each modal is most likely to occur in, and quantified analyses of their semantic functions. By way of illustration, *should* has three main functions in Mindt's corpus, with approximately the proportions indicated.

		%
1	Advisability/desirability	55
	(e.g. *You should plant potatoes*)	
2	Hypothetical event or result	36
	(e.g. *I should have gone back*)	
3	Politeness/downtoning	9
	(e.g. *I should like to support those views*)	

Overlaying the modal meaning of *should* are other meanings including temporal meaning, as follows:

		%
1	Past-time orientation	38
	(e.g. *I told him I should have joined the group*)	
2	Future-time orientation	25
	(e.g. *This should be done soon*)	

Table 3.21 Use of modals in the *LOB Corpus* Section J in various verb-phrase structures (%)

Modal structures	will	would	can	could	may	might	shall	should	must
Modal alone	1	1	1	2			5		1
Modal + infinitive	66	80	43	49	55	63	87	52	55
Modal + *be* + past participle	30	11	56	45	41	27	8	43	37
Modal + *be* + present participle	1	1							
Modal + *have* + past participle	1	5		3	4	6		3	6
Modal + *be* + *being* + past participle	1			1					1
Modal + *have* + *been* + past participle		2				4		2	
Modal + *have* + *been* + present participle									
Modal + *have* + *been* + *being* + past participle									

		%
3	Present-time orientation	19
	(e.g. *I don't think we should wait any longer*)	
4	Timelessness	18
	(e.g. *Height should always be measured without shoes*)	

Corpus-based research on modal verbs has thus begun to reveal how the distribution of their grammatical patterns and semantic roles are related to genre, and suggest what kinds of pedagogical emphases are likely to facilitate language learning.

3.2.3 Voice

Another dimension of verb-form use which has been illuminated by corpus-based studies is voice in English verbs. Francis and Kučera (1982: 554) provided an analysis of the proportion of active and passive voice predications in the different genres of the *Brown Corpus*. Table 3.22 shows the striking extent to which the passive is used more frequently in informative (A–J) than in imaginative (K–R) prose. In informative prose, 14.6% of the total predications are passive, while in imaginative prose only 4.2% are passive. Within the informative genres, the miscellaneous section (government documents and reports of various kinds) and the learned (academic texts) section have an even higher proportion of passive-voice use than the other genres (24.15% and 21.95% passives respectively), whereas the average for the whole corpus is 11.07%.

An earlier corpus study based mainly on part of the *SEU Corpus* by Svartvik (1966), one of the pioneers of corpus-based grammatical analysis, showed the extent to which the use of the passive varied in different registers. As shown in Table 3.23, Svartvik examined over 3,600 passives in texts totalling 323,000 words from eight registers. The number of passives per thousand words of text ranges from 3.0 in advertising to 23.1 in science, with one scientific text having 32 passives per thousand words. However, Svartvik noted (1966: 152) that the texts which belong to a particular register 'are remarkably similar' in the number of passives per thousand words. Further, Svartvik suggested that for the passive voice

> the major stylistic determining factor in the frequency of its use seems to lie in a distinction such as that between informative and imaginative prose, rather than in a difference of subject matter or between the spoken and written language. (1966: 155)

This conclusion is similar to that reached from the analysis made by Francis and Kučera (1982) working with a completely different corpus, as shown in Table 3.22. Interestingly, Svartvik found that among the 'agentive passives' in the corpus which can be systematically related to 'active' forms, 80% occur without an agent. This places the agent in a less prominent light than the one it has in pedagogical tradition, where

Table 3.22 Active and passive predications in the *Brown Corpus* (based on Francis & Kučera, 1982: 554)

Genre	Total number of tokens		%	
	Actives	Passives	Actives	Passives
I Informative prose				
A. Press: reportage	6,902	1,000	87.34	12.66
B. Press: editorial	4,662	586	88.83	11.17
C. Press: reviews	2,863	293	90.72	9.28
D. Religion	3,007	401	88.23	11.77
E. Skills and hobbies	5,680	944	85.75	14.25
F. Popular lore	8,145	1,165	87.49	12.51
G. Belles lettres	13,446	1,589	89.43	10.57
H. Miscellaneous	3,244	1,033	75.85	24.15
J. Learned	10,415	2,929	78.05	21.95
				14.6
II Imaginative prose				
K. General fiction	7,194	362	95.21	4.79
L. Mystery and detective	6,540	259	96.19	3.81
M. Science fiction	1,501	106	93.40	6.60
N. Adventure and western	7,798	290	98.41	3.59
P. Romance and love story	7,961	273	96.68	3.32
R. Humour	2,021	149	93.13	6.87
				4.2
Whole corpus	91,379	11,379	88.93	11.07

Table 3.23 The use of passives in different registers
(adapted from Svartvik, 1966: 155)

Text source	No. of words in sample	Total no. of passives	Passives per 1,000 words
Science	50,000	1,154	23.1
News	45,000	709	15.8
Arts	20,000	254	12.7
Speech	40,000	366	9.2
Sports	30,000	269	9.0
Novels	80,000	652	8.2
Plays	30,000	158	5.3
Advertising	28,000	83	3.0
Total	323,000	3,645	11.3

the passive with agent is generally introduced before the agentless passive. The remaining 20% are equally divided between those which take an animate *by*-agent and those which take an inanimate *by*-agent. Svartvik also provided distributional data on the verb-phrase structure of all the agentive passive clauses which make up his corpus. Table 3.24 summarizes the distribution. The first three of the eight structures which

Table 3.24 Verb-phrase structure of agentive passives
(adapted from Svartvik, 1966: 151)

Example of verb-phrase structure	No. of tokens	% of passives
is/was eaten	1,455	54
modal + *be eaten*	796	30
has/had been eaten	389	14
is/was being eaten	32	1
modal + *have been eaten*	17	1
modal + *be being eaten*	0	0
has/had + been being eaten	0	0
modal + *have been being eaten*	0	0
Total		100

Note: Under 'modal' in this adaptation of Svartvik's data is included items such as *have to, appear to, be going to, have got to*. The most frequent modals in these passive constructions are *can* (177), *may* (102), *could* (84), *will* (79), *should* (69), *must* (54), *have to* (52), *would* (48), *be to* (45).

are systematically possible account for 98% of the agentive passives, while all the rest clearly have a very low probability of occurrence.

The learned section (J) of the *Brown Corpus* has already been identified in Table 3.22 as a text category with a high proportion of passives. An analysis of the 2,929 passives from this section shows that about half occur with the simple present tense (*is eaten*), and that about 85% of all the passives occur without an agent. Moreover, the agents, where they occur, are all non-personal (e.g. *may be achieved by several methods*). The 10 most frequent verbs which take the passive in Section J are *use, give, see, consider, call, take, determine, note, assign* and *select*, and of these *use, see, consider, call, take* and *note* never appear with an agent.

3.2.4 Verb and particle use

A study by Akkerman (1984) on phrasal verbs shows which verb and particle combinations are most frequent in Sections A–J of the *Brown Corpus* and the extent to which idiomatic use is dependent on sequences of particles after the verb. Table 3.25 shows the 25 particles in the *Brown Corpus* which form part of phrasal verbs. *Up* and *out* account for 47.4% of all particles which follow verbs. *Off, back, down, on* and *in* together make up another 32.9%.

Akkerman also explores which of the particles coming second in a sequence of two particles are obligatory and which are optional for making the sequence idiomatic. Thus, for example, *for* in the sequence *go in for* is obligatorily part of the sequence, whereas *with* in *fall out with* does not appear to change the meaning of the sequence *fall out*, which still means 'disagree' or 'quarrel'. In about two-thirds of the phrasal verb occurrences in the *Brown Corpus* sample where there are two particles, the second one is optional in the sense that the meaning of the phrasal verb is not dependent on it to preserve the idiomaticity. Combinations in which the first particle is *around, down* or *away* seem to particularly need a second particle to preserve idiomaticity.

3.2.5 Subjunctive

Johansson & Norheim (1988: 27) suggested that 'the subjunctive is one of the few areas of grammar where there are differences between standard British and American English'. On the basis of the *Brown* and *LOB* corpora, they examined the occurrence of *were*-subjunctives and mandative subjunctives (used in *that*-clauses after a number of suasive verbs and adjectives such as *advise, demand, order, suggest*). Their data showed that the mandative subjunctive is more common in American English (e.g. *It is important that he join us*) whereas British English shows a preference for the use of *should* in such contexts (e.g. *He insists that it should be placed in a special museum*).

Table 3.25 Particles used with verbs in the *Brown Corpus* (from Akkerman, 1984: 63)

Particle	Total no. of tokens	As particle in verb + 1 particle combination		As first particle in verb + 2 particle combinations		Overall (%)
		Absolute	Relative (%)	Absolute	Relative (%)	
up	474	416	23.4	58	34.1	24.3
out	450	438	24.6	12	7.1	23.1
off	131	124	7.0	7	4.1	6.7
back	130	114	6.4	16	9.4	6.7
down	129	115	6.5	14	8.2	6.6
on	127	118	6.6	9	5.3	6.5
in	124	106	6.0	18	10.6	6.4
away	86	73	4.1	13	7.6	4.4
over	81	74	4.2	7	4.1	4.2
forth	26	25	1.4	1	0.6	1.3
about	25	25	1.4	–	–	1.3
along	25	23	1.3	2	1.2	1.3
forward	25	20	1.1	5	2.9	1.3
around	24	21	1.2	3	1.8	1.2
aside	24	24	1.3	–	–	1.2
ahead	20	17	1.0	3	1.8	1.0
by	15	15	0.8	–	–	0.8
through	14	12	0.7	2	1.2	0.7
across	6	6	0.3	–	–	0.3
inside	5	5	0.3	–	–	0.3
behind	3	3	0.2	–	–	0.2
outside	3	3	0.2	–	–	0.2
alongside	2	2	0.1	–	–	0.1
above	1	1	0.1	–	–	0.1
below	1	1	0.1	–	–	0.1
Total	1,951	1,781	100.0	170	100.0	100.0

Use of the *were*-subjunctive was similar in both American and British varieties of English and was strongly preferred to the past indicative *was* in hypothetical conditionals (e.g. *if it were available . . .*) and in clauses introduced by *as if* and *as though*. Since some grammarians have suggested that linguistic change is resulting in the demise of such subjunctive use, further corpus-based analysis of more recent corpora should be used to throw light on this matter.

3.2.6 *Prepositions:* of, at, from, between, through, by

About one word in every eight in almost any English text is a preposition. Mindt and Weber (1989) have calculated that in the *Brown Corpus*, 12.21% of all words are prepositions. The corresponding figure for the *LOB Corpus* is 12.34%. Prepositions make an important contribution to intra-propositional cohesion by linking lexicalized concepts in terms of place, duration, association, agency, time, cause and other relationships. Although there are about 100 single and multi-word (complex) English prepositions it has long been recognized that only a small number occur frequently in texts, with one preposition, *of* typically accounting for almost 30% of all prepositional tokens. In the *Brown* and *LOB* corpora, the 14 most frequent prepositions occur with the distribution shown in Table 3.26, and account for about 90% of prepositional use.

Table 3.26 The 14 most frequent prepositions in the *Brown* and *LOB* corpora

	Brown Corpus (%)	*LOB Corpus* (%)
of	29.8	28.6
in	17.1	16.4
to	9.1	8.8
for	7.4	7.1
with	6.0	5.8
on	5.1	5.1
at	4.4	4.4
by	4.3	4.6
from	3.6	3.8
into	1.5	1.3
about	1.0	1.0
through	0.7	0.6
over	0.7	0.6
between	0.6	0.7
Total	91.3	88.8

Note: Although *as* and *than* are also frequent, differences in tagging in *Brown* and *LOB* make comparison difficult.

When the high frequency and difficulty of acquisition of the English prepositional system is considered, it is somewhat surprising that there have not been more corpus-based studies of how the system is used. Studies of particular prepositions have already shown, however, that corpora can reveal previously undescribed systemic and distributional information. This section illustrates aspects of the information revealed in studies of six of the high frequency prepositions listed in Table 3.26, the prepositions *of, at, from, through, between* and *by*.

Sinclair (1991) has discussed the extent to which non-corpus-based descriptions of the very high frequency preposition *of* have proved to be unsatisfactory. On the basis of a pilot analysis of the large *Birmingham Corpus* he argued that *of* is 'sensitive to what precedes more than to what follows' (83). By way of example, we might compare the possible collocational 'bonding' relationship between *of* and the nouns which precede and follow it in the first two sentences of this paragraph (*descriptions of, the basis of, a pilot analysis of* compared with *of the very high frequency preposition, of a pilot analysis*). The preliminary conclusions reached showed the dominant pattern of use is where *of* combines with preceding and following nouns to expand the nominal group. Thus it seems to be the case that *of*, by far the most frequent of all English prepositions, is not normally used in the dominant prepositional structure, namely the prepositional phrase which forms clausal adjuncts.

On the other hand, analysis of the use of *at, from, by, between* and *through* reveals prepositional behaviour which conforms more closely to that described in descriptive grammars. However, the prepositional phrase occurs in collocations to an extent that tends to blur the boundary between grammar and lexis. Table 3.27 lists the phrases beginning with *at* which occur four or more times in the *LOB Corpus*. The phrases listed account for 2,575 (47%) of the tokens of *at* in the corpus. A further 932 tokens of *at* occurred in a single collocational framework preceding the names of towns, institutions or events (e.g. *at Ascot*) but none of them occurred four or more times and so they are not included in Table 3.27. If these tokens of *at* + (the) + proper noun of place are included, and if the 236 tokens of *at* + personal pronoun are similarly included in Table 3.27 as a single collocational framework (*at her; at us*), then 3,743 (68.4%) of the occurrences of *at* in the *LOB Corpus* are covered by the one table.

Table 3.27 Immediate right collocates of *at* occurring four or more times in the *LOB Corpus* (from Kennedy, 1990: 219)

at least	249	at first	50	at the meeting	
at + numeral	181	at any rate	34	(of)	25
at all	175	at night	34	at that time	24
at last	111	at the moment		at the age of	24
at once	98	(of)	34	at the back (of)	22
at the same time	92	at the top	31	at any time	21
at the end (of the)	88	at times	30	at the bottom (of)	20
at home	83	at the beginning		at the present	
at the time	77	(of)	30	time	20
at which	61	at this time	28	at about ___	19
at present	57	at work	26	at the expense of	19

Table 3.27 continued

at school	18	at the centre (of)	7	at a rate of	4
at this stage	18	at the corner (of)	7	at a later stage	4
at this point	17	at one end (of)	7	at a loss	4
at one time	17	at the heart of	7	at all costs	4
at a point	15	at the hotel	7	at all levels	4
at length	15	at a temperature		at arm's length	4
at the head of	15	(of)	7	at around ___	4
at the same ___	15	at a meeting (of)	6	at college	4
at the side (of)	14	at any moment	6	at each other	4
at the door	14	at best	6	at fault	4
at a time	13	at dawn	6	at high	
at a time when	13	at his desk	6	temperatures	4
at Cambridge	13	at rest	6	at low	
at what	12	at stake	6	temperatures	4
at the point (of)	12	at technical		at his feet	4
at the University	11	colleges	6	at its best	4
at dinner	11	at the edge (of)	6	at long last	4
at that moment	11	at the sound (of)	6	at midnight	4
at. (clause final)	10	at the thought (of)	6	at peace	4
at hand	10	at Manchester	6	at the base (of)	4
at large.	10	at Oxford	5	at the dance	4
at that	10	at Covent Garden	5	at the election	4
at the foot (of)	10	at Christmas	5	at the hospital	4
at the start	10	at the turn of	5	at the house	4
at the surface	10	at the school	5	at the last moment	4
at various ___	9	at the wheel	5	at the most.	4
at random	9	at the worst	5	at the level of	4
at sea	9	at the India Office	5	at the ready	4
at the front (of)	9	at the July meeting	5	at the root (of)	4
at ease	9	at the church	5	at the other	4
at first sight	9	at the close of	5	at Eton	4
at all times	8	at the cost of	5	at the way	4
at a cost of	8	at the far end	5	at the tailplane	4
at intervals	8	at the first	5	at the Foreign	
at the office	8	at the gate	5	Office	4
at the rate (of)	8	at the rear (of)	5	at the Tate Gallery	4
at this moment	8	at heart	5	at universities	4
at London Airport	8	at most	5	at will	4
at the table	7	at right angles	5	at one point	4
at the weekend	7	at a later date	5	at one.	4
				Total	2,575

The *LOB Corpus* is not big enough to present a clear picture of the collocational nature of *at* phrases. As Table 3.27 shows, some phrases such as *at least* or *at last* occur many times. Some phrases such as *at the India Office*, or *at the tailplane*, occur several times reflecting the topics included in the text samples selected for the corpus. They do not seem to be strongly formulaic, however. Some phrases in the corpus, such as *at an early stage, at short notice, at a safe distance, at much the same rate, at the last minute, love at first sight*, seem familiarly collocational, and yet because they each occur only twice in the corpus do not meet the arbitrary criterion of four occurrences required for inclusion in Table 3.27. If *at* is typical of other prepositions, the corpus reveals a much more lexically centred nature of prepositions than grammatical descriptions normally suggest. Furthermore, the corpus reveals that prepositions as a grammatical class behave very differently from each other in a number of ways. We have already noted that *of* tends to collocate with preceding items rather than following.

Table 3.28 compares the most frequent left collocates of *at, from, between* and *through* in the *LOB Corpus*. It shows that the prepositions tend to collocate with particular words. This is clear even when only immediately contiguous collocates are included in the analysis. There are also striking differences shown in the word classes which precede *between* and *through*. Most of the left collocates of *between* in Table 3.28 are nouns, whereas the most frequent words preceding *through* are verbs.

Table 3.28 Number of tokens of the most frequent immediate left collocates of *at, from, between* and *through* in the *LOB Corpus*

+ at		+ from		+ between		+ through	
look (v.)	201	away	136	difference	59	go	36
be	195	come	110	relationship	25	pass	33
and	111	apart	99	distinction	19	come	20
that	51	and	62	relation	16	be	15
stare (v.)	49	far	50	gap	12	and	13
up	45	be	47	agreement	11	get	12
arrive	44	derive	37	contrast	11	break	10
not	43	range	35	distance	11	him	10
but	35	up	33	place	11	run	10
it	35	arise	30	be	10	way	9
down	34	back (adv.)	29	comparison	9	it	8
(numeral)	32	obtain	26	exist	9	fall	7
live	30	it	25	meeting	9	lead	7
glance	29	take	24	contact	8	look (v.)	7
out	29	out	23	link	8	out	7

Note: Nouns and verbs are lemmatized.

Table 3.29 shows the relative proportions of various word classes immediately preceding each of the four prepositions in the whole of the *LOB Corpus*. It suggests that the normal grammatical description of prepositions as a class actually masks significant differences. The contrast between those prepositions more commonly preceded by nouns and those preceded by verbs is the most notable.

Table 3.29 Word classes occurring immediately before *at, from, between* and *through* in the *LOB Corpus* (adapted from Kennedy, 1990)

| Word class | % of tokens | | | |
	at	from	between	through
Nouns or pronouns	42	45	66	29
Verbs	32	29	16	43
Adjectives	3	5	2	4
Other word classes	17	17	10	15
Clause initial	7	4	6	9

The corpus can also be used to show the relative distribution of the various senses or semantic functions of the prepositions. Comprehensive dictionaries list the various meanings of prepositions and for the most frequent of this word class, for words such as *of, in, on*, 40 or 50 distinct meanings are listed. Prepositions are often considered to have a core or primary locative function (e.g. *It's **on** the table; they're **near** the door; it's **under** the house*), and it is recognised that they can also be used with an extended metaphorical function in non-locative senses (e.g. *on Friday; on account of, near death, under these circumstances*). However, analysis of how *at, between, through* and *by* function in the *LOB Corpus* suggests that it is in extended or metaphorical contexts that a significant proportion of the use of these prepositions occurs. Tables 3.30–3.33 summarize the approximate proportions of the occurrences of these four prepositions used for different semantic functions in the *LOB Corpus*.

Thus corpus-based studies of prepositions reveal that many of them occur frequently in recurring collocations, and that systematic analysis of the phrases which prepositions form part of reveals a variety of different semantic roles. However, little is yet known about how prepositional use might vary according to genre or regional variety and whether the analysis of the grammatical and semantic ecology of prepositions outlined in Tables 3.29–3.33 is reasonably robust. If such generalizations can be sustained beyond their occurrence in a particular corpus, and we can be confident that there is a greater amount of patterning than has hitherto

Table 3.30 Major semantic functions in which *at* occurs in the *LOB Corpus*

Function	% of *at* tokens
Location	
(a) *at* showing position	37
e.g. *He is at the office.*	
I saw it at the British Museum.	
(b) *at* showing direction	12
e.g. *She glanced at her watch.*	
She smiled at him.	
Time	
(a) *at* showing a point in time	13
e.g. *at 11 o'clock; at the moment; at the end*	
(b) *at* showing a period of time	10
e.g. *at that time; at night*	
Event/activity	6
e.g. *at the coronation; at this conference*	
Quantity/degree	16
e.g. *at 120° F; at least*	
State/manner	1
e.g. *at loggerheads with; at ease*	
Causation	1
e.g. *dismay at the amount of damage*	
Miscellaneous	4
e.g. *at any rate; leave it at that*	
n = 5951	100

been noted, then there will be implications for the content of language teaching, not least because of the high frequency of occurrence of members of this word class.

3.2.7 *Conjunctions:* since, when, once

Whereas prepositions are used to link concepts within propositions, or are part of adverbial adjuncts to propositions, conjunctions have an important role in interclausal cohesion. Corpus-based work on the use of subordinating conjunctions which introduce clauses marking temporal, causal and conditional relationships suggests that there are interesting differences in their nature and use. This can be illustrated by considering aspects of the use of words such as *since*, which is used as a preposition, adverb and conjunction, *when*, which is used primarily as a subordinating conjunction, or *once*, which is used as an adverbial and conjunction. It

Table 3.31 Major semantic functions in which *between* occurs in the *LOB Corpus* (adapted from Kennedy, 1991: 106)

Function	% of *between* tokens
Location	
(a) Between two or more places, entities or states e.g. *the channel between Africa and Sicily* *let nothing get between her and her ambition*	25
(b) Between points on a scale or range e.g. *temperatures between 1000° and 1450° C*	6
Movement	
(a) Going from one place or state to another e.g. *she ran between the dining room and the kitchen*	3
(b) Going between entities e.g. *he was observed . . . walking between the metals*	2
Time	
(a) Occurring at some time between two events or points in time e.g. *98 changes of Cabinet between 1834 and 1912*	4
(b) Duration, occupying a period between two events or points in time e.g. *to keep myself going between terms at college*	5
Other relationships	
(a) Bond between entities, states or places e.g. *an alliance between the Castilian and Leonese nobility*	11
(b) Interaction between entities or states e.g. *communication between management and employees*	17
(c) Similarity e.g. *the resemblances between Lawrence's inner life and his own*	2
(d) Differences e.g. *the discrepancy between expected and observed scores*	18
(e) Comparison e.g. *a comparison between different car manufacturers' guarantees*	2
Dividing or sharing e.g. *the division of the world between two ideological camps*	5
n = 867	100

Table 3.32 Major semantic functions in which *through* occurs in the
LOB Corpus
(adapted from Kennedy, 1991: 107)

Function	% of *through* tokens
Unimpeded motion	
(a) Through a hole or passage	10
e.g. *they went through a gate*	
movement of blood through arteries	
(b) Through an area	9
e.g. *when he was passing through London*	
the footpath through the fields	
(c) Through an entity or substance	6
e.g. *she ran a comb through her hair*	
Magda chugged through the dark	
(d) Through a point	5
e.g. *through each point there pass three lines*	
(e) Through a system or circuit	4
e.g. *a sweet thrill ran through every nerve*	
(f) Searching through something	3
e.g. *to look through the files he scrabbled*	
through his drawers	
Penetration of a barrier or obstruction	18
e.g. *the sun burst through the blue-grey clouds*	
he breaks through the Kantian dogma	
has survived its progress through Congress	
Perception through an obstruction	7
e.g. *to look through one of the windows*	
his eyes met hers through the thin veil of smoke	
Time	
(a) Through a period of time	5
e.g. *going through the whole of his life*	
(b) Through a process or event	3
e.g. *go through the same routine*	
Agent–intermediary–instrument	25
e.g. *I should have met him through Robert Graves*	
through the medium of the English language	
evidence obtained through the examination	
of stones	
secure cooperation through compromise	
Causation	5
e.g. *time lost through the flooding of the workings*	
her eyes were red through overmuch crying	
dilapidation through lack of maintenance	
n = 776	100

Table 3.33 Major semantic functions in which *by* occurs in the *LOB Corpus*

Function	% of *by* tokens
Agent marker	
(a) After passive verb	53
e.g. *the conference was boycotted by the two parties*	
It is brought about by an increase in the population	
(b) After a noun showing author or doer	11
e.g. *after Saturday's home defeat by Oldham*	
has presented a bronze head by E. Pentland	
Means or manner	
(a) After passive verb	5
e.g. *it is achieved by a heavy reliance on symbolism*	
(b) After non-passive verb	11
e.g. *I knew by the look on his face*	
Mr Kruschev left Kiev by rail	
He made (them) happy by beating Brown	
Location	2
e.g. *She lingered by the door*	
Time	4
e.g. *do it by Friday*	
Measurement	3
e.g. *five by four equals twenty*	
Miscellaneous	11
e.g. *What is meant by 'in time'*	
He is a plumber by training	
n = 5386	100

is, of course, not easy to separate lexical grammar from syntax when subordinating conjunctions are concerned.

SINCE

Since is one of a number of mainly temporal words which can function as a preposition or as a conjunction. Table 3.34 shows the distribution of *since* in various corpora and genre within corpora and illustrates the extent to which usage can vary in different contexts.

Table 3.34 The distribution of functions of *since* in different genres (%)

Function	LLC	LOB	LOB J (academic)	Brown J (academic)	Brown A–C (press)
Conjunction	52	51	69	86	42
Preposition	45	46	27	12	55
Other (adverb)	3	3	4	2	3

Since can have temporal and causal uses (e.g. *I've lived here since July; Since we don't agree we'd better get other advice*). The heavy preponderance of the use of *since* as a conjunction in academic texts may reflect the greater occurrence of subordination in such texts and the importance of causation and reasoning in academic writing. Of the 542 tokens of *since* in the *LOB Corpus*, 65% express temporal reference and 35% express causation. However, in the academic genre (Section J) 36% of the uses of *since* are temporal, while 64% express causation. In the academic section of the *Brown Corpus*, only 14% of the tokens of *since* have temporal reference, with 86% marking causation. In the *LLC* of spoken British English, on the other hand, 76% of the 161 tokens of *since* are temporal and 24% are causal.

There are also notable differences between corpora in the way *since* as a preposition and as a conjunction is used in temporal and causative expressions in academic texts. This is seen in Table 3.35.

Table 3.35 The use of *since* in temporal and causative expressions (%)

Corpus/Genre	Time Prep.	Conj.	Adv.	Cause/Reason Prep.	Conj.	Adv.
LOB J	77	10	13	0	100	0
Brown J	86	0	14	0	100	0

In the British academic texts as represented in the *LOB Corpus*, *since* as a conjunction is used for expressing both temporal and causal relationships, whereas in the American academic texts represented in the *Brown Corpus since* as a conjunction does not appear to be used for temporal reference.

WHEN

Analysis of how *when* is used in different corpora illustrates the commonly found stability in different contexts in the use of high frequency function words and the considerable variety of semantic relationships which can be marked. All the tokens of *when* were examined in context in the *London–Lund Corpus, LOB Corpus* and Sections A–C (the journalistic sections) of the *Wellington Corpus* of New Zealand English, which parallels the structure of the *Brown* and *LOB* corpora. The three sources, containing a total of 4,183 tokens of *when* in approximately 1.6 million words of running text, are quite different. The *LLC* contains recordings of many participants in a wide range of public and private conversations, commentaries, lectures, meetings and trials recorded between 1958 and 1976. In this corpus there is a tendency for there to be opinion and generalized description with the false starts, repetitions and other discourse features characteristic of spoken texts. The *LOB* and *Wellington* corpora, which are both of written English, on the other hand, have a much greater narrative emphasis, including reports and descriptions of particular events which have occurred, and are largely couched in well-formed sentences.

Figure 3.8 and Table 3.36 show the eight main semantic uses of *when* and their relative proportions of occurrence in each of the corpora. Senses

---

1   *When* marks the simultaneous occurrence of events or states or the time at which one event occurs in relation to another.
    Mr Douglas was away when that decision was made.

2   *When* marks the simultaneous duration of two states or processes occurring throughout a period. Synonymous with *while*.
    It is the same blank expression people have when they're watching television.

3   *When* marks sequence and is synonymous with *after*. Sometimes there is an element of causation.
    When you cut it out it will go away.
    And when you finished you went away.

4   *When* marks sequence and is synonymous with *before* or *by the time that*.
    She had only been in her room a few minutes when there was a knock.

5   *When* marks indefinite or timeless frequency or iteration and is synonymous with *whenever*.
    When mildew appears it should be treated.
    He used to throw his children bananas to eat when they were hungry.

6   *When* is synonymous with *given that* or *since*.
    Why should someone move here when he has to pay fifty thousand pounds?
    And how could it, farmers would ask, when the money they make is so slight?

7   *When* marks contingency and is synonymous with *if*.
    Each song is almost scary, especially when you consider that this was recorded only months before.

8   *When* marks concession and is synonymous with *although*.
    They often think of buying expensive aerials when they need not do so.

Figure 3.8   Senses of *when*

Table 3.36 Distribution of the senses of *when*

Senses of *when*	LLC (spoken British English)		LOB (written British English)		Wellington (written New Zealand English)		Total	
	Tokens	%	Tokens	%	Tokens	%	Tokens	%
1 at the time	357	28.1	689	27.2	94	24.5	1,140	27.3
2 while	261	20.6	383	15.1	67	17.5	711	17.0
3 after	257	20.3	763	30.1	113	29.4	1,133	27.1
4 before	53	4.2	146	5.8	27	7.0	226	5.4
5 whenever	157	12.4	199	7.9	32	8.4	388	9.3
6 given that	97	7.6	88	3.5	27	7.0	212	5.1
7 if	59	4.7	222	8.8	15	3.9	296	7.1
8 although	28	2.2	40	1.6	9	2.3	77	1.8
	1,269	100	2,530	100	384	100	4,183	100
Total number of words in the corpus	435,000		1,000,000		200,000		1,635,000	

1 and 2, which mark simultaneity, together account for 44% of the tokens of *when*. Senses 3 and 4, which mark the very different relationship of sequentiality, account for 33% of tokens. The more contingent senses, 5–8, account in total for about 23% of the tokens. Further, senses 3 and 4, while both marking sequentiality, actually mark two contrasting sequential notions, priorness and subsequence, with *after* being about five times as frequent as *before*.

In comparing the results in the three different corpora, while there is some difference in the relative proportions of tokens in each category especially as between the spoken English of the *LLC* and the two written corpora, the overall picture is remarkably consistent. The first three categories account for over two-thirds of the tokens of *when*, although none of the eight categories is insignificant. Particularly striking is the similarity in the distribution of the senses of *when* in both a spoken corpus and a written corpus collected in the United Kingdom mainly in the 1960s, and part of a written corpus collected on the other side of the world over twenty-five years later. The greater proportion of *when* as a synonym for *after* in the *LOB* and *Wellington* corpora may, of course, be a reflection of the reporting-narrative nature of particular genre in the corpora rather than necessarily reflecting the written medium as such.

When is a very frequent word in English, one of the hundred or so which make up half of all the words we use. According to Carroll et al. (1971) it is the 35th most frequent word to which schoolchildren are exposed in their reading. *When* is the 44th most frequent word in the *LOB Corpus*. The data presented in Table 3.36 suggest that the use of *when* to mark different senses is remarkably similar in three different corpora covering a range of genres assembled at different times, in different places, and from different media. If we were to seek to understand why *when* is sometimes hard for language learners, this analysis suggests that the semantic variety of its lexical roles could be one source of the difficulty. Although syntactic relationships can be counted in a computer corpus automatically, study of the distribution of sense is still obviously dependent on a great deal of manual analysis.

ONCE

As a temporal conjunction synonymous with *after* (or *as soon as*), *once* occurs 83 times in the *LOB Corpus*. Table 3.37 summarizes the distribution of these occurrences. *Once* introduces finite clauses 66 times (80%) and non-finite elliptical constructions on 17 occasions (20%). In the *LOB Corpus*, *once* occurs as a conjunction 54 times in Sections A–J (informative prose), accounting for 65% of occurrences. It is not clear why Sections K–R (imaginative prose), which make up only 25% of the total corpus, are disproportionately represented with 29 tokens (35% of the occurrences of *once*). In finite clauses in the *LOB Corpus once* is followed

Table 3.37 *Once* as a conjunction in the *LOB Corpus*

	Informative prose (A–J)	Imaginative prose (K–R)	Total LOB	%
I **Once in finite clauses**				
once + simple present	10	7	17	21
once + simple present passive	7	0	7	8
once + simple past	2	6	8	10
once + simple past passive	6	0	6	7
once + present perfect	8	4	12	15
once + present perfect passive	6	0	6	7
once + past perfect	4	4	8	10
once + past perfect passive	1	1	2	2
Total	44	22	66	80
II **Once in elliptical clauses**				
once + past participle e.g. *once firmly settled he was willing to go*	6	1	7	8
once + present participle e.g. *once going the job was tidied up*	0	1	1	1
once + adverbial e.g. *once inside she stood chewing* *once over a certain age she was known as Mrs*	4	5	9	11
Total	10	7	17	20
GRAND TOTAL	54	29	83	100

only by the verb forms shown in Table 3.37. The passive forms are almost exclusively in Sections A–J. Thirty-two percent of the verb forms following the conjunction *once* in *LOB* are passive, a proportion which is much higher than the occurrence of passives in the corpus as a whole.

3.2.8 More *and* less

More is one of the fifty or so most frequent words in English, and although *less* is considerably less frequent, it too is among the high frequency words of the language. Standard grammars of English show

that *more* and *less* serve a variety of functions for comparing and quantifying. Their grammatical role varies from being sub-modifiers of some
adjectives and adverbs on the one hand to acting as determiners and
pro-forms on the other. When they occur in their comparative role they
are sometimes followed by *than*. Anyone interested in a description of
more and *less* for pedagogical purposes might well be excused, however,
for wondering how these various uses are distributed in the language.

Regrettably, as with most other grammatical features we have considered, we still lack systematic and comprehensive accounts with details
of the distribution of the features in representative corpora. Until such
accounts become available, however, smaller-scale studies can be used
to point the way towards the kinds of information which will eventually
be made available through the analysis of large corpora. Table 3.38 shows
the proportion of the 2,184 occurrences of *more* and 456 occurrences of
less in the *LOB Corpus* which occupy various grammatical roles. A number
of points of interest are apparent. *More* and *less* have remarkably similar
word-class distributions in the corpus, and where they function as sub-
modifiers or determiners before adjectives, adverbs or nouns, in only
about a quarter of the instances is there a subsequent *than*. That is, *more
likely, more important, more rapidly, less rainfall, less time, less significant* typically occur without *than* following. The high incidence of pro-forms (e.g.
they want more) is also noteworthy. Table 3.38 shows that fixed phrases

Table 3.38 Grammatical roles of *more* and *less* in the *LOB Corpus*

Grammatical role	*more* (%)	*less* (%)
Submodifiers		
more/less + adj.	28.34	25.00
more/less + adj. + *than*	8.33	10.52
more/less + adv.	6.31	4.16
more/less + adv. + *than*	1.87	0.87
Determiners		
more/less + noun	11.48	7.22
more/less + noun + *than*	3.15	2.63
Proforms	27.7	30.92
Fixed phrases	5.93	12.91
Other	6.89	5.77
Total	100.00	100.00

such as *what's more, more or less,* and *none the less* also make up a not insignificant proportion of the uses of *more* and *less* in the *LOB Corpus*.

A somewhat different approach to the corpus-based analysis of quantification was used by Kennedy (1987a). In a close manual analysis of a small corpus of over 60,000 words from mainly journalistic sources, some 9,135 of the word tokens in the corpus were identified as quantifying. These were classified into a number of subcategories as shown in Table 3.39. It is noteworthy that 14.46% of the words in a corpus are used to quantify in some way. This suggests that the semantic category of quantification is of considerable importance in communication, and reflects the fact that this semantic function is performed by a wide range of syntactic classes, including not only determiners, but also adjectives, nouns, verbs and adverbs. Some 1,407 different types for expressing quantification were found in the 60,000-word corpus. The subcategory of 'totality' thus includes not only the quantifiers *all* and *every*, but also examples such as the following: *the **total** population, the **entire** audience, think **globally**, a **full** break in relations, **universally** praised.*

From the perspective of language education, the high frequency of tokens for expressing non-specific quantification (e.g. *a few people, a substantial number of complaints*) should have significance for curriculum designers. A similar conceptually based analysis of the distribution of words in corpora was undertaken for the linguistic devices which are used for the expression of temporal frequency (Kennedy, 1987b). By way of illustration, Table 3.40 shows the relative frequency of words used for expressing the notion of usual occurrence in the academic sections (J) of the *Brown* and *LOB* corpora.

3.3   Grammatical studies centred on the sentence

When we move beyond the word as the main focus of study to a focus on the linking of words together in phrases, clauses and sentences, corpus-based research has been no less revealing. Just as word-focused corpus studies reveal important differences in the relative frequency of use of word classes such as nouns, verbs, adjectives and adverbs in informative written English when compared with imaginative writing (see Table 3.5), so have they also revealed considerable genre differences in the use of syntactic patterns and in sentence length. Corpus studies have demonstrated for the first time that facile notions that syntactic constructions are in free variation are clearly not correct. As Tottie has shown in her study of negation, for example, there are important differences between spoken and written English in the sentence grammar of negation (see Section 3.3.2.5). Studying grammar in a corpus is sometimes more of a challenge than studying lexis. In part this is because the tagging and parsing of corpora to facilitate the automatic

Table 3.39 Relative frequencies of use of categories of quantification (from Kennedy, 1987a: 272)

Category of quantification	No. of different 'types' in 60,000 words	No. of quantification tokens	% of quantification tokens	% of words in corpus
A Specific quantities/degrees				
1 Numerical				
Cardinals	190	757	8.29	1.20
Ordinals	10	97	1.06	0.15
Fractions	11	30	0.33	0.05
Percentages	44	106	1.16	0.17
2 None	21	160	1.75	0.25
3 Individual	39	264	2.89	0.42
4 Totality	73	440	4.82	0.70
Total	388	1,854	20.30	2.93
B Non-specific quantities/degrees				
1 Approximation	16	107	1.17	0.17
2 Small quantities/degrees	75	385	4.21	0.61
3 Large quantities/degrees	231	1,640	17.95	2.60

Table 3.39 continued

Category of quantification	No. of different 'types' in 60,000 words	No. of quantification tokens	% of quantification tokens	% of words in corpus
4 Unspecified quantities/ degrees	273	1,514	16.57	2.40
5 Non-specific parts of a whole	26	309	3.38	0.49
6 Adequacy	8	35	0.38	0.06
Total	629	3,990	43.68	6.32
C Relative quantities/degrees				
1 More (non-specific)	123	1,690	18.50	2.68
2 Equivalence (specific)	24	76	0.83	0.12
3 Less (non-specific)	76	221	2.42	0.35
Total	223	1,987	21.75	3.15
D Measurement and calculation of quantity	114	1,123	12.29	1.78
E Miscellaneous	53	181	1.98	0.29
GRAND TOTAL	1,407	9,135	100.0	14.46

Table 3.40 Relative frequency of synonyms for *usually* in the academic sections of the *Brown* and *LOB* corpora (number of tokens in 320,000 words) (adapted from Kennedy, 1987b: 82)

Synonym	Frequency
(in) general	124
normal	119
usually	105
common	104
generally	78
typical	38
ordinary	30
usual	27
normally	26
commonly	24
regular	18
for the most part	10
custom	8
more often	8
more often than not	8
ordinarily	6
mostly	6
regularly	6
customary	5
routine	5
in most cases	4

analysis of texts, and the development of software for analysis, has not been so widely available or user-friendly as untagged text and the standard concordancing software.

3.3.1 Sentence length

Kučera and Francis (1967: 370) and Francis and Kučera (1982) were among the first to demonstrate from corpus analysis that sentence length is related to genre. In the *Brown Corpus* the mean number of words per sentence in the informative prose categories (A–J) is much greater than in imaginative prose (K–R). Although informative prose sentences are typically considerably longer than imaginative prose sentences in the *Brown Corpus*, there is much closer consistency in the number of predications per sentence regardless of genre. This absence of a strong relationship between sentence length and syntactic complexity in the corpus is suggested in the figures in Table 3.41, which show the mean number of words per predication. All the informative prose genres show a larger number of words per predication than the imaginative prose genres. Francis and Kučera suggest that it is the length and complexity of nominal groups and a larger number of non-finite predications in informative prose which possibly account for the longer sentence length in informative prose.

Table 3.41 Sentence length and predications in the *Brown Corpus* (adapted from Francis & Kučera, 1982: 552)

Genre	Words per sentence	Predications per sentence*	Words per predication
I Informative prose			
A. Press: reportage	20.72	2.63	7.88
B. Press: editorials	19.66	2.73	7.21
C. Press: reviews	21.06	2.62	8.03
D. Religion	21.21	2.90	7.33
E. Skills and hobbies	18.53	2.59	7.15
F. Popular lore	20.26	2.81	7.22
G. Belles lettres	21.35	2.93	7.29
H. Miscellaneous	24.07	2.80	8.59
J. Learned	22.31	2.84	7.85
Subtotal	21.06	2.78	7.57
II Imaginative prose			
K. General fiction	13.82	2.41	5.74
L. Mystery and detective	12.62	2.29	5.50
M. Science fiction	12.94	2.23	5.81
N. Adventure and western	12.75	2.30	5.54
P. Romance and love story	13.41	2.44	5.49
R. Humor	17.52	2.82	6.21
Subtotal	13.38	2.38	5.62
WHOLE CORPUS	18.40	2.64	6.96

* Predication is defined as 'any verb or verbal group with a tensed verb having a grammatical subject . . . and infinitives, gerunds and participles' (Francis & Kučera, 1982: 550).

In their earlier analysis, Kučera and Francis (1967: 377) had suggested that a high proportion of simulated spoken language or quoted material in imaginative texts tends to be strongly related to the shorter sentence length. More recent work by de Haan (1993) based on a sample from the *Nijmegen Corpus* has shown that in fiction texts with a greater amount of dialogue, the mean sentence length does indeed tend to be shorter than in those with fewer sentences of dialogue.

In a study of a one-million-word corpus of written American English extracted from the Associated Press newswire service and probably broadly representative of modern news reporting, Sharman (1989) found that the mean sentence length was 23.7 words (with a range from 3 to 70 words), a figure slightly larger than the mean length in Section A of the *Brown Corpus*.

3.3.2 Syntactic processes

When we move to corpus-based evidence on the syntactic structure of sentences, there has been much less quantitative information available from corpus studies than might have been expected. However, a number of studies have shown what a rich field remains to be explored in the description of grammatical structures and processes.

3.3.2.1 CLAUSE PATTERNING

Altenberg (1993) examined over 5,000 recurrent verb–complement combinations from the *London–Lund Corpus* of spoken English, to discover, among other things, what grammatical types of verb complementation were most common and what communicative functions they fulfil. As shown in Table 3.42, copular and monotransitive verb–complement types dominated. Although the incidence of adjectival complementation and simple direct object patterns in Table 3.42 is very striking, Altenberg has emphasized that the frequencies cannot necessarily be taken to represent the distribution of verb-complementation in general because of the criteria used for selecting his sample of recurrent types from the spoken corpus. This is because many of these types function as discourse items in spoken interaction to show agreement, reassurance or evaluation, to make requests or apologies (e.g. *that's right, it's all right, that would be lovely, excuse me, I'm sorry, wait a minute*). It is clear that many of these types are near-fossilized collocations with perhaps idiomatic status, which makes syntactic analysis somewhat otiose. The high incidence of the copular patterns is of course consistent with the dominance of *be* among English verbs noted earlier in the studies of Ota (1963) and others.

An analysis of over 15,000 sentences from the 130,000 word *Nijmegen Corpus* by Oostdijk and de Haan (1994a) is a richly detailed account of the most common clause patterns in this corpus of modern written English. About half of the clauses in the corpus are matrix clauses and half are embedded. Of the matrix clauses, 97.8% are finite, 1.5% are non-finite, and 0.7% are elliptical. For the embedded clauses, 57.9% are finite, 36.3% are non-finite and 5.8% are elliptical.

Table 3.42 Distribution of recurrent verb–complement patterns in the *LLC*
(adapted from Altenberg, 1993: 230)

Complementation patterns	No. of tokens	%	
Copular			
SVC (adj.)	2,282	45.6	
SVC (nom.)	674	13.5	
SVA	274	5.5	
Subtotal			64.5
Monotransitive			
SVO	1,048	20.9	
SVO (V = *have*)	374	7.5	
Subtotal			28.4
Complex transitive			
SVOC (adj.)	74	1.5	
SVOC (nom.)	9	0.2	
SVOA	141	2.8	
SVO + *to* infinitive	2	0.0	
SVO + bare infinitive	2	0.0	
SVO + *-ing* clause	4	0.1	
SVO + *-ed* clause	5	0.1	
Subtotal			4.7
Ditransitive			
SVOO	50	1.0	
SVO + prep. + O	65	1.3	
Subtotal			2.3
TOTAL	5,004		100

Key: S = Subject; V = Verb; C = Complement; A = Adverbial; O = Object.

Spoken and written texts totalling 895,000 words from the *SEU Corpus* were used by Mair (1990, 1991) to explore the nature and distribution of non-finite clauses which function as verb complements (e.g. *It enabled them to complete the job*), or as subjects (e.g. *To disregard the past is very often the surest way of becoming its slave*). It is not possible here to do justice to the detailed re-examination of complementation which this study provides. The discursive, qualitative approach which characterizes this corpus-based analysis quite deliberately plays down the quantitative information that characterizes most recent corpus-based research. Mair notes that the vast majority of all informational subject clauses are extraposed (e.g. *It is essential to ensure that the engine starts smoothly* rather than *To ensure that the engine starts smoothly is essential*), reflecting perhaps a principle of end-focus from a functional sentence perspective, or perhaps preferences in sentence organization for processing purposes. In this study the 10 most frequent adjectives governing infinitival subject clauses are, in order of frequency, *difficult, possible, easy, necessary, good, hard, interesting, important, impossible, nice*. The first 5 adjectives account for over half of all tokens of this structure in the corpus.

In his discussion of infinitival object clauses with subject-to-object raising (e.g. *I expected her to succeed*), Mair notes that 17 verbs govern all 366 of the active-voice constructions in the corpus, namely (in descending order of frequency) *want, allow, enable, expect, get, like, cause, require, have, order, wish, can't bear, hate, mean, need, permit, suffer*. Although these constructions are distributed fairly evenly in both spoken and written texts, there are some striking differences for individual verbs. *Get*, for example, is found in the spoken texts for 39 of its 49 tokens. There are 193 tokens of the 10 passive verbs in the corpus which occur with subject-to-object raising, namely (in descending order of frequency) *suppose, allow, expect, intend, mean, order, enable, need, permit, require*.

Mair's study of syntax within discourse with actual examples from the corpus is a study of authentic acts of communication. The resulting discussion of why certain choices are made, such as whether to extrapose or not, is thus necessarily sometimes indeterminate. Nevertheless, Mair (1991: 80) concludes that such analysis is a strength rather than a weakness of a corpus-based approach. 'Corpus analysis should not be quantitative and statistical only. The role of the corpus, after all, is not only to provide a limited and representative data-base for statistical analysis, but also to provide authentic and realistic data, the close reading of which will allow the linguist to approach grammar from a functional and discourse perspective.'

Following Mair's model, it would be useful to have further equally systematic corpus-based descriptions of complementation using corpora which represent other varieties of English. For example, it is sometimes suggested that in informative prose the verb which precedes a finite *that*-clause is more likely to be a 'communication' verb such as *say, state, claim, predict, deny, report, argue*, whereas in spoken conversation 'affective' or 'cooperative' verbs such as *think, feel, hope, mean, doubt, realize, wish, believe* tend to predominate. Similarly it may be the case that in both imaginative written prose and in speech, where speakers' thoughts, feelings or beliefs are being expressed, the complementizer *that* is more likely to be omitted than in informative genres where the words of someone else are being related or reported.

More information is needed on the relative frequency of different kinds of complementation, when and where extraposition or *that*-deletion occur, and the distribution of the verbs which govern complements, to flesh out existing descriptions of the use of complementizers.

3.3.2.2 NOUN MODIFICATION

A detailed corpus-based description of postmodification in the English noun phrase by de Haan (1989) also provides a good example of the value of a distributional analysis of syntactic processes. The 130,000 word *Nijmegen Corpus* was analysed and found to contain 2,430 postmodifying clauses. Almost 98% of the postmodifying clauses had one or other of the simpler clause patterns SV (37%), SVO (38%) or SVC/SVA (23%), as against about 92% of all the non-postmodifying clauses in the corpus, suggesting perhaps that embedding tends to favour less complex sentence patterns.

The analysis showed that about 70% of noun phrases function as subjects or prepositional complements and that noun phrases with postmodifying clauses tend to be disfavoured in subject functions. There is also a tendency noted in the data for postmodification to be less frequent in non-final positions of sentences. This is possibly because the subject or topic (which normally comes near the beginning of the sentence) is familiar enough not to need identification or elaboration through postmodification, or perhaps because brief subjects are easier to process. From this informational or functional perspective it is not surprising that where postmodification of a subject noun phrase does occur it is more likely to be non-restrictive or appositional than restrictive or defining.

De Haan (1991) also shows that about 70% of postmodifying relative clauses in the corpus are restrictive. In his data from the *Nijmegen Corpus*, the relativizers zero and *that* are found only with restrictive relative clauses, with zero being twice as frequent as *that*, while *which* is the most frequent link word overall, accounting for 45% of restrictive clause linkwords and over 55% of non-restrictive clause linkwords. Preliminary analysis of other corpora with a wider range of genres suggests that de Haan's data has a lower than expected incidence of *that*, and a correspondingly higher incidence of *which* reflecting perhaps formal written style or a preponderance of inanimate antecedents in his corpus.

An insightful corpus-based study by Meyer (1991a) analyses the syntactic, semantic and pragmatic characteristics of apposition, the grammatical process or relation between two noun phrases, which may nevertheless be marked by a variety of syntactic forms. Using a corpus of about 360,000 words compiled from the *SEU*, *Brown* and *London–Lund* corpora, Meyer was able to compare apposition in American and British varieties of written English, in different genres and in speech and writing. He found that although the predominant syntactic realization of apposition was by two

juxtaposed NPs (e.g. *Sybil, our neighbour . . .*), 45% of appositions were
by other structures (e.g. *Garden pests, including the fruit fly . . .*).

In addition to describing the syntactic structures and functions of
apposition Meyer (1991b) has categorized the semantic classes of the
2,841 tokens of apposition in his corpus. Table 3.43 shows that in only
59% of the tokens did the second unit of the apposition structure provide greater specificity. A quarter of the tokens provided equally specific
information and 16% were actually less specific.

Table 3.43 Semantic classes of apposition
(Meyer, 1991b: 176)

Semantic class	*Brown*	*LLC*	*SEU*	Total	
More specific					
Identification	323	239	451	1,013	
Appellation	212	21	124	357	
Particularization	49	49	40	138	
Exemplification	42	80	55	177	
Total	626	389	670	1,685	(59%)
Less specific					
Characterization	208	37	205	450	(16%)
Equally specific					
Paraphrase	165	258	143	566	
Reorientation	26	32	13	71	
Self-correction	1	62	6	69	
Total	192	352	162	706	(25%)
Total	1,026	778	1,037	2,841	(100%)

Table 3.44 shows that apposition was more likely to occur in some
genres than in others. If we assume that the role of apposition is to provide additional information, it seems that some genres, from journalistic
and academic contexts in particular, tend to require more apposition to
maintain communicative efficiency. Meyer (1991b: 179) suggests that
apposition is most necessary in genres which typically have less shared
knowledge between interlocutors or writer and reader. Table 3.44 suggests that in general, written texts assume less shared knowledge, while
spoken texts, especially from equal or intimate interlocutors in the *LLC*,
require fewer appositions. The fact that some written fiction produced
even fewer appositions than some of the spoken texts suggests that some
fiction may involve the reader by assuming shared knowledge or famil-
iarity with the novelist's 'world'. Although apposition is only one part

Table 3.44 Total number of appositions per genre
(Meyer, 1991b: 179)

Genre	No. of appositions	Appositions per 1000 words
Fiction (*SEU*)	201	5.0
Intimates (*LLC*)	158	5.3
Equals (*LLC*)	169	5.6
Fiction (*Brown*)	244	6.1
Learned, scientific (*Brown*)	132	6.6
Disparates (*LLC*)	223	7.4
Intimates/equals (*LLC*)	228	7.6
Learned, humanistic (*Brown*)	180	9.0
Learned, scientific (*SEU*)	197	9.9
Press (*SEU*)	394	9.9
Press (*Brown*)	470	11.8
Learned, humanistic (*SEU*)	245	12.3
Total	2,841	7.9

of the noun-phrase system in English, this study illustrates the extent to which much more insightful descriptions of the syntax and semantics of sentences might be possible and what might be expected from corpus-based descriptions of other syntactic processes.

Postmodification of nouns by finite and non-finite clauses and by prepositional phrases and adjective phrases has been the subject of a study by Biber et al. (1994). The corpus investigated was slightly smaller than the *Nijmegen Corpus* used by de Haan, and consisted of texts totalling about 115,000 words from three registers taken from the *LOB Corpus* and a private corpus of letters.

The data in Table 3.45 suggests that in these registers at least, postnominal modification by prepositional phrases is overwhelmingly more frequent than full, finite relative clauses – restrictive and non-restrictive, with or without relative pronouns as linkwords. Even in the fiction and personal letter genres, where postnominal modification is much less frequent than in editorials, the distributions of the various types are similar. It might be that both prepositional phrases and participial clauses can be viewed as elliptical constructions, that is, as kinds of reduced relative clauses, but nevertheless, the evidence from this study suggests that the pattern of use favours the elliptical rather than the fully explicit and marked postnominal clause modifiers. Biber et al. have noted that academic prose tends to make more use of relative clauses than most registers yet, even in academic prose, prepositional phrases are more common than relatives.

Table 3.45 Frequencies of different types of postnominal modifiers in three registers (per 1,000 words) (from Biber et al., 1994: 173)

Postnominal modifier	Editorials (27 texts)	Fiction (29 texts)	Letters (6 texts)
that relative clauses restrictive	1.8	0.7	0.5
WH relative clauses restrictive	5.4	2.1	1.1
WH relative clauses non-restrictive	1.9	2.2	0.3
Relative clauses with no relative pronoun	0.1	0.1	0.2
Participial postnominal modifiers (past and present)	4.9	1.8	0.2
Prepositional phrases as noun modifiers	38.2	15.2	16.8
Prepositional phrases as verb modifiers	44.1	56.2	45.8

3.3.2.3 CONDITIONALITY

Hill (1960) noted that at least 324 different combinations of finite verb forms could occur in the main and subordinate clauses of conditional sentences where the subordinate clause was introduced by *if*. Wang (1991) studied the distribution of these verb-form combinations in the 2,017 tokens of *if*-conditions in the *Brown Corpus* and the 2,307 tokens in the *LOB Corpus*. He found that only 76 of the 324 possible combinations described by Hill actually occurred in *Brown*, and 103 in *LOB*. The 24 most frequent combinations are listed in Table 3.46.

The first eight combinations (1–4) account for over 50% of all the tokens in each corpus, and the 24 combinations included in 1–10 account for about 75%. The striking similarity between American and British written usage in the distribution of the grammatical structure of these conditionals is parallelled by an analysis of their semantic function, shown in Table 3.47.

In each corpus, about half of the *if*-conditionals have so-called factual senses (e.g. *If you heat air it rises, I get a headache if I eat too many nuts*). A further 25% of uses have a predictive sense (e.g. *If you're not careful you'll fall down*). The remaining tokens of *if*-conditionals in the corpora are what are variously called hypothetical, imaginative, or unreal conditions. Approximately 14% in each corpus are improbable conditions (e.g. *I would take a coat if I thought it would rain*). The remainder are counterfactuals (e.g. *If I were you, I'd stay here; He would have drowned if we hadn't*

Table 3.46 Verb-form combinations in conditional sentences in the *Brown* and *LOB* corpora
(adapted from Wang, 1991: 58)

	Verb form in *if*-clause	Verb form in main clause	% of *if*-tokens *Brown*	*LOB*
1	Simple present	Simple present	22.0	22.0
2	Simple present	*will/shall/be going to* + stem	13.2	12.5
3	Simple past	*would/could/might* + stem	11.3	11.1
4	Simple past	Simple past	6.7	6.8
5	Simple present	*should/must/can/may/ought to* + stem	10.0	6.4
6	Past perfect	*would/could/might have* + past participle	3.9	4.1
7	*were (to)*	*would/could/might* + stem	4.0	4.0
8	*can* + stem	Simple present	1.1	3.2
9	Simple present	*would/could/might* + stem	1.9	2.4
10	Simple present	Imperative	1.7	2.0
	Total		75.8	74.5

Table 3.47 Semantic categories of conditional sentences in the *Brown* and *LOB* corpora
(adapted from Wang, 1991: 65)

Semantic category	% of *if*-conditional sentences *Brown* (US English)	*LOB* (UK English)
Open conditions		
Factual	47.3	48.3
Predictive	28.3	26.3
Hypothetical conditions		
Improbable	14.2	14.3
Counterfactual	10.2	11.1
Total	100	100

got him out of the water). Open conditions are about three times as frequent as hypothetical conditions in these corpora. Regrettably for students of English in many parts of the world, pedagogy sometimes tends to focus on the less frequently used structures and functions. Indeed, in many grammars and course books the most common type of conditional (simple present + simple present) is ignored entirely.

Clause ordering in the conditional sentences in *Brown* and *LOB* is shown in Table 3.48. There is a strong tendency for the *if*-clause to come before the main clause, a tendency slightly stronger in *Brown* than in *LOB*. However, in conditional sentences where the subordinating conjunction is *unless* rather than *if*, the *unless*-clause precedes the main clause for only 37.5% of tokens in *Brown* and significantly less again in *LOB* (24.7%).

Table 3.48 Clause order for conditional sentences in the *Brown* and *LOB* corpora (%)

	Brown	*LOB*
Initial *if*-clause	77.5	70.5
Initial *unless*-clause	37.5	24.7

3.3.2.4 CAUSATION

The marking of causation in English has been the subject of a number of corpus-based studies. There are numerous linguistic devices which can mark causation, many of which are lexicalized (e.g. *cause, because, result in, arise from, thanks to, give rise to, so, since, responsible for*). There are also various syntactic structures which can mark causal relationships, including phrases (e.g. *Because of the rain, the game was cancelled*) and clauses (e.g. *I went to the museum because I had a couple of hours to spare*). In addition to causal structures being marked explicitly with words such as *because*, causation is frequently conveyed by implicature (e.g. *In 1985 the use of poisoned bait was introduced to control rats. By 1990 there were reduced numbers of several bird species*). In this example, causation may be inferred from the juxtaposition of the sentences. One of the many functions of formal education is to help children learn when they might reasonably conclude that causation is implied in texts and when it would be unreasonable to draw such conclusions.

As Altenberg (1984, 1987) has noted, the choice between the many different ways of expressing causation in English is seldom free, but is influenced by various semantic, pragmatic, stylistic, cognitive and textual variables. His study of the distribution of ways of expressing causation in different contexts is a notable example of corpus-based analysis of syntactic and semantic processes. Altenberg studied the explicit marking of causation in a 100,000-word sample of spontaneous English conversation from the *London–Lund Corpus* and a similar-sized sample of informative prose from the *LOB Corpus*. The two corpora contrast not just in terms of their spoken or written textual sources, but in terms of such variables as participant interaction and intimacy, degree of formality, purpose, and opportunity for planning.

Altenberg focused on syntactically expressed causation, particularly by four main patterns, namely adverbial linkage (e.g. *hence, so*), prepositional linkage (e.g. *because of*), subordination (e.g. *because, since*) and clause integration (e.g. *that's why*). Of the 98 different types identified, 82 occur in *LOB* and 52 in the *LLC*. Even with fewer types, causation is more frequently marked in the *LLC* than in the *LOB* sample. Altenberg found that, of the four syntactic ways of marking causation, subordination accounts for about half of the tokens in each corpus, and adverbial links about a third.

Table 3.49 shows the 15 most frequent causal link types in the two corpora. Certain devices are very frequent (e.g. *because, so*). Some devices are very infrequent and only occur with one or two tokens in the combined 200,000 word corpus. (e.g. *as a consequence, accordingly*). Some conjuncts (e.g. *on account of, by reason of*) are reported as being completely absent from the corpus.

The two most frequent devices, *because* and *so*, account for 74% of all causal devices in the *LLC* sample but only 19% of the causal devices in the sample from *LOB*. As Altenberg (1984: 39) noted, there is clear stylistic patterning apparent, with more stylistic variation in the written corpus, 'while the predominantly private, intimate and personal character of the spoken situation, with its restricted possibilities for advance planning, produces a more informal language and less concern for stylistic variation'. An especially interesting feature is that the conjunction *for*, the second most common strategy in writing, does not appear once in the speech sample. The conjunction *since* and the adverbs *thus* and *therefore* are similarly greatly under-represented in spoken English.

In the samples from both *LLC* and *LOB* investigated by Altenberg, there was a slight preference for the result to be expressed before the cause (RC), in that 54% of the sentences expressing causation used this order. Altenberg's study shows, however, that particular causal devices tend to be associated with particular orders of the presentation of causal information in speech or writing. For example, in spoken texts *so* tends to be associated with CR order, and *because* with RC order. The finding can be compared with Fang and Kennedy's (1992) finding that in the whole *LOB Corpus*, only 6% of the subordinate clauses introduced by *because* are in the initial position. That is, *I hurt my leg because I fell off my bike* is much more frequent than *Because I fell off my bike I hurt my leg*. The considerable variation in preferred ordering of CR or RC according to the causal linking devices used indicates a need for further research. Causal sequencing may be partly related to a pragmatic association of the causal relation with topicalization, and to the nature of interaction in the case of spoken English.

Table 3.49 Distribution of the 15 most frequent causal links in the *London–Lund* and *LOB* corpora (from Altenberg, 1984: 44)

Links	Total			LLC			LOB			Diff coeff*
	N	%	Rank	N	%	Rank	N	%	Rank	
because	425	32	1	355	45	1	70	13	1	0.67
so	265	20	2	233	29	2	32	6	6	0.76
for (conj)	64	5	3	0	0	–	64	12	2	-1.00
therefore	62	5	4	15	2	7	47	9	3	-0.52
so Adj/Adv that	47	4	5	25	3	4	22	4	7	0.06
so that	45	3	6	32	4	3	13	2	12	0.42
since (conj)	38	3	7	5	1	14	33	6	5	-0.74
thus	35	3	8	0	0	–	35	7	4	-1.00
-ing-clause	30	2	9	12	2	8	18	3	10	-0.20
because of NP	28	2	10	18	2	5	10	2	14	0.29
for NP	28	2	10	9	1	10	19	4	8	-0.36
as	26	2	12	7	1	12	19	4	8	-0.46
for V-ing	25	2	13	11	1	9	14	3	11	-0.12
too Adj/Adv to	21	2	14	9	1	10	12	2	13	-0.14
that's why	21	2	15	17	2	6	4	1	20	0.62
Total (all links)	1,331	100		797	100		534	100		0.20

Note: The difference coefficient in this table indicates the relative frequency of the links or linking types in the two corpora. It has been calculated in the following way (cf. Hofland & Johansson, 1982: 14):

$$\frac{\text{Freq: } LLC - \text{Freq: } LOB}{\text{Freq: } LLC + \text{Freq: } LOB}$$

The coefficient may range from +1.00 to –1.00. A plus value indicates over-representation in *LLC*, a minus value over-representation in *LOB*.

Table 3.50 Explicit devices marking causation in the *LOB Corpus* (from Fang & Kennedy, 1992: 68)

Types	Tokens	Types	Tokens	Types	Tokens
because	635	outcome	20	precipitate	4
why	443	give rise to	19	produce of	4
so	425	give	18	root	4
for	365	inspire	17	rouse	4
therefore	296	on the ground(s)		stir	4
effect	278	that	14	stir up	4
cause	265	thereby	14	account for	3
reason	258	as a result	13	as a consequence	
thus	227	make for	11	of	3
result	212	contribute to	10	ascribe to	3
since	189	provoke	10	consequent	
as	166	by reason of	8	on/upon	3
because of	142	derive from	8	corollary	3
so . . . that	139	prompt	8	spark off	3
then	135	what with	8	underlie	3
so that	127	accordingly	7	aftermath	2
due to	123	by virtue of	7	as a consequence	2
for (that) reason	93	generate	7	attribute to	2
lead to	83	incur	7	for reasons of	2
from	81	raise	7	incite	2
hence	52	responsible for	7	in consideration	
as a result of	48	as a matter of	6	of	2
being	47	in consequence	6	on that account	2
under	46	out of	6	on that score	2
consequence	45	source	6	put down to	2
produce	45	arise out of	5	seeing that	2
consequently	44	bring on	5	spring from	2
result in	44	compel	5	upshot	2
create	41	engender	5	with the con-	
through	38	on the ground(s)		sequence that	2
bring about	37	of	5	at the bottom of	1
in view of	36	on the strength of	5	awaken	1
now that	32	with the result		by consequence	1
arise from	29	that	5	consequential to	1
owing to	26	yield	5	cos	1
arouse	25	evoke	4	emerge from	1
present	23	excite	4	from reasons of	1
such . . . that	23	inasmuch as	4	mainspring	1
induce	22	in consequence of	4	spark	1
result from	22	motivate	4	stem from	1
thanks to	21	occasion	4	the whys and	
in the light of	20	pose	4	wherefores	1
on account of	20				

Fang and Kennedy (1992) identified over 130 ways in which causation is marked in English and found 5,862 tokens of 119 of these types explicitly marking causation in the whole of the *LOB Corpus*. Table 3.50 shows the relative frequency of these. Because this analysis contained marked nominal and verbal types such as *effect, cause, reason* excluded from Altenberg's analysis, the rank ordering in the two studies cannot be easily compared. However, in this much bigger written corpus, the dominant role of the major items *because, so, for, therefore, since, so that* is similar to Altenberg's findings. The most frequent 23 types accounted for 82% of the 5,862 causation tokens in the corpus.

The information which can now be retrieved from available corpora on an important semantic notion such as causation can add considerably to the information available from even the best reference grammars. Quirk et al. (1985), for example, describe some 40 linguistic devices which can be used for expressing causation. Not only is it possible to expand this taxonomy considerably but also to provide a picture of the distribution of these devices in particular varieties of the language.

Clause order in sentences which contain a subordinate clause shows considerable variation according to whether the conjunction marks temporal, causal or conditional relationships and according to the genre or variety of the text. For example, by way of comparison with the data in Table 3.48, in the whole *LOB Corpus*, where the subordinate conjunction is *because*, the subordinate clause precedes the main clause for only 6% of sentences. In the academic prose section of *LOB* (J), *when*-clauses precede the main clause for 24% of tokens. On the other hand, in the same Section J of *LOB*, subordinate clauses beginning with *until* precede the main clause for only 3.5% of tokens. There is clearly room for further systematic corpus-based investigation in different varieties of English to describe the patterns of clause ordering in sentences which contain subordinate clauses, and to determine whether the differences indicated are inherent in the types of clause or are associated with regional, sociolinguistic or register variation.

3.3.2.5 NEGATION

A pioneering quantitative analysis of the structure and use of negation in British English was undertaken by Tottie (1991a), who explored grammatical, semantic and pragmatic aspects of this linguistic phenomenon. Using informative prose sections of the *LOB Corpus*, spoken and written texts from the *SEU Corpus*, Tottie undertook a study of the pragmatics of negation – when, why and how it is used. The study focused on differences between spoken and written English specifically in the use of affixal and non-affixal forms (e.g. *impossible* versus *not possible*) and in the use of *not*-negation and *no*-negation (e.g. *He didn't have any time* versus *He had no time*). The study is a detailed, intricate and complex one which explores many aspects of the semantics and pragmatics of negation and does not simply count the formal realizations of negation.

For the purposes of the present work however, where the focus is on the contribution of corpus studies to our understanding of distributional aspects of linguistic phenomena, there are a number of particularly relevant findings in Tottie's descriptive work which bring together some of the benefits of computer corpus based analysis and statistically–based variable rule analysis.

In 50,000-word samples of spoken and written English from the *SEU Corpus*, Tottie found that in spoken texts, negatives occurred with a frequency of 27.6 occurrences per 1,000 words, whereas in written texts the frequency was 12.8 per 1,000 words. In seeking to account for the fact that negatives occur over twice as frequently in speech as in writing, Tottie rejected stylistic, semantic and syntactic determinants to account for the differences. The nature of spoken discourse, involving interaction, mutual monitoring, role reversal, correction, support, denial, and a higher tendency of 'mental' verbs such as *know, think* to collocate with negation, is contrasted with the low degree of interaction characteristic of written communication.

In the conversations in the *SEU* and the expository prose from the *LOB Corpus* there was a statistically significant difference ($p < .001$) between the use of *not*-negation and *no*-negation. Whereas 66% of the speech sample tokens of negation used *not*, only 37% of the writing tokens used *not*. This preference for *no*-negation in written genres is very striking. From an examination of earlier varieties of English, however, Tottie (1991a: 235) suggested that *not*-negation is tending to replace *no*-negation, with this tendency showing up most strongly in speech and in less frequent verbs which have not tended to form such strong collocations.

Tottie also found important differences between speech and writing in the case of affixal negation. Whereas in her sample of written British English, 33% of negation tokens were affixal (e.g. *unlikely, illogical*), only 8% of spoken negation tokens were affixal (p. 46). This difference is attributed possibly to greater planning time and less fragmentation in the construction of written text. In written texts the proportion of affixal negation of adjectives (the largest single word class with affixal negation) was about two-thirds of the total number of negative sentences with adjectives. In spoken texts, only one-third of such sentences have affixal negation, perhaps reflecting a greater proportion of attributive adjectives in writing. Tottie further shows that the use of *not-/no*-negation is not always a matter of stylistic choice, but that a substantial proportion of negations (spoken 10%, written 34%) do not allow variation between *not* and *no* forms (pp. 186–188). Some negations always seem to collocate with only one of the *not* or *no* variants. (e.g. *no point*, **There is no lot of money available*).

Table 3.51 illustrates the extent to which verbs polarize into those which have a high proportion of *no-* or *not*-negation and those with a low proportion, with a particularly strong disparity between copular and existential *be* (1991a: 194). Overall Tottie's study of negation provides an excellent set of baseline data on a large number of variables associated with the structure and use of this important linguistic phenomenon. Further studies of how negation is handled in different varieties of English, using larger corpora and multivariate analysis involving other linguistic variables associated with negation should extend the rich insights provided in Tottie's research.

Table 3.51 Distribution of negation types with *be, have* and lexical verbs
(from Tottie, 1991a: 194)

Verb	Negation type	Spoken sample	Written sample
be 'copula'	*not*-neg	58	65
	no-neg	14 (19%)	36 (36%)
		72	101
Existential *be*	*not*-neg	5	2
	no-neg	35 (88%)	111 (98%)
		40	113
Stative *have*	*not*-neg	12	2
	no-neg	21 (64%)	48 (96%)
		33	50
Non-stative *have*	*not*-neg	8	2
	no-neg	2	6
		10	8
Lexical verbs	*not*-neg	113	98
	no-neg	27 (19%)	88 (46%)
		140	186
Totals	*not*-neg	196	169
	no-neg	99	289
		295	458

3.3.2.6 CLEFTING

The use of corpora to compare spoken and written genres in their use of particular syntactic processes is illustrated in Collins (1987). Cleft and pseudo-cleft sentences permit the highlighting and topicalization of sentence elements as in the following examples:

Non-cleft: *Fred gave Max a ride.*
Cleft: *It was Fred who gave Max a ride.*
              It was Max who Fred gave a ride to.
              It was a ride that Fred gave Max.
Pseudo-cleft: *What Fred did was give Max a ride.*

Collins reported that in a study of cleft and pseudo-cleft constructions in the *LLC* and *LOB* corpora, pseudo-clefts were more than three times as frequent as clefts in spoken texts whereas clefts outnumbered pseudo-clefts in writing by 1.3 to 1. In the more private or intimate texts of spoken conversation, pseudo-clefts were particularly favoured, while clefting in written texts was most prominent in the texts which expressed factual material rather than texts which recorded opinions. Thus variation in the use of clefting and pseudo-clefting is seen to move somewhat systematically according to genre and medium along a scale from intimacy to formality, or perhaps from interactive dialogue between equals to more public non-interactive domains of use.

3.4 Pragmatics and spoken discourse

The development of corpus linguistics from the 1960s coincided with a developing interest in the social and pragmatic functions of spoken language, and in the study of discourse units that could be part of, or larger than, the sentence. Whether sociolinguistic or pragmatic variables are associated with the choice by a speaker at the dinner table who says *May I have the salt please* rather than *Would you mind passing the salt* and whether either utterance functions as a request or a covert criticism of the cook, will depend on circumstances. What we say and how we say it is influenced by who we are talking to and where and when the interaction is taking place.

Whereas the units of written discourse have typically been the word, phrase, clause and sentence, spoken discourse has typically been studied in tone units, which contain significant discourse particles, pausing, overlap and other phenomena in addition to lexical and syntactic features. The literature on the linguistic analysis and description of discourse is replete with often quite small qualitative case studies which illustrate the characteristics of spoken interaction and the semantic and pragmatic functions of utterances.

Until the mid-1990s, corpus-based studies which quantify the use of discourse features were severely constrained because there was only one reasonably large, publicly available corpus of spoken English, the *London–Lund Corpus*, which had sufficient markup of prosodic and discourse features to make automatic analysis possible. The *London–Lund Corpus* has been an indispensable treasure trove for the analysis of discourse, in spite of limitations in the representativeness of its participants and the situations of discourse which we noted earlier. Many of the most significant studies based on the *London–Lund Corpus* have come from a group of scholars associated with Lund University in Sweden, where the machine-readable version of the spoken sections of the *SEU Corpus* was prepared. Svartvik (1990b) has described both the preparation of the electronic corpus and some of the studies of discourse at Lund based on the corpus. Altenberg (1990), for example, demonstrated the sheer volume of discourse items, which have fundamental pragmatic functions in speech for planning and structuring interactive discourse, for softening or intensifying what is being said and for providing feedback through backchannelling. Altenberg studied a 50,000-word sample from the *London–Lund Corpus*, and found a total of 4,516 such discourse items, as shown in Table 3.52. These items, as a category, are more frequent than such well-established word classes as prepositions, adverbs, determiners, conjunctions and adjectives. Yet, discourse items are not easily described by traditional grammatical structure with its focus on propositions rather than pragmatics.

Svartvik (1980) described the behaviour in conversation of one of these devices, the word *well*, in a 45,000-word sample from the *LLC*, as in:

... and I sáid well I | don't reàlly think I could wrìte (S1.3.6)
... oh wéll | of course | he'll be working with óverseas students ...
    (S1.2.45)

Well as a discourse particle ranked as the 14th most frequent lexical item in conversation (Svartvik 1992a), yet the word is rarely or never used in this sense in written English. As Svartvik points out, its importance is as a device to maintain social relationships or as a hesitation device to give the speaker time to plan and keep a turn in an interaction. The pragmatic functions of *well* identified in the corpus included polite disagreement, qualified refusal, reinforcement, modification, indirect and partial answers, and delaying tactics.

> The common denominator of the uses of *well* in the corpus seems to be that of shifting topic focus in discourse. It signals that the speaker is going to shift ground, i.e. that he is going to modify one or more assumptions or expectations which have formed the basis of discourse so far. *Well* signals a modification or partial change in the discourse, i.e. it introduces a part of the discourse that has something in common with what went before but also differs from it to some degree.
> (Svartvik, 1980: 177)

Corpus-based studies of the structure of spoken discourse have also been described by Aijmer (1996), who earlier reported on the function

Table 3.52 Distribution of discourse items in a sample of 50,000 words from the *LLC*
(from Altenberg, 1990: 183)

Types	Frequency
Responses	2237
yes	727
m(hm)	658
no	259
yea(h)	217
oh	170
quite	35
I see	29
that's right	22
ah	17
right	15
others	88
Hesitators	1,226
ə (:)h	767
ə (:)m	430
m	29
Softeners	438
you know	212
you see	119
I mean	102
others	5
Initiators	401
well	365
now	35
others	11
Hedges	95
sort of	82
sort of thing	10
others	3
Expletives (*God, heavens,* etc.)	52
Thanks	21
thank you	17
thanks	4
Apologies	19
sorry	12
others	7
Attention signals (*hey, look*)	6
Response elicitors (*eh, right*)	6
Politeness markers (*please*)	5
Orders (e.g. *give over*)	5
Others (greetings, etc.)	5
Total	4,516

of the hedging devices *sort of* and *kind of* in the *London–Lund Corpus* (Aijmer, 1984). These are among the most frequent hedging devices and are typical of those which allow the speaker planning time in informal conversation and which make reference deliberately less precise. In 34 texts from the *LLC*, each of 5,000 words, there were 553 occurrences of *sort of*, ranging between 3 and 73 tokens per text (e.g. *she could sort of slip things in inside pockets*), showing the influence of genre, topic, and degree of formality.

Although *sort of* can function as a hedge before content word classes such as nouns, verbs, adjectives and adverbs, 62% of the tokens in Aijmer's 170,000-word corpus were modifiers of NPs (e.g. *they're sort of pieces, I had a sort of dinner given for me . . .*). On 26 occasions, *sort of* collocated with *you know* (e.g. *I've always believed in having a sort of you know . . . evenings for doing one's hobbies*).

Sort of and *kind of* can soften the intensity of discourse, promote informality, and give the speaker more planning time. They can also protect the speaker from being accused of being too categorical, of exaggerating, or being inaccurate, in that the speaker pre-empts potential criticism by saying he or she is only approximating. The effect of the use of *sort of* or *kind of* can thus facilitate communication by making the impact of an utterance less disruptive. Aijmer (1986) has further explored the role of *sort of* and many other hedges in the *LLC* and *LOB* corpora and considered their function when they occur in different positions in the sentence. Table 3.53 shows the relative frequency of some of the most common hedges in her 170,000 word sample from the *LLC* and the whole of the *LOB Corpus*. Of the hedges listed in Table 3.53, only *in any way, somehow* and *so-called* have a higher incidence in writing than in speech when the

Table 3.53 Frequencies in spoken and written corpora of some individual hedges
(from Aijmer, 1986: 10)

Hedge	LLC	LOB
sort of	553	117
kind of	81	153
as it were	15	17
in a sense	12	7
in a way	21	17
in any way	2	17
somehow	8	64
so to speak	9	4
more or less	18	36
so-called	3	31

size of each corpus is taken into account. All the others are overwhelm-ingly more frequent in speech.

Many other discourse studies which have used corpora have also focused on the use of individual word forms, perhaps in part because of available software which facilitated lexical retrieval and analysis. Stenström (1990), for example, has described how lexical items peculiar to spoken English function in text. Typically they do not contribute significantly to the propositional content but rather to the interactive and pragmatic functions of discourse, including turn-taking and the backchannels char-acteristic of spoken discourse. In 10 texts of spontaneous dialogue from the *LLC* totalling some 50,000 words, Stenström identified the 16 dis-course categories illustrated in Table 3.54.

Table 3.54 Categories of discourse items in the *LLC* (Stenström, 1990: 144)

Discourse item categories	Examples
Apologies	*pardon, sorry, excuse me, I'm sorry, I beg your pardon*
Smooth-overs	*don't worry, never mind*
Hedges	*kind of, sort of, sort of thing*
Expletives	*damn, gosh, hell, fuck off, good heavens, the hell, for goodness sake, good heavens above, oh bloody hell*
Greetings	*hi, hello, good evening, good morning, Happy New Year, how are you, how do you do*
Initiators	*anyway, however, now*
Negative	*no*
Orders	*give over, go on, shut up*
Politeness markers	*please*
Q-tags	*is it, isn't it*
Responses	*ah, fine, good, uhuh, oh, OK, quite, really, right, sure, all right, fair enough, I'm sure, I see, that's good, that's it, that's right, that's true, very good*
Softeners	*I mean, mind you, you know, you see, as you know, do you see*
Thanks	*thanks, thank you*
well	*well*
Exemplifiers	*say*
Positive	*mhm, yeah, yes, yup*

The extent to which discourse items are a characteristic of dialogue rather than spoken monologue (or written English) is illustrated in

Stenström's comparison of two texts from the *LLC*, one of a couple talking over lunch and the other a monologue in which a speaker reminisces to an audience. Table 3.55 shows that the dialogue contains an overwhelming preponderance of discourse items.

Table 3.55 Categories of discourse items in dialogue and monologue
(from Stenström, 1990: 149)

Item	Dialogue	Monologue	Total
Organizing			
well	37	10	47
Softeners	33	4	37
Expletives	13	1	14
Initiators	3	7	10
Hedges	7	–	7
Exemplifiers	1	–	1
Interpersonal			
Positive	97	–	97
Negative	28	–	28
Responses	20	–	20
Q-tags	16	–	16
Apologies	4	–	4
Orders	4	–	4
Politeness markers	2	–	2
Thanks	1	–	1
Total	266	22	288

A study by Stenström (1987) of *really* in a sample from the *London–Lund Corpus* and in the whole *LOB Corpus* is another fine example of corpus-based research on the function of discourse items. Whereas *really* occurs with a frequency of 3.17 per 1,000 words in the *LLC*, it occurs only 0.31 times per 1,000 words in the *LOB Corpus*. Fifteen percent of the uses of *really* in the *LLC* are as a discourse item (1990: 162) with five major functions including 'intensifier', 'evaluator', 'reopener', 'go-on', 'planner'. Stenström's analysis of *really* illustrates well how an item which is traditionally described in grammatical terms as a member of a word class can be alternatively and at least as insightfully described in terms of its interactive function. While in the *LOB Corpus*, Stenström found no instances of *really* as re-opener, go-on or planner, she found that in speech *really* not only occurs frequently with these functions but is significantly associated with particular positions and prosodic contours.

In their comprehensive grammar, Quirk et al. (1985: 589) described the adverbial category known as amplifiers. They distinguished two subcategories:

(a) 'maximizers' (*absolutely, completely, entirely, utterly*, etc.)
(b) 'boosters' (*very, awfully, terribly, bloody*, etc.)

Boosters do not have the absolute degree of intensity which maximizers have, and can modify words which are gradable or 'scalar' (e.g. *pleasant, beautiful*), whereas maximizers typically modify non-scalar items (e.g. *impossible, wrong*). A study by Altenberg (1991a) illustrates well how a corpus can be used to expand the perspective of even the most comprehensive descriptive grammar by showing how the categories are used, which items are most likely to be used and what items they are used with. Altenberg brought together work on the role of amplifiers in discourse with an account of the recurrent collocations in which they occur in the *LLC*.

Table 3.56 shows not only that boosters are almost five times as frequent as maximizers in spoken discourse but that a few very frequent types account for most of the occurrences. Among the maximizers, *quite* occurred in 58% of all collocations containing a maximizer. Although there are potentially a large number of boosters, only 15 occurred in the *LLC* in recurrent combinations, and only 7 of the 15 items accounted for 98% of the tokens. Overall, boosters combine with a wider range of words and are used more often than the maximizers.

The 25 most frequent amplifier collocations listed in Table 3.57 account for over 58% of all the collocations containing amplifiers in the *London–Lund Corpus*. By focusing only on recurring word combinations in this corpus-based study of amplifiers, Altenberg provides a rich picture of the use of intensification in spoken English. He shows that comparatively few amplifiers are used in collocations, but those that are, are heavily exploited. The study also reveals collocational restrictions such as the basic restriction of maximizers to non-scalar words and of boosters to scalar words, and the tendency of a maximizer such as *absolutely* to collocate with negatives or superlatives.

3.5 Corpus-based studies of variation in the use of English

Many of the quantitative studies referred to in earlier sections of this chapter showed striking differences in aspects of the use of English lexis or grammar in more than one genre, domain of use or national variety as represented in different corpora or different parts of a single corpus. So far the primary focus has been on the linguistic phenomenon, whether it was, for example, modal verb use or negation. Now we return to consider some of these comparisons between genres or varieties more directly.

Table 3.56 Amplifiers in recurrent combinations in the *LLC* (adapted from Altenberg, 1991a: 131–132)

	Number of collocates	
Amplifier	Types	Tokens
Maximizers		
quite	45	230
absolutely	24	70
perfectly	10	39
entirely	7	21
completely	5	16
totally	2	9
fully	2	6
dead	1	2
utterly	1	2
Total	97	395
Boosters		
very	204	1,669
so	66	372
very much	6	134
terribly	14	39
jolly	5	28
extremely	5	20
awfully	7	16
bloody	3	8
particularly	3	7
highly	3	6
deeply	2	4
heavily	2	4
badly	1	2
frightfully	1	2
incredibly	1	2
Total	258	1,945

Computer corpus-based studies of variation in English became possible with the availability of the *Brown Corpus* from 1964. Initially, comparative studies could focus only on lexical and grammatical differences between genres as defined in the 15 subsections of the corpus. More often, as we have seen, comparisons were made between the two major divisions, informative prose (Sections A–J) and imaginative prose

AN INTRODUCTION TO CORPUS LINGUISTICS

Table 3.57 Most frequent amplifier collocations in the *LLC* (from Altenberg, 1991a: 135)

Collocation	Frequency	Amplifier type
very much	343	booster
very good	128	booster
very well	105	booster
so much	92	booster
very nice	92	booster
thank you very much	87	booster
so many	68	booster
very difficult	61	booster
very interesting	56	booster
thanks very much	35	booster
very little	35	booster
quite sure	28	maximizer
very long	27	booster
very important	24	booster
very often	24	booster
very happy	23	booster
jolly good	17	booster
very different	17	booster
very few	16	booster
quite clear	15	maximizer
very hard	15	booster
very pleasant	15	booster
quite right	14	maximizer
very small	14	booster
quite certain	13	maximizer

(Sections K–R), within the single variety of written American English. However, the subsequent availability of the *LOB Corpus* made possible studies of regional variation, and then, with the availability of the *LLC*, comparison between spoken and written varieties of English based on corpus analysis became possible. When the *Helsinki Corpus* became available, it supported studies of diachronic variation. In this section we will consider some of the corpus-based studies which set out to identify and compare the linguistic characteristics of different varieties of English.

3.5.1 *Comparisons of spoken and written English*

Until the 1990s when new corpora containing spoken texts began to become available, the major corpus for research on spoken English and of comparison between spoken and written English was the prosodically analysed, machine-readable *London–Lund Corpus*. Svartvik (1990b) contains a comprehensive bibliography of publications which report research based on the *LLC*. It shows that there was a considerable number of studies of prosodic, lexical and grammatical aspects of spoken English, many of which have been associated with the Text Segmentation for Speech (TESS) project at Lund University.

An excellent example of a comparison of aspects of spoken and written English was reported by Altenberg's (1994) analysis of the differences in how a high frequency function word *such* is used in the *LLC* and the *LOB Corpus*. Like many other function words, *such* can be used in more than one word class and has semantic diversity within a word class. Altenberg (1994: 236–237) has shown that there are very distinct distributions in the two corpora. In the more formal written texts of the *LOB Corpus* (Sections A–J), the use of *such* is more than three times as common as in the spontaneous, more informal spoken texts of the *LLC*. However, this predominance of *such* in written texts is confined to the use of *such* as an identifier (e.g. *never had such a thing been thought of*), which is seven times as common in the *LOB Corpus* as in the *LLC*. On the other hand, the use of *such* as an intensifier predominates in the *LLC* (e.g. *it's such a bore*).

Altenberg's analysis included the relative frequencies of use in different genres of *LOB* as well as the private conversation and public genre sections of the *LLC*. For example, while intensifying *such* has a similar likelihood of occurrence in private conversations and public discourse in the *LLC*, identifying *such* is significantly less common in private conversation. Interpreting the differences in distribution in terms of an historical functional shift towards intensification illustrates the value of a corpus-based distributional analysis to reveal differences which are characterized by tendencies towards functional change rather than by absolute distinctions.

Striking differences between spoken and written texts in the distribution of the different senses of homomorphic words is also apparent when we compare the *LLC* and the *LOB Corpus*. By way of example, the word *pretty* has three main uses as an adjective or intensifying adverbial, as shown in Table 3.58. Whereas the written corpus has 44% of the occurrences of *pretty* associated with nouns such as *girls, shoes, picture*, the spoken corpus, also compiled in the 1960s, has only 4% of occurrences as an adjective. In spoken English, *pretty* functions mainly as an intensifier.

As more spoken language corpora become available for research, more dramatic differences in the lexicon between speech and writing are likely to become apparent. A hint of what can be expected from such research is contained in a brief comparison of parts of the *British National Corpus* reported by Summers (1992), who noted that the words *really, right* and

Table 3.58 Uses of *pretty* in the *London–Lund* and *LOB* corpora

Function of *pretty*	London–Lund Corpus		LOB Corpus	
	Tokens	%	Tokens	%
adjective (*pretty flower*)	5	4	45	44
intensifier before adjective (*pretty horrible weather*)	95	79	37	36
intensifier before adverb (*pretty clearly seen*)	20	17	21	20
Total	120	100	103	100

just have dramatically different frequencies per million words in speech and writing, as shown in Table 3.59.

Table 3.59 Lexical differences in speech and writing

	Spoken English	Written English
really	2,249	425
right	4,623	720
just	5,122	1,092

A good example of comparison of the use of certain grammatical items in spoken and written corpora is Johansson's (1993) study of the use of restrictive and non-restrictive relative combinations introduced by *whose* and *of which*. She found that both of these relative markers occur about five times more frequently in written English than in spoken English, with *whose* occurring three times more often than *of which*.

There are clearly major differences between speech and writing when lexical use is compared. Grammatical studies suggest that the picture may not be so clear. A study by Greenbaum and Nelson (1995) of the complexity of clause relationships in speech and writing compared six genres in an 84,000-word sample from the British section of the *International Corpus of English*. Spontaneous conversations had the highest proportion of simple clauses and the lowest proportion of subordination and coordination. For all other genres, including personal handwritten letters, academic writing, and broadcast discussions there were no significant distinctions between speech and writing in any of a variety of measures of syntactic complexity used. The conclusion reached is that within each mode, there is considerable variation, and this variation tends to be greater than that between speech and writing as such. This conclusion is similar to that reached earlier by Biber (1988).

Subsequent work by Greenbaum et al. (1996) has shown how revealing a close manual analysis of a modest-sized corpus can be for comparative studies. Complement clauses are the most frequent subordinate clauses, with *that*-clauses preferred over clauses with zero complementizers in formal categories of speech and writing. The most notable distinction reported, and one of considerable significance for language education, was that in spoken texts the majority of complement clauses are finite, while, in writing, non-finite complements are the most frequent.

A very different direction in comparative studies of speech and writing based on corpora was taken in a study by Biber (1988), based on pioneering earlier work on the typology of text types (Biber & Finegan, 1986), in which a multi-feature, multi-dimensional, statistical basis for the study of linguistic variation was outlined. In an important series of studies these authors have demonstrated the value of computational analysis of corpora to show that variation and text classification are matters of degree rather than all-or-none phenomena.

Biber (1988) and (1989) described how 67 'linguistic features' were identified in an almost one-million-word sample from *LOB* and the *LLC*. These linguistic features are listed in Figure 3.9 and were counted in each of the 481 texts sampled. Using factor analysis, the patterns of co-occurrence of the 67 linguistic features were then identified to establish a number of major dimensions on which texts could vary. Particular texts or groups of texts could in this way be seen as having linguistic dimensions in common.

Thus, instead of defining genre or register on the basis of mode, domain of use, or function (speech vs writing; conversation vs public speech; newspaper writing vs fiction), Biber's approach has been to find which texts have common syntactic and lexical features and to establish typologies of texts according to whether they reflect the factorial dimensions. Text types are defined so that they are maximally similar or distinct linguistically rather than functionally. These differences are then interpreted functionally, so that text types are considered to represent functional types with particular linguistic characteristics. Biber has argued that 'the variation among texts within speech and writing is often as great as the variation across the two modes' (1988: 24). Rather than treating newspaper texts, for example, as representing a genre, Biber has suggested that 'genre distinctions do not adequately represent the underlying text types of English . . . ; linguistically distinct texts within a genre represent different text types; linguistically similar texts from different genres represent a single text type' (1989: 6).

AN INTRODUCTION TO CORPUS LINGUISTICS

Figure 3.9 Features used in Biber's multi-feature, multi-dimensional analysis of variation
(from Biber, 1988: 73–75)

A. Tense and aspect markers
    1. past tense
    2. perfect aspect
    3. present tense

B. Place and time adverbials
    4. place adverbials (e.g. *above, beside, outdoors*)
    5. time adverbials (e.g. *early, instantly, soon*)

C. Pronouns and pro-verbs
    6. first-person pronouns
    7. second-person pronouns
    8. third-person personal pronouns (excluding *it*)
    9. pronoun *it*
    10. demonstrative pronouns *(that, this, these, those* as pronouns)
    11. indefinite pronouns (e.g. *anybody, nothing, someone*)
    12. pro-verb *do*

D. Questions
    13. direct WH-questions

E. Nominal forms
    14. nominalizations (ending in *-tion, -ment, -ness, -ity*)
    15. gerunds (participial forms functioning as nouns)
    16. total other nouns

F. Passives
    17. agentless passives
    18. *by*-passives

G. Stative forms
    19. *be* as main verb
    20. existential *there*

H. Subordination features
    21. *that* verb complements (e.g. *I said that he went.*)
    22. *that* adjective complements (e.g. *I'm glad that you like it.*)
    23. WH-clauses (e.g. *I believed what he told me.*)
    24. infinitives
    25. present participial clauses (e.g. *Stuffing his mouth with cookies, Joe ran out the door.*)
    26. past participial clauses (e.g. *Built in a single week, the house would stand fifty years.*)
    27. past participial WHIZ deletion relatives (e.g. *the solution produced by this process*)
    28. present participial WHIZ deletion relatives (e.g. *the event causing this decline is . . .*)
    29. *that* relative clauses on subject position (e.g. *the dog that bit me*)
    30. *that* relative clauses on object position (e.g. *the dog that I saw*)
    31. WH-relatives on subject position (e.g. *the man who likes popcorn*)
    32. WH-relatives on object position (e.g. *the man who Sally likes*)
    33. pied-piping relative clauses (e.g. *the manner in which he was told*)
    34. sentence relatives (e.g. *Bob likes fried mangoes, which is the most disgusting thing I've ever heard of.*)
    35. causative adverbial subordinators (*because*)
    36. concessive adverbial subordinators (*although, though*)
    37. conditional adverbial subordinators (*if, unless*)
    38. other adverbial subordinators (e.g. *since, while, whereas*)

continued

Figure 3.9 continued

I. Prepositional phrases, adjectives and adverbs
    39. total prepositional phrases
    40. attributive adjectives (e.g. *the big horse*)
    41. predicative adjectives (e.g. *the horse is big*)
    42. total adverbs

J. Lexical specificity
    43. type/token ratio
    44. mean word length

K. Lexical classes
    45. conjuncts (e.g. *consequently, furthermore, however*)
    46. downtoners (e.g. *barely, nearly, slightly*)
    47. hedges (e.g. *at about, something like, almost*)
    48. amplifiers (e.g. *absolutely, extremely, perfectly*)
    49. emphatics (e.g. *a lot, for sure, really*)
    50. discourse particles (e.g. sentence-initial *well, now, anyway*)
    51. demonstratives

L. Modals
    52. possibility modals (*can, may, might, could*)
    53. necessity modals (*ought, should, must*)
    54. predictive modals (*will, would, shall*)

M. Specialized verb classes
    55. public verbs (e.g. *assert, declare, mention, say*)
    56. private verbs (e.g. *assume, believe, doubt, know*)
    57. suasive verbs (e.g. *command, insist, propose*)
    58. *seem* and *appear*

N. Reduced forms and dispreferred structures
    59. contractions
    60. subordinator *that* deletion (e.g. *I think [that] he went*)
    61. stranded prepositions (e.g. *the candidate that I was thinking of*)
    62. split infinitives (e.g. *he wants to convincingly prove that . . .*)
    63. split auxiliaries (e.g. *they are objectively shown to . . .*)

O. Coordination
    64. phrasal coordination (NOUN *and* NOUN; ADJ *and* ADJ; VERB *and* VERB; ADV *and* ADV)
    65. independent clause coordination (clause-initial *and*)

P. Negation
    66. synthetic negation (e.g. *no answer is good enough for Jones*)
    67. analytic negation (e.g. *that's not likely*)

The multi-dimensional structure of variation, with each 'dimension' consisting of a distinct set of co-occurring linguistic features, is characterized in terms of five main dimensions (1993a: 229).

1 Informational vs involved production
2 Narrative vs non-narrative concerns
3 Explicit (situation-independent) vs situation-dependent reference
4 Overt expression of persuasion
5 Abstract vs non-abstract style

Biber has also explored other dimensions associated with academic hedging/qualification and informational elaboration. His analysis of the factorial structure of the main dimensions shows how different text categories can be shown to reflect different dimensions. (Figure 3.10 shows the factorial structure of dimensions 1 and 5 of Biber's model.) On dimension 1, both scientific and medical prose have very high scores on features such as heavy nominalization and prepositional use and low occurrence of such features as private verbs (*think, feel, suppose*) or *that*-deletion. On dimension 5, scientific and medical texts also have substantial scores, which reflect the high occurrence of such features as conjunctions, agentless passives, and past participial WHIZ deletion (e.g. *the person named in the report*). Figure 3.11 from Biber et al. (1994: 182) shows how 10 spoken and written registers have strikingly different linguistic characteristics when the texts are mapped to show just dimensions 1 and 5 of the model.

The fact that a spoken and a written text can have more in common linguistically than two spoken texts or two written texts should not be surprising, but the empirical basis provided means that prior assumptions based on intuition or commentary can be given a linguistic rather than a functional or thematic starting point.

Biber's approach to variation in speech and writing, which combines corpus-based analysis with a greater use of computational support than most corpus linguists have used, has produced a methodology which can be used to show the extent to which any texts are similar or different. Biber has also explored this approach with historical, regional and cross-linguistic variation. An important application of the approach has been to variation in referential strategies in speech and writing (Biber, 1992), taking automatic analysis of text beyond the normal focus on vocabulary and grammar.

Further refinement of the model can be expected to remove some of the more problematic aspects of this approach. It is not hard, for example, to add to the 67 linguistic features in Figure 3.9 which form the basis of the typology, although Biber and Finegan (1991) have argued that the linguistic variables are not arbitrarily selected, but are statistically related to their function in texts. Some of the text types established by the factor analysis do not seem to be clearly different from each other. For example, the types 'learned' and 'scientific' exposition (Biber, 1989) may differ only in some cases because of a higher incidence of active verbs in the 'learned' text type.

Further, as Svartvik (1992a) has suggested, from the point of view of ordinary users of a language, the gap between spoken and written language may be greater than Biber's analysis suggests because outside of a corpus, speech is a process not a product, and is thus subject to dynamic characteristics including real-time constraints which are radically different from the constraints associated with written language. The interactive nature of dialogue, often involving less explicit marking, together with the role of prosody and the highly significant role of discourse items

CORPUS-BASED DESCRIPTIONS OF ENGLISH

Dimension 1: involved vs informational		
more involved	private verbs	.96
	that-deletion	.91
	contractions	.90
	present-tense verbs	.86
	2nd person pronouns	.86
	do as pro-verb	.82
	analytic negation	.78
	demonstrative pronouns	.76
	general emphatics	.74
	1st person pronouns	.74
	pronoun *it*	.71
	be as main verb	.71
	causative subordination	.66
	discourse particles	.66
	indefinite pronouns	.62
	general hedges	.58
	amplifiers	.56
	sentence relatives	.55
	WH-questions	.52
	possibility modals	.50
	non-phrasal coordination	.48
	WH-clauses	.47
	final prepositions	.43
	(adverbs	.42)
	(conditional subordination	.32)
	nouns	−.80
	word length	−.58
	prepositions	−.54
	type/token ratio	−.54
	attributive adjectives	−.47
	(place adverbials	−.42)
	(agentless passives	−.39)
more	(past participial WHIZ deletions	−.38)
informational	(present participial WHIZ deletions	−.32)

Dimension 5: abstract vs non-abstract style		
abstract	conjuncts	.48
	agentless passives	.43
	past participial clauses	.42
	by-passives	.41
	past participial WHIZ deletions	.40
	other adverbial subordinators	.39
	(predicative adjectives	.31)
non-abstract	type/token ratio	−.31

Figure 3.10 Factorial structure of two text-type dimensions
(based on Biber, 1988: 102)

189

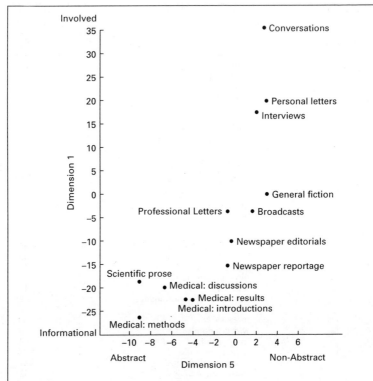

Figure 3.11 Linguistic characterization of 10 spoken and written registers with respect to dimension 1, 'Involved versus informational production', and dimension 5, 'Non-abstract versus abstract style' (from Biber et al., 1994: 182)

noted earlier, are all well-attested characteristics of spoken language which are not normally part of written language, but are outside the scope of Biber's model.

3.5.2 Comparisons of regional varieties of English

Systematic corpus-based study of linguistic and pragmatic differences between regional varieties of English will be greatly enhanced by the availability of the various sub-corpora of the *ICE* project discussed in Section 2.3.3.4. Up to the mid-1990s the major basis for comparison of regional varieties using corpora has been the *Brown* and *LOB* corpora and those such as the *Kolhapur*, *Wellington* and *Macquarie* corpora which have similar structures.

Comparisons of British and American written texts based on the *Brown* and *LOB* corpora have tended to find fewer grammatical differences between these varieties than many people would have expected. Apart from phonological differences, which cannot of course be compared in these two corpora of written texts, the main differences are lexical, although these differences do not show among the most frequent lexical items. Table 3.3 shows that the 50 most frequent words in the *Brown* and *LOB* corpora are almost the same. There are only two exceptions and these are minor. The word *so* is the only word in the *LOB* top 50 which does not occur in the *Brown* top 50. *So* is ranked 52 in the *Brown Corpus*. On the other hand, *more* is number 48 in the *Brown Corpus* but it is ranked number 51 in *LOB*.

LOB and *Brown* made possible the corpus-based comparative study of equivalent varieties of American and British English, even though they represent only a selection of genre types, the texts are of written not spoken varieties, and there is some variation in use between categories within each corpus. Some represent printing type (e.g. newspapers), others represent readership (popular lore, belles lettres) and others represent topic type (e.g. religion, science fiction).

Linguistic and cultural differences between these two corpora from the 1960s have been identified by Johansson (1980: 26) by comparing the occurrence of lower frequency content words which were more likely to be found in one corpus rather than the other. Johansson adopted a simple difference coefficient to indicate whether a word might be considered to be over- or under- represented in a corpus.

$$\frac{Freq.\ \text{LOB} - Freq.\ \text{Brown}}{Freq.\ LOB + Freq.\ Brown}$$

In indicating the relative frequency of a word in the two corpora the coefficient value varies between +1.00 and −1.00 and a positive value indicates over-representation in *LOB* and a negative value indicates over-representation in *Brown*. The list of words in Figure 3.12 confirms the intuitions many speakers of New Zealand English have about which words are more likely to be found in British usage or American usage. New Zealand undergraduates can assign about 90% of these accurately as being characteristic of either American or British English.

An imaginative attempt to compare vocabulary use in the *Brown* and *LOB* corpora as a window on possible social, political and cultural differences between American and British English is contained in the report of a study by Leech and Fallon (1992). By using the same formula employed by Johansson (1980) to indicate whether a word was over- or under-represented in a corpus, Leech and Fallon studied the distinctive vocabulary of specific domains including sport, travel and transport, administration and politics, social hierarchy, the military, law and crime,

---

+0.50 to +1.00

accommodation, acquaintances, advertisement, afterwards, alderman, amongst, barrister(s), beforehand, booklet, borough(s), borstal, castle, chap(s), cheque, cinema(s), commonwealth, constable, constituency, councillor(s), cricket, cupboard, draught, estates, excellency, exchequer, exhaust, expenditure, firstly, flats, forecast(s), fortnight, gaol, gentry, grey, grid, guinea(s), hairdresser, hitherto, holiday, icing, incomes, jug(s), keen, kin, lads, lodgings, lorry, ltd., madam, maiden, minister, ministry, monarch(y), mum, owing, packet, parish, parliament(ary), petrol, premises, prisoner, railway(s), registrar, rightly, ruler, scales, scheme(s), secondly, shareholders, shilling, sir, specially, spectacles, tea, thirdly, turnover, vicar, ware, whence, whilst, withdrawal, yacht

−0.50 to −1.00

accommodations, afterward, ain't, apartment(s), assignment(s), attorney, auto, automobile(s), barbecue, baseball, basement, billion(s), boost, bulletin, businessman, cafeteria, calendar, campus, candy, carryover, cents, chores, closet, commerce, confederate, congress(ional), congressman, cop(s), cowboy, currently, dealer(s), desegregation, detergent, determine, dollar(s), downtown, driveway, elevator, ethnic, fallout, fled, formulas, freight, gasoline, gonna, gotten, governor, graduate, grandma, gray, guy, highway(s), jazz, Jr., kid, legislature, lest, liquor, lobby, locate, location(s), lots, lumber, missile, movie(s), Negro, network, onto, percent, phoney, prairie, railroad(s), ranch, realtors, Republican(s), salesman, salesmen, sauce, shear, sidewalk, someday, sponsor, streetcar, therapist, trailer(s), transportation, truck(s), turnpike, unwed, uptown, utility, vacation(s), veterans, wagon(s), wildlife, yell

Figure 3.12 Some words with a high difference coefficient in the *LOB* and *Brown* corpora
(from Johansson, 1980: 27–28)

---

news media, business, science and technology, education, the arts and religion. The broad picture which emerges from a comparison of the two corpora, compiled from texts published in 1961, is a picture at that time of US culture 'masculine to the point of machismo, militaristic, dynamic and actuated by high ideals, driven by technology, activity and enterprise – contrasting with one of British culture as more given to temporizing and talking, to benefitting from wealth rather than creating it, and to family and emotional life, less actuated by matters of substance than by considerations of outward status. However much of a caricature, this is not an unconvincing portrayal for those of us who have lived with or in both cultures through recent decades' (1992: 44–45).

Non-trivial syntactic differences between British and American English have been notably harder to find in corpus-based studies. Johansson and Hofland (1989: 23) noted that the relative pronoun *that* is more common in American than in British usage, whereas *which* is more common in British than in American usage. However, because the total number of these relative pronouns is higher in *LOB* than in *Brown*, they made the point that it is not clear whether there are fewer relative clauses used in American English or more relative clauses with zero relativizers, or maybe both.

Mindt and Weber (1989) compared the *Brown* and *LOB* corpora for prepositional use. There were no significant differences in the distribution and use of the six most frequent prepositions (*of*, *in*, *to*, *for*, *with*, *on*). Furthermore, the 81 prepositions which occur in both corpora make up 99.9% of all preposition tokens. The authors concluded that there is a very close distributional correspondence between British and American English in this important grammatical category, which accounts for about 12% of all the words used in each corpus.

A similarly close correspondence between British and American English has already been noted in Table 3.46 which summarizes a study of verb-form use in complex English sentences where the conditional clause is introduced by *if*. Other researchers have noted that there are relatively few non-trivial grammatical differences between British and American English which could affect comprehensibility. A tendency to use more nominalizations in American English has been noted by Trudgill and Hannah (1982) among others.

However Biber's multi-feature approach to a comparison of British and American English reveals a different picture. A preliminary study by Biber (1987) showed that when the patterns of co-occurrence of grammatical features are studied, it is possible to find linguistic evidence to support the intuitive impression that the two varieties are different on more than phonological, lexical and discoursal grounds. Biber compared almost 800 texts from nine written genres from the *Brown* and *LOB* corpora (including press reportage, academic prose and romantic fiction) using an early version of the 'dimensions' established by factor analysis for his comparison of spoken and written English (see Figure 3.10). Biber reported that there are systematic differences between British and American prose as contained in the two corpora. The British genres, for example, have a lower incidence of nominalizations, conjuncts, passives, *it*-clefts, and a higher incidence of place and time adverbials, relative pronouns and subordinator deletion. The American written genres show a consistently higher level of abstractness and formality than their British counterparts in both fiction and non-fiction. Biber (1987: 115) suggests that the systematic differences between British and American written genres along an abstract vs situated dimension may reflect a higher incidence of such linguistic features as nominalization and prepositional phrases in American writing for integrating large amounts of information in clauses. The illustration of how regional varieties can differ on just one of the dimensions identified by Biber has, of course, to be considered along with differences on other dimensions.

Descriptions of major phonological differences between British and American English are fairly well-known, and at the segmental level are effectively summarized in the pronunciation keys to major dictionaries. Tottie (1991b) has used a corpus-based analysis to extend the comparison to pragmatic aspects of conversational style, specifically to compare how British and American speakers give feedback to maintain conversation but without seeking to interrupt or take over the speaker's turn. Even though analyses of corpora had shown that such backchannel items as *m* or *yes* are among the most frequent items in speech (see Section 3.4), they have attracted little research. Tottie's preliminary study showed that in the texts of her corpora, there were major differences in the items used. In American English *yeah*, *mhm*, *hm* and *right* account for 89% of the tokens used. In the British sample from the *LLC*, *yes*, *m*, *no* and *yeah* accounted for 90% of the tokens. American interlocutors gave three times as many backchannels per minute as did the British, and female participants used a greater variety of types. These findings suggest that more extensive comparisons will be worthwhile when new corpora of varieties of spoken English become available.

Linguistic prescriptivism has properly not been fashionable in the second half of the twentieth century but there are nevertheless numerous aspects of English where there is disputed grammatical usage in different regional varieties. Corpus-based descriptions can throw light on many of these matters. For example, *different* can be followed by *from*, *to* or *than*, and language users sometimes have strong views on what they think is normative. Rundell and Stock (1992) provide corpus-based evidence on what words follow *different* in the 30-million-word *Longman-Lancaster Corpus*, which includes spoken and written English from British, American and other sources mainly from the late 20th century. Of the 14,704 tokens of *different* in the corpus, 1,302 are followed by a preposition. Table 3.60 shows the relative frequencies of *from*, *to* and *than* after *different*, and compares Rundell and Stock's findings with use in the smaller one-million-word *Brown* and *LOB* corpora or the half-million-word *LLC*. A consistent pattern emerges. In all corpora, large and small, spoken and written, British and American – even in texts collected throughout a period of 25 or more years – *different from* is much more common than *different to* or *different than*. *Different than* is more common in American than in British texts but is not restricted to American usage. On the evidence of the *Brown Corpus different to* was not likely to be found in American written English in 1961. Table 3.60 provides evidence from yet another area of English of the remarkable stability of the grammar of English from a regional and short-term historical perspective. It also raises the question of how big a corpus needs to be for reliable grammatical information. The evidence of Table 3.60 for the use of *different* suggests that a one-million-word corpus may not be too small for valid and reliable corpus-based grammatical studies, depending on the frequency of the items under investigation.

American and British written English has been compared for the use of modal verbs in different genres in the *Brown* and *LOB* corpora. Nakamura (1993) found significant differences in the use of *could*, *would* and *will* in British and American written usage as represented by the whole corpora. The major difference in distribution occurs in the use of these modals in the texts which make up informative and imaginative genres.

Table 3.60 *Different* in four corpora

	Longman–Lancaster Corpus		Brown Corpus (written US 1961)		LOB Corpus (written UK 1961)		London–Lund Corpus (spoken UK 1960–)	
	Tokens	%	Tokens	%	Tokens	%	Tokens	%
different from	1,193	91.6	40	76.9	38	86.4	31	83.8
different to	75	5.8	0	–	4	9.1	3	8.1
different than	34	2.6	12	23.1	2	4.5	3	8.1
Total	1,302		52		44		37	

In the *Brown Corpus*, for example, *would* was the most frequently used modal in imaginative prose, but was not found to characterize imaginative prose in the *LOB Corpus*.

Comparative studies of the use of modal verbs and other grammatical classes such as adjectives (e.g. *likely*) and adverbs (e.g. *possibly*) which can express modality have been rare because of difficulties in getting corpora which contain similar text types or were compiled at similar times. However, in spite of these and other problems, comparative studies have been undertaken. We have already considered the comparison between the spoken and written use of modals undertaken by Coates (see Section 3.2.2). Shastri (1988) reported that in the *Kolhapur Corpus*, Indian English by and large conforms to modal usage in the *Brown, LOB* and *SEU* corpora.

Collins (1991a, b) has also undertaken studies of modality in an Australian English corpus of about a quarter of a million words and made certain comparisons with studies of British and American use based on parts of the *LLC, LOB* and *Brown* corpora. Table 3.61 illustrates possible regional differences in the use of one of these modals, *must*. Collins shows that in spoken Australian English the epistemic use of *must* is over five times as frequent as the root ('obligation') use, i.e. *you must be joking* is more frequent than *you must tell someone about it*. Collins suggests that *have (got) to* has become the main exponent of obligation at least in informal genres of Australian English. He also shows that for *should* the root use appears to dominate in Australian English to a greater extent than in the other varieties. While the corpora of these varieties of English are not entirely comparable for various reasons cited by Collins, this study is suggestive of the kinds of study which need to be undertaken and which will be facilitated by use of the *ICE* corpora when the various carefully matched sections are completed.

With the completion of the *Wellington Corpus* of New Zealand English and the *Macquarie Corpus* of Australian English, comparisons with the

Table 3.61 *Must* in Australian, British and American English (from Collins, 1991a: 154)

Use	AusE			BrE			AmE
	Speech	Writing	Total	Speech	Writing	Total	Writing
Root	16 (9.1%)	47 (26.7%)	63 (35.8%)	106 (24.3%)	153 (35.1%)	259 (59.4%)	51 (75.0%)
Epistemic	88 (50.0%)	18 (10.2%)	106 (60.2%)	92 (21.1%)	74 (17.0%)	166 (38.1%)	16 (23.5%)
Indeterminate	0 (0.0%)	7 (4.0%)	7 (4.0%)	2 (0.5%)	9 (2.1%)	11 (2.5%)	1 (1.5%)
Total	104 (59.1%)	72 (40.9%)	176 (100.0%)	200 (45.9%)	236 (54.1%)	436 (100.0%)	68 (100.0%)

parallel *Brown*, *LOB* and *Kolhapur* corpora became possible. Bauer (1993b) in an initial comparison of lexical usage in parts of the newspaper sections of the New Zealand, Australian, American and British corpora has noted that New Zealand usage seems to be divided between British and Australian usage. *Film* is preferred to *movie* in New Zealand as it is in Britain, whereas Australian English, while showing a preference for *film*, also has enough occurrences of *movie* to suggest some affinity with American usage.

Thus, as with other studies which compare different regional varieties of English, the evidence so far has shown not that speakers of New Zealand or Australian English have major differences in their grammatical or lexical systems, but rather that they may use particular items or constructions in different proportions from those of other regional varieties.

3.5.3 Variation in registers and genres

In addition to being able to identify ways in which regional varieties of English may differ from each other, computer corpora show promise for studying the stylistic distinctiveness of texts from the point of view of different registers and genres. Crystal (1991) highlighted a problem with a great deal of non-computer-corpus-based sociolinguistic and stylistic work when he suggested that it would be a good idea to generalize a method of 'stylistic profiling' which moved beyond the individualistic and often idiosyncratic case studies typical of many of these non-corpus-based studies.

There was a long series of genre variation studies particularly in the 1960s and 1970s on such topics as the language of advertising or the law and also many anthropological linguistic studies from the time of Boas and Sapir to more recent sociolinguistic studies which were based on purpose-built corpora of written texts, interviews or collected citations. Frequently in these descriptive studies there was surprisingly little or no quantitative or distributional analysis associated with the case study approach to linguistic description. A second major problem already mentioned was that genres were often defined using extralinguistic grounds, in a tradition deriving from classical Greek literary theory which divided works into epic, poetic and dramatic genres, and numerous sub-genres (such as tragedy, comedy, satire). More recently various approaches to the notion of genre have used the term to label various 'folk genres' describing texts from various sources which may be conveniently seen as having something in common (e.g. novels written by women; writing in English by speakers of other languages; political protest writing; fantasy). The term 'genre' is thus now also used to refer to discourse types other than those associated with traditional literary uses. While the term 'register' is sometimes used interchangeably with genre, it has tended to be used to refer to a variety of a language associated with a particular social function such as the language used in a particular kind of workplace. Romaine (1994: 20) has suggested that

> The concept of register is typically concerned with variation in language conditioned by uses rather than users and involves consideration of the situation or context of use, the purpose, subject matter and content of the message, and the relationship of the participants.

Genre and register differences between texts can be defined using extra-linguistic criteria based on function, purpose, communication, situational contexts, role relationships among participants, format, subject matter, degree of intimacy among participants, or simply conventions recognized by users of a language. A sermon may simply 'feel' different from a political speech. It is also possible, however, to be concerned about the linguistic bases of these putative differences.

We have already considered in connection with the study of variation in speech and writing the linguistically defined approach to 'text types' developed by Biber (1988) and Biber and Finegan (1991) involving a multi-feature/multi-dimension model established by multivariate statistical procedures. By showing that English genres can be defined or characterized linguistically and not just notionally or subjectively, Biber showed that some traditional genres can have more linguistic variation within them than exists between so-called different genres. 'Newspapers', for example, can include several quite distinct text types defined according to the co-occurrence of particular linguistic features. Further, as Biber and Finegan (1991) suggest, genre or text-type variation studies are inevitably text-based, whereas grammatical study of a whole corpus may give results which differ little from the results obtained from an equally large sample of unconnected sentences.

In the 1990s there came into being a new generation of very large corpora such as the *British National Corpus* or the *Bank of English*, which contain larger samples from a more balanced and extensive variety of text types and which are at least 100 times larger than the early computer corpora. These make it possible for more detailed reliability studies and for further exploration of the linguistic basis for text types. Further, in light of Biber's work, which showed marked linguistic differences across registers, it is clear that more valid linguistic descriptions of corpora as representations of the language as a whole 'must be based on corpora representing the range of registers' (1993a: 220). The point is that while generalizations about a language as a whole are desirable and necessary, such generalizations can conceal systematic differences which exist between registers. For example, particular collocations which occur with both high and low frequency words tend to be associated with particular registers.

Naturally, the probability of occurrence of a particular word or grammatical combination is dependent on the register it occurs in. This has obvious implications for automatic grammatical tagging or parsing based on stochastic modelling. Biber (1993a: 220) notes, for example, that while relative clauses are frequent in official documents and formal prepared speeches, they are rare in conversation, whereas subordinate adverbial clauses are relatively frequent in conversation but rare in official documentation or in press reporting. In the *LOB Corpus*, the word *admitted* is finite past tense in 77% of occurrences in imaginative sections (K–R) but non-finite past participle in 67% of occurrences in the informative prose sections (A–J).

Biber and Finegan (1994) used multi-dimensional analysis to reveal significant linguistic differences characterizing successive parts of a single text. As various researchers have noted, academic articles reporting experimental research tend to have a four-part IMRD structure – introduction, methods, results, discussion. Biber and Finegan analysed the linguistic characteristics of 19 medical research reports from 1985. They found that on eight linguistic features (*that* verb complements, 'public' verbs, first-person pronouns, possibility modals, present tense, past tense, agentless passives and downtoners) there were significant differences between the four IMRD sections in the extent to which the eight linguistic features co-occur. Although all sections of medical reports lie at the extreme 'informational' end of communication in contrast with more involved or interactive discourse, the point is that a register is not necessarily a homogeneous entity on linguistic grounds but part of a continuum of various combinations of linguistic features. Any text, even within a register which is clearly established on non-linguistic grounds (say, 'informal conversation between two close friends'), may have different linguistically defined subsections. It may move from greetings, to a statement of information by one participant, to an invitation, to reassurance, to persuasion, to agreement, with perhaps a subtext of humour and solidarity, each with characteristic linguistic features.

3.5.4 Studies of language change

The various diachronic corpora described in Section 2.3.2.4 have been the basis of many studies of the development of the morphosyntax and lexis of English. Something of the range of these studies is seen in a number of edited volumes including Rissanen et al. (1993) and Kytö et al. (1994). Research on diachronic corpora has not been restricted to vocabulary and syntactic change. Nevalainen and Raumolin-Brunberg (1994) describe the study of personal letters from Renaissance England for evidence of the effect of sociolinguistic factors, including gender, age, social status and relation to the recipient of the letter, which may have contributed to language change.

In addition to the necessary compilation of diachronic corpora, an activity which has consumed much of the time of diachronic corpus linguists from the mid-1980s, there have been numerous descriptive studies of usually sharply focused aspects of English. There is space to mention only a small number here. Rissanen (1992: 191), for example, compared the occurrence of periphrastic *do* in affirmative statements (*He did see his uncle yesterday*) with that of the progressive *be + ing* construction in the texts from the *Helsinki Corpus* written between 1500 and 1710. Table 3.62 shows that both constructions increased proportionately between the first two 70-year sub-periods containing texts of approximately equal total length, while in the texts from the second half of the 18th century (1640–1710) the occurrence of periphrastic *do* declines markedly. The use of the progressive continues to increase. Rissanen notes that although this data does not prove the two tendencies to be linked, 'it does not seem unlikely in view of the general development of verbal syntax in this crucial period of the history of English' (1992: 191).

Table 3.62 Occurrence of periphrastic *do* in affirmative statements and of the progressive form in Early Modern English sub-periods in the *Helsinki Corpus* (excluding Bible translations) (from Rissanen, 1992: 191)

	EModE1 1500–1570	EModE2 1570–1640	EModE3 1640–1710
do (aff. stat.)	285	447	185
be + ing	25	38	85

An interesting study from a series of pilot studies based on the *Helsinki Corpus* is Peitsara (1993: 219), which shows that the agent phrase in the English passive marked by the preposition *by* achieved a surprisingly early dominance over the alternative preposition agent markers (*from, mid, of, through* and *with*) in the period 1350–1640.

The use of agentive phrases increased over the period from 0.58 per 1,000 words to 1.02 per 1,000. Detailed analysis of occurrence in different genres showed that the agentive phrases were more frequent in more formal genres including statutes, sermons and official correspondence. Initially *of* and *by* were approximately of equal frequency. There were differences between genre, with *of* predominating in philosophy, religious instruction and imaginative narrative. By 1500 the use of *by* was overall three times as frequent as *of* and by 1640 the use of *by* was eight times as frequent as *of*. This corpus-based analysis thus tends to suggest that *by* had established dominance somewhat earlier than has sometimes been believed. Although variation continued even within texts, *of, through, with* and *from* did not continue to have the agent-marking grammatical function to anything like the same extent.

Another good example of how a diachronic corpus can be used to throw light on the history of English syntax is contained in Rissanen (1991), which illustrates the possible association of change with variation. The use of *that* and zero as object noun clause links is traced in the *Helsinki Corpus* from Late Middle English to the 17th century. The corpus evidence suggests that rather than zero being a later 'omission of *that'*, both zero and *that* are ways of linking object clauses to superordinate clauses, and they go back to very early periods in the language.

Incidentally, Rissanen shows how much manual work is still required in such a study of an untagged corpus in which zero elements are part of the analysis; and why high-quality grammatical tagging and parsing are of such importance to the next stage of corpus-based research. The study focuses on variation between zero and *that* after four very frequent verbs – *say, know, think* and *tell* (e.g. *He said (that) he had been ill*) – although it is suggested that the distributions described also hold for other high frequency verbs such as *see* and *hope*. It is suggested that zero was rare in Old English and Early Middle English texts but may have always been the unmarked (more frequent) object clause link in speech, as indicated by its high frequency in verse from Late Middle English. Tables 3.63 and 3.64 show the increased use of zero in written texts, and also indicate differences in the spread of zero with different verbs. Zero developed faster with the 'cognitive' verbs *think* and *know* than with *say* or *tell*. Rissanen also shows that there was a clear preference for zero as a link in particular speech-related genres such as trial records, sermons and comedies. Comparison with written Late Modern English as evidenced in the *LOB Corpus* shows that the increasing use of zero seemed

Table 3.63 Zero and *that* as object clause links in Late Middle English
(Rissanen, 1991: 279)

Verb	1350–1420		1420–1500	
	zero	*that*	zero	*that*
say	35	187	52	107
tell	2	23	8	21
know	1	30	15	24
think	5	30	12	14
Total	43 (14%)	270	87 (34%)	166

Table 3.64 Zero and *that* as object clause links in Early Modern English
(Rissanen, 1991: 279)

Verb	Mod 1 (1500–70)		Mod 2 (1570–1640)		Mod 3 (1640–1710)	
	zero	*that*	zero	*that*	zero	*that*
say	44	80	90	69	102	30
tell	8	20	34	44	56	50
know	23	17	31	27	29	17
think	22	13	86	25	67	11
Total	97 (43%)	130	241 (59%)	165	254 (70%)	108

to come to a halt. After *say* in the *LOB Corpus, that* occurs almost twice as often as an object clause link as does zero. This observation may of course reflect the composition of the two corpora rather than an historical trend. Rissanen discusses the shift in terms of a possible stylistic shift towards more formal ways of writing and syntactic complexity.

Studies of stylistics and the overall linguistic characteristics of an author or period in the history of the language also seem to be highly suited to the multi-dimensional approach developed by Biber and Finegan which was described earlier. Rather than tracing the evolution of a single lexical or morphosyntactic feature it is the systematic co-occurrence of a set of several features characterizing a style or register which is the focus of interest. Biber and Finegan (1988) described the linguistic characteristics of over 80 texts in a corpus of 90,000 words of English prose from the 18th to the 20th century, and showed how these linguistic characteristics of narratives, essays and personal letters changed over the centuries. On two of the dimensions of variation it is suggested that there were quite dramatic stylistic shifts over the three centuries. Eighteenth-century narratives, essays and letters were much more highly explicit, elaborated and context-independent in reference (e.g. with WH-relative clauses on objects, and fewer time and place adverbials) than later examples of these genres, which it is claimed are more markedly situation-dependent. On the dimension of 'abstract versus non-abstract style' a similar style shift occurred over the period studied. The 18th-century narratives and essays are much more highly 'abstract' in style (characterized by the co-occurrence of such features as conjuncts, agentless passives, past participial clauses and WHIZ-deletions) than later examples of these genres. Eighteenth-century and 20th-century letters show less dramatic change.

In this section of the book we have seen that descriptions of aspects of English lexis, morphology, syntax and discourse, based on the distributional analysis of corpora, have added new dimensions to our knowledge of the language. Corpus-based research has not yet explored systematically all aspects of the language. Nevertheless, there is evidence enough to show that new corpus-based descriptions of English such as Greenbaum (1996a) will increasingly be able to give information on the relative frequency of occurrence of items in different varieties of the language. This in turn promises to influence those involved with the teaching of English, in curriculum design, teacher education and classroom instruction. We will explore these and other applications in Chapter 5.

CHAPTER FOUR

Corpus analysis

Corpus-based approaches to language have introduced new dimensions to linguistic description and to various applications by permitting some degree of automatic analysis of text. The identification, counting and sorting of the words, collocations and grammatical structures which occur in a corpus can be carried out quickly and accurately by computer, thus greatly reducing some of the human drudgery sometimes associated with linguistic description, and vastly expanding the empirical basis. During the last decade a great deal of effort has been put into developing software and procedures for automatic corpus annotation. In this chapter, the annotation or pre-analysis of text by lemmatization, tagging and parsing is outlined, and then the major procedures used in corpus analysis are described, including listing, sorting, counting and concordancing. Finally, mention is made of some of the major software tools and packages available for analysing corpora.

At the outset, it should be recognized that there is a wide gulf between the computing resources available for corpus analysis in large commercial, or industrial research facilities, and those typically available for research by graduate students and scholars in most departments of linguistics, English language or applied linguistics. In large research enterprises such as those linked to commercial dictionary projects, teams of researchers typically have at their disposal powerful work stations, linked to fast network resources with huge storage capacities, and purpose-built software. They may also have programmers on hand to deal with problems and to develop new kinds of software for corpus analysis. The speed of change in such contexts can be seen in comparing the resources employed over the last decade or so. Clear (1987) has described the analytical processes developed for handling what were at the time huge amounts of text used in the *Cobuild* project, and the need for new analytical techniques for use by lexicographers working with an electronic corpus. In the *Cobuild* project, new dimensions were added to the lexicographer's craft by the development of software for producing wordlists and concordances and for sorting, classifying, sampling and manipulating huge amounts of data in various ways.

Within a few years the scope of such corpus-based lexicographical analysis had expanded in further directions with hardware and software which brings together information from within a corpus and matches it with other lexicographical or statistical information from external databases. Atkins (1992), for example, has described the *Hector* project, which involves the manual tagging of word senses in text as part of a large lexicographical project for Oxford University Press. In an illustrated description of the detailed stages and decisions which must be taken by the lexicographer using state-of-the-art procedures and powerful software developed for the project, Atkins points out that compiling a lexical database entry for a word such as *punch*, which had about 700 occurrences in a tagged 17-million-word corpus, nevertheless required at least a couple of days' work, and that the very richness of the data able to be retrieved nowadays has greatly complicated the work of the lexicographer. At the same time such richness has provided the basis for vastly improved dictionaries in terms of accuracy, comprehensiveness and perhaps above all ability to indicate collocations and other distributional characteristics of words and word sequences.

Much of the recent innovation in corpus analysis has come from such commercially linked research projects associated especially with the major British publishers of dictionaries, exploring the nature and distribution of words.

A second source of development has been computational linguistics. Researchers from within this interdisciplinary branch of language study have grappled with developing systems and software for the automatic analysis of grammar and meaning, for text analysis, text synthesis, machine translation and other applications employing computationally based processing of natural language. Corpus-based approaches have developed, focusing typically on such tasks as grammatical tagging and parsing, using either rule-based or probabilistic models. (See Section 5.2.)

Several overviews of issues and problems in corpus analysis have been published along with accounts of some of the tools and methods used. An important account of the development of research into probabilistic tagging and parsing undertaken at the Unit for Computer Research on English Language (UCREL) at Lancaster University from 1979 to 1986 is contained in Garside et al. (1987). An alternative rule-governed approach to the automatic analysis of English at the University of Nijmegen has been described by Oostdijk (1991). Briefer discussions by Burnard (1992b), Mair (1991) and Leech (1991) take quite divergent views on directions in corpus analysis. Burnard's essentially optimistic overview of the development of tools for automatic analysis reflects faith in the role of better programming and software to solve problems in analysis.

Mair on the other hand sees automatic analysis as being intrinsically limited in its sensitivity to the nature of discourse. Leech suggests which developments in annotation and analysis are most needed by researchers. He points out that, apart from concordancers and to a lesser extent grammatical tagging systems, there is a dearth of easily available software for retrieving data from corpora and for undertaking linguistic analyses of various kinds. Perhaps the biggest challenge is the need for user-friendly, easily interpretable, robust corpus parsers. As Leech (1993a) has noted in an analysis of the formal requirements for corpus annotation, it would be an advantage if there was as much as possible standardization or harmonization of terminology, annotation systems and means of analysis. During the present developmental phase of tools, systems and methods of analysis, it is probably too much to expect any standardization, especially while there are strongly competing linguistic theories and models of language processing, and in any case it could be argued that competing systems may be the necessary basis for identifying advantages and disadvantages of each.

Some of these issues are explored in later parts of this chapter. The main focus will be on the processes and procedures available for academic research of the type normally carried out on personal computers, using standard software. It will be clear, nevertheless, that, while corpus annotation makes possible the automatic counting of particular word classes or grammatical patterns in a corpus, thus forming the basis for probabilistic parsing of new texts, work in corpus analysis is still very much work in progress.

4.1 Corpus annotation and processing

4.1.1 Lemmatization

If we want a computer to recognize, count or sort the number of words in a text, this may seem to be a straightforward enough task. However, as already discussed in Section 3.1.2, the notion of what a word is has a number of possible interpretations which are well known to students of language. At the most basic level, the 'graphic' word on a page can be defined as a sequence of letters or alphanumeric characters with a space or punctuation mark on each side. In this sense the following paragraph can be said to contain 36 words.

> Words can show differences in use in different contexts. In one context a word like *bank* could refer to the side of a river, while in another, *bank* could be something you do with your money.

It is immediately apparent, however, that these 36 word forms contain several which are related to each other, namely:

word	Words
can	could
differences	different
context	contexts
in	In
you	your

Moreover, counts of graphic words produce some anomalies. For example, *New Zealand* would be counted as two words, and *the United States of America* as five. Hyphenated words such as *by-election* or *by-product* may be counted as two words in each case unless the *by-* occurs at the end of a line, in which case, they may be counted as one word.

The distinction between 'types' and 'tokens' is an important one in counting linguistic items, types being different items and tokens being instances of a type. Thus, the sentence *Words can show differences in use in different contexts* contains eight types. The type *in* has two tokens. However, it is not always clear what constitutes a type. In our 36-word paragraph above, for example, if we decide to consider *context* and *contexts* as variant forms of the same word with or without number marking, or *can* and *could* as the same word with differences in the tense morpheme, then our word count of types and tokens will be affected. That is, if by 'word' we mean 'different words', then the number of words in our example is less than 36. We might wish to argue that the 12 words listed above are really instances from six word families. In addition, the word *a* occurs twice, *in* occurs four times (not all with the same meaning), and *bank* occurs twice but in different word classes (noun and verb) and with completely different meanings.

Transcriptions of spoken language texts by different transcribers can also lead to inconsistencies in graphic word counts. Examples include whether a word is transcribed consistently as *fullback, full-back* or *full back, all right* or *alright, on to* or *onto, okay* or *OK, percent, per cent* or *%*. If words such as these occur with high frequency and are inconsistently transcribed, then the total word count can be significantly affected. Problems in standardizing word forms in transcriptions of spoken texts are discussed by Nelson (1995).

As a way of dealing with these and other potential problems which can affect the counting of linguistic items, analysts commonly treat word forms which are inflectionally or derivationally related to each other as if they are instances of a single word family, known as a lexeme or a lemma. As noted in Section 3.1.2, lemmatization is a process of classifying together all the identical or related forms of a word under a common headword, just as in dictionary-making many of the various morphological inflections or derivations of a word are listed under a single entry. At the same time, many analysts will wish to ensure that homonyms such as *bank* in the above example do not get classified into the same lemma. However, although human analysts can fairly easily recognize different word forms as belonging or not belonging to a common family, it is not at all straightforward attempting to lemmatize automatically by machine. Automatic lemmatizers have nevertheless been developed for several of the large lexicographical and natural language processing projects over the last two decades. Francis and Kučera (1982) provided a lemmatized list of words in the *Brown Corpus* with each headword listed in alphabetical order and subentries for inflectional variants which belong to the same word class (see Figure 3.3). The list was assembled 'largely automatically by computer' (1982: 6).

Lemmatizing can, of course, be done manually, but if a corpus is large, manual analysis can be too formidable a task to contemplate. Eventually analysts should have available reliable, robust and comprehensive automatic lemmatizers suitable for individual use on personal computers. One reason they have not been available is that reliable automatic lemmatizing depends on reliable grammatical tagging and, as we shall see in 4.1.2, most automatic tagging still requires considerable manual input to achieve total accuracy. Grammatical tagging is necessary to indicate to the lemmatizer whether, in a particular case, *banks* is a noun plus plural morpheme or a verb plus third-person singular morpheme, or whether *that* is a determiner or a relative pronoun. It is not enough simply to undertake 'stemming' – that is, removing or ignoring affixes. A 'stemmer' instructed to ignore *-ing* could assume that there is a verb *br*, with a present participle suffix *-ing*, or that *hoping* consists of *hop* + *-ing*. A lemmatizer has to be able to classify together *good/better/best* or *go/goes/went/gone/going*; *tall* and *taller* have to be shown to belong together, but *caper* should not be broken down into *cap* + *-er*; while *sealed* may be analysed as *seal* + *-ed*, *misled* must not be broken down into *misl* + *-ed*. Similarly, *uplifting* may be analysed as *uplift* + *-ing*, while *outstanding* should not be analysed as *outstand* + *-ing*. It is unlikely that researchers will wish to find *seem* and *seemly* in the same lemma. They may also want an automatic lemmatizer to recognize the *de-* in *dethrone, decouple* or *detoxify* as a prefix while seeing the *de-* of *design, decide* or *deposit* as part of the stem.

In order to handle the complexities of English morphology, including irregularities in verb inflections, automatic lemmatizers have typically employed two processes, often in combination. The first process employs a case-by-case method to deal with irregularity, by means of a set of a thousand or so rules. Thus, for example, *go, gone, going, goes, went* can by such a rule be classed under the headword *go*; whenever *better* appears in a text it is listed or counted under the headword *good*; *broke* is classified under *break*.

The second approach to automatic lemmatization is by means of affix stripping. Garside et al. (1987: 157 ff) indicated the necessary complexity of the suffix-stripping rules for the automatic lemmatization of the word forms in the tagged *LOB Corpus*. If a word form does not appear as part of the affix rule system, or is not listed as a specific exception, then the word is listed as a lemma in the same form in which it appears in the text.

Automatic lemmatization of the word forms in a corpus is still in a developmental phase and requires substantial manual input involving subjective decisions, as Sinclair (1991: 41) has noted. Lemmatization can be a useful process for certain purposes but, as we have seen, is neither uncomplicated nor always appropriate, and can in fact mask important differences. For example, if *circumstance* and *circumstances* are correctly seen as variants of a single lemma and merged accordingly, the fact that the plural form accounts for most occurrences in written texts can be lost sight of. It is not always clear that the common practice of listing the forms of a lemma under the noun or verb stem form is necessarily appropriate. For example, the most frequent form may not be the verb *differ* or the noun *difference*, but rather the adjective *different* in a given corpus. That is, which form should be the headword and which belongs to a sub-category is not always obvious.

4.1.2 Word-class tagging

When the first computerized corpus for linguistic analysis, the *Brown Corpus*, was compiled in the 1960s, it was inevitable that the word frequency lists derived by computer from the one million words of 'raw' text would have certain shortcomings. The computer could count and sort word forms, but in doing so it buried or distorted some important facts about the language. Specifically, as we saw in 4.1.1, unless they could be lemmatized, variant inflected forms of nouns and verbs especially would be treated as entirely different word types. Conversely, homographs could not be distinguished. The frequency count of the number of occurrences of the word form *can* in the corpus would include the noun which refers to a metal container as well as the modal auxiliary verb. De Rose (1991: 9) reported on just how frequent grammatical category ambiguity is in the *Brown Corpus*: 'About 11% of word types and 48% of word tokens occur with more than one category label'. He suggested that a larger corpus may show even larger proportions of categorial ambiguity. In the *Brown Corpus* wordlist based on 'raw' text, all occurrences of a verb form such as *removed*, whether as a finite past tense or as a non-finite past participle, were simply counted together. Because manual annotation of each word token with its word class in the corpus would be prohibitively expensive, the solution adopted for the *Brown Corpus* was to design a computer program to annotate automatically every word in the corpus with a 'tag' to show the word class to which it belonged in context. This first project to annotate a major corpus by computer was carried out between 1970 and 1978. Greene and Rubin (1971) describe the computer program known as TAGGIT, which they developed for this purpose. The 87 tags assigned to the word forms in the corpus are shown in Figure 4.1.

As Francis and Kučera (1982: 9) have pointed out, because the purpose of tagging the *Brown Corpus* was primarily to facilitate automatic or semi-automatic syntactic analysis, the tagging was designed especially to mark syntactically significant features. The tagset included major word classes and their inflectional variants, major function words, certain important individual lexemes such as *not*, certain punctuation marks and a small number of discourse markers. In light of subsequent developments in word-class tagging, where in most cases it was found necessary to greatly expand the tagset, the concern of Francis and Kučera that 'a system of 45 "parts of speech" [may seem] rather overspecified' was clearly unfounded.

The TAGGIT program proved able to assign the correct tag automatically to 77% of the word tokens in the *Brown Corpus*. The remaining 23%,

Figure 4.1 The tagset used for tagging the *Brown Corpus*
(Francis & Kučera, 1982: 6–8)

Tag	Description	Examples
.	sentence closer	. ; ? !
(	left parenthesis	([
)	right parenthesis	)]
*	*not, -n't*	
–	dash	
,	comma	
:	colon	
ABL	pre-qualifier	*quite, rather*
ABN	pre-quantifier	*half, all*
ABX	pre-quantifier, double conjunction	
AP	post-determiner	*many, next*
AT	article	*a, the, no*
BE	*be*	
BED	*were*	
BEDZ	*was*	
BEG	*being*	
BEM	*am, -'m*	
BEN	*been*	
BER	*are, -'re*	
BEZ	*is, -'s*	
CC	coordinating conjunction	*and, or*
CD	cardinal numeral	*two, 2*
CS	subordinating conjunction	*if, although*
DO	*do*	
DOD	*did*	
DOZ	*does*	
DT	singular determiner	*this, that*
DTI	singular or plural determiner	*some, any*
DTS	plural determiner	*these, those*
DTX	determiner, double conjunction	*either, neither*
EX	*there* (existential)	
FW	foreign word (hyphenated ahead)	
HL	word in headline (hyphenated after)	

continued

Figure 4.1 continued

Tag	Description	Examples
HV	*have*	
HVD	*had* (past tense), *-'d*	
HVG	*having*	
HVN	*had* (past participle)	
HVZ	*has, hath, -'s*	
IN	preposition	
JJ	adjective	
JJR	comparative adjective	
JJS	semantically superlative adjective	*chief, main, top*
JJT	morphologically superlative adjective	
MD	modal auxiliary	*can, may, could*
NC	cited word (hyphenated after)	
NN	singular or mass noun	
NN$	possessive singular noun	
NNS	plural noun	
NNS$	possessive plural noun	
NP	singular proper noun	
NP$	possessive singular proper noun	
NPS	plural proper noun	
NPS$	possessive plural proper noun	
NR	adverbial noun	*home, west, tomorrow*
NR$	possessive adverbial noun	
NRS	plural adverbial noun	
OD	ordinal numeral	*second, 2nd*
PN	nominal pronoun	*everybody, nothing*
PN$	possessive nominal pronoun	
PP$	possessive personal pronoun	*my, your, our*
PP$$	second possessive personal pronoun	
PPL	singular reflexive personal pronoun	*myself, herself*
PPLS	plural reflexive pronoun	*ourselves, themselves*
PPO	objective personal pronoun	*me, us, him*
PPS	3rd singular nominative pronoun	*he, she, it*
PPSS	other nominative pronoun	*I, we, they*
QL	qualifier	*very, too, extremely*
QLP	post-qualifier	*enough, indeed*
RB	adverb	
RBR	comparative adverb	
RBT	superlative adverb	
RN	nominal adverb	*here, then*
RP	adverb or particle	*across, off, up*
TL	word in title (hyphenated after)	
TO	infinitive marker	*to*
UH	interjection, exclamation	
VB	verb, base form	
VBD	verb, past tense	
VBG	verb, present participle, gerund	
VBN	verb, past participle	
VBZ	verb, 3rd singular present	
WDT	WH-determiner	*what, which*
WP$	possessive WH-pronoun	*whose*
WPO	objective WH-pronoun	*whom, which, that*
WPS	nominative WH-pronoun	*who, which, that*
WQL	WH-qualifier	*how*
WRB	WH-adverb	*how, when*

some 230,000 words, had to be tagged 'manually by a series of persons over a period of nearly ten years' (Francis & Kučera, 1982: 9). The *Brown* tagset is organized mainly on a categorial rather than functional basis. An automatic processor has little basis for being able to detect a relative clause with a zero relative marker in such a system. Within corpus linguistics, and more especially among computational linguists over the last two decades, ways of improving automatic word-class tagging as an essential prerequisite for further syntactic analysis has been a major preoccupation.

There is no obvious way of improving the accuracy of rule-based taggers of the kind developed by Greene and Rubin except through manual intervention. That is, the set of tags and the rule-based program have to be modified to take account of what actually occurs in the texts. Over the last decade however, automatic grammatical tagging has been able to improve greatly on the pioneering achievements of Greene and Rubin, through the development of an approach based on the probability of occurrence of particular sequences of words or tags. Although the dominant generative paradigm in modern linguistic theory has rejected probabilistic models as an inadequate basis for accounting for grammatical competence, it is somewhat ironical that

> The most successful grammatical tagging systems appear to be those based on a simple finite state grammar with probabilities (derived from corpus frequency data) assigned to the transitions between states, i.e. a Markov process model. (Leech, 1991: 16)

In the first instance, the tagged *Brown Corpus* and the TAGGIT program for automatic grammatical tagging were used to form the basis of a project at Lancaster, Oslo and Bergen Universities between 1978 and 1983 to tag the *LOB Corpus* of written British English. A new automatic tagging system, the Constituent Likelihood Automatic Word-tagging System (CLAWS), based on probabilistic principles, was a result of this project. The first version, CLAWS 1, used 133 basic word and punctuation tags, many of them identical to the 87 tags used in TAGGIT but allowing for greater delicacy of analysis. It was claimed that CLAWS 1 'made an error in 3% to 4% of word-tokens, and in these cases its output had to be manually corrected' (Garside et al., 1987: 9).

The CLAWS word-tagging system, which has been described in detail by Garside (1987) and Marshall (1987) has been further developed at Lancaster University's Unit for Computer Research on the English Language (UCREL) with versions for different purposes which have more or fewer word tags. The grammatical tagging proceeds in three stages. After the corpus is converted to a format designed for tagging, the tagging program automatically assigns a grammatical word-class tag to each word token, before a final manual post-editing is undertaken to correct errors.

```
A01  4  ^ a_AT move_NN to_TO stop_VB \0Mr_NPT Gaitskell_NP from_IN
A01  4  nominating_VBG any_DTI more_AP labour_NN
A01  5  life_NN peers_NNS is_BEZ to_TO be_BE made_VBN at_IN a_AT meeting_NN
A01  5  of_IN labour_NN \0MPs_NPTS tomorrow_NR ._.
A01  6  ^ \0Mr_NPT Michael_NP Foot_NP has_HVZ put_VBN down_RP a_AT
A01  6  resolution_NN on_IN the_ATI subject_NN and_CC
A01  7  he_PP3A is_BEZ to_TO be_BE backed_VBN by_IN \0Mr_NPT Will_NP
A01  7  Griffiths_NP ,_, \0MP_NPT for_IN Manchester_NP
A01  8  Exchange_NP ._.
```

Figure 4.2   A fragment of a tagged version of the *LOB Corpus*, horizontal format (from ICAME: Norwegian Computing Centre for the Humanities, Bergen)

Initially, after the automatic tag-assignment stage, if the program recognizes that a particular word form is a homograph, which in the lexicon can belong to more than one grammatical word class, then tag disambiguation is necessary. The original CLAWS 1 tagger worked with a lexicon of about 7,200 word forms and their potential word-class tags. To cope with words not in the lexicon, the tagger had heuristic devices such as a suffix list linked to possible word classes (e.g. *-ness* for a noun). Probabilities derived from earlier corpus tagging showed the part of speech a particular homograph was most likely to belong to. For example, in the *LOB Corpus* the word *sample* is 56 times more frequent as a noun than as a verb, whereas the word *work* is only about six times as likely to occur as a noun than as a verb. There is also a probability matrix which shows, on the basis of earlier corpus analyses, the transition probabilities between adjacent tags. That is, the matrix gives the frequency with which any tag is followed by any other tag in an earlier corpus used for 'training' the tagger. If a particular word, say *pretty*, is tagged as an adjective, CLAWS shows that there is a high probability of it being immediately followed by a noun. On the other hand, if *pretty* is tagged as an adverb, there is a higher probability of it being immediately followed by an adjective or by another adverb. In Figure 4.2, which is a small extract from the horizontal format of the *LOB Corpus* tagged by CLAWS 1, the tags in the first three lines represent the following grammatical word classes:

AT   singular article (*a, an, every*)
NN   singular common noun
TO   infinitival *to*
VB   uninflected base form of verb
NPT   singular titular noun with word-initial capital
NP   singular proper noun
IN   preposition
VBG   present participle
DTI   singular or plural determiner
AP   post determiner
NNS   plural common noun

BEZ   *is, 's*
BE   *be*
VBN past participle

The numbers at the left identify the texts and line numbers in the corpus.

Tagging enables automatic retrieval for the analysis of particular uses of a word form. For example, the word *move* is most frequently used as a verb. In Figure 4.2, however, it is tagged appropriately as a noun (_NN). With a tagged corpus, all uses of the word *move* as a verb (or as a noun) can be retrieved. Similarly, anyone doing research on how a word such as *since* functions as a preposition in English is faced with a problem unless the corpus is tagged. The following examples show that *since* can be used as a preposition, conjunction or adverb.

I've been waiting since 5 o'clock.   (preposition)
Since they can't agree, we'll have to call in a mediator. (conjunction)
He left home in 1975 and he hasn't been back since.   (adverb)

As long as the automatic tagger is an accurate one or there has been manual correction, a grammatically tagged corpus can quickly and easily be searched for only those uses of the word *since* where it functions as a preposition.

Lancaster University's UCREL has become one of the major centres for research on the automatic analysis of corpora and was among the pioneers in adopting the approach to analysis based on the statistical probabilities of occurrence of linguistic elements, rather than an approach based on logical or grammatical rules. As Sampson (1987) and others have pointed out, the probabilistic approach is firmly based on prior processing of corpora, usually on a large scale, whereas the non-probabilistic approaches to tagging tended to develop tagging rules from invented examples which supposedly explicate the putative grammatical structures of the language. The problem for the development of automatic tagging based on such grammatical rules is that no grammar of English has yet come anywhere near being able to describe all and only the sentences of the language as found in authentic discourse.

Over a decade of experience at UCREL in the development of probabilistic word-class tagging was put to a test which many corpus analysts might not have been willing to contemplate, namely the tagging of the 100-million-word *British National Corpus*. Leech et al. (1994) have described the experience of applying the CLAWS tagging system to such a vast amount of text. As we have seen, CLAWS was initially developed to tag the one-million-word *LOB Corpus*, and even so required manual post-editing to take the accuracy of tagging beyond about 96%. With a 100-million-word corpus, it would take a person who could check 1,000 words in 40 minutes over 40 years to manually post-edit such a tagged text to improve the accuracy of tagging (Leech et al., 1994: 49). This clearly would be beyond the scope of a normal research project and of little use in developing a system for on-line processing of text for applications such as natural language processing or automatic translation.

For the tagging of the *BNC*, a later version of CLAWS was developed to further eliminate as many as possible of the errors made by the earlier CLAWS taggers. This was done by reducing the size of the tagset to about 60 tags, developing new 'portmanteau' tags, expanding the lexicon used as part of the tagger to about 10,000 items, and greatly enhancing the 'idiom list' of word sequences. These modifications are described in detail in Leech et al. (1994: 54 ff). At the beginning of the process the tagger assigns potential tags. In the case of a word such as *the*, the tagger assigns only the tag AT0, meaning that *the* can only be an article in that context. The word *leaves*, on the other hand, would be tagged NN2 and VVZ, meaning that it could be a plural common noun or the third-person singular of a verb. Certain word sequences such as *paint brush, know how* or *in lieu of* from a predetermined 'idiom list' are then tagged as units. Then the tagger has to make a single 'best guess' for each word token where more than one potential tag has been assigned. The 'best guess' as to which tag or sequence of tags goes with a particular sequence of words is calculated automatically from a matrix of transitional probabilities.

> For each sequence of tags *ti, tj*, there is an estimated probability (based on previous analysis of corpus data) that *ti* will be immediately followed by *tj*, rather than some other tag. For each sequence of n tags, the likelihood of the whole sequence can be calculated as a product of the individual transitional probabilities in the string.
> (Leech et al., 1994: 53)

The device of a portmanteau tag was used in the tagging of the *Brown Corpus*, and has been used in later versions of CLAWS tagging. Essentially it is a tag which indicates that the word class to which the lexical item belongs is one or other of two or more alternatives. Thus the portmanteau tag AVP-PRP means that the tagged word is either an adverb particle or a preposition. Portmanteau tags are a recognition of the fact that most errors in grammatical tagging come from the inability of the tagger to distinguish between the items of a small number of pairs of potential tags. The problem of whether an *-ed* form is a finite past tense or a past participle is typically a difficult one for automatic taggers (e.g. *The car raced through the city centre crashed*). Similarly, distinguishing between the use of *this* and *that* as determiners or pronouns is avoided in the CLAWS 5 tagset by categorizing them with a portmanteau tag.

The general tagging procedure can be seen from Figures 4.3 to 4.5. In Figure 4.3, the original text is a fragment from a transcribed recording of spoken English, formatted in SGML (see Section 2.6.5) and ready for word-class tagging by CLAWS. In Figure 4.4, the text has been tagged automatically using the CLAWS system. Each word has an unambiguous

<u id=D0036 who=W0001>		There's no petrol in the car. </u>		
<u id=D0037 who=W0002>		You mean <pause> every time I have that car I have to <ptr t=P7> put petrol in. <ptr t=P8></u>		
<u id=D0038 who=W0001>		No I <ptr t=P8> put it in the last two times. Twenty quid's worth. So you'll have <pause> you watch my little car. <pause>		

Figure 4.3   A fragment of the *BNC* after SGML markup and before CLAWS word-class tagging

---

Figure 4.4   A fragment of the *BNC* after word-class tagging with CLAWS

0000079	010	There	>03	[EX0/100] AV0/0
0000079	011	's	<97	VBZ
0000079	020	no	03	[AT0/100] ITJ/0 AV0%/0 NN1%0
0000079	030	petrol	03	NN1
0000079	040	in	03	[PRP/99] AVP@/1
0000079	050	the	03	AT0
0000079	060	car	03	NN1
0000079	061	.	03	.
0000079	062	</u>	01	NULL
0000080	001	**22;1760;u	01	NULL
0000080	002	---------------------		
0000080	010	You	03	PNP
0000080	020	mean	03	[VVB/100] AJ0/0 NN1@/0
0000080	021	<pause>	01	NULL
0000080	030	every	03	AT0
0000080	040	time	03	[NN1/100] VVB%/0
0000080	050	I	03	[PNP/99] NP0@/0 CRD@/0 ZZ0@/0
0000080	060	have	03	VHB
0000080	070	that	03	[DT0/100] AV0%/0 CJT/0
0000080	080	car	03	NN1
0000080	090	I	03	[PNP/99] NP0@/1 CRD@/0 ZZ0@/0
0000080	100	have	03	VHB
0000080	110	to	98	TO0
0000080	111	**10;1783;ptr	01	NULL
0000080	120	put	98	VVI
0000080	130	petrol	03	NN1
0000080	140	in	03	[AVP@/59] PRP/41
0000080	141	.	03	.
0000080	142	**10;1794;ptr	01	NULL
0000080	143	</u>	01	NULL
0000081	001	**22;1805;u	01	NULL
0000081	002	---------------------		
0000081	003	**10;1828;ptr	01	NULL
0000081	010	No	03	[ITJ/87] AT0/11 AV0%/2 NN1%/0
0000081	020	I	03	[PNP/85] NP0@/13 CRD@/1 ZZ0@/1
0000081	021	**10;1839;ptr	01	NULL
0000081	030	put	03	[VVD/83] VVB/17 VVN/1 NN1%/0
0000081	040	it	03	PNP
0000081	050	in	03	[PRP/94] AVP@/6
0000081	060	the	03	AT0
0000081	070	last	03	[ORD/100] NN1%/0 VVB@/0
0000081	080	two	03	CRD
0000081	090	times	03	[NN2/100] VVZ%/0 PRP%/0

continued

Figure 4.4 continued

0000081	091	.	03	
0000081	092	----------------------		
0000081	100	Twenty	03	CRD
0000081	110	quid	>03	[NN0/92] NN1/5 UNC/3
0000081	111	's	<99	POS
0000081	120	worth	03	[NN1/95] PRP/5
0000081	121	.	03	.
0000081	122	----------------------		
0000081	130	So	03	[CJS/95] AV0/5
0000081	140	you	>03	PNP
0000081	141	'll	<03	VM0
0000081	150	have	98	VHI
0000081	151	<pause>	01	NULL
0000081	160	you	03	PNP
0000081	170	watch	03	[VVB/100] NN1/0
0000081	180	my	03	DPS
0000081	190	little	03	[AJ0/67] DT0/33 AV0/0
0000081	200	car	03	NN1
0000081	201	.	03	.
0000081	202	<pause>	01	NULL

Note: @ and % are 'rarity markers'.

```
<u id=D0036 who=W0001>
<s c="0000079 002" n=00057>
There_EX0 's_VBZ no_AT0 petrol_NN1 in_PRP the_AT0 car_NN1 ._PUN
</u>
<u id=D0037 who=W0002>
<s c="0000080 002" n=00058>
You_PNP mean_VVB <pause> every_AT0 time_NN1 I_PNP have_VHB that_DT0
car_NN1 I_PNP have_VHB to_TO0 <ptr t=P7> put_VVI petrol_NN1 in_AVP-PRP
._PUN <ptr t=P8>
</u>
<u id=D0038 who=W0001>
<s c="0000081 002" n=00059>
<ptr t=P7> No_ITJ I_PNP <ptr t=P8> put_VVD it_PNP in_PRP the_AT0 last_ORD
two_CRD times_NN2 ._PUN
<s c="0000081 092" n=00060>
Twenty_CRD quid_NN0 's_POS worth_NN1 ._PUN
<s c="0000081 122" n=00061>
So_CJS you_PNP 'll_VM0 have_VHI <pause> you_PNP watch_VVB my_DPS
little_AJ0 car_NN1 ._PUN <pause>
```

Figure 4.5 A fragment of the *BNC* after post-CLAWS processing by SANTA CLAWS

---

tag or a set of potential tags, with the probability of occurrence assessed by CLAWS for each potential tag. Thus the first time *in* occurs, the tagger assesses its probability as a preposition (PRP) to be 99% and as an adverb particle (AVP) to be 1%. The second time *in* occurs, the probability that it is an adverb particle is given as 59%, and as a preposition 41%. The

AN INTRODUCTION TO CORPUS LINGUISTICS

third time *in* occurs the tagger has assessed the probability of it being a preposition to be 94%, with only a 6% chance of it being an adverb particle. In its context, *mean* is judged to be the base form of a verb (VVB) with 100% confidence, even though in other contexts *mean* can be an adjective (AJ0) or a singular noun (NN1). *Little* is rated as most probably an adjective in this context (67%). It is rated as less likely to be a determiner (33%) and certainly not an adverb here.

In Figure 4.5 the CLAWS output has undergone further processing with additional software (*SANTA CLAWS*) which, for each word, either accepts one particular tag from the options available or inserts a portmanteau tag (see the second use of *in* which is tagged (AVP-PRP)). For comparison with the original tagset used for tagging the *Brown Corpus* (see Figure 4.1) the tagset of about 60 tags and 20 portmanteau tags used for the word-class tagging of the *BNC* is shown in Figure 4.6.

The reduced tagset in CLAWS 5 reduces the delicacy of analysis available for CLAWS 1 (e.g. the indicative use of the verb *move* and the imperative are not distinguished) but, because fewer distinctions have to be made, the tagger should make fewer errors.

Because of the huge size of the task in tagging the *BNC*, only selective manual post-editing of the automatically tagged output was initially possible, with concentration on the sources of error which were known to be most likely. Automatic tagging cannot yet be claimed to be error free but, given the complexity of language, probabilistic tagging has been remarkably successful, with an error rate of less than about 4% overall in the case of CLAWS. Problems associated with automatic word-class tagging are considered further in Section 4.1.3.

Figure 4.6   The tagset of CLAWS 5 used for tagging the *BNC*

AJ0   adjective (unmarked) (e.g. *good, old*)
AJC   comparative adjective (e.g. *better, older*)
AJS   superlative adjective (e.g. *best, oldest*)
AT0   article (e.g. *the, a, an*)
AV0   adverb (unmarked) (e.g. *often, well, longer, furthest*)
AVP   adverb particle (e.g. *up, off, out*)
AVQ   WH-adverb (e.g. *when, how, why*)
CJC   coordinating conjunction (e.g. *and, or*)
CJS   subordinating conjunction (e.g. *although, when*)
CJT   the conjunction *that*
CRD   cardinal numeral (e.g. *3, fifty-five, 6609*) (excluding *one*)
DPS   possessive determiner form (e.g. *your, their*)
DT0   general determiner (e.g. *these, some*)
DTQ   WH-determiner (e.g. *whose, which*)
EX0   existential *there*
ITJ   interjection or other isolate (e.g. *oh, yes, hmm*)
NN0   noun (neutral for number) (e.g. *aircraft, data*)
NN1   singular noun (e.g. *pencil, goose*)
NN2   plural noun (e.g. *pencils, geese*)

continued

Figure 4.6 *continued*

NNN	<<PROCESS TAG>> numeral noun, neutral for number (dozen, hundred)*/	
NN2	<<PROCESS TAG>> plural numeral noun (hundreds, thousands)*/	
NNS	<<PROCESS TAG>> noun of style (e.g. president, governments, Messrs.)	
NP0	proper noun (e.g. *London, Michael, Mars*)	
NULL	the null tag (for items not to be tagged)	
ORD	ordinal (e.g. *sixth, 77th, last*)	
PNI	indefinite pronoun (e.g. *none, everything*)	
PNP	personal pronoun (e.g. *you, them, ours*)	
PNQ	WH-pronoun (e.g. *who, whoever*)	
PNX	reflexive pronoun (e.g. *itself, ourselves*)	
POS	the possessive (or genitive morpheme) *'s* or *'*	
PRF	the preposition *of*	
PRP	preposition (except for *of*) (e.g. *for, above, to*)	
PUL	punctuation – left bracket (i.e. (or [)	
PUN	punctuation – general mark (i.e. . ! , : ; - ? ...)	
PUQ	punctuation – quotation mark (i.e. ' ' ")	
PUR	punctuation – right bracket (i.e.) or])	
TO0	infinitive marker *to*	
UNC	'unclassified' items which are not words of the English lexicon	
VBB	the 'base forms' of the verb *be* (except the infinitive), i.e. *am, are*	
VBD	past form of the verb *be*, i.e. *was, were*	
VBG	-ing form of the verb *be*, i.e. *being*	
VBI	infinitive of the verb *be*	
VBN	past participle of the verb *be*, i.e. *been*	
VBZ	-s form of the verb *be*, i.e. *is, 's*	
VDB	base form of the verb *do* (except the infinitive), i.e. *do*	
VDD	past form of the verb *do*, i.e. *did*	
VDG	-ing form of the verb *do*, i.e. *doing*	
VDI	infinitive of the verb *do*	
VDN	past participle of the verb *do*, i.e. *done*	
VDZ	-s form of the verb *do*, i.e. *does*	
VHB	base form of the verb *have* (except the infinitive), i.e. *have*	
VHD	past tense form of the verb *have*, i.e. *had, 'd*	
VHG	-ing form of the verb *have*, i.e. *having*	
VHI	infinitive of the verb *have*	
VHN	past participle of the verb *have*, i.e. *had*	
VHZ	-s form of the verb *have*, i.e. *has, 's*	
VM0	modal auxiliary verb (e.g. *can, could, will, 'll*)	
VVB	base form of lexical verb (except the infinitive) (e.g. *take, live*)	
VVD	past tense form of lexical verb (e.g. *took, lived*)	
VVG	-ing form of lexical verb (e.g. *taking, living*)	
VVI	infinitive of lexical verb	
VVN	past participle form of lexical verb (e.g. *taken, lived*)	
VVZ	-s form of lexical verb (e.g. *takes, lives*)	
XX0	the negative *not* or *n't*	
ZZ0	alphabetical symbol (e.g. A, B, c, d)	

Portmanteau tags

AJ0-AV0	AV0-AJ0	adjective/adverb
AJ0-NN1	NN1-AJ0	adjective/noun
AJ0-VVD	VVD-AJ0	adjective/verb
AJ0-VVG	VVG-AJ0	adjective/-ing
AJ0-VVN	VVN-AJ0	adjective/past participle
AVP-PRP	PRP-AVP	adverb/preposition
CJS-PRP	PRP-CJS	conjunction/preposition
NN1-NP0	NP0-NN1	noun/proper noun
NN1-VVG	VVG-NN1	noun/-ing
VVD-VVN	VVN-VVD	past tense verb/past participle

De Rose (1988, 1991) has evaluated the probabilistic approach to grammatical tagging which had been pioneered in the CLAWS system, and which he had also employed in developing a tagging system called VOLSUNGA. De Rose has shown that probability-based (or stochastic) tagging is remarkably robust under a variety of conditions. For English he also identified the following as the most frequent tagging errors:

past participle assigned instead of past tense of verb
singular noun assigned instead of verb
singular noun assigned instead of adjective
preposition assigned instead of subordinating conjunction
singular noun assigned instead of present participle of verb

With awareness of the word-class categories most likely to be a source of error in tagging, researchers can focus on them to develop improved systems.

It is beyond the scope of the present work to attempt to compare or evaluate the various systems which have been developed for the automatic word-class tagging of corpora (see Leech, 1993a). For a start, there is no one way to tag a text grammatically. The tagset employed inevitably reflects a particular theory of language. The theoretical assumptions we make about the relationship between morphology, syntax and semantics, for example, can affect the types of tags assigned to words. The size of the tagset reflects, of course, the necessary degree of delicacy of analysis for the purpose intended. In general, the greater the number of tag categories, the greater the potential for tagging error, but at the same time the greater the precision of analysis available. Such precision is necessary for natural language processing.

Just as the accuracy of the automatic tagging of a corpus has to be evaluated in terms of a particular tagset, it is at present also unrealistic to expect automatic tagging to be satisfactory without some manual post-editing. Even then there is room for variation. It is not a matter of intrinsic correctness, whether, for example, the words **metal** and **concrete** are tagged as nouns or adjectives in the following:

metal   It was held by a metal brace.
concrete The cowshed had a concrete floor.
          (cf. He made a concrete proposal.)

This is one reason why in huge tagging projects such as that developed for the *British National Corpus* portmanteau tags can be a useful way of avoiding making invidious choices. A revealing study by Baker (1995) has shown that even manual post-editing does not necessarily lead to complete agreement on appropriate grammatical tagging. Nine experienced post-editors were asked to check and correct, if necessary, certain sentences tagged by CLAWS. Overall consistency between the editors was 98%. That is, even manual post-editing did not achieve completely uniform tagging.

The various tagging systems developed since TAGGIT have mostly been designed for particular corpus-based projects, and to a considerable extent, therefore, have to be evaluated in those terms. The resulting tagging schemes have tended to be mutually incompatible, although some researchers have attempted to develop new algorithms to permit mapping between different tagging systems. Such a scheme which allowed different tagsets to be recognized and worked with would enlarge the amount of grammatically tagged text which individual research projects had at their disposal.

Another reason why it is not possible to fairly evaluate the various tagging systems is that most are not available outside the research or industrial projects for which they were developed. For very few is there enough published information on which to base a judgment as to their respective accuracy and efficiency. In addition to TAGGIT and CLAWS, four other important tagging projects are mentioned here, however, to indicate something of the scope of research in this area being undertaken at the University of Pennsylvania in the United States, Lund University in Sweden, Nijmegen University in The Netherlands and University College London in the United Kingdom.

As noted earlier, the most successful tagging systems have adopted a probabilistic approach and claim to be able to assign their respective tagsets to the word tokens in almost any texts with at least 95% accuracy. Many other researchers, especially from within the fields of artificial intelligence and cognitive science, influenced by work in generative grammar, initially pinned their faith on rule-based approaches to tagging. However, throughout the 1980s there was a growing recognition that it was difficult to get rule-based tagging to work outside well-chosen fragments of text, sometimes specially composed for the tagger. Corpus-based tagging of unrestricted text has shown repeatedly that the complexity of a language such as English is simply not yet able to be accounted for by rule-based approaches to tagging alone.

As Church and Mercer (1993: 7) have pointed out, the success of tagging using a probabilistic approach is evidenced by the number of programs which have adopted it, and particularly by the variety of fields of application, including speech synthesis, speech recognition, information retrieval, sense disambiguation and computational lexicography, as well as descriptive linguistics.

The annotation of the 4.5-million-word *Penn Treebank Corpus of American English* from 1989 to 1992 used a pared-down tagset of 36 word-class tags and 12 mainly punctuation tags based on the tagset developed earlier for the *Brown Corpus*. An explanation of the reasons for reducing the *Brown* tagset is contained in Marcus et al. (1993). Essentially, these changes could be made in light of the major purpose of the word-class tagging in the project, which is to provide input for a parser. Error rates of 2%–6% in automatic word-class annotation have been claimed before manual correction. Marcus et al. (1993) note that experience with the annotation of the *Penn Treebank* project showed that on grounds of speed, consistency and accuracy, manual correction of automatic tagging is superior to entirely manual tagging by trained annotators. The *Penn Treebank* tagset is contained in Figure 4.7.

1	CC	Co-ordinating conjunction	25	TO	*to*
2	CD	Cardinal number	26	UH	Interjection
3	DT	Determiner	27	VB	Verb, base form
4	EX	Existential *there*	28	VBD	Verb, past tense
5	FW	Foreign word	29	VBG	Verb, gerund/present participle
6	IN	Preposition/subordinating	30	VBN	Verb, past participle
		conjunction	31	VBP	Verb, non-3rd person singular
7	JJ	Adjective			present
8	JJR	Adjective, comparative	32	VBZ	Verb, 3rd person singular present
9	JJS	Adjective, superlative	33	WDT	WH-determiner
10	LS	List item marker	34	WP	WH-pronoun
11	MD	Modal	35	WP$	Possessive WH-pronoun
12	NN	Noun, singular or mass	36	WRB	WH-adverb
13	NNS	Noun, plural	37	#	Pound sign
14	NNP	Proper noun, singular	38	$	Dollar sign
15	NNPS	Proper noun, plural	39	.	Sentence-final punctuation
16	PDT	Predeterminer	40	,	Comma
17	POS	Possessive ending	41	:	Colon, semi-colon
18	PRP	Personal pronoun	42	(	Left bracket character
19	PP$	Possessive pronoun	43	)	Right bracket character
20	RB	Adverb	44	"	Straight double quote
21	RBR	Adverb, comparative	45	`	Left open single quote
22	RBS	Adverb, superlative	46	"	Left open double quote
23	RP	Particle	47	'	Right close single quote
24	SYM	Symbol (mathematical or scientific)	48	"	Right close double quote

Figure 4.7 The *Penn Treebank* tagset
(Marcus et al., 1993: 317)

Use of a large tagset for word-class tagging was described by Svartvik for the Text Segmentation for Speech (TESS) project at Lund University in Sweden, based on spoken texts from the *London–Lund Corpus*. Over 200 word-class categories were used for this probabilistic tagger which was designed to facilitate the syntactic analysis of spoken texts in particular. An error rate of 'between 3 and 6 per cent' is claimed (Svartvik, 1990a: 80) and this is a very high order of accuracy of automatic tagging considering the large number of grammatical categories. The TESS tagger used a statistical tagging algorithm which was similar to that developed for the CLAWS tagger (Eeg-Olofsson, 1990: 108). The high level of delicacy of the TESS tagset can be illustrated by considering its ability not only to distinguish the word form *as* when it is used as a preposition from when it is used as an adverb or conjunction, but in the latter case, where the conjunction *as* is semantically tagged to show its use to introduce different clause types, including temporal, reason, concession, similarity. Svartvik (1990a: 101–106) lists the complete TESS tagset.

Research on the automatic analysis of corpora has, since the early 1970s, been undertaken in the English Department at the University of Nijmegen in The Netherlands. Projects led by Jan Aarts have made Nijmegen an important centre for research in corpus analysis, and in particular since 1980, when the first Tools for Syntactic Corpus Analysis (TOSCA) project was launched (see Section 2.3.2.6). Syntactic description and analysis in its own right, rather than other applications, has been a prime objective of TOSCA research with word-class tagging an important preliminary to automatic parsing. The *TOSCA Corpus* has been grammatically tagged from a tagset of 322 tags using an automatic word-class tagger, including a large lexicon, with manual post-editing to correct the error rate of approximately 8%. Van Halteren and Oostdijk (1993) have provided an overview of the system of analysis used, and a useful discussion of the consequences of a large tagset for ambiguity of analysis. It has been noted by Oostdijk (1991: 3) that the Nijmegen approach to automatic analysis differs fundamentally from the approach adopted in many other corpus annotation projects such as CLAWS which have used a probabilistic approach to tagging, able to analyse any text in a given language. The Nijmegen research on the other hand has sought to develop automatic tagging not primarily on a probabilistic basis, but on the basis of a set of formal linguistically based rules which characterize sentences as strings of word classes, and without any necessary further applications other than providing the best possible descriptively adequate account of the language of the corpus.

An extended and modified version of the TOSCA tagset was adopted for the *ICE* project. Greenbaum (1993) and Greenbaum and Ni (1996) describe major differences in the tag categories between the TOSCA/ *ICE* and CLAWS tagsets, both of which are highly detailed. The *ICE* tagset distinguishes 22 word classes, many of which are subcategorized to give a total of 256 lexico-grammatical tags, 78 of which are for verb types alone and 15 punctuation and pause tags. Figure 4.8 contains a fragment of the *ICE* tagset showing the level of detail with which the texts are annotated for pro-forms. As Greenbaum (1993) noted, considerable post-editing of the output of the TOSCA/*ICE* tagger was undertaken when tagging the British section of the *ICE* project. The TOSCA tagger is commercially available from the English Department at the University of Nijmegen, and the *ICE* tagger is similarly available from the Survey of English Usage at University College London.

In the final analysis, the value or 'success' of the various approaches to word-class tagging may not be crucially dependent on theoretical differences. It is largely an empirical matter within a theoretical framework as to whether a tagging system is more or less successful in correctly

Tag	Category	Example
PROFM(conjoin)	proform, conjoin	a week or *so*; and *so forth*
PROFM(one,plu)	proform, *one*, plural	These *ones* are not mine
PROFM(one,sing)	proform, *one*, singular	I want the big *one*
PROFM(so,claus)	proform, *so*, clausal	I hope *so*; I hope *not*
PROFM(so,phras)	proform, *so*, phrasal	Joe is cold. *So* am I
PRON(ass)	pronoun, assertive	*some* books
PRON(ass,sing)	pronoun, assertive, singular	*something* nice
PRON(dem)	pronoun, demonstrative	*Such* things will never happen to me
PRON(dem,plu)	pronoun, demonstrative, plural	*those* chairs
PRON(dem,sing)	pronoun, demonstrative, singular	*this* cup
PRON(exclam)	pronoun, exclamatory	*What* a performance!
PRON(inter)	pronoun, interrogative	*What* are you up to?
PRON(neg)	pronoun, negative	*no* food; *none*; in the middle of *nowhere*
PRON(neg,sing)	pronoun, negative, singular	*nobody*
PRON(nom)	pronoun, nominal relative	You may take *whatever* you fancy
PRON(nonass)	pronoun, nonassertive	*any* mistake
PRON(nonass,sing)	pronoun, nonassertive, singular	*anything* edible
PRON(pers)	pronoun, personal	*you*
PRON(pers,plu)	pronoun, personal, plural	*we*
PRON(pers,plu,encl)	pronoun, personal, plural, enclitic	Let*'s* do it
PRON(pers,procl)	pronoun, personal, proclitic	*y'*know
PRON(pers,sing)	pronoun, personal, singular	*I*; *s/he*; *him/her*
PRON(pers,sing,procl)	pronoun, personal, proclitic	A cat came. *'T*was my neighbour's
PRON(poss)	pronoun, possessive	*your*; *yours*
PRON(poss,plu)	pronoun, possessive, plural	*our*; *ours*
PRON(poss,sing)	pronoun, possessive, singular	*his/her*; *his/hers*
PRON(quant)	pronoun, quantifying	*enough* food
PRON(quant,plu)	pronoun, quantifying, plural	*few* cows
PRON(quant,sing)	pronoun, quantifying, singular	*much* water; *little* soup; *many a* wolf
PRON(recip)	pronoun, reciprocal	*each other*; *one another*
PRON(ref,plu)	pronoun, reflexive, plural	*yourselves*
PRON(ref,sing)	pronoun, reflexive, singular	*yourself*
PRON(rel)	pronoun, relative	Pick the ones *that* you like
PRON(univ)	pronoun, universal	*all* my friends; *all* the water; *all* of it
PRON(univ,plu)	pronoun, universal, plural	*both* my parents; *both* of the two
PRON(univ,sing)	pronoun, universal, singular	*each* pig
PROPIT	prop *it*	*It*'s me; *It*'s raining; *It* would be best if you went
PROPIT(procl)	prop *it*, proclitic	*'T*was cloudy yesterday

Figure 4.8 A fragment of the *ICE* tagset

tagging a sentence, a text or indeed a whole corpus. In fact, because most rule-based approaches to automatic tagging have grown out of the conventional wisdom contained in grammars such as that by Quirk et al. (1985), it could be argued that probabilistic or discovery-based models of analysis are likely to be more successful in challenging and expanding the descriptive models of English than those which are rule-based.

Sampson (1987) has also argued persuasively that the possibility of designing comprehensive grammars which can take account of all texts may for practical purposes be insurmountable, given the complexity of natural languages. Ultimately, of course, the best approach to tagging will be the one that is robustly able to handle the widest variety of texts with the greatest accuracy, whether this approach is rule-based or probabilistic or a combination of the two.

4.1.3 Semantic aspects of tagging

As noted earlier, the degree of delicacy in tagging a corpus depends on the purposes for which the corpus is intended. Lexicographers, for example, may be interested in word-class details for each word form but may not have any obvious use for a full syntactic analysis or parsing. Natural language processing research, on the other hand, usually requires quite delicate automatic parsing. For whatever reason automatic tagging is required, there continue to be substantial problems. This is partly because polysemy, which is endemic in a language such as English, makes sense tagging and word-sense disambiguation very difficult. For most areas of computerized language analysis the discrimination of word senses is of fundamental importance and, even at the relatively low level analysis involved in grammatical tagging, the degree of delicacy of the tagset necessary for appropriate word-sense disambiguation poses formidable problems. If we compare the following two examples, it is apparent that in the first case *once* most probably means 'formerly', 'during a period in the past', whereas in the second it most probably means 'on one occasion'.

I lived there once.
I went there once.

To tag *lived* and *went* merely as verbs is clearly too crude to assist the sense disambiguation of *once*.

Issues in word-sense disambiguation are beyond the scope of this book but they have continued to be of great importance within computational linguistics, and have included how best to establish the different senses of a word form (e.g. whether there are really two senses of *once* in the above examples) and the role of different sources of knowledge for establishing and disambiguating word senses (e.g. word associations, collocations, grammatical context, context of use, probabilistic or rule-based methods of making sense readings of words in texts). Some of these issues have been reviewed by Gale et al. (1993).

Resolving semantic ambiguity by machine is not yet as far advanced as the automatic identification of the word class to which a word form belongs in context. The extent of the problem is well illustrated by Guthrie et al. (1994). The authors discovered that seven out of the eight major senses of the word *bridge* listed in the *Longman Dictionary of Contemporary English* (*LDOCE*) were used in a single newspaper, the *Wall Street Journal*, from 1987 to 1989. That is, it does not seem likely that the following senses of *bridge* are each restricted to particular domains or genres.

1 something that carries a road over a river, etc. (noun or verb)
2 part of a ship
3 upper part of the nose
4 part of a pair of glasses
5 part of a stringed musical instrument
6 a dental device
7 a card game
8 idiomatic uses (as in *don't cross your bridges* ...)

It is simply not easy to disambiguate words automatically using linguistic context or domain of use as a sole basis. Further, as Guthrie et al. note, some researchers have found that 'perhaps half of the words in a new text cannot be related to a dictionary entry' (1994: 85). Sometimes this is because a particular inflected form of a word is not listed in a dictionary as a separate entry. In addition, a significant number of words have metaphorical uses which have not been listed as dictionary entries. Ultimately, word-class and sense tagging are important for more sophisticated levels of automatic language analysis including syntactic parsing and natural language processing applications. As we have seen, some grammatical tagging systems such as that used in the TESS project already make use of semantic information, but to do this successfully automatically on a large scale with unrestricted input is a daunting task. In processing unrestricted text, sense tagging (whether probabilistic or rule-driven) simply cannot yet perform to a high level of accuracy. The problem can be illustrated if we compare the following examples:

We left the stable cases till later.
We painted the stable doors last spring.

In general use, *stable* is most commonly an adjective. In horse-racing circles, however, *stable* has high frequency of use as a noun. In both sentences, there is not enough evidence in the context for either word-class or sense of *stable* to be established automatically without wider contextual input and knowledge of the world.

This example revisits the question posed earlier of how accurate are the word-class tagging systems currently used. It is virtually impossible to establish reliably which taggers are most accurate without getting them all to perform identical tasks on identical bodies of unrestricted text. However, no such experiment has yet been undertaken, partly because some of the taggers have been developed by individual users and are simply not available for comparative evaluation. Moreover, accuracy can only be meaningful in relation to a particular tagset. As we have noted, the greater the number of tags, generally the harder it is to tag correctly. Furthermore, there is a vast difference between tagging the written texts which most taggers have been developed from and for, and tagging spoken texts which typically contain fragmentary utterances, false starts, and constructions which challenge the traditionally accepted notions of word class and syntactic structure as epitomized in the standard descriptive grammars of the language. Problems with accuracy of transcription and indecipherable speech also make the tagging of speech difficult. Taggers have to be familiar not only with word sequences but with lexical senses, as we have seen.

It is easy to forget that when claims are made about the impressive accuracy with which grammatical tags can be assigned by machine, the high success rates 'typically in the region of 96–7 per cent' (Leech, 1991: 15) are a result of averaging. As noted by Kennedy (1996a), certain very frequent words or word classes can be tagged with almost total accuracy, while for others it is possible to tag with accuracy rates of only 80%–85%, thus necessitating manual post-editing.

The 100 most frequent word types in the *LOB Corpus* account for 49% of all the one million word tokens in the corpus. About 65 of these 100 word types can be grammatically tagged without any indeterminacy. Thus, the word *the* is virtually always a definite article and this alone accounts for about 6.8% of all tokens in the *LOB Corpus*, 6.9% in *Brown* and 4.7% in the *London–Lund Corpus* of spoken English. *She* and *he* are always subject personal pronouns, *am, is, are, was, were* are unambiguously finite verb forms, and so on. The 65 word forms like this which can be assigned their correct word class with total or near total accuracy account for about a third of all word tokens in the *LOB Corpus*. That is, if we consider only 65 of the 100 most frequent types in the corpus, about 335,000 tokens can be accurately tagged automatically. The other 35 of the 100 most frequent word types in the corpus are like *had*, which can be a finite or non-finite verb, or *that*, which can be a determiner, an intensifier, a conjunction or a relative pronoun. If we assume 95% accuracy overall, the remaining 670,000 tokens in the corpus would have about 50,000 errors in tagging (an error rate of 7.5%). Over 7 out of every 100 word tokens in the corpus will thus be wrongly tagged. Again there will be the effect of averaging. For some words or word classes the tagging error rate will be much higher than 7.5%, while for other words such as days of the week there may be complete accuracy. Tagging errors are thus typically concentrated in particular items or groups of items.

We can appreciate the task and achievements of those who have developed automatic taggers if we consider the tagging of relatively high frequency words such as *once*. Three word-class uses of the word *once* were identified in the *LOB Corpus*: adverbial, conjunction and noun. These were tagged with an early version of CLAWS and manually post-edited (Garside et al., 1987: 33). The adverbial use is by far the most frequent, with over 80% of the tokens. When the *Wellington Corpus* was tagged automatically with a later version of CLAWS but without manual post-editing, some occurrences of *once* as a conjunction were tagged as adverbs and some adverbs as conjunctions. For example, in the following sentences *once* was wrongly classified as a conjunction:

Once there were Maori burial grounds in the site.
Once we went to Tasmania.
He told me he knew Peltzer, once the conqueror of Douglas Lowe.

On the other hand, *once* was wrongly tagged as an adverbial in the following sentences:

Once a function has been formed it can be used to classify.
They will respond to authority or guidance, especially once adolescence is reached.
He considered the infrastructure required once the Bill passed into law.

In *just this once* the word *once* was tagged as an adverb instead of a noun. About 20% of the tokens of *once* in the *Wellington Corpus* were initially mistagged by the machine as conjunctions or adverbs, necessitating manual correction. These errors occurred especially in sentences involving ellipsis or where *once* was sentence-initial.

The grammatical tagging of a polysemous word such as *once* also needs sense disambiguation to make the word-class tagging maximally useful. The considerable manual input required can be illustrated in further analysis of *once* as an adverbial where at least two quite distinct senses are possible. *Once* can refer to a single event or occurrence and can have past or future reference, or it can be used to refer to a former period of time.

Once = on one single occasion, e.g.:

Her eyes never once cast him the merest glance.
Surely I can take a Saturday morning once in the year.

Once = formerly, previously, at a time in the past, e.g.:

I was once a journalist.
I am writing from another place once named Tingralla.

In the *LOB Corpus*, as Table 4.1 shows, almost 45% of all the tokens of *once* used as adverbials are split evenly between these two senses. In the remaining 55% of occurrences, *once* occurs in adverbial phrases. Table 4.1 also summarizes the use of *once* as an adverbial in the *Wellington Corpus*. *Once* is used significantly more than in *LOB* to mean 'formerly'. The most significant difference between the British and New Zealand corpora is in the proportion of the adverbial uses of *once* in collocation with *at* (*at once*) with the sense 'immediately' (*Go away at once*). In *LOB*, 22.3% of occurrences of adverbial *once* are used in this way compared with

Table 4.1 *Once* as an adverbial in the *LOB* and *Wellington* corpora (based on Kennedy, 1996a)

	LOB Corpus		Wellington Corpus	
	Tokens	% of *once* as adverbial	Tokens	% of *once* as adverbial
once = on one single occasion	81	22.5	63	23.6
once = formerly, previously, at a time in the past	80	22.3	96	36.3
Adverbial phrase idioms				
once a/every/per (week)	6	1.7	16	6.0
once again	42	11.7	24	9.0
once more	27	7.5	15	5.6
once and for all (= conclusively)	4	1.1	3	1.1
once or twice (= occasionally)	5	1.4	3	1.1
more than once	5	1.4	3	1.1
once in a while (= sometimes)	1	0.3	3	1.1
once upon a time	1	0.3	1	0.4
at once (= immediately)	80	22.3	16	6.0
(all) at once (= simultaneously)	16	4.5	16	6.0
(all) at once (= suddenly)	2	0.6	0	–
(just) for once (= unusually)	9	2.5	7	2.6
Total *once* adverbial tokens	359	100	266	100

only 6% in the *Wellington Corpus*. The tagging of *at once*, however, does not assist sense disambiguation in the following sentences.

'Frank must go away at once,' she said. (*at once* = immediately)
I can't be everywhere at once. (*at once* = simultaneously)
Then all at once she remembered what she had heard. (*all at once* = suddenly)

As we have seen, taggers which operate in a probabilistic manner obviously have a more complicated task with word forms which can function in more than one word class. But further, as Biber (1993a: 220) has demonstrated, 'the probabilities associated with grammatically ambiguous forms are often markedly different across registers'. Register differences can thus affect the success of automatic word-class taggers and grammatical parsers. Biber notes, for example, that relative clauses are frequent in official documents and prepared speeches but rare in conversation. On the other hand, causative adverbial clauses are frequent in conversation but rare in official documents and press reports.

Problems involved in automatic tagging and the kind of manual input necessary in sense disambiguation suggests that a good deal of caution is needed if comparative studies are based on tagged corpora. It is essential that before corpora or parts of corpora are compared the analyst can be sure that the same tagger has been used and the same degree of manual post-editing has been carried out. At present, automatic tagging and cursory post-editing on their own appear to be inadequate except for totally determinate word types. As Sinclair (1992: 386) has commented, 'From experience so far, it appears likely that there will be a lot of indeterminateness in automatic analysis'.

Indeterminacy in natural language poses problems not only for automatic analysis but for manual analysis too. In the following sentence, *once* could mean 'on one occasion' or 'formerly':

According to the script she was once captain of the junior hockey team
at her school.

Here the indeterminacy is probably best resolved by knowledge of the world, but in the following two sentences it is presumably resolved by the grammatical context. In the first, *not once*, while denying a single occurrence, actually allows for more than one occurrence, while in the latter *not once* means 'never':

Most of them have bathed before not once but ten times.
Not once did anyone visit her.

The annotation of semantic relationships has been explored by researchers concerned with the marking of cohesion in texts. Fligelstone (1992) has described the initial stages of a project to develop a system for annotating texts in order to show anaphoric relations such as the association of third-person pronouns with their antecedents, and to mark recoverable ellipsis, e.g. *There are 9 categories in PGA statistical service. Assists isn't* **among them**. *If it were* [ellipsis of *among them*], *Ben Crenshaw* . . . Such work to develop ways of annotating cohesive relations in text may eventually lead to the development of an automatic anaphor resolver perhaps based on probabilistic principles. The *XANADU* editing software for marking cohesion, developed at Lancaster University for UCREL, is described by Garside (1993). As with the CLAWS word-class tagger, *XANADU* relies on both automatic and manual processing, and in fact works on the output of prior word-class tagging and manual skeleton parsing.

Another extension of automatic analysis of annotated texts from corpora has been explored in the field of content analysis, which is concerned with the distributional analysis of semantic aspects of texts. Wilson and Rayson (1993) have described a project designed to extend the CLAWS annotation system so as to assign semantic tags automatically to large bodies of transcribed speech from market research interviews.

4.1.4 Parsing

As we have seen, grammatical tagging assigns a tag to each word in a text to label the word class to which it belongs in context. Parsing is a more demanding task involving not only annotation but also linguistic analysis, according to some particular grammatical theory, to identify and label the function of each word or group of words in a phrase or sentence. A word tagged as a noun can function as the subject, object or complement of a verb, for example. A parsed corpus is necessary if we wish to retrieve, say, relative clauses identified by labelled bracketing of the syntactic function of these clauses in texts. Corpora which have been analysed in this way are often called **treebanks** because they are collections of labelled constituent structures or phrase markers. A parsed corpus provides a labelled analysis for each sentence to show how the various words function. Information about the functions of words in context is of course vital for language processing whether in our normal everyday use or in any attempt to use machines to simulate natural language processing. For example, a word processor which is designed to receive its input from the human voice rather than a keyboard must be able to distinguish between *right, rite, write* and *Wright* and can only do so if it can identify from the context whether the form it 'hears' is an adjective, verb, common noun or proper noun. It can do this partly by the collocational probability of word classes co-occurring in particular grammatical structures. For example, /raɪt/ is most likely to be *Wright* after *Ms* or *Mr*. On the other hand, *right* is most likely to be a noun if it occurs in the structure *on the right*, whereas in a context like *the right stuff*, the word *right* is most likely to be an adjective. The prepositional phrase *on the right* functions adjectivally in *The person on the right is her brother*, whereas it functions adverbially in *Our house is on the right*, and so on. Many applications will benefit from the availability of fully parsed corpora, even though their compilation, which typically involves much laborious manual analysis, has until recently produced quite small parsed corpora. Their application has been mainly as a research resource to help clarify some of the problems in processing natural language by machine. The major parsed corpora which were publicly available in the early

1990s have been described in an excellent overview by Sampson (1992a), who provided what he termed 'a consumer guide' to five of them, evaluating their strengths and weaknesses for different kinds of linguistic research and illustrating the format of each.

For some purposes, a fully exhaustive parse of text can be necessary. For others, it is much more economical and still adequate to sketch out only certain major functions and structures. For purposes of linguistic description it is desirable, if not essential, for the parsing process to be transparent and comprehensible. However, parsing is also crucial in various applications in natural language processing, including text-to-speech synthesis and machine translation (Patten, 1992). As long as the task is carried out, and with whatever level of detail or complexity proves to be necessary, it is a reasonably safe assumption that the power and speed of computers will be able to meet the need. At present, what is needed is fast, robust, reliable, automatic systems, techniques and software to undertake the parsing. In addition to applications in natural language processing, there is a need for reliable information on the major patterns in the sentence structure of English so that language pedagogy can be improved. This should not only be at the level of clause types (SVO, SVOO, SVOC, SVC, etc.) but also for descriptions of such processes as modification. For example, information may be needed on the proportion of English sentences in a particular text, genre or corpus which have adverbial modification by means of a prepositional phrase, and the proportion of prepositional phrases which function adjectivally and adverbially respectively, as in:

The woman **at the airport** was my aunt.
I watched the planes land **at the airport**.

At present, automatic parsing has not approached the level of accuracy achieved by automatic word-class taggers. However, as with word-class tagging, there have been two main approaches to the development of automatic parsers, based on probabilistic and rule-based principles. Automatic parsing is closely associated with word-class and sense tagging, and part of the challenge for developers of tagging and parsing systems has been to design software which will reliably identify from the domain, subject field, collocations, and syntactic structure in which a particular use of a word occurs, precisely what its sense is, and what is its grammatical function. On the basis of grammatical rules and probabilistic information from earlier manual parsing, the parser has to make the best match to produce the most complete or most likely analysis of a phrase or sentence. In many cases, a large number of alternative parses are possible.

Automatic parsing has tended to founder on certain features of natural languages which have predictably proved difficult, such as prepositional phrase attachment and coordination. Discontinuous elements and ellipsis are also notoriously difficult. The difficulty caused by ellipsis is exacerbated especially in spoken texts where 'incomplete' utterances, false starts and discourse items such as fillers occur. Not everything can be analysed linguistically (e.g. routines such as *good on you* as a way of congratulating or encouraging someone). Ihalainen (1991b: 213) gives an excellent example of how ellipsis can challenge a parser. He points out that in the following exchange, although the answer may appear to be a noun phrase, it is really equivalent to a prepositional phrase functioning as an adverbial:

Q. Where were you born?
A. A place called Latworthy.

As Carberry (1989) has demonstrated, however, there is an even greater challenge for automatic parsers in having to model intersentential ellipsis resolution, where in ordinary human communication we decode fragments on the basis of discourse expectations, beliefs, focusing strategies, and other pragmatic knowledge, as well as syntactic and lexical information. Sampson (1992b: 430) cites *Best before see base of can* as today being 'one of the highest frequency sentences of written British English'; yet a decade or so ago it might well have been grammatically impossible. In cases such as these a parser would almost certainly have trouble establishing the grammatical structure.

The dominance of generative grammar as a theory of language from the 1960s made it natural for researchers in natural language processing to assume initially that parsers could be derived from schemes of grammatical rules. A rule-based parser typically searches through the rules in a predetermined grammar and lexicon and seeks to specify which of the rules could be applied to produce a well-formed syntactic analysis of a given sentence in the corpus. The sentence would be considered ungrammatical if rules could not generate it. On the other hand, if more than one analysis were found, then the sentences could be considered to have an ambiguous grammatical interpretation which could only be resolved with further semantic or pragmatic information.

Patten (1992) reviewed the range of techniques developed, including top-down versus bottom-up processing of sentence phrase markers, and various alternative grammatical models. However, as he notes, while it is possible to build effective automatic parsers for certain sentences with small experimental grammars, 'the general problem of parsing unrestricted text with a large grammar has not been solved' (1992: 50). Sampson (1992b) and others have argued on the basis of work with the *LOB Corpus* that unrestricted natural language is grammatically much richer and less determinate than generative models of language have yet been able to take account of. The false starts and incompleteness of spoken utterances can make analysis even more difficult. It thus makes sense to avoid the model of a parser dealing with all-and-only sentences of a language – the strict notion of well-formedness being not applicable to real corpus data. The size of the task is illustrated in the manually parsed *Lancaster–Leeds Treebank*. Sampson found 747 different NP-types among the 8,328 NPs in the treebank. Of these, the most frequent type (Det + Nsg) constituted only 14% of the types. Phrase-structure parsers for English appear thus to be unwieldy and unworkably large if designed to deal with unrestricted text and not just 'test' sentences. Briscoe (1990) has however argued that English noun phrases are more regular than Sampson suggests and offered an alternative view that viable parsers might be developed using generative grammars.

The difficulty of successfully developing rule-based approaches to the automatic parsing of corpora, however, led some researchers to explore parsing from a probabilistic perspective. In particular, teams of researchers in the United Kingdom at the Universities of Lancaster and Leeds, and in the USA at IBM and the AT&T Bell Laboratories, have worked on developing probabilistic parsers based on laborious initial manual parsing to build up a database or treebank of parsed sentences. The purpose of the treebank is to provide statistics on the frequency of grammatical structures for the automatic parser to use subsequently in the probabilistic analysis of unrestricted text. By the 1990s it was widely accepted that probabilistic data-based techniques rather than hypothesis or rule-based techniques held the greatest promise for the development of automatic parsing. An indispensable account of one of the earliest projects in probabilistic parsing carried out at Lancaster University is Garside et al. (1987). About 45,000 words in 2,284 sentences, totalling about 4.5% of the *LOB Corpus*, with texts representing all 15 genres of the corpus, were parsed manually by Sampson, resulting in the *Lancaster–Leeds Treebank*. The mean sentence length was 22.1 words. Sampson (1987) described how a technique called simulated annealing could then subsequently be employed to find the optimal parse tree for any 'new' sentence as matched against the treebank. A fragment from the *Lancaster–Leeds Treebank* illustrating the result of the parsing is shown in Figure 4.9.

K16   116
[S[Nas I_PP1A Nas][R next_RI R][V wondered_VBD V][Fn if_CS [Nas she_PP3A Nas][V would_MD like_VB V][Ti& [Vi to_TO bear_VB Vi][R down_RPR][P on_IN [Ns Shaftesbury_NP Avenue_NPL Ns]P][Ti+ and_CC [V see_VB V][Ncs a_AT play_NN Ncs]Ti+]Ti&]Fn]._. S]

Figure 4.9   A fragment of the *Lancaster–Leeds Treebank*
(from Leech & Garside, 1991: 15)

As noted earlier, the *Lancaster–Leeds Treebank* was based on a context-free phrase-structure grammar which exhibited a huge number of grammatical rules, many of which occurred once only in the corpus (Leech & Garside, 1991). Subsequently, the *LOB Corpus Treebank* was created

with a parsing scheme based on the experience and statistics derived
from the *Lancaster–Leeds Treebank* project. It became available in 1991 as
an automatic, probabilistically parsed version of about 144,000 words
of text from the *LOB Corpus*. The *LOB Corpus Treebank* (also known as
the *Parsed LOB Corpus* or the *Lancaster Parsed Corpus*) was designed to
develop automatic probabilistic parsing procedures for the UCREL parsing system at Lancaster, and while the parsing scheme is similar to that
of the *Lancaster–Leeds Treebank,* the later work has a smaller simplified
set of subcategory symbols. A distinction is not made between singular
and plural noun phrases, for example. The *LOB Corpus Treebank* was a
pioneering analysed corpus in that it was the result of automatic parsing followed by manual correction of errors. Figure 4.10 consists of a
fragment from the *LOB Corpus Treebank.*

[S[N it_PP3 N][V arose_VBD V][P during_IN [N talks_NNS [P following_IN [N[G
President_NPT Kennedy's_NPS G] report_NN [P to_IN [N the_ATI British_JNP
Prime_NPT Minister_NPT N]P][Po of_INO [N the_ATI outcome_NN [Po of_INO
[N his_PPS recent_JJ visit_NN [P to_IN [N Paris_NP N]P]N]Po]N]P]N]P]._. S]

Figure 4.10   A fragment of the *LOB Corpus Treebank*
(from Leech & Garside, 1991: 18)

The UCREL team found, however, that the less delicate system of
analysis used for the *LOB Corpus Treebank* was not satisfactory, both
because the resulting statistical information was still not enough for driv-
ing a fully automatic probabilistic parser and because context-free phrase-
structure grammars induced from such a corpus were unmanageably
large. They concluded that while tagging could be done best automatically with manual post-editing, in the case of parsing it was more efficient
to do it manually using specially developed software to speed up data
entry. They developed, therefore, an even more simplified technique
which they called 'skeleton parsing'. Figure 4.11 is a fragment of the
Skeleton Treebank from the *Lancaster/IBM Spoken English Corpus.*

---

(4)   [S& Well_UH [V let_VM21 's_VM22 now_RT turn_VVO [N our_APPS
attention_NN1 N][P to_II [N cricket_NN1 N]P]V]S&] ,_, and_CC [S+ once_RR21
more_RR22 [N it_PPH1 N][V 's_VHZ been_VBN [Nr a_AT1 year_NNT1 [Fr
when_RRQ [N[N& test_NN1 matches_NN2 N&] ,_, and_CC [N+ the_AT
ubiquitous_JJ [one_MC1 day_NNT1] internationals_NN2 N+]N] ,_, [V
proliferated_VVD [P around_II [N the_AT world_NN1 N]P]V]Fr]Nr]V]S+] :_:

Figure 4.11   A fragment of the Skeleton Treebank of the *Lancaster/IBM Spoken
English Corpus*
(from Leech & Garside, 1991: 21)

Leech and Garside (1991) have described the principles, procedures
and use of skeleton parsing developed at UCREL. The amount of manual

input involved in this skeleton parsing, however, is worth noting in light of the ultimate desirability for fully automatic analysis. Although skilled manual parsers can achieve parsing speeds of 'well over a sentence a minute (where the average length of sentences is over 20 words)' (Leech & Garside, 1991: 24), learning to be a competent analyst took about three months, even for such minimalist analysis. The skeleton parsing technique has nevertheless been valuable in producing over three million words of machine-readable parsed text to help generate statistics for the development of fully automatic probabilistic parsers, which continue to remain as a somewhat distant goal for researchers on corpus analysis.

Souter and O'Donoghue (1991) have discussed research on developing a probabilistic parser compatible with systemic functional grammar. Analysis of the manually parsed *Polytechnic of Wales Corpus* of 60,800 words resulted in over 4,500 syntactic rules, most of which occurred infrequently. On the basis of what they termed 'the ungraceful failure of current rule-based techniques' (1991: 46), they have, like Sampson, rejected models which observe a strict distinction between rule-based 'grammatical and ungrammatical' and used instead a scale of observed frequency of occurrence of word strings.

One of the largest and most influential parsing projects has been undertaken at the University of Pennsylvania. Marcus et al. (1993) have described the *Penn Treebank* project, which is a 4.8-million-word collection of texts tagged for word class and partially parsed to give labelled bracketed structures. The texts are of written American English and come from the *Wall Street Journal*, the *Brown Corpus* (retagged), US Department of Energy abstracts, government and industry bulletins and manuals, a small amount of fiction from classic American authors and also some radio transcripts.

In the first phase of the *Penn Treebank* development, the parsing analysis was described as 'skeletal' in that it was a surface-structure analysis lacking some systematic detail. The small tagset and the parsing system resulted in quite a coarse analysis with some unlabelled nodes in the trees, but one which is reasonably accessible to human analysts.

Initially, partial automatic parsing is undertaken by Hindle's nonprobabilistic *Fidditch Parser*. Figure 4.12 provides an example of an analysed sentence from the *Penn Treebank* after the initial output of *Fidditch* has been manually simplified and corrected. Here is the sample sentence before tagging and parsing:

> Battle-tested industrial managers here always buck up nervous newcomers with the tale of the first of their countrymen to visit Mexico, a boatload of samurai warriors blown ashore 375 years ago.

The second phase of the *Penn Treebank* project, which began in 1993, resulted in a much richer grammatical annotation considerably removed from skeletal parsing. In particular it provides for some encoding of under-

```
((S
     (NP Battle-tested industrial managers
          here)
     always
     (VP buck
          up
          (NP nervous newcomers)
          (PP with
               (NP the tale
                    (PP of
                         (NP (NP the
                                   (ADJP first
                                        (PP of
                                             (NP their countrymen)))
                                   (S (NP *)
                                   to
                                   (VP visit
                                        (NP Mexico))))
                              '
                         (NP (NP a boatload
                              (PP of
                                   (NP (NP warriors)
                                        (VP-1 blown
                                             ashore
                                             (ADVP (NP 375 years)
                                                  ago)))))
                         (VP-1 *pseudo-attach*)))))))))
```

Figure 4.12   An analysed sentence from the *Penn Treebank*
after simplification and correction (from Marcus et al., 1993: 325)

lying structure through the automatic marking of predicate–argument structure, and also handles discontinuous elements. The *Penn Treebank* provides a very large amount of parsed text for the research community to work with.

There are several other analysed corpora from which research has been reported but not all are publicly available. They include the Lancaster-annotated *Associated Press Treebank*, which is a one-million-word partially parsed corpus of US newswire reports; the *Canadian Hansard Treebank*, which is a partially parsed corpus of about 750,000 words from the Canadian parliamentary proceedings; the *IBM Manuals Treebank*, which is a partially parsed corpus of about 800,000 words from computer manuals.

The first of the publicly available analysed corpora for research was compiled at the University of Gothenburg (Ellegård, 1978). A subset of a little over 10% of the *Brown Corpus* of written American English, containing 64 of the 500 *Brown* texts and totalling 128,000 words, was manually analysed using a form of dependency grammar. The *Gothenburg Corpus* codes both formal and functional properties of constituents, including some aspects of underlying structure. Sampson (1992a, c) has described some of the 'complexities and inadequacies' of the *Gothenburg Corpus* coding scheme and has himself led a project which aims to turn the somewhat neglected *Gothenburg Corpus* into a more accessible and useful resource for research by replacing the tagging and coding system, providing additional analysis including some semantic categories, more detailed underlying structure, and restoring the original orthographic details. Sampson's project – Surface and Underlying Structural Analyses of Naturalistic English (SUSANNE) – (Sampson, 1995) has probably the most complex and sophisticated analytic scheme of any of the analysed corpora available in the mid-1990s.

Sampson (1992c) has noted that available parsed corpora have been analysed with varying degrees of delicacy, not all of which show the deep structure or logical relationships in the analysed sentences, and yet such deep analysis is required for many applications of natural language processing for information technology. The *SUSANNE Corpus* analytic scheme is an attempt to specify norms and a comprehensive checklist of linguistic phenomena for the annotation of modern English in terms of both its underlying or logical structure as well as the surface grammar. Although the attempt at comprehensiveness in the analysis of the *SUSANNE Corpus* is one of its strengths for information-technology-directed research on natural language processing, at the same time, not surprisingly, the amount of detail does not make it easy for linguists interested in using the corpus for getting a descriptive picture of the grammar of English. Figure 4.13 illustrates the format of the analysis. However, perhaps a compensation for the relative difficulty of interpretability of the format of *SUSANNE* is that the compilers have made the corpus available without charge via the Internet, and in so doing have generously contributed to the tradition of more-or-less free access which has characterized many of the developments in corpus linguistics. Full details of the SUSANNE analytic scheme and information on how to get access to the corpus are contained in Sampson (1995), with a useful overview in Sampson (1994).

The fragment from the *SUSANNE Corpus* illustrated in Figure 4.13 has six data fields. Columns 1 and 2 show reference and status (e.g. whether the word is an abbreviation or symbol); 3 is a word-class tag (from a 352-item tagset based on the tagset used in the Lancaster parsers); 4 is the graphic word; 5 the lemma; and 6 the parse, or bracketed string. The parse string is split up line by line, according to the current word of the parsed sentence, but it may be easier to understand it as a labelled bracketing (or phrase marker) if the separate lines are imagined joined in one horizontal string.

As noted in Section 4.1.2, from the early 1980s work at Nijmegen on the 1.5-million-word *TOSCA Corpus* was directed towards syntactic analysis. Oostdijk (1991) provides a comprehensive description of the development of analysed corpora at Nijmegen and includes analyses of many sentences illustrating the approach taken to produce tagged text and the associated phrase markers. Figure 4.14 is an example of the type

A10:0620p	A	NNS	Dr.	–	[O[S[Nns:s.
A10:0630a	–	NP1s	Barnes	Barnes	.Nns:s]
A10:0630b	–	VVDv	said	say	[Vd.Vd]
A10:0630c	–	CST	that	that	[Fn:o.
A10:0630d	–	EX	there	there	
A10:0630e	–	VVDi	seemed	seem	[Vd.Vd]
A10:0630f	–	YG	–	–	[Ti:s<s152.s152>
A10:0630g	–	TO	to	to	[Vib.
A10:0630h	–	VB0	be	be	.Vib]Ti:s]
A10:0630i	–	NN1n	feeling	feeling	[Ns:S152.
A10:0630j	–	CST	that	that	[Fn.
A10:0630k	–	NN1n	evacuation	evacuation	[Np:s.
A10:0630m	–	NN2	plans	plan	.
A10:0630n	–	YC	+,	–	.
A10:0630p	–	RR	even	even	.
A10:0640a	–	IF	for	for	[P.
A10:0640b	–	AT1	a	a	[Ns:151.
A10:0640c	–	JJ	high	high	.
A10:0640d	–	NNJ1n	school	school	.
A10:0640e	–	RRQr	where	where	[Fr[Rq:p151.Rq:p151]
A10:0640f	–	EX	there	there	.
A10:0640g	–	VBDR	were	be	[Vwb.Vwb]
A10:0640h	–	NN2	lots	lot	[Np:s.
A10:0640i	–	IO	of	of	[Po.
A10:0640j	–	NN2	cars	car	.Po]Np:s]Fr]Ns:151]P]Np:s]
A10:0640k	–	YIL	<ldquo>	–	.
A10:0640m	–	VMd	+might	may	[Vdceb.
A10:0640n	–	XX	not	not	.
A10:0640p	–	VB0	be	be	.Vdceb]
A10:0640q	–	JJ	realistic	realistic	[J:e.J:e]
A10:0650a	–	CC	and	and	[Fn+.
A10:0650b	–	VMd	would	will	[Vdce.
A10:0650c	–	XX	not	not	.
A10:0650d	–	VV0v	work	work	.Vdce]Fn+]
A10:0650e	–	YIR	+<rdquo>	–	.Fn]Ns:S152]Fn:o]S]
A10:0650f	–	YF	+.	–	.O]
A10:0650g	–	YB	<minbrk>	–	[Oh.Oh]

Figure 4.13 A fragment of the *SUSANNE Corpus*
(Sampson, 1994: 175)

of analyses produced. Results are stored at Nijmegen University, where the corpus is available for consultation. Information about current *TOSCA Corpus* research is available via e-mail: hvh@lett.kun.nl. For the Nijmegen research, the descriptive grammar used in parsing has been based ultimately on that of Quirk et al. (1972, 1985). Van Halteren and Oostdijk (1993: 154) note that this system has been found to describe adequately most syntactic structures and processes found in the texts, including, for example, coordination, apposition, clefting, extraposition, verbless clauses, interrogatives, imperatives, subject–verb inversion and certain kinds of ellipsis. Only 'a small number of structures and phenomena has not yet been accounted for', and these are mainly constructions which occur relatively infrequently. However, as Oostdijk (1991: 214) notes, in practice the *TOSCA Parser* at that stage could assign appropriate analyses to a

```
        ┌─1 ┬─1─1─ ........................................................................... Somewhat
        │   └─2─ ............................................................................ sporadically
       ┌─2 ┬─1─ ................................................................................ at
       │   └─2 ┬─1─1─ ...................................................................... this
       │       └─2─ .......................................................................... time
  ┌─1 ─┤─3─ ..................................................................................... ,
  │    ├─4─1─ ............................................................................... Appleby
  │    ├─5 ┬─1─ ............................................................................. was
 ─*─┤     └─2─ ........................................................................... writing
  │    │   ┌─1─1─ ........................................................................... a
  │    └─6 ┤─2─ .......................................................................... book
  └─2─ ......................................................................................... .
```

NOFU, TXTU()
: UTT,S(REG,DECL)
:   A,AVP(GE)
:   AVPR,AVP(GE)
:   :AVHD,ADV(GE,ABS){Somewhat}
:   AVHD,ADV(GE,ABS){sporadically}
:   A,PP()
:   P,PREP(){at}
:   PC,NP()
:   :DT,DTP(SING)
:   : DTCE,DET(DEM,SING){this}
:   :NPHD,CN(SING){time}
:   NOFU,NOCA(IGN){,}
:   SU,NP()
:   NPHD,PRN(SING){Appleby}
:   VB,VP(MOTR)
:   AVB,AUX(PROG,PAST){was}
:   MVB,MLV(MOTR,PRESP){writing}
:   OD,NP()
:   DT,DTP(SING)
:   :DTCE,ART(SING){a}
:   NPHD,CN(SING) {book}
: PUNC,PUNCM(PER){.}

Figure 4.14 Format of a parsed sentence using the Nijmegen approach to the automatic analysis of English
(from Oostdijk, 1991: 162)

sample of fiction texts with about 88% accuracy, but with only about 56% accuracy to non-fiction texts.

The *TOSCA Parser* assigns trees to each sentence according to a formal 'extended affix grammar' which contains several thousand rules. The automatic parsing typically results in many ambiguous analyses. It was reported that only 20% of sentences receive a single analysis, while about 15% receive between 20 and 100 analyses. Alternative analyses for the same sentence have to be resolved manually with semantic or pragmatic information. The large amount of manual input to the parsing requires experienced and skilled analysts. Such manual input, deciding between alternative parses, can be hugely time-consuming and costly but ultimately for any such rule-based parser it can be worthwhile if it leads to improved specification of the grammatical rules and thus to more accurate and efficient automatic parsing in the future.

The *TOSCA Corpus* is stored in the *Nijmegen Linguistic Database* (*LDB*), which is a sophisticated software package designed for the storage and management of large collections of systematically analysed tree structures. The interactive software can be used to explore the structure of the trees, or to search for and count particular structures and to display these graphically. The *LDB* does not itself syntactically analyse a corpus. Although it was originally used for storing the analysed *Nijmegen* and *TOSCA* corpora, it has been used to store other parsed corpora including the *Lancaster–Leeds* and the *Polytechnic of Wales* corpora. Van Halteren and van den Heuvel (1990) have provided a manual on the use of the *LDB* software, which was the first software designed to handle large syntactically analysed corpora. With the *LDB* it is possible to undertake such tasks as identifying and counting all sentences in a corpus which do not have a grammatical subject, or counting the number of direct objects and comparing their internal structures. The longest direct object in the *Nijmegen Corpus* apparently contains 69 words. The *LDB* can also be used to carry out routine concordancing such as selecting every verb in a corpus which has a particular word (e.g. *often*) attached to it.

Even higher levels of accuracy in word-class tagging and syntactic parsing have been claimed for corpus-analysis software developed more recently at the University of Helsinki using a non-probabilistic approach known as Constraint Grammar Parsing (Karlsson, 1994; Karlsson et al., 1995). In the *Constraint Grammar Parser of English* (*ENGCG*), word-class tagging and syntactic parsing are closely related, with tagging being used as the basis for parsing and the whole process being viewed as progressive disambiguation, through a series of seven modules, of possible alternative readings using both morphological and contextual information. Kytö and Voutilainen give examples of the non-statistical approach in *ENGCG* using 'hand-written linguistic rules or constraints' (1995: 26) such as the following:

Discard all finite verb readings if the preceding word is an unambiguous determiner.
Discard all finite verb readings if the preceding word is *to*.

Most of the 139 grammatical tags used in *ENGCG* are consistent with those in Quirk et al. (1985), which, as in the case of the *TOSCA Parser*, provides the grammatical framework for the *Helsinki* parser.

Kytö and Voutilainen (1995: 25) provide an example of how the sentence *That round table might collapse* is handled by *ENGCG* from the initial morphological analysis which gives multiple possible readings for each word, through morphological disambiguation based on some 1,100 linguistically based constraints rather than probabilities, to a surface

AN INTRODUCTION TO CORPUS LINGUISTICS

syntactic analysis with tagging, and finally to syntactic disambiguation involving some 400 syntactic and other constraints.

Figure 4.15 shows the initial morphological analysis of the sample sentence with alternative readings, and then the output after syntactic tagging and disambiguation. Karlsson (1994) gives examples of more complex analyses. It should be noted that, unlike other parsers mentioned, the *ENGCG Parser* employs a dependency grammar analysis, and thus

```
'<*that>'
        'that' <*> <**CLB> CS @CS
        'that' <*> DET CENTRAL DEM SG @DN>
        'that' <*> ADV AD-A> @AD-A>
        'that' <*> PRON DEM SG
        'that' <*> <NonMod> <**CLB> <Rel> PRON SG/PL
'<round>'
        'round' <SVO> <SV> V SUBJUNCTIVE VFIN @+FMAINV
        'round' <SVO> <SV> V IMP VFIN @+FMAINV
        'round' <SVO> <SV> V INF
        'round' <SVO> <SV> V PRES -SG3 VFIN @+FMAINV
        'round' PREP
        'round' N NOM SG
        'round' A ABS
        'round' ADV ADVL @ADVL
'<table>'
        'table' N NOM SG
        'table' <SVO> V SUBJUNCTIVE VFIN @+FMAINV
        'table' <SVO> V IMP VFIN @+FMAINV
        'table' <SVO> V INF
        'table' <SVO> V PRES -SG3 VFIN @+FMAINV
'<might>'
        'might' <-Indef> N NOM SG
        'might' V AUXMOD VFIN @+FAUXV
'<collapse>'
        'collapse' N NOM SG
        'collapse' <SV> <SVO> V SUBJUNCTIVE VFIN @+FMAINV
        'collapse' <SV> <SVO> V IMP VFIN @+FMAINV
        'collapse' <SV> <SVO> V INF
        'collapse' <SV> <SVO> V PRES -SG3 VFIN @+FMAINV
'<$.>'

Finally, there is the sample sentence after full ENGCG parsing:

'<*that>'
        'that' <*> DET CENTRAL DEM SG @DN> ;; determiner
'<round>'
        'round' A ABS @AN> ;; premodifying adjective
'<table>'
        'table' N NOM SG @SUBJ ;; subject
'<might>'
        'might' V AUXMOD VFIN @+FAUXV ;; finite auxiliary
'<collapse>'
        'collapse' <SV> <SVO> V INF @-FMAINV ;; nonfinite main verb
'<$.>'
```

Figure 4.15 A sample of the output of the *ENGCG Parser* (from Kytö & Voutilainen, 1995: 25–28)

avoids the necessity of constituent structure trees to show syntactic relationships. The *Constraint Grammar Parser of English* has been applied to
the annotation of the massive *Bank of English Corpus* extension of the
Cobuild project.

Karlsson (1994) has reported a very high level of accuracy for word-
class tagging with an error rate not exceeding 0.3% for those 94%–97%
of words given an unambiguous tag. At the parsing level, accuracy is
not as high, with 15% of words being given more than one syntactic
label and 3% of words being given an incorrect label. Initial indications
suggest that the *ENGCG* analyses may not be delicate enough for some
purposes because there is a degree of underspecification in the tagging.
However, if these high levels of accuracy and speed of analysis for written standard English are able to be achieved across wide varieties of
texts, the *ENGCG* system may nevertheless offer many users the possibility of substantial advances in on-line automatic processing of text. Even
an error rate of 1%, however, represents one million errors of analysis
in a 100-million-word corpus, and this is no small number if the output
is to be used, for example, in translation projects. Further information on
developments in the *ENGCG* system of analysis is available by e-mail
from Atro.Voutilainen@Helsinki.fi.

Other systems for corpus annotation and analysis have been developed
for particular projects. For example, Eeg-Olofsson (1990) and Altenberg
(1990c) have described research on parsing and on the automatic segmentation of spoken text into tone units, as part of the TESS project
(Svartvik, 1990b). Annotation systems for corpora to facilitate research
on discourse and pragmatic aspects of language are still in their infancy,
but are clearly needed in light of the growing availability of corpora of
spoken language. Another development is the use of self-organizing algorithms, or statistical techniques whereby the computer itself 'learns' to
achieve an optimal analysis. Self-organizing systems of linguistic analysis based on corpora may result in new taxonomies of word classes
and grammatical structures which differ somewhat from the traditional
categories used.

In the meantime, corpus analysis is very much in a developmental
phase. Systems of analysis are often not very consumer-friendly and, as
we have seen, considerable training and expertise is often required to
interact with or handle them. Many are not freely available. The output
of more advanced levels of analysis such as parsing is often hard for
inexperienced analysts to interpret, because the output is represented in
a form which facilitates interpretation by the computer rather than the
human user.

Analysed corpora appear in a wide variety of formats, as can be seen
from the examples used in this chapter. In some, sentences can occupy
many lines with one word to a line. In others, tree diagrams wend their
way across the screen or page. In some, the tags or codes used for word

class or grammatical function are reasonably transparent abbreviations (e.g. VB for verb). In others, opaque numerical codes are used.

As Briscoe (1994: 97) noted, in spite of three decades of research on how to parse natural language automatically, 'no practical domain-independent parser of unrestricted text has been developed, to date'. In spite of the apparently competing philosophies of rule-based versus probabilistic approaches to parsing, Briscoe has suggested that approaches to parsing from a probabilistic perspective are not necessarily in opposition to approaches based on a generative grammar, but that the two approaches may be viewed as complementary. Briscoe and Carroll (1993) have outlined just such an approach involving unification-based or feature-based grammars, a direction also taken in Black et al. (1993), involving both automatic and manual analysis. During the years of research on automatic tagging and parsing, the lack of common standards for tagset size and ways of displaying phrase-structure trees has meant that it has been, and continues to be, difficult to assess the relative merits of the different parsers. Up till now most of the parsed corpora have been manually parsed to act as training bases or benchmarks from which to undertake research on how to automate the process of parsing. Where automatic parsing has been used, manual post-editing has also been necessary. As noted earlier, experience at Lancaster led UCREL researchers to claim machine-assisted manual analysis to be more efficient than manually corrected machine output.

Souter (1993) has reviewed the strengths and weaknesses of the different formatting styles used to display the sentences of existing parsed corpora of English. The case is well made for some greater standardization than has evolved during the developmental phase of corpus parsing. An appendix to Souter's review provides examples of the wide differences in the formats of some of the major publicly available parsed corpora. However, such is the exploratory nature of much of this research that there is little evidence that researchers will settle on a single standard model and format for automatic advanced parsing of texts in the foreseeable future at least. One outcome of this situation has been that many corpus researchers have been encouraged to continue to work with raw text and to focus on lexical grammar.

4.2 Procedures used in corpus analysis

A number of routine procedures are used to search a corpus, to recover information or to organize, catalogue or display the facts about language which are under investigation. The most basic format used in displaying information about the linguistic elements in a corpus is generated by means of listing and counting. The lists produced by software can be of a number of different kinds ranging from simple wordlists to more sophisticated analyses including the classic concordance format. We will consider examples of some of the frequently used formats.

4.2.1 Wordlists

Whether a corpus is huge and dynamic, or whether it aims to be representative through being carefully structured to contain samples from different genres of a language, or whether the corpus is sampled from a single genre or even a single short text, the same kinds of lexical analyses can be undertaken. Figure 4.16 is a short text from a newspaper which is used here to illustrate some of the analyses carried out with commercially available software, in this case the *Oxford Concordance Program* (*OCP*).

For reference purposes it can be useful to have a list of all the word forms or types in a text or corpus sorted alphabetically. Often the number of tokens or occurrences of each type is added. Table 4.2 is just such an example of a simple listing in alphabetical order with the number of tokens listed for each type in the short text in Figure 4.16.

Doomsday Rocks by Simon Tisdall

The possibility that a killer asteroid the size of Mount Everest could collide with Earth and cause an explosion equivalent in force to that of all existing nuclear warheads is provoking intense debate in American scientific circles. A team of NASA scientists last week urged Congress to consider funding for a global early warning system of giant telescopes to detect incoming 'doomsday rocks', as the asteroids are termed. One plan envisaged a ground-based international force of nuclear missiles to deflect would-be galactic gatecrashers.

United States scientists differ over the immediacy of the threat. But there is a growing consensus that 65 million years ago an asteroid roughly six to nine miles in diameter smashed into the Caribbean basin. The resulting dust cloud blotted out the sun for months and is blamed by some for killing the dinosaurs and other life forms. With Earth in a cosmic shooting gallery, 'the risk is real,' said Dr. David Morrison of NASA's Ames Research Centre in California.

More asteroids crossing Earth's path are being discovered each month, and increasing scientific attention is being paid to land craters previously assumed to be of volcanic origin. The largest known, in Ontario, is 124 miles across. The NASA team proposed a census of menacing rocks. They estimated that a full survey would find between 1,050 and 4,200 asteroids with a diameter of about three-fifths of a mile and enough force to cause a global rupture. A leading asteroid expert, Dr. Richard Binzel of the Massachusetts Institute of Technology, said in an interview that there was 'probably a one in 7,000 chance that an impact with global repercussions could happen in a person's lifetime'.

Figure 4.16   A sample text for analysis
(from *The Guardian Weekly*, 19 April 1992)

Table 4.2 is not lemmatized, and thus *a* and *an* are counted separately, as are *asteroid* and *asteroids*; *Earth* and *Earth's*; *is, are, was, be* and *being; mile* and *mile; month* and *months; NASA* and *NASA's*. Further, *1,050,*

Table 4.2 Alphabetical list of types from Figure 4.16

a	14	dinosaurs	1	land	1	rupture	1
about	1	discovered	1	largest	1	said	2
across	1	doomsday	2	last	1	scientific	2
ago	1	Dr.	2	leading	1	scientists	2
all	1	dust	1	life	1	shooting	1
American	1	each	1	lifetime	1	Simon	1
Ames	1	early	1	Massachusetts	1	six	1
an	4	Earth	2	menacing	1	size	1
and	6	Earth's	1	mile	1	smashed	1
are	2	enough	1	miles	2	some	1
as	1	envisaged	1	million	1	States	1
assumed	1	equivalent	1	missiles	1	sun	1
asteroid	3	estimated	1	month	1	survey	1
asteroids	3	Everest	1	months	1	system	1
attention	1	existing	1	More	1	team	2
basin	1	expert	1	Morrison	1	Technology	1
be	1	explosion	1	Mount	1	telescopes	1
being	2	find	1	NASA	2	termed	1
between	1	for	3	NASA's	1	that	6
Binzel	1	force	3	nine	1	the	13
blamed	1	forms	1	nuclear	2	there	2
blotted	1	full	1	of	13	They	1
But	1	funding	1	one	2	threat	1
by	2	galactic	1	Ontario	1	three-fifths	1
California	1	gallery	1	origin	1	Tisdall	1
Caribbean	1	gatecrashers	1	other	1	to	8
cause	2	giant	1	out	1	United	1
census	1	global	3	over	1	urged	1
Centre	1	ground-based	1	paid	1	volcanic	1
chance	1	growing	1	path	1	warheads	1
circles	1	happen	1	person's	1	warning	1
cloud	1	immediacy	1	plan	1	was	1
collide	1	impact	1	possibility	1	week	1
Congress	1	in	9	previously	1	with	4
consensus	1	incoming	1	probably	1	would	1
consider	1	increasing	1	proposed	1	would-be	1
cosmic	1	Institute	1	provoking	1	years	1
could	2	intense	1	real	1	000	1
craters	1	international	1	repercussions	1	050	1
crossing	1	interview	1	Research	1	1	1
David	1	into	1	resulting	1	124	1
debate	1	is	6	Richard	1	200	1
deflect	1	killer	1	risk	1	4	1
detect	1	killing	1	rocks	3	65	1
diameter	2	known	1	roughly	1	7	1
differ	1						

4,200 and *7,000* have each been counted as two items (*1* and *050*, etc.), while *65 million* and *United States* have also similarly each been counted as two items. An alphabetical list of all the lemmas would result in a smaller list containing 10 fewer separate types.

Table 4.2 can be arranged differently, as shown in Table 4.3. Sorting a list in terms of alphabetical order of the last letter in each word might initially seem somewhat bizarre or perverse. However, such an ordering of types can be useful for identifying words with similar suffixes, belonging in some cases to similar word classes. Thus the adjectives *scientific, cosmic, volcanic* and *galactic* are listed together, followed by all the *-ed* forms, some of which are, of course, simple past tense forms (e.g. *urged*) while others are past participles (e.g. *termed*). A corpus which has been accurately tagged could list these word classes separately. A sorting of the word types by word length, as shown in Table 4.4, although with only a short text, illustrates one of the laws attributed to Zipf (1935) that the length of a word in a language is in an inverse relationship to its frequency. A rank ordering of types according to descending (or, less commonly, ascending) order of frequency of occurrence as in Table 4.5 can be one of the most useful formats for a wordlist, especially to display information about corpus lexicons which can be used in applied linguistics, for example to identify the words most likely to be met by users of the language in particular domains.

In our text, in Figure 4.16, there were only about 280 words. Nevertheless, the eight most frequent words in the text are identical to the eight most frequent in the one-million-word *LOB Corpus* (compare Table 3.3 and Table 4.5), although there are differences in rank. Generalizations about word frequency are useful in fields such as language teaching. Frequency counts need to be interpreted with some care, however. In different domains there can be quite radical differences. In texts of conversation, for example, it is common to find second-person pronouns and discourse particles such as *okay, right, well* and *yeah* to rank in the top 20 words. We have already noted in Table 3.4 differences between the word frequencies in general academic texts and in the economics subject field. Word-form types displayed in wordlists are not, however, generally considered to be the best format for studying the lexicon in a corpus for the obvious reason that polysemy and word-class ambiguity are not able to be distinguished. For this reason, the procedure known as concordancing, providing the context in which each word token appears, has been the major tool used for accessing corpora.

4.2.2 Concordances

A concordance is a formatted version or display of all the occurrences or tokens of a particular type in a corpus. The type is usually called a

Table 4.3 List of types sorted according to alphabetical order (starting with the last letter in each word)

a	14	rupture	1	in	9	dinosaurs	1
California	1	intense	1	origin	1	Congress	1
NASA	2	cause	2	basin	1	across	1
scientific	2	debate	1	million	1	scientists	2
cosmic	1	Institute	1	explosion	1	Massachusetts	1
volcanic	1	size	1	attention	1	census	1
galactic	1	of	13	Simon	1	consensus	1
envisaged	1	menacing	1	Morrison	1	threat	1
urged	1	leading	1	sun	1	that	6
smashed	1	funding	1	known	1	impact	1
blamed	1	being	2	ago	1	deflect	1
termed	1	provoking	1	Ontario	1	detect	1
assumed	1	killing	1	to	8	giant	1
discovered	1	incoming	1	into	1	equivalent	1
ground-based	1	warning	1	nuclear	2	Mount	1
proposed	1	increasing	1	Dr.	2	expert	1
estimated	1	crossing	1	consider	1	last	1
United	1	resulting	1	differ	1	largest	1
blotted	1	shooting	1	other	1	Everest	1
paid	1	existing	1	killer	1	dust	1
said	2	growing	1	diameter	2	But	1
asteroid	3	each	1	over	1	out	1
David	1	Research	1	for	3	about	1
could	2	enough	1	as	1	interview	1
would	1	path	1	NASA's	1	six	1
and	6	with	4	was	1	doomsday	2
land	1	month	1	warheads	1	by	2
find	1	Earth	2	asteroids	3	immediacy	1
Richard	1	week	1	circles	1	They	1
cloud	1	risk	1	miles	2	survey	1
be	1	global	3	missiles	1	Technology	1
would-be	1	real	1	Ames	1	probably	1
chance	1	international	1	telescopes	1	roughly	1
force	3	Binzel	1	States	1	early	1
collide	1	all	1	three-fifths	1	previously	1
life	1	Tisdall	1	months	1	gallery	1
the	13	full	1	Earth's	1	possibility	1
mile	1	team	2	is	6	000	1
lifetime	1	system	1	rocks	3	200	1
some	1	an	4	forms	1	050	1
nine	1	American	1	repercussions	1	1	1
one	2	Caribbean	1	person's	1	4	1
are	2	plan	1	years	1	124	1
there	2	between	1	gatecrashers	1	65	1
More	1	happen	1	craters	1	7	1
Centre	1						

Table 4.4 List of types sorted according to word length

international	1	Research	1	killer	1	nine	1
Massachusetts	1	shooting	1	months	1	over	1
repercussions	1	volcanic	1	NASA's	1	paid	1
gatecrashers	1	warheads	1	origin	1	path	1
ground-based	1	would-be	1	States	1	plan	1
three-fifths	1	assumed	1	survey	1	real	1
possibility	1	between	1	system	1	risk	1
California	1	blotted	1	termed	1	said	2
discovered	1	circles	1	threat	1	size	1
equivalent	1	collide	1	United	1	some	1
increasing	1	craters	1	about	1	team	2
previously	1	deflect	1	basin	1	that	6
scientific	2	Earth's	1	being	2	They	1
scientists	2	Everest	1	cause	2	week	1
Technology	1	funding	1	cloud	1	With	4
telescopes	1	gallery	1	could	2	ago	1
asteroids	3	growing	1	David	1	all	1
attention	1	intense	1	early	1	and	6
Caribbean	1	killing	1	Earth	2	are	2
consensus	1	largest	1	force	3	But	1
dinosaurs	1	leading	1	forms	1	for	3
envisaged	1	million	1	giant	1	one	2
estimated	1	nuclear	2	known	1	out	1
explosion	1	Ontario	1	miles	2	six	1
immediacy	1	Richard	1	month	1	sun	1
Institute	1	roughly	1	Mount	1	the	13
interview	1	rupture	1	other	1	was	1
provoking	1	smashed	1	rocks	3	000	1
resulting	1	Tisdall	1	Simon	1	050	1
American	1	warning	1	there	2	124	1
asteroid	3	across	1	urged	1	200	1
Congress	1	Binzel	1	would	1	an	4
consider	1	blamed	1	years	1	as	1
crossing	1	census	1	Ames	1	be	1
diameter	2	Centre	1	dust	1	by	2
doomsday	2	chance	1	each	1	Dr.	2
existing	1	cosmic	1	find	1	In	9
galactic	1	debate	1	full	1	is	6
incoming	1	detect	1	into	1	of	13
lifetime	1	differ	1	land	1	to	8
menacing	1	enough	1	last	1	65	1
missiles	1	expert	1	life	1	a	14
Morrison	1	global	3	mile	1	1	1
person's	1	happen	1	More	1	4	1
probably	1	impact	1	NASA	2	7	1
proposed	1						

Table 4.5 List of types sorted by descending order of frequency

a	14	Binzel	1	ground-based	1	proposed	1
of	13	blamed	1	growing	1	provoking	1
the	13	blotted	1	happen	1	real	1
in	9	But	1	immediacy	1	repercussions	1
to	8	California	1	impact	1	Research	1
and	6	Caribbean	1	incoming	1	resulting	1
is	6	census	1	increasing	1	Richard	1
that	6	Centre	1	Institute	1	risk	1
an	4	chance	1	intense	1	roughly	1
With	4	circles	1	international	1	rupture	1
asteroid	3	cloud	1	interview	1	shooting	1
asteroids	3	collide	1	into	1	Simon	1
for	3	Congress	1	killer	1	six	1
force	3	consensus	1	killing	1	size	1
global	3	consider	1	known	1	smashed	1
rocks	3	cosmic	1	land	1	some	1
are	2	craters	1	largest	1	States	1
being	2	crossing	1	last	1	sun	1
by	2	David	1	leading	1	survey	1
cause	2	debate	1	life	1	system	1
could	2	deflect	1	lifetime	1	Technology	1
diameter	2	detect	1	Massachusetts	1	telescopes	1
doomsday	2	differ	1	menacing	1	termed	1
Dr.	2	dinosaurs	1	mile	1	They	1
Earth	2	discovered	1	million	1	threat	1
miles	2	dust	1	missiles	1	three-fifths	1
NASA	2	each	1	month	1	Tisdall	1
nuclear	2	early	1	months	1	United	1
One	2	Earth's	1	More	1	urged	1
said	2	enough	1	Morrison	1	volcanic	1
scientific	2	envisaged	1	Mount	1	warheads	1
scientists	2	equivalent	1	NASA's	1	warning	1
team	2	estimated	1	nine	1	was	1
there	2	Everest	1	Ontario	1	week	1
about	1	existing	1	origin	1	would	1
across	1	expert	1	other	1	would-be	1
ago	1	explosion	1	out	1	years	1
all	1	find	1	over	1	000	1
American	1	forms	1	paid	1	050	1
Ames	1	full	1	path	1	1	1
as	1	funding	1	person's	1	124	1
assumed	1	galactic	1	plan	1	200	1
attention	1	gallery	1	possibility	1	4	1
basin	1	gatecrashers	1	previously	1	65	1
be	1	giant	1	probably	1	7	1
between	1						

keyword but is sometimes referred to as a target item, node word or search item. Concordances can be generated with easily available software in two main ways. Using batch generation, a concordance can be made for each and every type in the corpus, or alternatively for a selected type or types. The computer program searches the text and finds every occurrence of each word type in the corpus and makes a file containing each such occurrence with a predetermined amount of context. Batch-generated concordances for all the words in a corpus can be expensive in terms of time taken to produce them and the amount of disk space needed. A second type of concordance can be faster and interactive. If the corpus has been pre-processed by computer to index each word, the software can be used to find almost instantly all the occurrences of a type, and the size of the context can also be easily altered. Develements in computer speed and software now enable even unindexed corpora to be analyzed rapidly. Concordances can be produced in a number of formats. The most usual form is the *Key Word in Context (KWIC) Concordance.*

Figure 4.17 is an example of a *KWIC* concordance for the type *on* from a small part of a single text from Section J (the learned and academic section) of the *Brown Corpus.* The tokens of *on* in context are displayed in the order in which they occurred in the text ('text order'). It can be seen that in this fragment the word *data* occurs three times before *on*; *information* precedes *on* twice. *On* is typically followed by a noun phrase, with *the* as the most frequent determiner.

2436	Let us speculate a little	on	the maximum size of the python
2449	and there is nothing at all	on	the amethystine python
2468	data	on	the boa constrictor about match
2476	The following information	on	snakes varying greatly
2482	United States, could supply data	on	the maturing period for
2508	amount of agreement	on	some of the giants.
2512	There are three levels	on	which to treat the subject
2514	proof and therefore may err	on	the conservative
2521	The third level leans	on	a belief that a lot of smoke
2536	but	on	the third level, and is chiefly
2544	Detailed information	on	record lengths of the giants
2548	as far as possible, data	on	these aspects of growth

Figure 4.17 A fragment of an unsorted concordance for *on* from the *Brown Corpus*

In a typical *KWIC* concordance the format has the keyword in the centre of the line as illustrated in Figure 4.17, but with more context each side of the keyword. In order to get a picture of the environments in which a keyword occurs in a corpus, the concordance can be sorted in such a way that all the same word sequences to the left or right of the keyword are displayed together as in Figures 4.18 and 4.19.

In Figure 4.18, which is a fragment from a concordance for *on* in the *LOB Corpus,* the context to the right of the keyword *on* in each line has been

Figure 4.18 A fragment of a right-sorted concordance for *on* from the *LOB Corpus*

	on	
61 cases exports from the semi-industrialised countries	on	average show J46 62 much the same movement in volume as
very small. J29 50 TABLE! J29 51 Parents in Area A were	on	average younger than parents in Area B: J29 52 TABLE! J
rman socialists gave the J41 91 party more than 1 apiece	on	average 720,000 in 1957; dues for J41 92 those in the h
t the export volume of wool from J46 68 these countries,	on	average, approximates to the world total, some J46 69 a
here too J22 96 venereal disease rates are of relevance.	On	average, she will have J22 97 had two or three years of
ew tables agree with the old to within J15 92 3 per cent	on	average, with occasional divergencies up to 6 per cent.
0s. 30d. to 500s. 90d. A16 164 and Villiers Engineering,	on	bad results, 10s. 30d. to 60s. 90d. A16 165 Full detail
177 relative was poor and in debt, and that he had been	on	bad terms with G07 178 Byron since the Separation, in w
, and made by Tyneside mothers F42 41 for their children	on	baking day; 'Checky pigs' from F42 42 Leicestershire: L
g and drag hinges, the former being freely J73 7 mounted	on	ball races and the latter having adjustable cork fricti
se struts carried at their ends a J73 74 spindle mounted	on	ball races, passing through and fixed to the J73 75 hel
ople and G31 167 factories where old men could sit about	on	barrows. These quiet G31 168 scenes showed him the Engl
1 B06 133 issues were confused, clear policy details- as	on	bases- were B06 134 decisively carried. B06 135 5Peace
G22 30 We chattered, we pointed out, and compared notes	on	beaches and G22 31 sand-castles and spades and shells,
wed no signs of K14 3 being interested in what was going	on	before his eyes, and the shoe K14 4 remained, untouched
hire-purchase payment A35 194 was due. A35 195 Speaking	on	behalf of her son before a Darlington court today a A35
try's G05 20 disaster, of pleading with cogent eloquence	on	behalf of his G05 21 countrymen. I was able next day to
e J36 39 discerned also in the Crowther Report's desire,	on	behalf of secondary J36 40 schools, to make the 0G.C.E.
avour of the Union, H19 96 endorsed that view. H19 97 4.	On	behalf of the Company Office, and that whilst they we
gn Office, afterwards G08 123 Lord Hardinge of Penshurst	on	behalf of the Foreign Office, and on G08 124 behalf of
ations made, either in general or in particular. H24 159	On	behalf of the Group, H24 160 2PLOWDEN H24 161 0Chairman.
have been good enough, 0Mr. Speaker, H19 176 to say that	on	behalf of the House you will conduct a certain amount H
fuels A36 149 available. A36 150 Welcoming the delegates	on	behalf of the Mayor Councillor Miss A36 151 Christine L
0widow, hotel owner, and millionairess, A10 163 is here	on	behalf of the New York State Racing Commission to A10 1
consider any report made in H14 162 respect of him by or	on	behalf of the Prison Commissioners, and H14 163 section
pon referred to the Court for H19 58 decision. H19 59 3.	On	behalf of the Union it was stated that they had when H1
ant to the Ministry A34 20 of Works, 0Mr. Charles Green,	on	behalf of the Walsingham Excavation A34 21 Committee, w

continued

Figure 4.18 continued

implies that 1all 0expenses B10 5 incurred by directors	on	behalf of their companies should be disclosed B10 6 to
riving Chiang Kai-shek's representative of a seat G76 57	on	behalf of Formosa. G76 58 Probably only a newly elected
G31 158 country. It falls to his Prime Minister to speak	on	behalf of G31 159 England. Not long afterwards another
ifteen years earlier by the 1946 Family Census conducted	on	behalf of H01 8 the Royal Commission on Population. The
! J29 163 Claims to give explicit direction and guidance	on	behaviour were J29 164 significantly greater in working
s of the brain, and the effect of the newer drugs C14 52	on	behaviour. This is a particularly controversial area in
, snuffed-out laughter conversation P22 121 they carried	on	behind her father's disapproving newspaper. He was P22
organised. E31 162 He congratulated the catering industry	on	being alive to this E31 163 need. He wished more indust
heir eyes on a seagoing L07 121 boat. Clive- he insisted	on	being called Clive- haggled with him L07 122 and within
Nor must we G43 173 forget the great singer who insists	on	being centre-stage or who G43 174 shouts a top note eve
6 158 what's been said I gather that he wasn't very keen	on	being in this P26 159 concert at all. Do you often have
r you from K26 142 coming.' K26 143 We congratulated him	on	being so infected with the joy of pure K26 144 scholars
ack G06 80 the outer skin would become so sensitive that	on	being touched it felt G06 81 as if something red-hot we
3 39 whose dancing you admire; maybe you just want to go	on	belonging to E13 40 "The Club", or maybe, having been s
in a G25 179 billycock hat, and 0Mr. Fitzwilliam looking	on	benevolently. G25 180 2012 G26 1 213 TEXT G26I G26 2 0A
the A36 18 increase should be postponed until a decision	on	betting levy A36 19 contributions to racecourse executi
th. For some A25 5 time now negotiations have been going	on	between the State Building A25 6 Society and a group be
11 218 today." L11 219 "I was wondering if you've a book	on	birds I could borrow." L11 220 MacLeod explained. L11 2
ce of this finding on J31 67 the validity of the results	on	birth control methods. J31 68 Questioning on family plai
ack of the desk top was a newspaper, folded N22 230 down	on	black headlines which read: N22 231 6FRANK DELGARRA, BA
there are none of the A40 121 modern aids to navigation	on	board so the skipper and his mate must A40 122 needs be
se. A28 188 6THE MAID A28 189 0No sooner was Providencia	on	board than yet another late-comer A28 190 was seen runn
men F23 174 working eight to a relay to carry stretchers	on	board the ships. F23 175 Round every ambulance and aid-
e were F22 114 near enough to run a rope away and get it	on	board the trawler. F22 115 In retrospect, it was an eas
by A13 6 the Glasgow tug Ocean Salvor. There was no one	on	board when she went A13 7 down. A13 B 0Salvage vessels
off. F22 98 Some of our ratings had already been placed	on	board 1Thracian F22 99 0by 1Warden0's motor boat, and h
eat unheard-of chunks of ripping G12 87 cake. Then came	on	board. Had no dinner. Couldn't after Gibbs' G12 88 cake
for eight days. But G10 97 there was any amount of drink	on	board- to us amazingly cheap- and G10 98 the other thre

Figure 4.19 A fragment of a left-sorted concordance for *on* from the *LOB Corpus*

Left context		Right context
ctric bill. It's up again. We'll R02 136 have to go easy	on	the immersion heater next quarter.' R02 137 Cecil gritt,
pt to bring sexual matters into better focus. Going easy	on	the G36 95 puritanism would be a commendable resolve, at
g in tax-free champagne whilst he had to go B02 139 easy	on	the immersion heater. 'What is it, Cecil? Don't you fee
to find out just how they go about C17 192 eavesdropping	on	the public. C17 193 An 0ABC spokesman was quite adamant
four Championship contests in the Usher Hall, Edinburgh,	on	E12 146 February 25, to replenish their repertoire of ms
is house opposite the Archer's G56 155 Hall in Edinburgh,	on	26th June 1794 from a sudden haemorrhage. G56 156 Gett
the G45 200 1Spectator 0in its original American edition	on	June 24, 1960. G45 201 4Records G45 202 Values of the Si
ted to read the article by your Commercial B10 57 Editor	on	butter August 21. I ought not to have to express my B10
ng April 1, 1963. A15 46 6LANDING FEES UP A15 47 4Effect	on	Costs A15 48 0The effect of this would have been to keep
ngs which seems likely to have an H09 150 adverse effect	on	training results. No less than 66.4 per cent of H09 151
summer of A38 16 1960 had a particularly adverse effect	on	the activities of motor A38 17 cycle dealers and results
e on G11 49 my father's outlook- not too large an effect	on	a mind so naturally G11 50 large, but they must have she
6 picnic. Gorin said such luxury had a beneficial effect	on	the working G49 57 man on his way to, and from, the fact
at regular intervals may well have a real C14 32 effect	on	the future through their power to draw the attention of
people who were made redundant. The demoralising effect	on	the staff H15 139 of the new towns was deplorable. Natun
nd now the beer with the curry, had their desired effect	on	us: or K02 20 rather, on Nigel and myself. Lee, I notice
unemployment will doubtless have a J44 26 greater effect	on	the change in wage rates if it is spread over all J44 2
for true" N02 199 This sidelight on Piers had its effect	on	Beryl. Without taking N02 200 it too seriously she found
put him down E17 175 again. E17 176 This had its effect	on	the Filipino, who slowed considerably in E17 177 the ney
Thus, the evil of cruelty D09 137 consists in its effect	on	the disposition of the doer and not in the D09 138 suff.
ke, and that the spanwise loading has more J74 43 effect	on	the downwash than the chordwise loading, and so the wind
r thrust and flapping angles and also the J73 149 effect	on	overall pitching moment. J73 150 6.2 1Thrust coefficient
ee solution appeared to have slightly J12 52 less effect	on	sodium efflux in the desheathed preparations might J12
J12 208 appear to show that the poison had little effect	on	the rate of J12 209 accumulation of the radioactive ions
elves, J71 117 which is very low, has very little effect	on	the torsional buckling J71 118 load and is neglected in
tion, though A11 199 there might be some marginal effect	on	the country rate, so far as he A11 200 could ascertain tl
dried in such a way as to have a E33 143 minimum effect	on	the flavour and nutritive value of the original E33 144
r of tenants. B25 48 But it can have only a minor effect	on	this resurgent housing B25 49 problem as a whole. Must

continued

Figure 4.19 continued

stinctiveness of J32 127 specific sounds has much effect	on	their selection in a sound J32 128 complement 0p. 12 0f.
r as he A11 200 could ascertain there would be no effect	on	the urban district council A11 201 rate, because any los
nt contrast to J34 208 syntactic function, has no effect	on	classification in French J34 209 1tout toute 0in sentence
For the most part, this pastime has no permanent effect	on	the G51 27 language, but occasionally, so strong is the
s in length of schooling have no J38 135 residual effect	on	reading performance during the first two years of J38 1;
36 tolerance. And the sight of them had the same effect	on	Shale it L19 37 always had- a kind of cynical contempt 1
l of 'excess demand' for labour had a significant effect	on	J44 182 wage rate changes in that period. J44 183 It ma)
revious schooling J38 145 still had a significant effect	on	reading scores, even after the J38 146 elimination of at
here is evidence that phytoplankton may have some effect	on	the J06 187 vertical migration of crustacean zooplankton
" L16 90 Winter said, "You always have a soothing effect	on	Wally. We L16 91 shouldn't have any more trouble for the
187 language, but it also has a most stimulating effect	on	the pupils' H03 188 morale and willingness to learn. H0
no weapon more G05 180 lethal than vodka. And the effect	on	the German people of the first G05 181 ten years of the
ow, it J31 147 seems most relevant to examine the effect	on	the internal consistency J31 148 of the 1all user 0grout
e talk." A06 107 6'DISASTER' A06 108 0"It had the effect	on	one former supporter that he now thinks A06 109 this Pr.
ne to Salisbury at the Foreign Office. J59 12 The effect	on	both of them, and on Cranbrook when he read it, was J59
me and it is made of similar J15 53 material. The effect	on	the data of using applicators of different J15 54 design
K09 52 'The natives have never been to Paris. The effect	on	them was K09 53 staggering.' K09 54 Father Felix said d;
dents and dangerous H23 221 occurrences and their effect	on	the operations of the Boards. H23 222 2021 H24 1 288 TE
mendments, none of economic significance in their effected	on	the J43 161 revenue. Introducing the bill in the Senate
A38 20 Although much of the group's business is effected	on	hire A38 21 purchase terms, the company's experience in
er of some E34 191 weeks will net always will be as effective	on	very grey hair when the E34 192 cuticle of the hair has
dous F42 23 boost just where it would be most effective-	on	the customer's F42 24 doorstep, he added. The British F
has J36 37 been deplored because of its adverse effects	on	education in the J36 38 primary school. A distaste for
rocess of selection can J36 194 have deleterious effects	on	the more essential process of education. J36 195 At even
to pieces as he N04 209 had done with disastrous effects	on	the morale of his crew; but he N04 210 had. Quite sudden
. The migrant labour system has "disintegrating effects"	on	D17 64 African life. D17 65 5. The wages of the vast ma
ital out of South Africa which will have serious effects	on	the G73 90 economy of the country. G73 91 Nevertheless,
discovery of how materials produce G64 131 their effects	on	us and how energy can be stored and controlled. G64 132

the basis for the sorting of the whole line by a simple alphabetical ordering. Consequently, recurring word sequences show up together. The numbers in the concordance identify the text from which the line came.

The context to the left of the keyword is the basis for the sorting which results in the format in Figure 4.19. For the study of significant collocations, both right- and left-sorted contexts are very important because they enable the researcher to identify at a glance the major recurring word sequences. Thus, from Figures 4.18 and 4.19 it can be seen that *on average, on behalf of, on being . . .* and *on board* each occur several times in the *LOB Corpus*, as do *easy on* and *effect(s) on*. As noted earlier in Section 3.1.3, for all but very high frequency words, large corpora are needed to identify significant collocational patterning.

A concordance can thus provide information on the company words keep in a corpus. It can also show different senses of a word type. In Figure 4.18, the *on* in *. . . on baking day* is temporal, whereas in *. . . on barrows* it is spatial, and in *. . . a book on birds on* is a synonym for *about*. In each case *on* is a preposition. In lexicography the use of concordancing to identify senses of word types, and as a source of citations to provide authentic examples of the use of words, is now fairly standard. By means of concordances, the distribution of senses of *right*, as in *right hand side of the road* or *right answer* can be revealed. Concordancing can also be used as a basis for calculating the relative frequencies of the different uses of a type, and this continues to be very important for curriculum design for language teaching purposes as well as for probabilistic approaches to the automatic analysis of corpora.

Concordancing is also relevant where a corpus has been annotated with word-class tags. Figure 4.20 shows a concordance of one section of the tagged *LOB Corpus* for the use of the type *present* as a noun.

```
F:Popular lore
F08:21      accept_VB a_AT valuable_JJ   present_NN   from_IN a_AT man_NN
F12:16   NN things_NNS are_BER at_IN     present_NN   ,_, but_CC walking_VBG out
F12:41    concentrate_VB on_IN the_ATI   present_NN   ._. ^ try_VB to_TO
F12:52         ._. ^ *'_*' your_PP$      present_NN   is_BEZ more_QL valuable_JJ
F15:37     time_NN or_CC of_IN the_ATI   present_NN   ,_, it_PP3 can_MD be_BE seen
F24:64      for_IN her_PP3O as_IN a_AT   present_NN   from_IN her_PP$ father_NN
F36:34        VBZ them_PP3OS at_IN       present_NN   from_IN sharing_VBG in_IN
F36:36         RB ,_, for_IN the_ATI     present_NN   ,_, this_DT first_OD
F36:73       people_NNS ._. ^ at_IN      present_NN   it_PP3 affects_VBZ a_AT
F38:79    of_IN what_WDT is_BEZ at_IN    present_NN   known_VBN are_BER given_VBN
```

Figure 4.20 A concordance for the noun *present* in Section F (popular lore) of the tagged *LOB Corpus*

The program has identified the noun by means of the tag _NN, and has selected only this use and not the adjective (_JJ) or verb uses (_VB). Of course, even within the noun uses shown in Figure 4.20, there are different senses, including *present* meaning 'gift' and *present* with a temporal meaning. Analysis of a tagged corpus can thus reveal not only collocational behaviour in terms of particular word sequences, but also in terms of the distribution of word-class sequences.

In the *KWIC* version of the tagged *LOB Corpus*, available through ICAME, the concordance is sorted alphabetically by the keyword and its tag, then by the next two words and their tags, and finally by the rest of the context to the right. All tags except the two following the tagged keyword have been removed. This *KWIC* version also contains statistics on the occurrence of all types in the corpus, including their different word-class uses in different genres.

The amount of context in which a keyword appears in a concordance is able to be specified in most concordance programs, typically in terms of the number of characters (including spaces). An A4 page width can take about 80 characters, which is similar to the width which is typically displayed on a computer screen. Wide-carriage paper used in line printers takes about 130 characters and gives a context even larger than landscape. Figures 4.18 and 4.19 are reproduced from wide-carriage format and show the advantages of more context.

In addition to being able to specify a keyword for a concordance, as illustrated in Figures 4.18–4.20, most programs have the facility for specifying the search item to be a part word, affix or a phrase. The wild card facility (usually specified by means of the symbol *) allows for an item to be the keyword in the context of an unspecified number of alphanumeric characters. Thus if the search item for a concordance is *ing*, the program will find all items ending in *ing*. Of course, although in this case the intention of the linguist may be to find all examples of the English present participle in an untagged corpus, the resulting concordance will not only list the tokens of all present participles in context but also words such as the noun *king* and verb *bring*, thus necessitating further editing. Some experimentation in choosing an optimal wild card pattern to maximize identification and selection of the desired items can be well rewarded. A search item *re*t* containing the wild card symbol will result in a concordance containing all words beginning in *re* and ending in *t*, including *rent, react, repeat, realist, resort, recalcitrant*, and so on.

So far, we have considered collocational patterning involving only immediately adjacent words. Many concordance programs, however, enable the researcher to specify the co-occurrence of words within a certain span before or after the keyword. For example, if the keyword is *tendency*, it is possible to specify that the concordancer find all occurrences of *tendency* where it occurs before or after the word *strong* within a span of, say, plus or minus five words. That is, the concordancer will find and display strings such as the following:

There is a *strong tendency* for it to snow late in winter.
The *tendency* is nevertheless very *strong.* . . .
how *strong* the *tendency* is, remains to be seen.

Collier (1993) has described major issues in collocational analysis arising from the statistical significance of differences between expected and
observed frequencies of items in specified concordance environments.
He has also shown clearly the size and scope of the problem of concordancing with mega-corpora involving thousands of types, with the risk
of research and researchers being overwhelmed by an overabundance
of data. The use of indexing and banks of collocates are suggested as
ways of helping overcome this problem when studying collocations in
a huge corpus. Random sampling of tokens of high frequency items may
also be necessary when working with very large amounts of data.

There is room for the development of improved, more sophisticated,
user-friendly, publicly available software for corpus analysis which brings
together some of the best of the functions which are available in different
software systems. Sinclair (1992) has set out a desideratum of tools which
could assist corpus analysis, including lexical parsers, phrase finders,
devices for identifying lexical compounds, and devices for identifying,
for typological purposes, the groups of linguistic elements which characterize particular genres.

Functions which are likely to prove particularly valuable include software which facilitates post-editing of concordances. A tagged corpus
is superb for making a concordance containing just one use of a word
form. For example, as we have seen, if the tagging is accurate or has
been manually checked, a concordancer can select as directed the word
once only when it occurs in a corpus as a conjunction (*once we get home
we'll have lunch*) or when it occurs as an adverb (*I once visited Prague*) or
when it occurs as a noun (*I've met him just the once*). However, tagged
(or parsed) corpora, as we have seen, are not easy to read, and it can be
useful to be able to strip the tags out after the concordance has been
made, for further analysis of the text. Researchers working with a spoken
corpus, such as the *London–Lund Corpus*, which has been tagged for prosody, have for similar reasons sometimes had occasion to strip the prosodic
markup out of the concordanced version for certain kinds of research.
The software developed for the *ICE* project includes facilities for stripping
tags and other markup from the corpus (Greenbaum, 1996b).

4.2.3 *Statistics in corpus analysis*

Software for corpus analysis typically provides basic descriptive statistics
on the number of word forms or tokens in the corpus or section of the
corpus, the number of different word types and the type–token ratios.
Other descriptive statistics are sometimes provided on mean sentence

length, and the number of sentences containing particular numbers of words, the number of sentences in the text, and the proportion of the sentences which have more than a specified number of words. As noted in Section 3.1.2, Johansson (1978, 1981) has used simple but useful measures of 'distinctiveness' to identify items which are associated with particular text types.

If there were facilities for more sophisticated statistical analyses, it would make some of the available corpus analysis software even more useful, so as to enable researchers to test quickly and easily whether differences between observed frequencies of occurrence of items in different genres are statistically significant, or whether the co-occurrence of two or more items in a sentence occurs at a greater-than-chance frequency. Further, if non-parametric techniques such as chi-square, or multivariate statistical analyses such as ANOVA were readily able to be applied to concordances with user-friendly software, it could improve the rigour of analyses and provide a more focused direction to corpus-based analyses of language. Biber and Finegan have worked on text typology involving factor analyses, and the Nijmegen group have been pioneers in the use of a range of statistical procedures to test the significance of differences in the frequency of grammatical items. These are examples of statistical research which has taken quantitative analyses of corpora well beyond the basic level of the counting of occurrences of items. McEnery and Wilson (1996) have surveyed some of the major statistical procedures used in corpus linguistics for showing the complex relationships which exist between linguistic variables.

4.3 Corpus search and retrieval software

Many researchers who work with corpora have had to develop software to address particular research needs and problems. The great majority of corpus linguists have however made use of commercially available software or freeware available through particular research groups. The available software has different strengths and weaknesses and individual products do not all handle the same functions. Many researchers tend to settle on one particular system they become familiar with, and make do with it. Corpus linguists interested in describing the distribution of lexical or grammatical phenomena often lack the computer programming skills to develop the software which would best serve their needs. Even fewer have been in a position to evaluate the merits and weaknesses of various high-level programming languages which have been used in corpus analysis, including Snobol, Pascal, Spitbol, Lisp, Prolog, Perl or Icon. Butler (1985) has provided a useful evaluation of some of these issues.

It is probably inevitable in a period when there have been massive changes in computer capacity and corpus size, and software has also been undergoing development, that software packages have sometimes proved to be less than optimally satisfactory. To compound the problems, the instruction manuals have not always been easy to use. Particular systems often have features which make them useful for particular kinds of task. From the point of view of the corpus linguist, there is usually some product which will best do the job in hand, and it is worth becoming familiar with the software described here in order to evaluate at first hand the particular merits of each. Most software has been designed for MS-DOS machines but some may run on the Macintosh under SoftPC. The compatibility of the Power PC with both Macintosh and MS-DOS systems widens the availability of software for individual users. Hofland (1991) and Higgins (1991) have provided useful evaluations and reviews of some of the major concordance programs for personal computers. In the remainder of this section, the facilities offered by some of the standard software tools which have been developed specifically for corpus analysis will be described.

4.3.1 *The* Oxford Concordance Program (OCP)

Of the commercially available software for corpus analysis, one of the most widely used, reliable, flexible and straightforward to use has been the *Oxford Concordance Program* (OCP), first available in 1981 for mainframe use, and subsequently released in a faster *Version 2* (Hockey & Martin, 1988a). A version for personal computers, *Micro-OCP* (Hockey & Martin, 1988b), was also released in an easily used, menu-driven format with all the functions and features of the mainframe version, including a built-in editor. Texts and command files can be moved easily between mainframe and personal computers.

OCP is a batch program for making wordlists, concordances and indexes. It will run on most mainframes, can handle large corpora files in any alphabetic language, and it can handle a wide variety of text formats as input. However, OCP works with 'raw' text and not with 'indexed' text, and this has consequences for the speed of processing. Software programs which work with indexed text have to have the corpus annotated by computer in such a way that each word in the corpus can be retrieved almost instantly. With a concordance which works with an indexed corpus, it is possible for the researcher to work interactively. For example, in a one-million-word corpus all tokens of a particular word, say *patient*, can be retrieved and displayed in a few seconds, and the amount of context in the concordance can be instantly varied. Concordancers such as OCP, however, do not work in this way. Whenever a linguistic item is searched for, the program has to go through the whole corpus and find all tokens in a pre-specified and fixed context size. As computers have become faster, analyses which used to take hours now take minutes, with the result that the comparative slowness of OCP is much less of a disadvantage than it used to be. Unfortunately, at the same time, corpora have become much larger. In a number of respects the issue of slowness with *OCP* is outweighed by its excellent sorting facilities, its flexibility in formatting, and the user-friendly, straightforward, easily learned commands, including defaults for commonly undertaken procedures. For lexicographical and morphological research on corpora up to a million words in size in particular, *OCP* has continued to be a benchmark for corpus analysis software.

OCP operates with three main files. The researcher specifies the name of the text file to be analysed, the command file which specifies what analyses are to be carried out, and the output file which will contain the product of the analyses. Command files can be easily set up to include or ignore certain parts of a corpus. Analysis can be carried out on a whole corpus or a specific text, section of a text or a line. The object of analysis can as easily be a single word (or list of words or part words), a phrase or phrases, or collocations associated with particular keywords. The collocations can be adjacent or separated from the keyword by up to a specified number of words. Full references as to text and line number of each token can be kept along with basic statistics on frequency of occurrence. The options for formatting the printout with *OCP* are more attractive and useful for linguistic analysis than the output of most other programs.

The users' manuals for *OCP* (Hockey & Martin, 1986a, b) are similarly clearer and more accessible than most such documentation and include examples of analyses. Butler (1985) and Davidson (1992) provide clear illustrative examples of how the many functions of *OCP* can be used to analyse corpora, and Lancashire (1991) provides an incisive description of the scope of the program. Information on *OCP* is available from Oxford Computing Services, 13 Banbury Road, Oxford OX2 6NN, United Kingdom. *Micro-OCP*, the version for PCs, is distributed by Oxford University Press.

4.3.2 WordCruncher

Since the 1980s almost certainly the most widely used software for interactive concordancing has been *WordCruncher*. Developed commercially for PCs from a concordancer produced originally at Brigham Young University, Utah, *WordCruncher* can provide extremely fast retrieval of lexically based aspects of large corpora. It has two separate programs. *WC Index* (formerly called *Index ETC*) is a batch process which is used initially to index a text file or corpus to produce a series of specially annotated files which in turn are the basis for the very fast access to information on word frequency and collocations. *WC Index* runs on a plain ASCII file and early versions took about 20 minutes to index 100 K of text data. Because indexing takes place in RAM memory, there are limits to the size of texts which can be indexed, but separately indexed files can be subsequently merged. It used to be a fairly common experience for novices to find indexing texts with *WordCruncher* to be difficult, but later versions with access through Windows will reportedly be able to index files of any size, and have enhanced features such as easier mobility around the analysed text.

The second program, *WC View*, runs as a menu to locate data in the pre-indexed text. It provides fast, almost instantaneous retrieval of all the tokens of morphemes (e.g. *-ly*), words, phrases, and collocations of both adjacent and discontinuous collocates, even when there are thousands of tokens of the particular search item in the corpus. In viewing the retrieved items, *WordCruncher* can provide many options for the amount of context, ranging from a single line to about fifty. Collocations can be retrieved within a user-defined context of plus or minus *n* words in the same line, sentence or page. Various options include basic statistics on item frequency in a whole corpus or section of a corpus. Attractive screen displays also show referencing clearly. Particular tokens of a keyword can be selected out of a display with a keystroke and made part of another file which can be printed or moved into a word processing program for further editing or processing. This facility is particularly useful for teaching purposes, both as a source of citations for descriptive linguistic purposes, or for second and foreign language teaching.

WordCruncher is excellent for rapidly exploring a large text, particularly for lexically based phenomena. Although it works well with text which has been annotated with word-class tags, *WordCruncher*, like most software, is not as satisfactory for exploring syntactic phenomena. Similarly, in spite of the interactive feature and its speed, *WordCruncher* has not been as notable for its flexibility for sorting and formatting the output of analyses. Information on *WordCruncher* is available through Johnston and Company, Electronic Publishers, PO Box 6627, Bloomington, Indiana 47407, USA.

4.3.3 TACT

A third, widely used research-oriented software system for corpus analysis is *TACT*. Developed at the University of Toronto by Bradley and Presutti and first released in 1989, *TACT* is shareware which, like *OCP* and *WordCruncher*, runs on MS-DOS machines. An excellent manual by Bradley (1991) gives full details of the various facilities available in the software. *TACT* was originally devised for literary research to assist in content analysis through vocabulary studies. For example, it can show where vocabulary is distributed in a text, and which characters in a literary work tend to be associated with the use of particular words and with what frequency.

However, *TACT* has also been found to be a sophisticated and flexible program for descriptive linguistic studies. Like *WordCruncher*, *TACT* works with pre-indexed text and is thus both fast and interactive. It uses one program, *MAKBAS*, to undertake the indexing. Creating the pre-indexed text by means of *MAKBAS* is not entirely straightforward, but once done it makes it possible for the *TACT* analysis software to undertake a large number of types of analysis by means of menus which provide more flexible, varied and sophisticated analyses than most programs offer. By means of simple keystrokes, *TACT* will display lists of all the word forms in a text with the number of tokens, or all the tokens of particular words or phrases. Any word type or token can be displayed with user-defined and variable amounts of context from a line to a screenful or more. The software will show by means of graphs whether there is a tendency for particular words to occur in particular parts of a text. *TACT* can calculate z-scores to measure the relationship between observed and expected frequencies of the co-occurrence of items in a corpus. An objective basis for studying collocation is one advantage of this facility, which identifies collocations with items occurring within five words before or after the keyword.

The text-referencing system in *TACT* is flexible and robust and the screen displays of analysed text can be stored easily as separate files or printed. Typical of the user-friendly features of *TACT* are the facility to display a *KWIC* concordance or index display and a text window simultaneously on a split screen. *TACT* is also able to work easily to identify and list all the tokens of pre-specified word-class tag combinations in a corpus or part of a corpus. For example, in the *LOB Corpus* all examples of adjectives pre-modified by an adverb (e.g. *very noisy, rather unusual,* etc.) can be identified and displayed.

Information on the most recent release of *TACT* with its accompanying documentation is available through the Modern Language Association in New York or from the Centre for Computing in the Humanities, Robarts Library, University of Toronto, Toronto, Ontario M5S 1A5, Canada.

4.3.4   Other widely used software for special purposes

A number of corpus analysis software systems have been developed for special purposes or applications. The *Child Language Analysis* (*CLAN*) software system written for use with the *CHILDES Database* (MacWhinney & Snow, 1990) is non-interactive software which can handle batch processing for a number of simple functions such as wordlists and *KWIC* concordances relevant for research on the acquisition of language.

COALA is a more complex software system especially suitable for the semi-automatic analysis of transitional linguistic systems such as occur during the acquisition of a language. Among its functions, *COALA* offers computer assistance to manual parsing of interlanguage data.

(Pienemann, 1992). It runs on PC and Macintosh environments and is controlled through menus. *COALA* includes an interactive system for the annotation of corpora, including parsing. It functions as a relational database which can link files and perform many integrated functions involving analysis at various linguistic levels, including, for example, identifying morpheme boundaries, or parsing certain structures such as noun phrases and subject complements. Information about *COALA* can be obtained from Manfred Pienemann, Department of Modern European Languages, Australian National University, Canberra, ACT 0200, Australia, E-mail: compuling@anu.edu.au.

CONC 1.7 is a freeware *KWIC* concordancer for Macintosh computers which has been found to be a useful tool for linguistic analyses where the researcher wishes to explore a text and move between windows of text and concordance windows. It permits user-determined searches and various types of sorting options. It has been used to retrieve particular phonological features from texts, such as all occurrences of particular obstruents in certain environments. Further information on *CONC 1.7* is available from the International Academic Bookstore, 7500 W Camp Wisdom Road, Dallas, TX 75236, USA.

Free Text Browser is also designed for Macintosh computers and is run under HyperCard. It provides basic, straightforward, fast indexing of large texts and a concordancing facility which enables the user to move quickly back and forward to context windows. Some users have noted that revision of the system to provide more options for sorting and printing analyses could further improve this useful concordancer, which is available with pre-indexed corpora on the ICAME CD-ROM (see below).

Some software which has been developed is especially suitable for educational purposes, including what is sometimes referred to as classroom concordancing. The *Longman Mini Concordancer* (*LMC*) (Chandler & Tribble, 1989) is a simple concordancer which is very fast and easy to use and particularly accessible for language learners who are exploring the distribution of vocabulary in a text and for seeing authentic corpusbased examples of words in context. When initially released, *LMC* could handle texts up to 50,000 words in length. Because it operates within RAM it is not suitable for the processing of large corpora. It is nevertheless an excellent tool for classroom use. It takes only a few minutes to prepare texts and then, by use of a menu, gives instant access to wordlists and concordances with various sorting options, including concordances sorted from the ends of words with wild cards to enable students to find, for example, all regular past tense / past participle forms. Left- or right-sorted concordances make it easy for students to see major collocational patterns in text.

MicroConcord is a more recent MS-DOS concordancer designed specifically for educational applications by Scott and Johns and well-documented in Murison-Bowie (1993). One of the convenient features of *MicroConcord* is that it can search any corpus of several million words very quickly in ASCII format without indexing, and indeed was published initially with two 'corpus collections' each of one million words of text from *The Independent* newspaper and academic texts respectively. One aspect of the initially released software which limits its value for research purposes is that it can store only about 1,500 tokens in context of a type being searched for. This limitation will, of course, usually only be relevant for the retrieval of very high frequency words and grammatical patterns. *MicroConcord* provides a large range of options for searching, sorting, browsing, editing and formatting the analyses of words, part words or strings of words in varied context sizes for *KWIC* concordances or sentences. A particularly well-developed function is the ability to search quickly for and count the collocates of items within a range of up to five words before or after the keyword.

Laufer and Nation (1995) have described *VocabProfile*, an MS-DOS program for comparing the vocabulary overlap of different texts and the proportion of any text made up of words from pre-determined frequency lists. *VocabProfile* enables a researcher or language teacher to check what proportion of the vocabulary in a text is taken from, say, the most frequent 1,000 or 2,000 words of English or from a specified genre-specific technical vocabulary.

Researchers who need a fast, interactive facility for corpus analysis, especially at the lexical or morphological level of analysis, and who wish to compare the way linguistic features behave in different corpora, have a superb facility available in the ICAME CD-ROM (see Section 2.7). This CD-ROM contains *TACT* as well as *WordCruncher* and *Free Text Browser* software along with most of the major first-generation corpora including *Brown, LOB, London–Lund, Kolhapur* and *Helsinki*, all in various versions pre-indexed for both *TACT* and *WordCruncher*. The huge capacity of the CD-ROM, with at least 650 M of storage capacity, and the speed of analysis of pre-indexed corpora have created a powerful facility for corpus-based research by individuals using relatively modest personal computing facilities.

4.3.5 New generation software

A new generation of search and retrieval software became available from the mid-1990s, combining a number of features and, in most cases, able to handle large corpora. A powerful and versatile tool for corpus management and analysis is *LEXA*, developed by Raymond Hickey (1993). *LEXA* runs on an MS-DOS personal computer and the suite of programs, including a statistical package and corpus preparation software, contains some 60 interrelated programs for many kinds of linguistic analysis and for the retrieval of a wide variety of lexical, grammatical and thematic information from corpora. The programs range from a lemmatizer and tagger to software which lists all the types in a text or corpus with frequency distribution. The software can also transfer user-tagged items to a database for further processing, identify and retrieve all tokens of user-specified grammatical patterns or particular word strings, or make concordances in various formats. The use of Windows technology and menus makes *LEXA* easy to learn to use. However, one of the strongest features of the total *LEXA* package is the association of facilities which make possible a wide range of statistical operations on the various types of linguistic analysis undertaken. As noted earlier, the analysis of differences in the distribution of linguistic items in texts by corpus linguists has often not been subjected to rigorous criteria for statistical significance. Hickey has made available in the *LEXA* software a package of the mainly non-parametric tests typically used by linguists, including chi-square, Pearson product–moment correlation coefficient, Spearman rank correlation coefficient, and the Mann-Whitney U-test. These and other tests can be used to reveal the extent to which the analyst can be confident that observed quantitative differences in the distribution of linguistic items are a result of chance or not. Initially designed for diachronic research on the *Helsinki Corpus*, the *LEXA* software can however be used for research on any text corpus which has pure ASCII format. Further information on *LEXA*, including voluminous documentation, is available from ICAME, Norwegian Computing Centre for the Humanities, Harald Haarfagres gt.31, N-5007 Bergen, Norway. E-mail: icame@hd.uib.no.

Corpus analysis software has been developed at University College London specifically for the *International Corpus of English* project, but it can also be used with other corpora. The *ICE Corpus Utility Program* (*ICECUP*) has been designed to take advantage of the rich word-class tagging and markup of the corpora in the *ICE* project, as well as the experience of linguists who have used earlier software for their research, and who have become aware of additional facilities needed to undertake linguistic analysis. The major features of *ICECUP* have been described in Quinn (1993) and Quinn and Porter (1994) and in Greenbaum (1996b). The *ICECUP* software employs an indexed corpus for speed of processing, menus and Windows technology for ease of operation, and can perform the whole range of selecting, sorting and displaying features associated with the most widely used interactive concordances. These features include searching for, counting, sorting by frequency or alphabetical order before or after the keyword, and displaying in lists or concordances words, affixes, word combinations, word-class tags and tag combinations. *ICECUP* displays have clear references, variable contexts and the ability to be displayed with or without word-class tags and other markup. The facility to search a corpus or part of a corpus for strings of items either as collocations or grammatical structures is a notable feature of *ICECUP*. Split-screen concordances which show both an individual token in a *KWIC* line as well as that same token in a larger (expandable) context make it unnecessary to move between screens as in most other interactive concordancers. The subcorpus facility makes it easy to study parts of a corpus defined in sociolinguistic terms or by genre. Information on *ICECUP* is available from the Survey of English Usage, University College London, Gower Street, London WC1E 6BT.

More recently, three powerful search and retrieval software tools have become available. All use Windows technology. *WordSmith* was developed by Mike Scott (1996) and is available through Oxford University Press. It builds on the strengths of the earlier *MicroConcord* and overcomes the limitations in capacity. The ability to undertake more detailed analyses of the frequencies of concordanced items and the ability to extract collocational information easily make *WordSmith* an attractive package. In addition, it is capable of searching on complex 'search arguments' including tags, wildcards, *and/or/not* operators, and discontinuous sequences. A demonstration version is available on the World Wide Web at: http://www1.oup.co.uk/elt/catalogu/multimed/4589846/4589846.html.

SARA is the software package distributed with the *British National Corpus*. Capable of searching this huge corpus, it is compatible with SGML and is aware of annotations. That is, it can search on annotations such as word-class tags while masking them from the user.

XKwic (also known as *CQp*) is an advanced search and retrieval package developed in Stuttgart, and capable of handling very large corpora (Christ, 1994). Like other recently developed state-of-the-art software, *XKwic* is capable of rapid complex searches.

These new tools have made it possible for researchers to begin to exploit the opportunities provided by the new generation of large corpora. They can be expected to lead to improved descriptions of languages and to have an important influence on various other applications of corpus-based analysis.

CHAPTER FIVE

Implications and applications of corpus-based analysis

In the preceding chapters of this book we have considered some important techniques, procedures and issues in the compilation and analysis of corpora and have explored some of the ways in which corpus-based descriptions have thrown light on the structure and use of English. There are now many corpora available for linguistic description and for various other applications. The stance we have taken has been that, while a corpus can be a new kind of research domain involving new methodologies, the use of corpora does not in itself constitute a new or separate branch of linguistics. Rather, corpus linguistics is essentially descriptive linguistics aided by new technology. However, whether or not corpora are used as the basis for description, descriptive linguistics has always influenced and been influenced by theories of language and had applications apart from the production of lexicons and grammars. Further, it would have been surprising if the introduction of any technology as revolutionary as computing had not had consequences for the study of language. It is now clearly apparent that the ability to use computers to find, sort, analyse and quantify linguistic features and processes in huge amounts of text with great speed has already had an impact in a number of fields in the language sciences. Altenberg's ICAME bibliography, referred to at the start of Chapter 3, shows that in addition to descriptive studies of phonology, grammar, vocabulary and discourse, corpora of English have been used for lexicography and for research on social, regional, diachronic and stylistic variation, first and second language acquisition, and natural language processing, including tagging and parsing, speech recognition and machine translation.

Atkins et al. (1992) classified the potential users of corpora into three main groups – those interested in the language of texts, those interested in the content of texts, and those interested in the texts themselves. Any such classification inevitably has fuzzy boundaries but, in general, it is a useful way of showing the extent to which corpus-based analysis has consequences beyond linguistic description.

The availability of large bodies of text in electronic form has sparked off a dramatic increase in corpus-based research on language within computational linguistics, the interdisciplinary field of scholarship which seeks to study and simulate with computers, the processes and procedures by which we interpret and produce natural language. Computational linguists have focused on the language of texts from two directions. Initially, extant linguistic descriptions were used as a basis for devising 'knowledge-based' rules for the automatic linguistic analysis of texts. More recently, self-organizing approaches to analysis based on probabilities of occurrence in corpora have been used, but both approaches have needed each other. As Atkins et al. (1992: 14) have noted, research suggests that 'self-organizing statistical techniques gain much in effectiveness when they act on the output of grammatically-based analysis'. Researchers working on text derived from speech, information retrieval or machine translation have found it valuable to use corpora as test-beds for models and systems devised for the automatic analysis or processing of natural language. For applied linguists concerned with language teaching, a corpus can not only be one source of authentic text to which learners of a language might be exposed, but also the corpus can be analysed to discover the relative weight which might be given to lexical or grammatical items and processes in curricula and teaching materials.

Among researchers using corpora because of an interest in the content of texts rather than the language itself, we might include those studying topics or trends in the study of particular subject matter by groups of language users. Historians, sociologists and literary critics interested in the source or history of ideas, text attribution, plagiarism or stylistic characteristics are possible examples. A student of government policy in New Zealand, for example, might use a corpus which is based on newspapers to trace changes over a period of time in the use of the word *crown* from when it referred to the monarch to when it referred to representative government.

Research which makes use of corpora because of a need to access particular texts for mainly literary studies has been described by Butler (1985) and Burrows (1992) and is reflected in some of the work reported in the journals *Computers and the Humanities* and *Literary and Linguistic Computing* and in major surveys such as Lancashire (1991).

In addition to the studies in linguistic description which formed the basis of Chapter 3, several areas or branches of the language sciences have thus been affected by the availability of corpora. The present chapter focuses mainly on implications and applications of corpus-based research as it affects the goals of linguistic theory, the methodology of linguistic description, developments in computational linguistics, and the theory and practice of second language teaching.

5.1 Goals of linguistic description and the effect of corpora on methodology

5.1.1 Language as possibility and language as probability

For much of the last four decades, many linguists have recognized the validity of Chomsky's observations on the nature of language and the consequences of these observations for the goals of linguistic theory and description. It has been widely accepted that the proper goal of linguistics is to account for our 'competence' or knowledge of language and to model this competence in terms of rules and constraints. The empirical basis for linguistic description has tended to be introspective judgments about the legitimacy of example sentences as evidence for the existence of putative rules or processes in a language. That is to say, such examples have to pass the empirical test of the judgment of native speakers as to whether they are possible within the language. The plausibility and appropriateness of even the well-formed sentences, and the likelihood of their being used, was not an issue or even part of the theory. Observers have been asked to judge whether sometimes bizarre sentences such as the following are well-formed, acceptable or possible, and to account for these judgments.

Does it worry you that the aardvark didn't eat all its food?
Does that the aardvark didn't eat all its food worry you?
You are worried by that the aardvark didn't eat all its food.
Does for the aardvark not to have eaten all its food worry you?

Linguistic description in this context is thus conceived of as a description of competence, our knowledge of the system we use, through an attempt to account for what Chomsky (1965: 57) claimed to be:

> the fundamental fact about the normal use of language, namely the speaker's ability to produce and understand instantly new sentences that are not similar to those heard in any physically defined sense, or in terms of any notion of frames or classes of elements, nor associated with those previously heard by conditioning, nor obtainable from them by any sort of 'generalization' known to psychology or philosophy.

However, as corpus-based studies have repeatedly shown, the 'normal use of language' does include considerable use of recurrent prefabricated constructions. Further, description of the system we use is not the only legitimate goal of the study of language. The linguistic system is both derived from and instantiated by specific instances of use. It is thus perfectly legitimate to describe language both in terms of the system we use and our use of this system, and for the description thus to encompass language as possibility as well as probability of use. Moreover, when language is described in terms of probability of occurrence, it is not a denial of our ability to create or understand unique utterances. Rather, the fact that items or sequences of items tend to occur in particular contexts may be seen to help account for the possibility of communication, in that we are not totally dependent on working with unique items or combinations thereof. Further, as Leech (1991) pointed out, although linguists who followed Chomsky often rejected the relevance of probabilistic models of language for the goals they set for linguistic theory, these models have in fact worked remarkably well, especially for certain uses of probabilistic information in computational linguistics.

In contrast to Chomskyan approaches to language, corpus-based descriptions are based on non-elicited linguistic performance as the source of evidence for theories of language, and so far have largely focused on particular languages rather than universals of language. However, although the goals and focus of study have typically differed, the two approaches can be seen as complementary rather than conflicting. The study of performance data has, after all, been very much part of sociolinguistic and ethnomethodological research, even though the use of case-study data has sometimes been insufficient for wider generalization. Computer corpus-based approaches to language use well-established scientific procedures involving observation, analysis, theory building and subsequent verification, and bring a new distributional perspective to linguistic description. Such a distributional perspective has of course been taken for granted in most other scientific fields. Indeed the persistence of linguistic description without quantitative information about the relative frequency of use of the linguistic elements in various contexts is perhaps as surprising as it would be if demographic descriptions failed to indicate the size of the different population groups in a community. There is little doubt that without a distributional perspective many of the applications of corpus linguistics, most especially those involving natural language processing and language education, would not have occurred.

Chafe (1992) has argued, nevertheless, that corpus linguistics should not be concerned with distribution of the elements of language as an end in itself, but should also show concern for what the distribution might signify. Chafe (1992: 96) defines a corpus linguist as

> a linguist who tries to understand language, and behind language the mind, by carefully observing extensive natural samples of it and then, with insight and imagination, constructing plausible understandings that encompass and explain those observations.

The use of both introspection and corpus-based analysis can contribute to linguistic analysis and description. Corpora cannot tell us everything about how a language works. For example, they cannot be used as a basis for stating what structures or processes are not possible and, so far, intuitive judgments as well as corpus data are needed to establish the difference between phrases such as *run a risk* and *take a risk*, as

Fillmore (1992) demonstrates in a detailed discussion of the syntactico-semantic structure of those phrases and other uses of the word *risk*.

The fact that an item or structure does not appear in even the largest corpus does not necessarily mean that it cannot occur, but could suggest the corpus might be inadequate or the item infrequent. Neither does the fact that a construction occurs in a corpus necessarily establish its grammaticality. Spoken texts in particular have always challenged the grammatical–ungrammatical distinction. Aarts (1991) has shown with an excellent set of examples that some sentences in a corpus do not conform to what is represented in intuition-based descriptions of what is possible, but these 'ungrammatical' or marginal contributions often have quite high frequency of occurrence. Intuitive judgments will often reject as being not well-formed many constructions which occur in a transcribed spoken corpus. Whether utterances which involve phonetic or syntactic reductions such as *where you going?, wannanother one?* or *Good that you got here early* have to be accounted for grammatically will probably depend in the final analysis on frequency of occurrence and intuitive judgments as to what is 'normal'.

One of the main implications of corpus-based analysis is that the boundary between lexis and grammar has become much less clear. As discussed in Section 3.1.3, work on collocations has shown that new definitions of what constitutes a word, and of the units of sentence construction may be needed. This also has consequences for research on language acquisition in forcing a reconsideration of what it is children acquire and, on second language teaching, in reconsidering what the units of learning and instruction might be. A case for the study of grammar and vocabulary as a unitary probabilistic system was made by Halliday, with collocation being sometimes more grammatical and at other times more lexical in nature, and with register being 'a syndrome of lexico-grammatical probabilities' (1992: 68).

As we have seen in Chapter 3, use of corpora can do some things well, including identifying previously unnoticed linguistic items or processes. The methodologies which best exploit the potential of corpora are still not as well established as is needed, and there is room for wider use by corpus linguists of more sophisticated statistical analysis of data. Corpus-based research has not surprisingly hitherto tended to be mainly concerned with the distribution of forms rather than with semantic aspects of language. Ingenious ways still need to be found to get a corpus to reveal how semantic notions such as causation or topicalization, condition or contingency are expressed and distributed in a corpus. We have noted that the relative frequency of items can be used to help define register or genre on linguistic grounds, but further work is also needed on the co-occurrence of linguistic items or processes. Thus, we need to know not only how conditions are expressed and how often each of the particular forms which mark conditionality are used in a particular genre, but whether there is any relationship between the use of these forms and the use of other items or processes.

One consequence for linguistics of the availability and use of corpora is likely to be the effect on the education of undergraduate and graduate students and teachers. The content of courses in these areas is already undergoing change, with greater emphasis on the study of variation in language use, a field already opened up over several decades within sociolinguistics. Students and teachers are likely to benefit from instruction which is corpus-related, including being taught to access corpora as sources of evidence. As more and more linguistics students become familiar with using computers to address research questions, and others become comfortable with the use of more user-friendly software, we can expect the use of corpora to become more of a mainstream activity, as Knowles (1990) and Fligelstone (1993) have suggested.

5.1.2 *The description of English*

It has already been noted that for lexicography the use of corpora has become indispensable for identifying types, the development of new senses for types, and the relative frequency of use of these different senses. In the future, more use is likely to be made of the dictionary as an electronic lexical database, constantly updated and able to be searched by users (or by machines for automatic processing) in a wide variety of ways. The CD-ROM version of the *OED* second edition gives some idea of the potential. The latest editions of learners' dictionaries such as *LDOCE* and *Cobuild* already include some corpus-based data on frequency and there is scope for this kind of information to be greatly enhanced and expanded in imaginative new ways.

In spite of the large number of corpus-based descriptions of English grammar contained in the ICAME bibliography, it is clear that there are many aspects of English grammar and use which have not yet been approached from a corpus perspective. Descriptions of a fairly heterogeneous collection of aspects of English grammar have been based on corpora, often on the basis of only one genre of the *Brown, LOB* or *London–Lund* corpora. Some of the corpus-based analysis carried out prior to 1980 was statistically deficient (e.g. in the size or representativeness of the corpus) and needs to be replicated with new corpora. What is needed is systematic, comprehensive descriptive and comparative studies of formal and functional aspects of English in a range of genres and sociolinguistic and regional varieties.

A taste of what such corpus-based descriptions can achieve is contained in two quite different studies of English modal verbs by Coates (1983) and more recently by Mindt (1995), who used a much larger corpus. (see Section 3.2.2) In each case the studies have provided distributional analysis which shows how the modal system is used, the relative semantic significance of the different modals and the linguistic environments in which they occur.

The research topics in a machine-readable corpus are potentially as various and wide ranging as are the facts about a language and the use of that language. It can be valuable and instructive for students to be invited to study a page of printout of a concordance and to suggest research questions about the behaviour of particular words or structures. However, there is also a need for systematic and comprehensive corpus-based research agendas across the whole grammatical system. It is not possible to know in advance what is going to be discovered in a corpus, for there is always the possibility of discovering new patterning and distributions for known linguistic items or processes. Figure 5.1 lists some of the major units and processes in English at the levels of grammar and discourse which would normally be expected to be part of a systematic corpus-based description of English. Reference grammars

---

Word classes
  e.g. adjectives, adverbs, determiners, nouns, prepositions, pronouns, verbs

Word morphology and functions
  e.g. tense, aspect, number

Word types

Lemmas

Collocations

Phrase classes
  e.g. noun phrases, verb phrases, prepositional phrases, adjective phrases, adverb phrases

Clause elements
  e.g. subject, direct object, complement, adverbial (adjuncts, conjuncts, disjuncts)

Clause patterns
  e.g. SV, SVO, SVC, SVA, existential constructions

Clause processes
  e.g. extraposition, clefting, passivization, negation (e.g. *no* vs *not*), ellipsis

Sentence types
  e.g. declarative, interrogative (*yes/no*, *wh*-), imperative

Complex sentences
  e.g. co-ordination, subordination (nominal clauses, relative clauses, adverbial clauses, comparative clauses)

Ways in which information is organized and structured in discourse

Discourse particles

Form and function
  e.g. interrogative vs questions

Cohesion

Figure 5.1 Outline of major grammatical and discoursal units and structures which might be studied in a corpus
(from Kennedy, 1996b: 223)

---

such as Quirk et al. (1985) provide more detailed taxonomies, and these items can also, of course, be the focus of corpus-based comparative studies of the use of English in different domains, modes, genres, and sociolinguistic and regional varieties.

In addition to comprehensive corpus-based research programmes, there are also many opportunities for smaller-scale research studies, including dissertations and theses. As noted in Kennedy (1996b), even very small class exercises in which students or teachers in training undertake corpus analysis to compare, say, the distribution of *different from*, *different to* and *different than* in different varieties of English can demonstrate more about the hazards of prescriptivism than whole lectures or chapters about the nature of language use and language change. Larger studies, more suitable for theses or dissertations, may explore topics such as collocational distributions with particular prepositions or intensifiers, or whether subordinate clauses are more or less likely to precede or follow main clauses in complex sentences in different varieties of the language. As shown in Section 3.3.2, initial work in this largely unexplored field suggests that preferred clause ordering may differ according to whether the subordinating conjunction marks temporal, causal, conditional, concessional or other semantic relations. Descriptions of English intensifiers can similarly move beyond outlines of the grammar which note the positional use and relative distribution of intensifiers such as *very*, *pretty*, *rather*, *terribly* to incorporate material found rarely even in dictionaries, including the tendency shown in corpora for the use of *pretty* in some domains to be associated with 'negative' adjectives (*pretty awful*, *pretty terrible*, *pretty miserable*), while *terribly* tends to be associated with 'positive' adjectives (*terribly exciting*, *terribly impressive*).

Distributional accounts might also be undertaken, for example, of attributive vs predicative use of adjectives, and participle vs adjective modification of nouns.

The potential opportunities for corpus-based descriptive studies can be illustrated when we consider how comparisons are made. There is a very large number of linguistic devices available in English for making comparisons of many kinds (e.g. *There aren't as many x as y; There is less x than y; The amount of x exceeds the amount of y*). Little is known about the preferred ways of making comparisons in different contexts, even though the number of linguistic devices available in English is far greater than the normally recognized comparative and superlative morphemes. Mitchell (1990) outlined a possible systematic taxonomy for analysis which combines both grammatical and semantic criteria. Alongside such a system we might consider whether users of English, when making comparisons, are more or less likely to make the comparison in terms of superiority, inferiority or equality, or the denial of these (e.g. *Fred has more money than Max; Max has less money than Fred; Max doesn't have as much money as Fred*, etc.). Systematic descriptions of the distribution of these various ways of making comparisons which go beyond describing what is systemically possible would certainly have implications for language teaching and may also be of value for understanding psycholinguistic processes.

As suggested in Kennedy (1996b), research questions such as the following are likely to continue to be central in corpus-based descriptive studies: What are the linguistic units, patterns, systems or processes in the language, genre or text and how often, when, where, why and with whom are they used? Whether the texts have spoken or written origins, corpus-based studies have characteristically focused on four main types of analysis and description:

1   Word-based studies which explore the ecology of lexis both in terms of the occurrence and frequency of occurrence of items. Work by Renouf and Sinclair (1991), Kjellmer (1994) and others suggests that the expansion of lexical studies to include collocations is likely to be one of the most innovative and productive areas of corpus-based research.
2   Studies of the co-occurrence of grammatical word-class tags as expressions of syntactic patterning and as the basis for quantitative studies of the use of syntax.
3   Studies of the co-occurrence of groups of linguistic items or processes to show by means of factor analysis the linguistic characteristics of genre. Biber (1988) has pioneered the use of this approach to establish text types, which differs from the usual domain or topic-based approaches.
4   Studies of the structure of discourse, especially of spoken interaction, and of the basis of cohesion in spoken and written texts.

5.2   Corpus linguistics and computational linguistics

Although systematic coverage of computational linguistics is beyond the scope of this book, it is one of the most challenging and potentially most significant fields contributing to and making use of corpus-related research. The impact of corpora on computational linguistics can be gauged if we consider the extent to which the content and direction of research within the field has changed within less than a decade. Beginning in the 1950s with attempts to use computers for machine translation between languages, research and development in computational linguistics has involved scholars mainly from computer science, artificial intelligence and linguistic theory. Natural language processing was typically approached through traditional levels and processes of language used by linguists for analysing language, including morphology, syntax and lexis. In his overview of the field, Grishman (1986) reflected the major approaches and issues of the time. He identified three particular applications as being central in the development of computational linguistics, namely machine translation, automatic information retrieval from natural language texts and the interface between humans and machines. Other applications referred to included the testing of grammars proposed by theoretical linguists, text generation and the modelling of language understanding. Grishman's book included the computer modelling of syntactic rules in terms of the phrase-structure grammars familiar to linguists, semantic analysis in terms of models from formal logic such as predicate calculus, and information structure beyond the sentence. The word 'corpus' did not appear in the index and the use of corpora did not have a place in the methodologies described.

Within five years, however, two issues of *Computational Linguistics*, the most prominent journal in the field, were published as special issues on using large corpora. To understand why corpus-based research became mainstream so rapidly for research in natural language processing, we need to recognize that scholars working in various fields within computational linguistics increasingly found that the linguistic rule-based paradigms being proposed were simply not adequate to model normal language use, whereas stochastic approaches both worked better with new, previously unanalysed text, and held greater promise. Church and Mercer (1993) have provided an excellent overview of the issues which led to this interest in corpus-based statistical approaches to language analysis within computational linguistics to complement and enhance the results of rule-based paradigms. Klavens and Resnik (1996) have edited a volume of papers exploring the relationship between statistical and rule-based approaches to language, and how each can contribute to theory and to solving practical problems in computational linguistics.

Linguists have, of course, been well aware of the immense complexity of the structure and processes of natural languages, and the limited extent to which explicit, formal linguistic rules have been able to capture this structure. It is scarcely surprising then that attempts to capture the complex processes involved in human communication by means of computer modelling and simulation of the pragmatic, discoursal, semantic, grammatical, lexical, phonological and phonetic aspects of language have proved to be very difficult, without dealing with the adaptability and unpredictability of language in use. Further difficulties include how we handle ellipsis, anaphora, anomaly (including performance characteristics such as false starts), ambiguity, polysemy, metaphor, idiom, relevance and knowledge of the world. We are still a long way, for example, from getting a computer to recognize the functions of discourse and coherence, and why (1) is readily considered to be coherent and well-formed but (2) might be harder to contextualize:

1	A	There's the door.	2	A	There's the moon.
	B	I'm in the bath.		B	I'm in the bath.
	A	I'll take it then.		A	I'll take it then.

In (1) the discourse might relate to who answers a knock at the door, whereas in (2) the context might relate to who takes a photograph.

The rules of discourse depend on how the functions of utterances are interpreted, which in turn depends on experience of the use of language in context. Where there are multiple functions possible, it is hard to do automatic processing by rules. It is thus perhaps not surprising that researchers in various areas of computational linguistics have welcomed the availability of large corpora and improved computing technology to explore solutions to the practical problems of natural language processing.

Among the areas of research within computational linguistics where increasing interest has been shown in corpus-based methodologies have been techniques for text analysis associated with automated word-class tagging, morphological analysis, parsing, word sense disambiguation, parallel (bilingual) text alignment, anaphora resolution and the structure of discourse beyond the sentence. Applications of this research have been in areas as diverse as those associated with information retrieval, including the automated content analysis of texts, automated document analysis, abstracting and lexicography; speech recognition and synthesis; machine translation; and the induction and evaluation of grammars. Some of the issues and current developments are described in Armstrong (1994) and in the special issues of *Computational Linguistics* referred to above (1993, vol. 19, nos. 1 & 2).

Within computational linguistics, corpora have been used most successfully to enhance rule-based systems of analysis where disambiguation of items or structures is required. We have already seen in Section 4.1 how some of the most advanced word-class taggers and syntactic parsers have used statistical data on the probability of one item rather than another occurring in a particular context, and in so doing have improved the accuracy of the tagger or parser. That is, the device uses an abstract mathematical model of human behaviour rather than attempting to model and make use of linguistic knowledge (or competence) in order to tag or parse a text.

Sampson (1993) has described the ability to parse as being central to natural language processing. Whether it is a speech recognition or machine-translation system which is being designed, something has to be able to work out the grammatical structure of the spoken or written text. That is, the natural language processing system has to be able to work out relationships such as what is the logical subject of a sentence, and not only deal with surface structure relationships. In the case of spoken texts, the problems are compounded by the characteristic false starts and incomplete utterances.

In this context, the role of manually tagged corpora has been to 'train', test and refine automated taggers and parsers. The aim is then that the taggers be used in various applications without restriction on text (see Garside et al., 1987). The development by Marcus et al. (1993) of a parser which can encode aspects of both deep and surface structure relationships has already been referred to in Section 4.1.4. Black et al. (1993) reviewed various approaches to parsing and have shown that although those which use corpus-derived statistical probabilities rather than linguistic rules hold most promise, corpora are crucial test-beds for all approaches. Briscoe and Carroll (1993) have reported encouraging progress on a fully auto-matic procedure for ranking the large number of possible syntactic ana-lyses produced by grammatical parsers. They have proceeded in stages through semi-automatic analysis, using a corpus to fine-tune or 'train' the device – the goal being to produce a syntactic analysis which can support semantic interpretation. Church et al. (1991) have explored the statistical significance of the co-occurrence of items in corpora to reveal both formal syntactic and semantic collocational tendencies.

Working out statistical probabilities of occurrence from corpora is not without its problems, however. Biber (1993a) illustrates how with grammatically ambiguous forms (e.g. simple past vs past participle) the probability of one rather than the other occurring is often very differ-ent across registers. For example, in the *LOB Corpus, admitted, observed, remembered* and *expected* function as simple past tense in fiction for 77%, 91%, 89% and 54% of their occurrences respectively. On the other hand, these same word forms occur in expository prose as past participles in passives with respective probabilities of 67%, 45%, 72% and 77%. This kind of information is very important for probabilistic parsers and shows how natural language processing needs corpora which adequately rep-resent the domains of intended application. Generalizations or statistical information about languages derived from corpora which represent a range of registers tends to 'average' the results and can therefore mask important differences between language varieties.

Natural language processing systems have been particularly success-ful so far in applications such as spelling, style or grammar checking (Roach, 1992; Bateman & Hovy, 1992). However, it is the long-standing dream of machine translation in real time which has tended to capture the imagination and, increasingly, the investment of research funding. Developments have been summarized in a number of overviews, includ-ing Slocum (1985), Hutchins (1986), Hutchins and Somers (1992) and Lewis (1992). Although the initial work in machine translation begun in the 1950s received reduced research funding from the mid-1960s, by the mid-1980s the sheer amount of technical material needing to be translated was supporting a revival of research. As Slocum (1985) noted, in 1984 alone, approximately half a million pages of text were translated auto-matically or assisted by machine, and in the European Community by

1982 a third of the entire administrative budget was being spent on translation. In subsequent years, the need for machine translation has increased even more. The complexity of human languages is such, however, that we should be under no illusion that fully automatic, high-quality translation is about to become a reality. Nowadays a number of approaches to machine translation which have been refined through corpus-based research have been able to efficiently produce imperfect, medium-quality translations which benefit from subsequent post-editing. Machine-aided translation (MAT) which takes advantage of Windows technology, rapid access to large, more sophisticated, lexical databases, and parallel text screens are among the 'tools' which can also support human translators.

Corpus-derived statistics have been used by Brown et al. (1993) to develop mathematical modelling of the processes involved in machine translation, and to thus explore the probabilistic approaches used successfully in other areas of natural language processing. They used aligned English–French corpora. Gale and Church (1993) have described research on the alignment or matching of sentences in parallel bilingual corpora. Parallel aligned corpora have also been the basis for exploring the feasibility of 'example-based machine translation' (Sadler, 1989). One procedure explored is for sentences or sentence fragments in a text to be matched with an equivalent in a large bilingual aligned database. This apparently somewhat awkward approach to translation can only work successfully of course as long as the required sentences or units exist in the corpus. The practical, corpus-based progress in machine translation in the face of still imperfect semantic, pragmatic and syntactic representation in artificial intelligence-modelling has, as in other areas of computational linguistics, given an important boost to research in corpus linguistics during the 1990s, and promises to contribute to developments across a wide range of applications of natural language processing.

5.3 Corpus-based approaches to language teaching

Second language teaching theories and practices are influenced by facts and opinions about the conditions necessary for successful language learning, the background, attitudes and goals of particular learners, the techniques and procedures which are believed to facilitate language learning most efficiently, and what we believe needs to be learned in order to be a language user. For much of the last three decades, mainstream language teaching theory has focused on the process of learning through communication, rather than through the more traditional focus on the forms of language. That is, the focus of language teaching shifted away from principled ways of learning vocabulary and grammar on to learning how to do things with words. The rediscovery that language existed to communicate both propositional and social meaning thus led to a pedagogical emphasis on messages and the messengers rather than the linguistic system which carried them.

The reasons for this pedagogical focus on communication have included a recognition that many learners in the latter part of the century need to learn second languages for purposes of spoken interaction and not only as a way of accessing knowledge or cultural experience through written sources. There has also been less certainty than previously over what the units of language acquisition might be, partly as a result of major developments and shifts in linguistic theory. Other contributing factors have included a widespread recognition of the sociolinguistic parameters of language acquisition and use, resulting in the need to take account of variation, dissatisfaction with the teaching of a language as an unapplied system based on grammatical descriptions, increasing recognition of the role of interaction in the acquisition process, and a growing awareness of the nature and dimensions of discourse. The result has been quite a widespread tendency – in second language acquisition theory at least – for the central role of the language teacher to shift from being a source of knowledge about the language to that of becoming an organizer of tasks or opportunities for learning. These learning tasks or situations, rather than descriptions of language, have thus tended to determine the linguistic dimensions of learning.

However valuable may have been the focus on learning language as communication (particularly in increasing language fluency), there has been growing recognition that systemic accuracy is also relevant, and consequently there has been a more recent revival of interest among language teachers in what is being learned: the content of language learning. This refocusing has come at a time when corpus-based research is well placed to inform the content of language teaching. As we have seen in earlier sections of this book, there is increasing evidence from corpus studies of English to suggest which language items and processes are most likely to be encountered by language users, and which therefore may deserve more investment of time in instruction. Curriculum designers and classroom teachers need to have access to this information through better reference materials and syllabuses.

For those concerned with the teaching and learning of second or foreign languages in particular, information on the distribution of the elements and processes of a language can influence pedagogy in a number of ways. First it can influence the content of language teaching by affecting selection of what to teach, the sequencing of pedagogy, and the weight given to items or parts of the language being taught, thus contributing directly to the content of instruction. Secondly, through the consciousness-raising of teachers about language and language use, it can show that likelihood of occurrence, or frequency of use, is an important measure of usefulness. Corpus studies can also contribute to language teaching methodology by influencing the approach to instruction and making available techniques and procedures which encourage self-access and individualized instruction through interaction with authentic, analysed text from a corpus database.

5.3.1 The content of language teaching

There is a possibly apocryphal story told of the language learners' phrase book which contained the sentences *Stop the carriage. The postillion has been struck by lightning*, an extreme example of English which may prove to be of dubious use for most language learners. Corpus-based teaching materials can help avoid such oddities or apparent phrasal hapax legomena because the texts are authentic and each word can be displayed in or extracted from its original context.

As we have seen in Section 3.1.1, corpus-based research on the distribution of vocabulary left a mark on English language teaching from the 1920s to the 1950s. Many of the researchers were language teachers. As a result of this corpus-based research, by the 1960s language teachers were relatively familiar with distributional approaches to the languages they taught. Virtually without exception, these early studies found that a few lexical or grammatical types accounted for most of the tokens in texts. Most types occurred so rarely that it was doubtful that the investment of teaching time justified the return in terms of usefulness. By concentrating on the usual, rather than the exceptions, in the use of linguistic items or processes, it was argued that teachers could best assist learners acquire the second or foreign language. It became widely accepted that, at the elementary and intermediate stages of instruction, high frequency items in the language rather than intrinsically difficult items should receive the main pedagogical focus in the content and sequencing of the curriculum, in the weight of emphasis in the classroom and in the assessment of achievement and proficiency. In his corpus-based study of verb-form morphology in American English, designed to provide insights for pedagogical purposes, Ota (1963: 14) was typical of a number of researchers when he chose to study 'the probable and improbable rather than the possible and impossible'.

Most of these early corpus-based descriptions used written texts and counted the forms not the senses of items. The descriptions showed what users of the language were likely to read rather than what they might want to say or write. These analyses based on frequency of occurrence needed to be complemented, as Mackay (1965) argued, by consideration of the semantic range of items, their coverage of genres, and their learnability. Curricula based on written texts needed to be supplemented by spoken texts to capture the routines used in social interaction (e.g. *How are you?*), fundamental communicative functions (e.g. *How do you get to the airport?*) and discourse items for such essential purposes as turn-bidding and hedging (Svartvik, 1991).

The potential significance of corpus-based studies for language teaching can be illustrated by recalling those we have considered associated with verb-form use. This is because verbs are frequent in spoken and written English, accounting for about 20% of all the words used, and because verb-form morphology is also a significant part of the learning burden for learners of English. As Tables 3.13–3.25 suggest, the teaching of verb forms as a paradigm or system totally distorts their functional significance. George (1963c: 16) pointed out that 'a typical first year English course' may introduce the verb forms for imperative, negative imperative, present progressive, simple present habitual, present perfect, simple past narrative and some means of referring to the future (e.g. *going to* + stem). These forms account for only about 20% of all the verb-form occurrences in his Hyderabad corpus. On the other hand, if the course were based on the seven most frequently occurring items in that corpus, it would cover almost 60% of the verb-form tokens.

The Hyderabad study was based on the analyses of written texts and is probably not typical of other varieties. It seems likely nevertheless that some of the English verb forms covered in syllabuses do not justify the considerable pedagogical attention they typically receive, by being taught as part of the complete system of verb-form use. Thus, for example, *shall*, *ought to* and *need* are not frequently used. Similarly, where 'now' is the time reference, over 95% of the verb forms in written English are the simple present and only about 5% are present progressive. However, in many parts of the world the progressive is taught early as the form for 'now'. As Table 5.1 shows, the main use of the finite simple present in written texts is not to express habitual or iterative meaning as is often taught (e.g. *I travel to work by train every day*), but rather actual present (e.g. *I agree with you*) or neutral time (e.g. *My name is Fred*).

Table 5.1 Uses of the finite simple present tense
(adapted from George, 1963a)

Use	%
Present or actual moment	57.7
Neutral (devoid of time reference)	33.5
Habitual-iterative	5.5
Others	3.3
Total	100.0

In a much more recent study, Grabowski and Mindt (1995) analysed the use of 160 irregular verb forms in the *Brown* and *LOB* corpora and produced a list ranked in order of frequency with learners of English in mind. As is well recognized, some of these verbs such as *do, go, make* are among the most frequent in English, while others such as *beseech* and *smite* are uncommon in most contexts. Because the irregular verbs are normally a challenge for most learners, the corpus-based rank-ordering provided by Grabowski and Mindt can be a useful guide for the selection and gradation of these items for pedagogy. When the very frequent operators *be, have, do* are included (accounting for 60% of the irregular verb tokens), the 20 most frequent irregular verbs account for 83.6% of all irregular verbs in the written corpora. The lemmatized list of the most frequent irregular verbs in rank order is: *be, have, do, say, make, go, take, come, see, know, get, give, find, think, tell, become, show, leave, feel, put.* Against this background, English language teachers may not be surprised to learn that the 4,240 regular verb types in *Brown* and *LOB* (96.4% of the verb types) account for only 42.3% of the verb tokens. Learning the most frequent irregular verb forms therefore gives a good return for the investment of learners' time, and the rank-ordered list provided by Grabowski and Mindt provides a useful alternative to the alphabetically ordered lists which learners in many countries have been required to learn, even though they have rarely needed to use many of these forms.

It can be argued that statistics such as these on verb-form frequency reflect their particular textual sources, and that corpora of spoken varieties of English or more informal written sources would certainly lead to different relative frequencies. However, the broad picture from these studies is clear. Most English verb forms do not seem to be frequent enough to warrant pedagogical attention until quite advanced stages of the second language acquisition process. Learners' time might well be better spent on acquiring a bigger vocabulary or paying more attention to sociopragmatic aspects of competence which are inadequately treated in most curricula. For pedagogy, corpus-based descriptions also have advantages over comparative grammars which can further distort the distributional picture by focusing on idiosyncratic differences between languages, and on the unusual at the expense of the usual.

The studies of modal verbs by Coates and Mindt described in Section 3.2.2 have shown the distribution of these frequent auxiliary verbs in spoken and written English, and the relative use of their many different semantic functions. This important information has not yet had the influence which might have been expected on curriculum design, textbook writing and classroom practice. Holmes (1988) furthermore has argued, on the basis of a comparison between a corpus analysis and the linguistic devices taught in textbooks for expressing epistemic modality, that there can be a significant mismatch between normal use of English and what is taught to second language learners. While the important epistemic uses of modal verbs are frequently undertaught, there also tends to be an almost total absence of pedagogical focus on the frequently used lexical verbs (e.g. *appear, believe, doubt, suppose*), nouns (e.g. *possibility, tendency, likelihood*) and adverbials (e.g. *perhaps, of course, probably*) to express epistemic modality.

This kind of mismatch between use and pedagogy has also been strikingly illustrated in a study by Ljung (1990). When the lexical content of 56 textbooks commonly used for the teaching of English as a foreign language at upper secondary schools in Sweden was compared with the most frequent items in the *Cobuild Corpus*, it was found that the TEFL texts tended to expose the learners to a limited number of clichéd human interest stories involving an atypically high proportion of words denoting simple, concrete objects, physical actions, emotions and subjective judgments at the expense of often more frequent items in *Cobuild* denoting abstractions, mental processes and social phenomena. That is, there was a strong tendency for words such as the following to be over-represented in the learners' texts: *boat, desk, ticket, football, nurse, sick, shut, sing, quietly*. On the other hand, words such as the following high frequency items tended to be under-represented: *activity, attempt, community, detail, direction, evidence, knowledge, purpose, source, depend, similar, benefit, slightly*. It could of course be argued that, because it contains a preponderance of written texts, the *Cobuild Corpus* may inevitably emphasize more abstract vocabulary.

Twenty per cent of the most frequent 1,000 words in the corpus of learners' texts did not occur in the most frequent 1,000 words in *Cobuild* and vice versa. This application of corpus analysis in the context of foreign language teaching also shows that there is no clear increase in vocabulary difficulty between textbooks designed for later as compared with early secondary school years. Ljung (1991) has also discussed the results of his analysis in terms of Biber's model of text types. In these terms, the corpus of learners' textbooks has the characteristics of 'situated' rather than 'abstract' content and a strong 'narrative' or reported style which, it is suggested, does not prepare learners of English for genres such as those represented in the news media, reports and manuals of information.

Incompatibilities between corpus-based descriptions of English and the pedagogical emphasis given to linguistic items or processes have also been strikingly illustrated by Biber et al. (1994), who have shown that although prepositional phrases are overwhelmingly more frequent than finite or non-finite relative clauses as noun modifiers, textbooks for teaching English as a second or foreign language typically spend much more space and pedagogical focus on relative clauses. A similar incompatibility can be demonstrated in many genres for the relative emphases given to active and passive voice, agent marking by means of *by*-phrases, and determiner use. It continues to be somewhat surprising that in the teaching of conceptual categories such as 'totality' (a subcategory of quantification), pedagogical focus is typically concentrated on traditionally taught grammatical quantifiers such as *all* and *every*, while at the same time in spoken or written corpora totality is commonly marked lexically with words such as *entire, global, completely, whole, universal, throughout*.

An important insight from corpus-based research is the extent to which genre or text type can affect the linguistic content of texts, with potential implications therefore for instruction. As Sutarsyah et al. (1994) have shown, advanced learners of English wishing to study English for the specific purpose of undertaking business studies or economics are unlikely to receive exposure to relevant vocabulary if they are part of a general English for academic purposes course. In comparing a corpus consisting of texts from many academic fields with one of roughly the same size consisting of a single economics text, there were almost two-and-a-half times as many different word types in the general text as in the specialized text, suggesting that as far as vocabulary is concerned the learners working through the general academic texts meet new words that would rarely recur, and that English for academic purposes courses that go beyond the 3,000 commonest words may be of little value for learners with specific purposes. Table 5.2 shows that learners exposed to the economics specialized text get about five times as much exposure to the

Table 5.2 Rank order of the 50 most frequent content words used in an economics text compared with their occurence in general acadmic English
(adapted from Sutarsyah, 1993: 135)

	Rank order		Frequency	
Word	Economics	General academic English	Economics	General academic English
price	9	479	3,080	90
cost	14	471	2,251	91
demand	17	411	1,944	102
curve	21	525	1,804	83
firm	23	991	1,743	41
supply	24	509	1,590	86
quantity	25	807	1,467	53
margin	27	*	1,427	24
economy	29	224	1,353	172
produce	31	234	1,237	167
income	33	442	1,183	96
market	36	372	1,104	110
labour	40	313	1,004	131
increase	41	113	1,002	277
consume	42	623	995	70
total	47	362	946	114
change	48	92	927	316

Table 5.2 continued

	Rank order		Frequency	
Word	Economics	General academic English	Economics	General academic English
rate	49	104	915	293
capital	51	842	907	50
work	52	58	906	480
make	54	37	893	656
output	58	852	861	50
use	59	27	829	974
average	61	475	777	90
industry	61	191	777	186
production	63	552	772	84
revenue	65	*	763	10
product	66	390	749	106
profit	67	*	733	27
high	69	65	715	408
goods	72	*	705	21
point	73	96	702	313
year	74	43	700	577
show	76	60	677	455
part	77	74	667	372
good	78	414	659	102
equal	79	376	628	109
trade	80	518	621	85
pay	81	320	618	130
example	82	118	599	263
difference	84	55	562	496
see	85	79	559	360
people	86	136	555	241
wage	87	589	552	75
rise	89	500	534	87
buy	90	*	521	35
low	93	120	497	260
fall	94	377	492	109
govern	96	236	478	166
figure	99	268	455	148
			47,435	9,841

* = not in the first 1,000 words of general academic English

50 most frequent content words in that text than they would in a corpus consisting of texts from general academic sources. In fact, the 50 words in Table 5.2 occur so frequently in economics that almost one word in every six running words in that text comes from this list of 50 words. The same list accounts for only 3% of the words in the general academic corpus.

More research is needed on lexical distribution in specialized subject fields based on corpora rather than single texts. There is, of course, also a need for compilation of a wider range of such specialized corpora.

There are few aspects of language structure and use which cannot be described from a distributional perspective, and potentially, therefore, corpus-based description should make an important contribution to the content of second language teaching. Such analysis can be used not only for syllabus design and the sequencing of pedagogical materials. Corpus-based description can also be used for the consciousness-raising of classroom teachers about the dimensions of the learners' task and for prioritizing the emphasis given to various learning goals in the classroom. Intuitions about the use of language can frequently be misleading, as we have seen repeatedly in preceding chapters. A major contribution of work in corpus linguistics to language teaching is thus to provide quantitative evidence on the distribution of the component parts of the language, as a yardstick against which to evaluate subjective judgments about the goals and content of instruction.

5.3.2 *Language teaching methodology*

In addition to its impact on the linguistic content of language pedagogy, corpus-based research also has the potential to have a direct effect on language teaching methodology. As we have seen, for over three decades the analysis and description of corpora has accumulated facts about lexis, grammar and discourse at a time when language teachers were being encouraged to expose learners to authentic spoken discourse or written texts and to the negotiation of meaning with interlocutors. The details of analysed wordlists, or statistics on the relative frequency of items or processes in the language provided by corpus analysis, have been in a sense out of step with mainstream meaning-based approaches to language teaching.

Grammar had of course rarely been entirely neglected in the various changes in approach to language pedagogy since the 1960s, but it was a renewal of interest in the role of vocabulary in language learning and teaching which provided computer corpus-based research with the first opportunity to influence language teaching methodology. From the late 1980s there was a revival of interest among applied linguists in the place of vocabulary in second and foreign language learning, with major overviews such as Nation (1990) and Nattinger and De Carrico (1992), and edited collections of articles such as Carter and McCarthy (1988) exploring expanded notions of the nature of the lexicon and its pedagogical implications. Sinclair and Renouf (1988) went so far as to advocate corpus-based lexical syllabuses for language learning. They suggested that 'the question of lexical selection has passed many course writers by' (1988: 150) and that, for learners of English at least, the main pedagogical emphasis should be on the most frequent words in the language (supplemented by words of particular use in specific domains), their central patterns of usage (as shown by corpus analysis) and the collocations they are typically part of. They noted, for example, that *see* occurs most frequently as in *I thought they were all away, you see*, rather than as in 'seeing through the eyes' or 'I see what you mean', and yet this use is rarely represented adequately in English language courses.

The recurrent and pervasive phrasal regularities in English, often consisting of prefabricated word sequences, suggest that an important task for language learners is to internalize such sequences. Collocations, where grammar and lexis meet in the phrase, are now taken seriously in language pedagogy because they can be identified empirically by the methodologies developed in corpus analysis. This knowledge, incorporating a wider notion of the word, can also contribute to the revival of lexically based approaches to language teaching by including both systemic and distributional data (Kennedy, 1990). Bahns (1993) has suggested that a contrastive approach to the teaching of collocations, by which learners of different first languages are taught different collocations, might help address the problem of learning the huge number of collocations which exist in a language such as English. Learners of second languages sometimes transfer semantic collocations for the first language inappropriately to the second. For example, the following sentences have been produced by Cantonese learners of English:

There is a greater risk of *getting a fire* in crowded offices.
You should evacuate a building as soon as a *fire happens*.
Special equipment is needed to *destroy the fire*.
You should not *water an electrical fire*.

In each case the verb is not one which would normally collocate with *fire* in English.

Another reason why a focus on linguistic form has gathered support is because exposure to language in use without a linguistically itemized syllabus to guide learning is not necessarily efficient. There is rarely the time available for second language learners to be able to get the equivalent exposure which native speakers of a language have had in acquiring a language, through exposure to the language in use. And, in any case, there are few fields of human learning where it would be considered reasonable and efficient for learning to depend on exposure without instruction. Willis (1990) is among those who have taken up the case for the central role of lexis in syllabus design and language teaching methodology, and has been associated with commercial applications based on corpus analysis in the *Cobuild* project.

Of course, if a corpus-based description of a language is inadequate because the corpus is not truly representative of the language, then the pedagogical implications are reasonably serious. Owen (1993) has thus argued that some of the syntactic and collocational descriptions of lexis derived from the *Cobuild Corpus* are not necessarily typical, and that over-dependence on a corpus as a basis for the development of pedagogical grammar can lead to 'irrelevance, oversight and misrepresentation' (p. 185). It could, however, be argued that it should not be surprising that at a developmental stage corpus-based approaches to pedagogy may contain inaccuracies and lack of balance, but such shortcomings already exist in curricula based on intuition, traditional descriptions, tasks or other bases, as Halliday, Sinclair, Svartvik and others have repeatedly argued.

Corpora should be used judiciously for pedagogical purposes, informing instruction rather than determining it so as to avoid the risk of a return to prescriptivism. Frequency of occurrence in corpora should be only one of the criteria used to influence instruction. Sometimes, according to the goals of the learners, less frequent items or processes in a language may deserve more attention than the most frequent, simply because they are known to be learning problems with a wide range of uses. The facts about language and language use which emerge from corpus analyses should never be allowed to become a burden for pedagogy.

In spite of an obvious increase in the use of corpora during the 1990s, it would be misleading to suggest that the use of corpora has become part of the mainstream in language teaching theory and practice. In part this is because meaning-focused instruction has been widely accepted, and there has been a reluctance by many teachers to return to instruction with a central focus on the forms of language. There are already signs that the fruits of corpus-based research may help reconcile these approaches to language teaching. A second reason perhaps why the potential contribution of corpus linguistics is yet to be realized in pedagogy is because of a perceived need for users of corpora to be computer literate. With newly available corpora and software, however, doing corpus analysis is becoming easier by the day. In any case, while most language classrooms do not have access to the equipment necessary for computer-assisted language learning, and while teachers baulk at exploring corpora whether for lack of equipment, time or inclination, the results of corpus analysis of the type referred to in this book can be made available in traditional ways through curricula and printed teaching materials.

There are, however, other matters which need to be addressed if corpus linguistics is to gain wider acceptance among language teachers. In the first place is the issue of validity. Most language teachers are now aware of the importance of variation in language use, and are therefore somewhat reluctant to ignore differences arising from domain or genre, or the needs of learners for specific purposes, in favour of generalized descriptions of English. Many teachers are wary of distributional data on, say, conditionals based on a written corpus, and question whether the results would be the same if the analysis had been based on a spoken English corpus, or an intimate dyadic interaction. We need more genre-sensitive studies and more specialized corpora in addition to the larger representative corpora as a basis for analysis.

The size of a corpus clearly affects its reliability. Sometimes analyses based on quite small corpora are published, and this generates uncertainty as to whether the findings should be generalized or taken very seriously. The availability of the second-generation corpora should greatly improve the reliability of corpus-based analysis because of their size and methods of compilation.

While the possibility of the automatic analysis of corpora offers an exciting prospect, corpus research which combines computerized analysis and counting, with manual analysis, can be particularly useful for language teaching. For example, while a computer corpus study of 'causation' can be interesting and indeed important in giving us information on, say, the relative frequency in use of the various devices such as *because* or *since* which can mark causation, the fact is that causation is frequently unmarked in English and is expected to be inferred. Two or more propositions are simply juxtaposed and the listener or reader is expected in a particular case to infer a causal link, e.g. *The hole in the ozone layer over Antarctica is larger this year. The incidence of skin cancer is expected to rise.* Language teachers who properly view language as a system which functions to communicate propositional, illocutionary and sociolinguistic meaning need to have distributional information on aspects of language which require manual as well as computerized analysis.

Although scientifically interesting research findings on how a single word is used in a particular domain may seem too trivial to be of pedagogical significance, this is not the fault of corpus linguistics, but perhaps one of the reasons why greater pedagogical use is not made of corpus research. One of the challenges facing those who work with corpora in the 1990s is to carry out a systematic and comprehensive programme of research on the structure and use of particular languages and to make the results easily accessible. The kinds of studies referred to in this book show what can be done. Many of these studies need updating but there can be little doubt that, if the research is carried out, then it will earn the gratitude of language teachers.

It has been suggested throughout this book that corpus linguistics involving computers for text storage and analysis can produce descriptions of language which have important implications for language teaching, both in helping to identify the content of instruction and in methodological approaches to instruction. Computers can, of course, also be used as language teaching aids in classrooms and self-access learning centres without involving corpora. Since the mid-1970s advocates of computer-assisted language learning (CALL) have, however, suggested that the use of corpora might be relevant as a direct source of input for learners. It is important to distinguish between computer corpus research as a proven source of knowledge about language, and CALL, which is a teaching aid which may have potential for some learning situations. It would be unfortunate if the frustration and cynicism sometimes expressed by language teachers in relation to CALL were to be associated with corpus linguistics simply because computers are involved in each case.

Initially, when CALL was pioneered, it was dominated by the drills and practice associated with behaviourism. There was no connection with corpus linguistics, and CALL proponents were often enthusiastic amateur programmers who devised question-and-answer, tutorial-mode exercises and tests on vocabulary, grammar and translation. The mainstream of language teaching was not greatly impressed. Cloze-type and other gap-filling exercises and tests and the use of word-processing techniques such as spelling checks similarly had no necessary connection with corpora. The advantage of the use of CALL for such purposes was that learners could work at their own pace in programmed and often individualized instruction. The use of HyperCard to teach Chinese characters, stroke order, character recognition and tones is a good example of the value of such programmed instruction. The comparative lack of progress in CALL which Last (1992), Kaliski (1992) and others noted was partly a consequence of new technology being unable to fulfil expectations which had been raised to unrealistic levels. Some of the techniques used, for example, were reminiscent of the pattern practice of discredited, unfashionable but not always ineffective earlier audiolingual approaches to language teaching and were simply incompatible with the current orthodoxy of communicative language teaching.

In the 1990s however, CALL has grown beyond these beginnings, partly because of the wider availability of microcomputers, and attempts have been made to individualize syllabus design and instruction using techniques some of which are very much associated with corpus linguistics. Hubbard (1992) has provided a useful framework of what needs to be taken account of in CALL design. His taxonomy lists major factors which second language acquisition research has shown to be relevant for language learning, ranging from linguistic assumptions (e.g. whether the sentence is a relevant unit of learning), learning assumptions (e.g. the role of reinforcement), learner variables (e.g. preferred learning style), syllabus type (e.g. structural or functional), and level of difficulty of text, through to procedural matters such as techniques for presenting learning material or giving feedback. That is, instead of adapting CALL to what a computer program can do, an attempt is made to get CALL to take account of the necessary conditions for successful language learning. Computers cannot yet make judgments as to whether learners are comprehensible or sensible or other normal characteristics of real-world language use in interaction. However, modern CALL has nevertheless largely moved on from the drill master, quiz master approach to programmed instruction to give learners more control over what is learned, thus promoting what is sometimes called autonomous language learning in self-paced, more interactive, meaning-dominated, task-oriented activities. Stevens (1992) has described three kinds of courseware used in CALL, only one of which involves the use of corpora. These include problem-solving tasks which range from the use of cloze procedure to computer games, which are not always tolerated by older learners who may not see the purpose of such activities. Secondly, word processors with spelling checkers to help develop writing skills have been used especially with more mature language learners. Thirdly, CALL software which involves the exploration of text to acquire knowledge, and test intuitions about language, has been attractive for well-motivated learners although there is little research evidence yet of beneficial effects on language learning. The most widely used corpus-based technique or activity associated with learner-controlled exploratory interaction is concordancing. The use of a concordance to analyse a corpus has, of course, been an important technique or tool in lexicography and other fields, as we have seen in Section 4.2.2. One of the pioneers to attempt to adapt concordancing to language teaching was Johns (1986), and since then there have been imaginative proposals for the use of concordances in the classroom. The most influential of these have been by Tribble and Jones (1990) and Murison-Bowie (1993), both of which contain clear and informative examples of exercises which make use of concordancing. It is suggested that, with concordancing, the teacher's role is to guide and co-ordinate students' activity as they research the language in a kind of data-driven, inductive, consciousness-raising exploration of texts. Using a concordancer, the learner can locate or be confronted with all the tokens of a particular type which occur in a text or corpus, observe how the tokens of words or phrases function in context, and note the most frequent senses, and the company the types typically keep as part of collocations or grammatical patterns. Thus a learner might wish to see whether *happy* is most typically followed by *about, with, for, at,* or any other preposition; whether *rather* and *pretty* are synonymous intensifiers; or whether *left* most often occurs as a past tense form of *leave* or as an adverb, adjective or noun. Flexibility in sorting and formatting a concordance can be an added attraction for sophisticated, highly motivated language learners who are disposed towards inductive learning. Aston (1995) has reviewed some of the ways in which learners can be exposed to corpus-based analyses which help them infer rules and provide the necessary relevant repeated exposure to linguistic items in use.

However, excessive claims should not be made about concordancing. It is not a language teaching methodology nor a panacea but one among many techniques or aids which may be used to facilitate learning for some learners. Some learners clearly prefer to pick things up through interaction and reading and through predigested 'secondary' sources of information about the target language in the form of dictionaries and, to a lesser extent, grammars.

Like all language teaching techniques, corpus-based concordancing has ultimately to be judged on its results. Learners of a language can get access to authentic text from books, newspapers and recordings as well as from a corpus, and interaction with a corpus database is no more 'real text' than these other sources of comprehensible input. Evaluation of learning will therefore be crucial for deciding the future of corpus-based approaches to language learning. It is not necessarily a virtue for a language learner to work with data which has not been pre-analysed by grammarians. A learner who looks at tokens of *if* to see how conditionals are formed and used may miss entirely all the other ways by which conditionality is expressed through juxtaposition, or marking by *unless, and, or*, etc. Language in use is divergent and unpredictable and exposure to too much unanalysed detail can both confuse and trivialize important linguistic processes for language learners, and lead to uncoordinated, unfocused and inefficient learning.

As we have seen throughout this book, corpus linguistics has begun to exploit the opportunities for new types of linguistic description provided by the development of computing, with consequences for linguistic description, natural language processing and language pedagogy. The use of computerized corpora as a basis for developing models and descriptions of language and for various applications may prove to be among the most far-reaching achievements of the language sciences in the contribution made to reconciling the confusion of Babel, while at the same time permitting the maintenance of linguistic and cultural diversity within heterogeneous human societies.

References

Aarts, J. (1991) 'Intuition-based and observation-based grammar', in Aijmer & Altenberg (1991): 44–62

Aarts, J., Haan, P. de and Oostdijk, N. (eds.) (1993) *English Language Corpora: Design, Analysis and Exploitation* Amsterdam: Rodopi

Aarts, J. and Meijs, W. (eds.) (1984) *Corpus Linguistics: Recent Developments in the Use of Computer Corpora in English Language Research* Amsterdam: Rodopi

Aarts, J. and Meijs, W. (eds.) (1986) *Corpus Linguistics II. New Studies in the Analysis and Exploitation of Computer Corpora* Amsterdam: Rodopi

Aarts, J. and Meijs, W. (eds.) (1990) *Theory and Practice in Corpus Linguistics* Amsterdam: Rodopi

Aijmer, K. (1984) '*Sort of* and *kind of* in English conversation' *Studia Linguistica 38*: 118–128

Aijmer, K. (1986) 'Discourse variation and hedging', in Aarts & Meijs (1986): 1–18

Aijmer, K. (1996) *Conversational Routines in English: Convention and Creativity* London: Longman

Aijmer, K. and Altenberg, B. (eds.) (1991) *English Corpus Linguistics: Studies in Honour of Jan Svartvik* London: Longman

Akkerman, E. (1984) 'Verb and particle combinations: particle frequency ratings and idiomaticity' *ICAME News 8*: 60–70

Algeo, J. (1988) 'A computer corpus for a dictionary of Briticisms', in Kytö et al.: 45–59

Altenberg, B. (1984) 'Causal linking in spoken and written English' *Studia Linguistica 38*: 20–69

Altenberg, B. (1987) 'Causal ordering strategies in English conversation', in Monaghan, J. (ed.) *Grammar in the Construction of Texts* London: Frances Pinter, 50–64

Altenberg, B. (1990) 'Spoken English and the dictionary', in Svartvik (1990b): 177–191

Altenberg, B. (1991a) 'Amplifier collocations in spoken English', in Johansson & Stenström (1991): 127–148

Altenberg, B. (1991b) 'A bibliography of publications relating to English computer corpora', in Johansson & Stenström (1991): 355–396

Altenberg, B. (1991c) 'The London–Lund corpus of spoken English: research and applications: using corpora' *Proceedings of the Seventh Annual Conference of the*

AN INTRODUCTION TO CORPUS LINGUISTICS

UW Centre for the New OED and Text Research Oxford: Dictionary Department, Oxford University Press, 71–83

Altenberg, B. (1993) 'Recurrent verb–complement constructions in the London–Lund corpus', in Aarts et al. (1993): 227–245

Altenberg, B. (1994) 'On the functions of *such* in spoken and written English', in Oostdijk & de Haan (1994b): 223–240

Anderson, A. H. et al. (1991) 'The HCRC map task corpus' *Language and Speech 34*, 4: 351–366

Armstrong, S. (ed.) (1994) *Using Large Corpora* Cambridge, Mass.: MIT Press

Aston, G. (1995) 'Corpora in language pedagogy: matching theory and practice' in Cook, G. and Seidlhofer, B. (eds.) *Principle and Practice in Applied Linguistics* Oxford: Oxford University Press

Atkins, B. T. S. (1992) 'Tools for computer-aided corpus lexicography: the Hector project' *Acta Linguistica Hungarica 41*, 1–4: 5–71

Atkins, B. T. S., Clear, J. and Ostler, N. (1992) 'Corpus design criteria' *Literary and Linguistic Computing 7*, 1: 1–16

Bahns, J. (1993) 'Lexical collocations: a contrastive view' *ELT Journal 47*, 1: 56–63

Baker, J. P. (1995) 'The evaluation of multiple post-editors: inter-rater consistency in correcting automatically tagged data' *Technical Paper No.7* Lancaster: UCREL, Lancaster University

Barkema, H. (1993) 'Idiomaticity in English NPs', in Aarts et al. (1993): 257–278

Bateman, J. A. and Hovy, E. H. (1992) 'Computers and text generation: principles and uses', in Butler (1992): 53–74

Bauer, L. (1991) 'Who speaks New Zealand English?' *ICE Newsletter 11*

Bauer, L. (1993a) *Manual of Information to Accompany the Wellington Corpus of New Zealand English* Wellington: Department of Linguistics, Victoria University of Wellington

Bauer, L. (1993b) 'Progress with a corpus of New Zealand English and some early results', in Souter & Atwell (1993): 1–10

Bell, A. (1991) *The Language of News Media* Oxford: Blackwell

Benson, M., Benson, E. and Ilson, R. (1986) *The BBI Combinatory Dictionary of English* Amsterdam: John Benjamins

Biber, D. (1987) 'A textual comparison of British and American writing' *American Speech 62*: 99–119

Biber, D. (1988) *Variation across Speech and Writing* Cambridge: Cambridge University Press

Biber, D. (1989) 'A typology of English texts' *Linguistics 27*: 3–43

Biber, D. (1990) 'Methodological issues regarding corpus-based analyses of linguistic variation' *Literary and Linguistic Computing 5*: 257–269

Biber, D. (1992) 'Using computer-based text corpora to analyze the referential strategies of spoken and written texts', in Svartvik (1992b): 213–252

Biber, D. (1993a) 'Using register-diversified corpora for general language studies' *Computational Linguistics 19*, 2: 219–241

Biber, D. (1993b) 'Representativeness in corpus design' *Literary and Linguistic Computing 8*, 4: 243–257

Biber, D., Conrad, S. and Reppen, R. (1994) 'Corpus-based approaches to issues in applied linguistics' *Applied Linguistics 15*, 2: 169–189

Biber, D. and Finegan, E. (1986) 'An initial typology of English text types', in Aarts & Meijs (1986): 19–46

Biber, D. and Finegan, E. (1988) 'Drift in three English genres from the 18th to the 20th centuries: a multidimensional approach', in Kytö et al. (1988): 83–103

Biber, D. and Finegan, E. (1991) 'On the exploitation of computerized corpora in variation studies', in Aijmer & Altenberg (1991): 204–220

Biber, D. and Finegan, E. (1992) 'The linguistic evolution of five written and speech-based English genres from the 17th to the 20th centuries', in Rissanen et al. (1992): 688–704

Biber, D. and Finegan, E. (1994) 'Intra-textual variation within medical research articles', in Oostdijk & de Haan (1994b): 201–222

Biber, D. and Finegan, E. (1995) 'The Archer corpus' *ICAME Journal 19*: 148

Black, E., Garside, R. and Leech, G. (1993) *Statistically-Driven Computer Grammars of English: The IBM/Lancaster Approach* Amsterdam: Rodopi

Blackwell, S. (1993) 'From dirty data to clean language', in Aarts, et al. (1993): 97–106

Boguraev, B. and Briscoe, E. J. (eds.) (1989) *Computational Lexicography for Natural Language Processing* London: Longman

Bongers, H. (1947) *The History and Principles of Vocabulary Control* Woerden: Wocopi

Boyce, M. T. (1996) 'Compiling a corpus of contemporary broadcast Maori' *New Zealand Studies in Applied Linguistics* 2: 79–92

Bradley, J. (1991) *TACT User's Manual* Toronto: University of Toronto

Briscoe, T. (1990) 'English noun phrases are regular: a reply to Professor Sampson', in Aarts & Meijs (1990): 45–60

Briscoe, T. (1994) 'Prospects for practical parsing of unrestricted text: robust statistical parsing techniques', in Oostdijk & Haan (1994b): 97–120

Briscoe, T. and Carroll, J. (1993) 'Generalized probabilistic LR parsing of natural language with unification-based grammars' *Computational Linguistics 19, 1*: 25–59

Brown, P. F., Della Pietra, S., Della Pietra, V. and Mercer, R. (1993) 'The mathematics of statistical machine translation: parameter estimation' *Computational Linguistics 19, 2*: 263–312

Bryan, M. (1988) *SGML: An Author's Guide to the Standard Generalized Markup Language* Wokingham: Addison-Wesley

Burnage, G. and Dunlop, D. (1993) 'Encoding the British National Corpus', in Aarts et al. (1993): 79–95

Burnard, L. (1988) 'The Oxford Text Archive: principles and prospects', in Genet, J.-P. (ed.) *Standardisation et Echange des Bases de Données Historiques* Paris: Editions du CNRS, 191–203

Burnard, L. (1992a) *Corpus Document Interchange Format: Version 1.2* Oxford: Oxford Computing Centre, BNC Working Paper TGC.W30

Burnard, L. (1992b) 'Tools and techniques for computer-assisted text processing', in Butler (1992): 1–28

Burrows, J. F. (1992) 'Computers and the study of literature', in Butler (1992): 167–204

Butler, C. S. (1985) *Computers in Linguistics* Oxford: Blackwell

Butler, C. S. (ed.) (1992) *Computers and Written Texts* Oxford: Blackwell

Carberry, S. (1989) 'A pragmatics-based approach to ellipsis resolution' *Computational Linguistics 15, 2*: 75–96

Carroll, J. B., Davies, P. and Richman, B. (eds.) (1971) *The American Heritage Word Frequency Book* New York: American Heritage Publishing Co.

Carter, R. and McCarthy, M. (eds.) (1988) *Vocabulary and Language Teaching* London: Longman

Carterette, E. C. and Jones, M. H. (1974) *Informal Speech* Berkeley: University of California Press

Chafe, W. (1992) 'The importance of corpus linguistics to understanding the nature of language', in Svartvik (1992b): 79–97

Chafe, W., Dubois, J. and Thompson, S. A. (1991) 'Towards a new corpus of spoken American English', in Aijmer & Altenberg (1991): 64–82

Chandler, B. and Tribble, C. (1989) *Longman Mini-Concordancer* London: Longman

Chomsky, N. (1957) *Syntactic Structures* The Hague: Mouton

Chomsky, N. (1959) 'Review of Skinner, B. F. *Verbal Behavior*' *Language 35, 1*: 26–58

Chomsky, N. (1965) *Aspects of the Theory of Syntax* Cambridge, Mass: MIT Press

Christ, O. (1994) 'A modular and flexible architecture for an integrated corpus query system', in *Proceedings of COMPLEX '94* 3rd Conference on Computational Lexicography and Text Research, Budapest

Church, K. W., Hanks, P., Hindle, D. and Gale, W. (1991) 'Using statistics in lexical analysis', in Zernik, P. (ed.) *Lexical Acquisition: Using On-Line Resources to Build a Lexicon* Hillsdale: Lawrence Erlbaum

Church, K. W. and Liberman, M. (1991) 'A status report on the ACL/DCI', in *Using Corpora* Proceedings from the new OED conference. Waterloo, Ontario: University of Waterloo Centre for the New OED and Text Research: 84–91

Church, K. W. and Mercer, R. L. (1993) 'Introduction to the special issue on computational linguistics using large corpora' *Computational Linguistics 19, 1*: 1–24

Clear, J. (1987) 'Computing', in Sinclair (1987): 41–61

Coates, J. (1983) *The Semantics of the Modal Auxiliaries* London: Croom Helm

Coleman, A. (1929) *The Teaching of Modern Foreign Languages in the United States* New York: Macmillan

Collier, A. (1993) 'Issues of large-scale collocational analysis', in Aarts et al. (1993): 289–298

Collins Cobuild English Language Dictionary (1987) London: Collins

Collins Cobuild English Grammar (1990) London: Collins

Collins, P. (1987) 'Cleft and pseudo-cleft constructions in English spoken and written discourse' *ICAME Journal 11*: 5–17

Collins, P. (1991a) 'The modals of obligation and necessity in Australian English', in Aijmer & Altenberg (1991): 145–165

Collins, P. (1991b) '*Will* and *shall* in Australian English', in Johansson & Stenström (1991): 181–200

Crowdy, S. (1993) 'Spoken corpus design' *Literary and Linguistic Computing 8, 4*: 259–265

Crowdy, S. (1994) 'Spoken corpus transcription' *Literary and Linguistic Computing, 9, 1*: 25–28

Cruden, A. (1769) *Complete Concordance to the Old and New Testaments* London: Lutterworth Press (3rd edition)

Crystal, D. (1991) 'Stylistic profiling', in Aijmer & Altenberg (1991): 221–238

Davidson, L. (1992) 'Using large text data-banks on computers', in Roach, P. (ed.) *Computing in Linguistics and Phonetics: Introductory Readings* London: Academic Press

Davis, C., Deegan, M. and Lee, S. (eds.) (1992) *Resources Guide* Oxford: CTI (Centre for Textual Studies)

De Rose, S. J. (1988) 'Grammatical category disambiguation by statistical optimization' *Computational Linguistics* 14: 31–39

De Rose, S. J. (1991) 'An analysis of probabilistic grammatical tagging methods', in Johansson & Stenström (1991): 9–14

Dušková, L. (1977) 'On some differences in the use of the perfect and the preterite between British and American English' *Prague Studies in Mathematical Linguistics* 5: 53–68

Dušková, L. and Urbanová, V. (1967) 'A frequency count of English tenses with application to teaching English as a foreign language' *Prague Studies in Mathematical Linguistics* 2: 19–36

Edwards, J. A. (1992) 'Design principles in the transcription of spoken discourse', in Svartvik (1992b): 129–144

Edwards, J. A. (1993) 'Survey of electronic corpora and related resources for language researchers', in Edwards & Lampert (eds.): 263–310

Edwards, J. A. and Lampert, M. D. (eds.) (1993) *Talking Data: Transcription and Coding in Discourse Research* Hillsdale: Lawrence Erlbaum

Eeg-Olofsson, M. (1990) 'An automatic word-class tagger and a phrase parser', in Svartvik (1990b): 107–136

Ellegård, A. (1978) *The Syntactic Structure of English Texts* Göteborg: Acta Universitatis Gothoburgensis

Ellis, A. J. (1889) *The Existing Phonology of English Dialects* London: Trübner & Co.

Fang, A. C. (1993) 'Building a corpus of the English of computer science', in Aarts et al. (1993): 73–78

Fang, X. and Kennedy, G. (1992) 'Expressing causation in written English' *RELC Journal 23*, 1: 62–80

Faucett, L., Palmer, H. E., West, M. and Thorndike, E. L. (1936) *Interim Report on Vocabulary Selection* London: P. S. King

Fillmore, C. J. (1992) ' "Corpus linguistics" or "Computer-aided armchair linguistics" ', in Svartvik (1992b): 35–60

Firth, J. R. (1957) 'A synopsis of linguistic theory, 1930–1955', in *Studies in Linguistic Analysis* Oxford: Blackwell, 1–32

Fligelstone, S. (1992) 'Developing a scheme for annotating text to show anaphoric relations', in Leitner (1992): 153–170

Fligelstone, S. (1993) 'Some reflections on the question of teaching, from a corpus linguistics perspective' *ICAME Journal 17*: 97–109

Francis, W. N. (1992) 'Language corpora BC', in Svartvik (1992b): 17–32

Francis, W. N. and Kučera, H. (1964) *Manual of Information to Accompany 'A Standard Sample of Present-Day Edited American English, for Use with Digital Computers'* (revised 1979) Providence, RI: Department of Linguistics, Brown University

Francis, W. N. and Kučera, H. (1982) *Frequency Analysis of English Usage: Lexicon and Grammar* Boston: Houghton Mifflin

Fries, C. C. (1940) *American English Grammar* Monograph 10, New York: National Council of Teachers of English

Fries, C. C. (1952) *The Structure of English* London: Longman

Fries, C. C. and Traver, A. A. (1940) *English Word Lists: A Study of their Adaptability for Instruction* Washington: American Council on Education

Gale, W. and Church, K. (1993) 'A program for aligning sentences in bilingual corpora' *Computational Linguistics 19*, 1: 75–102

Gale, W., Church, K. and Yarowsky, D. (1993) 'A method for disambiguating word senses in a large corpus' *Computers and the Humanities 26, 5 & 6*: 415–439

Garside, R. (1987) 'The CLAWS word-tagging system', in Garside et al. (1987): 30–41

Garside, R. (1993) 'The marking of cohesive relationships: tools for the construction of a large bank of anaphoric data' *ICAME Journal 17*: 5–27

Garside, R., Leech, G. and Sampson, G. (eds.) (1987) *The Computational Analysis of English. A Corpus-Based Approach* London: Longman

George, H. V. (1963a) *Report on a Verb-Form Frequency Count* Monograph 1, Hyderabad: Central Institute of English

George, H. V. (1963b) 'A verb-form frequency count' *English Language Teaching 18, 1*: 31–37

George, H. V. (1963c) *A Verb-form Frequency Count: Application to Course Design* Monograph 2, Hyderabad: Central Institute of English

Goldfarb, C. F. (1990) *The SGML Handbook* Oxford: Clarendon Press

Gougenheim, G., Michéa, R., Rivenc, P. and Sauvageot, A. (1956) *L'Elaboration du Français Elémentaire* Paris: Didier

Govindankutty, A. (1973) 'The computer and Dravidian linguistics' *ALLC Bulletin 1, 3*: 3–5

Grabowski, E. and Mindt, D. (1995) 'A corpus-based learning list of irregular verbs in English' *ICAME Journal 19*: 5–22

Granger, S. (1993) 'International corpus of learner English', in Aarts et al. (1993): 57–72

Greenbaum, S. (1991) 'The development of the International Corpus of English', in Aijmer & Altenberg (1991): 83–91

Greenbaum, S. (1992) 'A new corpus of English: ICE', in Svartvik (1992b): 171–179

Greenbaum, S. (1993) 'The tagset for the International Corpus of English', in Souter & Atwell (1993): 11–24

Greenbaum, S. (1996a) *The Oxford English Grammar* Oxford: Oxford University Press

Greenbaum, S. (ed.) (1996b) *Comparing English Worldwide: The International Corpus of English* Oxford: Clarendon Press

Greenbaum, S., Leech, G. and Svartvik, J. (eds.) (1980) *Studies in English Linguistics for Randolph Quirk* London: Longman

Greenbaum, S. and Nelson, G. (1995) 'Clause relationships in spoken and written English' *Functions of Language 2, 1*: 1–21

Greenbaum, S., Nelson, G. and Weitzman, M. (1996) 'Complement clauses in English', in Thomas & Short (1996): 76–91

Greenbaum, S. and Ni, Yibin (1996) 'About the ICE tagset', in Greenbaum (1996b): 92–109

Greenbaum, S. and Svartvik, J. (1990) 'The London–Lund Corpus of Spoken English', in Svartvik (1990b): 11–59

Greene, B. B. and Rubin, G. M. (1971) *Automated Grammatical Tagging of English* Providence, RI: Department of Computer Science, Brown University

Grishman, R. (1986) *Computational Linguistics: An Introduction* Cambridge: Cambridge University Press

Guthrie, L., Guthrie, J. and Cowie, J. (1994) 'Resolving lexical ambiguity', in Oostdijk & Haan (1994b): 79–93

Haan, P. de (1989) *Postmodifying Clauses in the English Noun Phrase. A Corpus-Based Study* Amsterdam: Rodopi

Haan, P. de (1991) 'On the exploration of corpus data by means of problem-oriented tagging: postmodifying clauses in the English noun phrase', in Johansson & Stenström (1991): 51–66

Haan, P. de (1993) 'Sentence length in running text', in Souter & Atwell (1993): 147–161

Halliday, M. A. K. (1985) *Introduction to Functional Grammar* London: Edward Arnold

Halliday, M. A. K. (1991) 'Corpus studies and probabilistic grammar', in Aijmer & Altenberg (1991): 30–43

Halliday, M. A. K. (1992) 'Language as system and language as instance: the corpus as a theoretical construct', in Svartvik (1992b): 61–77

Halteren, H. van and Heuvel, T. van den (1990) *Linguistic Exploitation of Syntactic Databases* Amsterdam: Rodopi

Halteren, H. van and Oostdijk, N. (1993) 'Towards a syntactic database: the TOSCA analysis system', in Aarts et al. (1993): 145–162

Hickey, R. (1993) 'Corpus data processing with Lexa' *ICAME Journal* 17: 73–95

Higgins, J. (1991) 'Which concordancer? A comparative review of MS-DOS software' *System 19, 1–2*: 91–117

Hill, L. A. (1960) 'The sequence of tenses with *if*-clauses' *Language Learning 10, 3*: 165–178

Hockey, S. and Ide, N. (1991) *Research in Humanities Computing* Oxford: Clarendon Press

Hockey, S. and Martin, J. (1988a) *Oxford Concordance Program. Users' Manual. Version 2* Oxford: Oxford University Computing Service

Hockey, S. and Martin, J. (1988b) *Micro-OCP* Oxford: Oxford University Press

Hofland, K. (1991) 'Concordance programs for personal computers', in Johansson & Stenström (1991): 283–306

Hofland, K. and Johansson, S. (1982) *Word Frequencies in British and American English* Bergen: Norwegian Computing Centre for the Humanities

Holmes, J. (1988) 'Doubt and certainty in ESL textbooks' *Applied Linguistics 9*: 21–44

Holmes, J. (1995) 'The Wellington Corpus of Spoken New Zealand English: a progress report' *New Zealand English Newsletter 9*: 5–8

Holmes, J. (1996) 'The New Zealand spoken component of *ICE*: some methodological challenges' in Greenbaum (1996b): 163–181

Hubbard, P. (1992) 'A methodological framework for CALL courseware development', in Pennington & Stevens (1992): 39–65

Hutchins, W. J. (1986) *Machine Translation: Past, Present and Future* Chichester: Ellis Horwood

Hutchins, W. J. and Somers, H. (1992) *An Introduction to Machine Translation* London: Academic Press

Ide, N. and Véronis, J. (eds.) (1995) *The Text Encoding Initiative: Background and Context* Dordrecht: Kluwer Academic Publishers

Ihalainen, O. (1991a) 'A point of verb syntax in south-western British English: an analysis of a dialect continuum', in Aijmer & Altenberg (1991): 290–302

Ihalainen, O. (1991b) 'The grammatical subject in educated and dialectal English: comparing the London–Lund Corpus and the Helsinki Corpus of Modern English Dialects', in Johansson & Stenström (1991): 201–214

James, G. (1996) *English in Computer Science* Hong Kong: Longman

Janssen, S. (1990) 'Automatic sense disambiguation with LDOCE: enriching syntactically analyzed corpora with semantic data', in Aarts & Meijs (1990): 105–135

Jespersen, O. (1909–49) *A Modern English Grammar on Historical Principles. I–VII* Copenhagen: Munksgaard

Johansson, C. (1993) '*Whose* and *of which* with non-personal antecedents in written and spoken English', in Souter & Atwell (1993): 97–116

Johansson, S. (1978) *Some Aspects of the Vocabulary of Learned and Scientific English* Gothenburg Studies in English 42. Gothenburg: Acta Universitatis Gothoburgensis

Johansson, S. (1980) 'The LOB Corpus of British English texts: presentation and comments' *ALLC Journal 1*: 25–36

Johansson, S. (1981) 'Word frequencies in different types of English texts' *ICAME News 5*: 1–13

Johansson, S. (ed.) (1982) *Computer Corpora in English Language Research* Bergen: Norwegian Computing Centre for the Humanities

Johansson, S. (1994) 'Continuity and change in the encoding of computer corpora', in Oostdijk & Haan (1994b): 13–31

Johansson, S., Atwell, E., Garside, R. and Leech, G. (1986) *The Tagged LOB Corpus. Users' Manual* Bergen: Norwegian Computing Centre for the Humanities

Johansson, S. and Hofland, K. (1989) *Frequency Analysis of English Vocabulary and Grammar* 2 vols. Oxford: Clarendon Press

Johansson, S., Leech, G. and Goodluck, H. (1978) *Manual of Information to Accompany the Lancaster–Oslo–Bergen Corpus of British English, for Use with Digital Computers* Oslo: Department of English, Oslo University

Johansson, S. and Norheim, E. H. (1988) 'The subjunctive in British and American English' *ICAME Journal 12*: 27–36

Johansson, S. and Stenström, A.-B. (eds.) (1991) *English Computer Corpora* Berlin: Mouton de Gruyter

Joos, M. (1964) *The English Verb: Form and Meaning* Madison: University of Wisconsin Press

Kaliski, T. (1992) 'Computer-assisted language learning', in Roach (1992): 97–109

Kaplan, R. B. (1980) 'The language situation in Australia' *Linguistic Reporter 22, 5*: 2–3

Karlsson, F. (1994) 'Robust parsing of unconstrained text', in Oostdijk & Haan (1994b): 121–142

Karlsson, F., Voutilainen, A., Heikkilä, J. and Anttila, A. (eds.) (1995) *Constraint Grammar. A Language-Independent System for Parsing Unrestricted Text* Berlin: Mouton de Gruyter

Kennedy, G. (1987a) 'Quantification and the use of English: a case study of one aspect of the learner's task' *Applied Linguistics 8*: 264–286

Kennedy, G. (1987b) 'Expressing temporal frequency in academic English' *TESOL Quarterly 21*: 69–86

Kennedy, G. (1990) 'Collocations: where grammar and vocabulary teaching meet', in Anivan, S. (ed.) *Language Teaching Methodology for the Nineties* RELC Anthology Series No. 24. Singapore: Regional Language Centre, 215–229

Kennedy, G. (1991) '*Between* and *through*: the company they keep and the functions they serve', in Aijmer & Altenberg (1991): 95–110

Kennedy, G. (1992) 'Preferred ways of putting things with implications for language teaching', in Svartvik (1992b): 335–373

Kennedy, G. (1996a) 'Over *once* lightly', in Percy et al. (1996): 253–262

Kennedy, G. (1996b) 'The corpus as a research domain', in Greenbaum (1996b): 217–226

Kjellmer, G. (1982) 'Some problems relating to the study of collocations in the Brown Corpus', in Johansson (1982): 25–33

Kjellmer, G. (1984) 'Some thoughts on collocational distinctiveness', in Aarts & Meijs (1984): 163–171

Kjellmer, G. (1987) 'Aspects of English collocations', in Meijs (1987): 133–140

Kjellmer, G. (1991) 'A mint of phrases', in Aijmer & Altenberg (1991): 111–127

Kjellmer, G. (1992) 'Grammatical or nativelike?' in Leitner (1992): 329–343

Kjellmer, G. (1994) *A Dictionary of English Collocations Based on the Brown Corpus* 3 vols. Oxford: Clarendon Press

Klavens, J. and Resnik, P. (eds.) (1996) *The Balancing Act: Combining Symbolic and Statistical Approaches to Language* Cambridge, Mass.: MIT Press

Knowles, G. (1990) 'The use of spoken and written corpora in the teaching of language and linguistics' *Literary and Linguistic Computing 5, 1*: 45–48

Knowles, G. (1993) 'The machine-readable spoken English corpus', in Aarts et al. (1993): 107–122

Knowles, G., Taylor, L. and Williams, B. (1992) *A Corpus of Formal British English Speech* London: Longman

Krámský, J. (1969) 'Verb form frequency in English' *Brno Studies in English 8*: 111–120

Krámský, J. (1972) 'A contribution to the investigation of the frequency of occurrence of nominal and verbal elements in English' *Prague Studies in Mathematical Linguistics 4*: 35–45

Kruisinga, E. (1931–32) *A Handbook of Present-Day English* Groningen: Noordhoff

Kučera, H. and Francis, W. N. (1967) *Computational Analysis of Present-Day American English* Providence, RI: Brown University Press

Kytö, M. (1991) *Manual to the Diachronic Part of the Helsinki Corpus of English Texts* Helsinki: Department of English, University of Helsinki

Kytö, M. (1993) 'A supplement to the Helsinki Corpus of English texts: the corpus of early American English', in Aarts et al. (1993): 3–10

Kytö, M., Ihalainen, O. and Rissanen, M. (eds.) (1988) *Corpus Linguistics, Hard and Soft* Amsterdam: Rodopi

Kytö, M. and Rissanen, M. (1992) 'A language in transition: the Helsinki Corpus of English texts' *ICAME Journal 16*: 7–27

Kytö, M. and Rissanen, M. (1996) 'English historical corpora: report on developments in 1995' *ICAME Journal 20*: 117–132

Kytö, M., Rissanen, M. and Wright, S. (eds.) (1994) *Corpora across the Centuries. Proceedings of the First International Colloquium on English Diachronic Corpora* Amsterdam: Rodopi

Kytö, M. and Voutilainen, A. (1995) 'Applying the constraint grammar parser of English to the Helsinki Corpus' *ICAME Journal 19*: 23–48

Lancashire, I. (ed.) (1991) *The Humanities Computing Yearbook 1989–90* Oxford: Clarendon Press

Lancashire, I. and McCarty, W. (eds.) (1988) *The Humanities Computing Yearbook 1988* Oxford: Clarendon Press

AN INTRODUCTION TO CORPUS LINGUISTICS

Last, R. (1992) 'Computers and language learning: past, present – and future?' in Butler (1992): 227–245

Laufer, B. and Nation, I. S. P. (1995) 'Vocabulary size and use: lexical richness in L2 written production' *Applied Linguistics 16, 3*: 307–322

Leech, G. (1991) 'The state of the art in corpus linguistics', in Aijmer & Altenberg (1991): 8–29

Leech, G. (1992) 'Corpora and theories of linguistic performance', in Svartvik (1992b): 105–122

Leech, G. (1993a) 'Corpus annotation schemes' *Literary and Linguistic Computing 8, 4*: 275–281

Leech, G. (1993b) '100 million words of English' *English Today 9*: 9–15

Leech, G. and Fallon, R. (1992) 'Computer corpora – What do they tell us about culture?' *ICAME Journal 16*: 29–50

Leech, G. and Fligelstone, S. (1992) 'Computers and corpus analysis', in Butler (1992): 115–140

Leech, G. and Garside, R. (1991) 'Running a grammar factory: the production of syntactically analyzed corpora or "treebanks" ', in Johansson & Stenström (1991): 15–32

Leech, G., Garside, R. and Bryant, M. (1994) 'The large-scale grammatical tagging of text: experience with the British National Corpus', in Oostdijk & Haan (1994b): 47–63

Leech, G., Myers, G. and Thomas, J. (eds.) (1995) *Spoken English on Computer* London: Longman

Leitner, G. (1991) 'The Kolhapur Corpus of Indian English – intravarietal description and/or intervarietal comparison', in Johansson & Stenström (1991): 215–232

Leitner, G. (ed.) (1992) *New Directions in English Language Corpora. Methodology, Results, Software Developments* Berlin: Mouton de Gruyter

Lewis, D. (1992) 'Computers and translation', in Butler (1992): 75–113

Light, R. (1994) *The SGML Tagger* Oxford: Oxford University Press

Ljung, M. (1990) *A Study of TEFL Vocabulary* Stockholm Studies in English 78. Stockholm: Almqvist & Wiksell

Ljung, M. (1991) 'Swedish TEFL meets reality', in Johansson & Stenström (1991): 245–256

Lorge, I. (1949) *Semantic Count of the 570 Commonest English Words* New York: Columbia University Press

Mackey, W. F. (1965) *Language Teaching Analysis* London: Longman

MacWhinney, B. (1991) *The Childes Project: Tools for Analyzing Talk* Hillsdale: Lawrence Erlbaum

MacWhinney, B. and Snow, C. (1990) 'The Child Language Data Exchange System' *ICAME Journal 14*: 3–25

Mair, C. (1990) *Infinitival Complement Clauses in English: A Study of Syntax in Discourse* Cambridge: Cambridge University Press

Mair, C. (1991) 'Quantitative or qualitative corpus analysis? Infinitival complement clauses in the Survey of English Usage Corpus', in Johansson & Stenström (1991): 67–80

Malinowski, B. (1935) *Coral Gardens and their Magic* Vol. 2 London: Allen & Unwin

Marcus, M., Santorini, B. and Marcinkiewicz, M. (1993) 'Building a large annotated corpus of English: the Penn Treebank' *Computational Linguistics 19, 2*: 313–330

Marshall, I. (1987) 'Tag selection using probabilistic methods', in Garside et al. (1987): 42–56

McEnery, T. and Wilson, A. (1996) *Corpus Linguistics* Edinburgh: Edinburgh University Press

Meijs, W. (ed.) (1987) *Corpus Linguistics and Beyond. Proceedings of the Seventh International Conference on English Language Research on Computerized Corpora* Amsterdam: Rodopi

Meyer, C. F. (1991a) *Apposition in Contemporary English* Cambridge: Cambridge University Press

Meyer, C. F. (1991b) 'A corpus-based study of apposition in English', in Aijmer & Altenberg (1991): 166–181

Milić, L. T. (1990) 'A new historical corpus' *ICAME Journal 14*: 26–39

Miller, G. A. (1951) *Language and Communication* New York: McGraw-Hill

Milton, J. C. and Tong, K. S. T. (eds.) (1991) *Text Analysis in Computer-Assisted Language Learning* Hong Kong: Hong Kong University of Science and Technology

Mindt, D. (1995) *An Empirical Grammar of the English Verb: Modal Verbs* Berlin: Cornelsen

Mindt, D. and Weber, C. (1989) 'Prepositions in American and British English' *World Englishes 8*: 229–238

Mitchell, K. (1990) 'On comparisons in a notional grammar' *Applied Linguistics 11*, 1: 52–72

Murison-Bowie, S. (1993) *Micro-Concord Manual: An Introduction to the Practices and Principles of Concordancing in Language Teaching* Oxford: Oxford University Press

Murray, K. M. E. (1977) *Caught in the Web of Words: James A. H. Murray and the Oxford English Dictionary* New Haven: Yale University Press

Nakamura, J. (1993) 'Quantitative comparison of modals in the Brown and LOB Corpora' *ICAME Journal 17*: 29–48

Nation, I. S. P. (1990) *Teaching and Learning Vocabulary* Boston: Heinle & Heinle

Nattinger, J. R. and DeCarrico, J. S. (1992) *Lexical Phrases and Language Teaching* Oxford: Oxford University Press

Nelson, G. (1995) 'Standardizing wordforms in the spoken ICE corpora' Working Paper of the ICE project, Department of English, University College London

Nevalainen, T. and Raumolin-Brunberg, H. (1994) 'Sociolinguistics and language history: the Helsinki Corpus of Early English Correspondence' *Hermes, Journal of Linguistics 13*: 135–143

Oostdijk, N. (1988a) 'A corpus for studying linguistic variation' *ICAME Journal 12*: 3–14

Oostdijk, N. (1988b) 'A corpus linguistic approach to linguistic variation' *Literary and Linguistic Computing 3*: 12–25

Oostdijk, N. (1991) *Corpus Linguistics and the Automatic Analysis of English* Amsterdam: Rodopi

Oostdijk, N. and Haan, P. de (1994a) 'Clause patterns in modern British English' *ICAME Journal 18*: 41–80

Oostdijk, N. and Haan, P. de (eds.) (1994b) *Corpus-Based Research into Language: In Honour of Jan Aarts* Amsterdam: Rodopi

Ota, A. (1963) *Tense and Aspect of Present-Day American English* Tokyo: Kenkyusha

Owen, C. (1993) 'Corpus-based grammar and the Heineken Effect: lexico-grammatical description for language learners' *Applied Linguistics 14*: 167–187

Palmer, F. R. (1965) *A Linguistic Study of the English Verb* London: Longman

Palmer, H. E. (1933) *Second Interim Report on English Collocations* Tokyo: Institute for Research in English Teaching

Patten, T. (1992) 'Computers and natural language parsing', in Butler (1992): 29–52

Pawley, A. and Syder, F. (1983) 'Two puzzles for linguistic theory: native-like selection and native-like fluency', in Richards, J. and Schmidt, R. (eds.) *Language and Communication* London: Longman, 191–226

Peitsara, K. (1993) 'On the development of the *by*-agent in English', in Rissanen et al. (1993): 219–233

Pennington, M. C. and Stevens, V. (eds.) (1992) *Computers in Applied Linguistics: An International Perspective* Clevedon: Multilingual Matters

Percy, C., Meyer, C. and Lancashire, I. (eds.) (1996) *Synchronic Corpus Linguistics* Amsterdam: Rodopi

Perdue, C. (1993) *Adult Language Acquisition* 2 vols. Cambridge: Cambridge University Press

Peters, A. (1983) *The Units of Language Acquisition* Cambridge: Cambridge University Press

Pienemann, M. (1992) 'COALA – a computational system for interlanguage analysis' *Second Language Research 8, 1*: 59–92

Poutsma, H. (1926–29) *A Grammar of Late Modern English* Groningen: Noordhoff

Quinn, A. (1993) 'An object-oriented design for a corpus utility program', in Aarts et al. (1993): 215–225

Quinn, A. and Porter, N. (1994) 'Investigating English usage with ICECUP' *English Today 10, 3*: 19–24

Quirk, R. (1968) 'The Survey of English Usage', Chapter 7 of *Essays on the English Language: Medieval and Modern* London: Longman

Quirk, R., Greenbaum, S., Leech, G. and Svartvik, J. (1972) *A Grammar of Contemporary English* London: Longman

Quirk, R., Greenbaum, S., Leech, G. and Svartvik, J. (1985) *A Comprehensive Grammar of the English Language* London: Longman

Renouf, A. (1987) 'Corpus development', in Sinclair (1987): 1–40

Renouf, A. (1992) 'What do you think of that? A pilot study of the phraseology of the core words in English', in Leitner (1992): 301–317

Renouf, A. (1993) 'A word in time: first findings from the investigation of dynamic text', in Aarts et al. (1993): 279–288

Renouf, A. and Sinclair, J. McH. (1991) 'Collocational frameworks in English', in Aijmer & Altenberg (1991): 128–143

Rissanen, M. (1991) 'On the history of *that*/zero as object clause links in English', in Aijmer & Altenberg (1991): 272–289

Rissanen, M. (1992) 'The diachronic corpus as a window to the history of English', in Svartvik (1992b): 185–205

Rissanen, M., Ihalainen, O., Nevalainen, T. and Taavitsainen, I. (eds.) (1992) *History of Englishes. New Methods and Interpretations in Historical Linguistics* Berlin: Mouton de Gruyter

Rissanen, M., Kytö, M. and Palander-Collin, M. (eds.) (1993) *Early English in the Computer Age: Explorations through the Helsinki Corpus* Berlin: Mouton de Gruyter

Roach, P. (ed.) (1992) *Computing in Linguistics and Phonetics: Introductory Readings* London: Academic Press

Romaine, S. (1994) *Language in Society: An Introduction to Sociolinguistics* Oxford: Oxford University Press

Rundell, M. and Stock, P. (1992) 'The corpus revolution' *English Today 30, 31 and 32*: 9–14, 21–32 and 45–51

Sadler, V. (1989) *Working with Analogical Semantics* Dordrecht: Foris

Sampson, G. (1987) 'Probabilistic models of analysis', in Garside et al. (1987): 16–29

Sampson, G. (1992a) 'Analyzed corpora of English: a consumer guide', in Pennington & Stevens (1992): 181–200

Sampson, G. (1992b) 'Probabilistic parsing', in Svartvik (1992b): 425–447

Sampson, G. (1992c) 'SUSANNE – a deeply analyzed corpus of American English', in Leitner (1992): 171–189

Sampson, G. (1993) 'The SUSANNE Corpus' *ICAME Journal 17*: 125–127

Sampson, G. (1994) 'SUSANNE: a domesday book of English grammar', in Oostdijk & Haan (1994b): 169–188

Sampson, G. (1995) *English for the Computer* Oxford: Oxford University Press

Sand, A. and Siemund, R. (1992) 'LOB – 30 years on' *ICAME Journal 16*: 119–122

Scott, M. (1996) *WordSmith* Oxford: Oxford University Press

Sharman, R. A. (1989) *Observational Evidence for a Statistical Model of Language* Report 205. Winchester: IBM UK Scientific Centre

Shastri, S. V. (1988) 'The Kolhapur Corpus of Indian English and work done on its basis so far' *ICAME Journal 12*: 15–26

Sinclair, J. (ed.) (1987) *Looking Up. An Account of the Cobuild Project in Lexical Computing* London: Collins ELT

Sinclair, J. (1989) 'Uncommonly common words', in Tickoo, M. L. (ed.) *Learners' Dictionaries: State of the Art* RELC Anthology Series No. 23. Singapore: Regional Language Centre, 135–152

Sinclair, J. (1991) *Corpus, Concordance, Collocation* Oxford: Oxford University Press

Sinclair, J. (1992) 'The automatic analysis of corpora', in Svartvik (1992b): 379–397

Sinclair, J. and Renouf, A. (1988) 'A lexical syllabus for language learning', in Carter & McCarthy (1988): 140–160

Slocum, J. (1985) 'A survey of machine translation: its history, current status and future prospects' *Computational Linguistics 11, 1*: 1–17

Souter, C. (1993) 'Towards a standard format for parsed corpora', in Aarts et al. (1993): 197–214

Souter, C. and Atwell, E. (eds.) (1993) *Corpus-Based Computational Linguistics* Amsterdam: Rodopi

Souter, C. and O'Donoghue, T. F. (1991) 'Probabilistic parsing in the COMMUNAL Project', in Johansson & Stenström (1991): 33–48

Sperberg-McQueen, C. M. and Burnard, L. (eds.) (1994) *Guidelines for Electronic Text Encoding and Interchange* Chicago and Oxford: Text Encoding Initiative

Stenström, A.-B. (1987) 'What does *really* really do?', in Monaghan, J. (ed.) *Grammar in the Construction of Texts* London: Frances Pinter, 65–79

Stenström, A.-B. (1990) 'Lexical items peculiar to spoken discourse', in Svartvik (1990b): 137–176

Stenström, A.-B. and Breivik, L. E. (1993) 'The Bergen Corpus of London Teenager Language (COLT)' *ICAME Journal 17*: 128

Stevens, V. (1992) 'Humanism and CALL: a coming of age', in Pennington & Stevens (1992): 11–38

AN INTRODUCTION TO CORPUS LINGUISTICS

Summers, D. (1991) *Longman/Lancaster English Language Corpus: Criteria and Design* Harlow: Longman

Summers, D. (1992) 'English in the raw' *Modern English Teacher 1*, 4: 14–16

Sutarsyah, C. (1993) 'The vocabulary of economics and academic English' Unpublished MA thesis. Victoria University of Wellington

Sutarsyah, C., Nation, I. S. P. and Kennedy, G. (1994) 'How useful is EAP vocabulary for ESP? – A corpus-based case study *RELC Journal 25*, 2: 34–50

Svartvik, J. (1966) *On Voice in the English Verb* The Hague: Mouton

Svartvik, J. (1980) 'Well in conversation', in Greenbaum et al. (eds.): 167–177

Svartvik, J. (1990a) 'Tagging and parsing on the TESS project', in Svartvik (1990b): 87–106

Svartvik, J. (ed.) (1990b) *The London–Lund Corpus of Spoken English: Description and Research* Lund: Lund Studies in English 82. Lund University Press

Svartvik, J. (1991) 'What can real spoken data teach teachers of English?' in Alatis, J. E. (ed.) *Georgetown University Round Table on Languages and Linguistics* Washington, DC: Georgetown University Press: 555–566

Svartvik, J. (1992a) 'Lexis in English language corpora', in Tommola, H., Varantola, K., Salmi-Tolonen, T. and Schopp, J. (eds.): 17–31

Svartvik, J. (ed.) (1992b) *Directions in Corpus Linguistics* Proceedings of Nobel Symposium 82, Stockholm, 4–8 August 1991. Berlin: Mouton de Gruyter

Svartvik, J. and Quirk, R. (eds.) (1980) *A Corpus of English Conversation* Lund Studies in English 56. Lund: Lund University Press

Taylor, L., Leech, G. and Fligelstone, S. (1991) 'A survey of English machine-readable corpora', in Johansson & Stenström (eds.): 319–354

Thomas, J. and Short, M. (eds.) (1996) *Using Corpora for Language Research* London: Longman

Thorndike, E. L. (1921) *Teacher's Wordbook* New York: Columbia Teachers College

Thorndike, E. L. and Lorge, I. (1944) *The Teacher's Wordbook of 30,000 Words* New York: Columbia University Press

Tommola, H., Varantola, K., Salmi-Tolonen, T. and Schopp, J. (1992) *Euralex '92. Proceedings I and II. Papers Submitted to the 5th Euralex International Congress on Lexicography in Tampere, Finland* 2 vols. Tampere: Tampereen Yliopisto

Tottie, G. (1991a) *Negation in English Speech and Writing* London: Academic Press

Tottie, G. (1991b) 'Conversational style in British and American English: the case of backchannels', in Aijmer & Altenberg (1991): 254–271

Tribble, C. and Jones, G. (1990) *Concordances in the Classroom. A Resource Book for Teachers* London: Longman

Trudgill, P. and Hannah, J. (1982) *International English: A Guide to Varieties of Standard English* London: Edward Arnold

Vossen, P. (1991) 'Polysemy and vagueness of meaning descriptions in the Longman Dictionary of Contemporary English', in Johansson & Stenström (1991): 105–124

Wang Sheng (1991) 'A corpus study of English conditionals'. Unpublished MA thesis. Victoria University of Wellington

Warren, L. (1992) 'Learning from the Learners' Corpus' *Modern English Teacher 1*: 9–11

West, M. (1953) *A General Service List of English Words* London: Longman

Willis, J. D. (1990) 'The lexical syllabus', in Sinclair, J., Hoey, M. and Fox, G. (eds.) *Techniques of Description* London: Collins

Wilson, A. and Rayson, P. (1993) 'The automatic content analysis of spoken discourse. A report on work in progress', in Souter & Atwell (1993): 215–226

Wong-Fillmore, L. (1976) 'The second time around: cognition and social strategies in second language acquisition'. Unpublished PhD thesis. Stanford University

Wright, J. (1898–1905) *English Dialect Dictionary* London: Oxford University Press

Wright, S. (1993) 'In search of history: English language in the eighteenth century', in Aarts et al. (1993): 25–40

Zhu Qi-bo (1989) 'A quantitative look at the Guangzhou Petroleum English Corpus' *ICAME Journal* 13: 28–38

Zipf, G. K. (1935) *The Psychobiology of Language* Boston: Houghton Mifflin

Zipf, G. K. (1949) *Human Behaviour and the Principle of Least Effort* Cambridge, Mass.: Addison-Wesley

Index

INDEX

INDEX